World Christianity in the Twentieth Century

DATE DUE

			PRINTED IN U.S.A.

SCM CORE TEXT

World Christianity in the Twentieth Century

Noel Davies and Martin Conway

scm press

The Authors have asserted their right under the Copyright,
Designs and Patents Act, 1988, to be identified as the Authors of
this Work

Bible quotations are from the Revised English Bible © Oxford
University Press and Cambridge University Press 1961, 1970.

British Library Cataloguing in Publication data

A catalogue record for this book is available
from the British Library

978 0 334 04043 9

First published in 2008 by SCM Press
13–17 Long Lane,
London EC1A 9PN

www.scm-canterburypress.co.uk

SCM Press is a division of
SCM-Canterbury Press Ltd

Typeset by Regent Typesetting, London
Printed in the UK by
CPI William Clowes Beccles NR34 7TL

Contents

Preface

'You will receive power when the Holy Spirit comes upon you; and you will bear witness for me in Jerusalem, and throughout all Judea and Samaria, and even in the farthest corners of the earth.'

(Acts 1.8)

'Go therefore to all nations and make them disciples; baptize them in the name of the Father and the Son and the Holy Spirit, and teach them to observe all that I have commended you. I will be with you always, to the end of time.'

(Matt. 28.19–20)

Our purpose in this book is to record and set out one major chapter in the story of the worldwide Christian mission. Over the nineteen centuries since Jesus' ministry, death and resurrection proclaimed the good news of the Kingdom of God, and Philip, Peter and Paul engaged in their mission in the first Christian century, much has been achieved. But it has been the twentieth century which has most nearly seen not the ending of the missionary task, far from it, but the arrival of that good news and the acceptance of it by at least some people in virtually every main human grouping in every part of the world. Still more, it has brought the acceptance, by Christians of virtually every culture and language around the planet, of the responsibility to transmit this same story both to their neighbours and fellow citizens, and to their children and grandchildren, as a story of universal truth and importance. What this new chapter of the worldwide mission will 'mean', as tomorrow's humanity looks back in the twenty-second and twenty-third centuries, can only be left to the good purposes of the Father to share as and when and how God chooses (Acts 1.7). But at least this book offers its readers an overall survey of the comparable adventures, with no shortage of tragic and even horrific moments, of those who have shared this same good news with many persons and peoples during the century recently completed.

Our aim has been to provide a comprehensive overview of the main developments within Christianity during the twentieth century, for the sake of readers who will face comparable challenges in the twenty-first century. No such review can be exhaustive. There is an inevitable element of selectivity, reflecting our particular areas of experience and expertise. Nor can such a work be completely original. We have both had wide experience of the world Church during the latter half of the century. Inevitably, however, we have also been deeply reliant, as any reader who is familiar with the field will immediately recognize, on authoritative resources in the various fields covered by this volume.

The idea for this book (and the accompanying *SCM Core Reader on World Christianity in the Twentieth Century*) arose from two courses of lectures on this theme given by Noel Davies for the Department of Religious and Theological Studies at Cardiff University. It became clear that there were no textbooks that covered the historical and theological issues that were the focus of such a course. Consultations with Barbara Laing of SCM Press (whose encouragement throughout this process we deeply appreciate, as well as that of her successor, Dr Natalie Watson and her colleagues, whose editorial and proof reading expertise has contributed enormously to this volume) gave rise to a proposal for the present texts, with the specific aim of providing focused resources for students of theology and religious studies and other general readers, to enable them to attain an overall perspective on world Christianity in the twentieth century, with all its complexities and challenges. It became clear that no one person could provide an adequately informed source of reliable information and analysis. Dr Martin Conway enthusiastically agreed to share in the project and so began a collaboration that has led to the present volume.

The two of us have worked closely together. While each of us has taken prime responsibility for different chapters of the book, we are both responsible for the whole. We have both spent most of our professional careers as servants of the ecumenical movement that has been such a new and vital feature of the witness and changing purposes of the Christian churches in the twentieth century. This will be relatively clear throughout the book. But we have not intended to limit our interest to that specific movement, which of course has had and still has its weaknesses, failures and needs for renewal and change, like any other human phenomenon. Within the limits of these two volumes, as of our competence, we offer what we hope can be seen as a relatively factual and objective survey, of course much helped by our own experiences as well as by what we have learned from others.

We are both British, one Welsh, one English, one lay, the other ordained, but have both travelled widely around the world, though not in every area or situation that will be mentioned in our text. We well realize that to be British is to have a conditioning that by no means makes us automatically trustworthy in every context! At the present time, humanity is – rightly – very sensitive to the many diversities that our different backgrounds, cultures and outlooks impart to us. Most of us are conscious of some of these, but not of others. We hope that the palette of friendships that each of us has been privileged to enjoy over the years will have helped to keep us fairly free of the kinds of Eurocentric, let alone Britain-centred, perspectives of which we are all too well aware.

Still more, we are both men, have not personally had to experience poverty or oppression, and are no longer in our most youthful years! We are not unaware that these factors will make it difficult for some readers to trust our account to be adequately sensitive to some of the tensions in what we are writing about. To this we can only say that we have tried our best, and so will always gladly welcome information about aspects of this vast subject where what we have written may seem to any reader inappropriate or plain wrong.

No less importantly, we are both Christians, indeed both from 'churches of the Reformation' (one Anglican, one Congregationalist) but with considerable experience of a wide range of different communities within the sadly divided worldwide Church. We write from the inside of this total faith and community about what has been happening over the twentieth century. We are well aware that to write about matters of conviction and obedience from inside the community in question is a very different matter from writing about these same things from outside that community. We do not apologize for this. We encourage those who feel that this 'insiders' view' needs complementing with a different sort of view, from outside, to put theirs forward too. Yet we write both for those who are Christian, and for those who would not say that they are, in the hope of offering reliable accounts of the larger context for the story with which so many of our readers will be wrestling in the twenty-first century.

Ideally, this book should be used alongside the companion *SCM Core Reader on World Christianity in the Twentieth Century*, which offers extracts from key documents and writings that illustrate and explain some of the fundamental points made in the chapters of the current volume. Cross references in each chapter point readers to these texts. So the maximum benefit will be derived from this book when used alongside the *Reader*. However, if readers do not have access to the *Reader*, then we hope that what we offer here tells its own story and provides an adequate and helpful perspective on the events that have shaped Christianity during the century. Any readers who wish to follow up particular aspects of the story will find guidance on further reading at the end of each chapter.

So we offer this book in recognition that there is an exciting story to be told, a development of Christian life and discipleship to be celebrated and, of course, constant failures for which Christians are called to repent. As authors, we offer it in gratitude that we have been able to share in a small way in parts of this story and have been given this opportunity of presenting to a wider readership something of the excitement and sorrow that we have experienced, as we have participated in the life of the world Church during the latter decades of the twentieth century. Above all, we offer it with thanksgiving to God for being able to recognize, in so much of the story that is told here, the work of the Holy Spirit, who has used the people of God among all nations and peoples – with all their gifts and failures – to bear witness to Christ and bring praise to his glory.

Introduction
An Overview of the Twentieth Century

Most of us are aware of much that we have inherited from the century just past, yet it may be helpful to try and indicate some of the features of that period that for us have shaped the total background of the events and people written about here. These paragraphs may feel dangerously schematic – human realities are invariably more complex and mysterious than they appear! Yet it is important to be aware of a range of events and qualities of the wider history before starting on the details of any specific part.

It was a century of constant, often unpredictable change, as illustrated by two climactic events at either end of the century. The Russo-Japanese war of 1904–05 showed how, within less than 50 years from the first 'unequal treaties' by which the USA forced Japan to open its ports, an Asian nation could by military force compel two of the 'great powers' of Europe, Russia and Germany, to cede to it territories and influence they would much rather have kept for themselves. This was, as we can now see with hindsight, a clear warning that from then on major wars were likely to involve interests in every part of the globe. So too, in September 2001, the wholly unexpected attack using a succession of airliners on the World Trade Center in New York and the Pentagon in Washington, the first violent attack on the continental United States by an external power since the War of Independence in the 1770s, shattered in a single day the USA's sense of itself as the one unassailable super-power, and gave notice of massive alienation between forces within the 'House of Islam' and the interests and expectations of the 'Western alliance' centred in the USA.

In between those two poles, lasting changes came about from the two World Wars. Not that the entire world was directly involved in either or both – the first saw almost no action in the Americas, and the second, much more widespread in its direct actions, still left most of sub-Saharan Africa physically unaffected. But they both greatly changed the assumptions and expectations of vast swathes of humanity in every part of the world.

The First World War was triggered by the assassination in Sarajevo, Bosnia, of the heir to the Austro-Hungarian throne, Archduke Franz Ferdinand. Initiated by a gunman reacting to inter-communal rivalries in the Balkans, which were to continue simmering for the rest of the century, it quickly came to involve the major European powers – Germany, Britain, France, Italy and Russia. Most of it saw bitter fighting at the opposite ends of Europe, on a relatively immobile line of trenches running through Belgium and Eastern France, with more mobility in the fighting to the east through Poland, Romania and Serbia. Before it ended, the Middle East had become involved through Arab uprisings, supported by the British and French, against the Ottoman Empire, which eventually led to the collapse of the little that was left of that long-dwindling empire, and its conversion into the self-confessed 'secular state' of Turkey. Germany's colonies in Africa – Togo, Cameroon, Tanganyika (now Tanzania) and South-West Africa (now Namibia) – were handed over to French, British and South African governments by mandates from the League of Nations created by the Versailles peace treaty. Only in East Africa had there been any prolonged fighting.

But the consequences were major. The Russian throne was swept aside by the Bolshevik revolution in late 1917, after which three years of bitter civil war left even the Bolshevik winners exhausted. The Austro-Hungarian Empire collapsed into five separate nations – Poland, Czechoslovakia, Hungary, Austria and Yugoslavia – with a host of disputed territories and unhappy minorities whose grievances were by no means all finally settled by the end of the century. Territorially, Germany was the least affected of the losing states, but again royal rule was overthrown in favour of a democratic system which proved unable, 15 years on, to withstand the popularity of the ferociously nationalist and totalitarian party of Adolf Hitler.

The Second World War was fought on an even larger scale. Partly because of the involvement of Japan in its bombing of the United States' fleet in Pearl Harbor in the Hawaiian islands in December 1941, which immediately rushed the USA into active participation. And partly because of the availability of naval power – in the submarines that caused such damage and fear to convoys travelling between Britain and North America, and in the long-distance warships that could range the oceans freely until they met heavier guns, torpedoes from submarines or aircraft launched from equally long-range aircraft-carriers. Again, sub-Saharan Africa was largely untouched by actual fighting, though the continent's northern coastal peoples saw huge armoured forces from Germany, France and Britain ranged against each other. The Japanese armies and navy, no less active and well prepared than the Germans, invaded huge swathes of Asia from Eastern China to the Philippines and New Guinea, and from the Marshall Islands and those of the South Pacific through to the Dutch East Indies, Thailand and Burma. They occupied territories neighbouring on Russia (the Soviet Union joined in the fighting in the Far East in the last month of the Pacific War in August 1945), Australia (which beat them back in New Guinea from September 1942 on) and even Eastern India, where British troops were daily expecting a new front in early 1942.

The aftermath of this war also was a changed world, with Europe divided down the middle – Germany quite literally so – between peoples swept up into the Communist camp under the Soviet Union's sway and those to the North and West almost all in close alliance with the USA. These latter came later to form among themselves the European Economic Community, now European Union. North America had been as fully involved, even stretched, as any, even if there was no fighting there. South America had witnessed the hunting and sinking of the German warship *Tirpitz* in the estuary between Buenos Aires and Montevideo, but had not been much involved.

Yet the mood of many of the previously colonial nations, under the British, French, Dutch, Belgian, Italian, Spanish and Portuguese empires had decisively shifted, with the realization that these 'master' nations were no less threatened and vulnerable than any other. So that along with the bitter division in Europe, the 20 years after the victories of May (over Germany) and July 1945 (over Japan) saw a long and irreversible succession of movements into independence by the peoples of 'the South' from their colonial eras.

India, the largest single colony, whether in area or in population, was handed over by the British to its own rulers in 1947, not without bitter fighting between the new states of India and Pakistan as millions of people decided they must cross the new border between them, both ways on. The one case where there was a prolonged war between colonizer and formerly colonized was in the thousand or so islands comprising Indonesia. Here the local people, having done at least as much to get rid of the Japanese as the Dutch, were not prepared to put up with being taken back into rule by the latter, and therefore waged a war of independence which reached its final success in 1949. The Belgians decided to abandon their claim over the Congo in mid–1960, the year which also saw the British move out of Nigeria (after the Gold Coast, becoming Ghana, in 1957) and the French give a real degree of independence to all 12 of their sub-Saharan colonies, as well as Madagascar. The Portuguese only ceded independence to Angola and Mozambique in 1975, after heavy fighting had been under way for years in both countries, and after an internal revolution inside Portugal had thrown out their dictator, Salazar.

Already in 1910 the British had ceded self-government to an all-white regime of the Union of South Africa, a pattern followed by the whites of (then) Rhodesia (now Zimbabwe) in 1923. So in those countries, the latter of which tried to take control of its northern neighbours (Northern Rhodesia and Nyasaland now Zambia and Malawi) in a Central African Federation which lasted barely ten years, from 1953 to 1963, it took rather longer to achieve real independence. Zimbabwe only achieved it in 1980 after a prolonged civil war. Zambia and Malawi were given it by the British much less painfully in 1964, but were left very weak economically. South Africa only achieved it after monumental struggles, if largely non-violent, by the eventual acceptance of the white regime in 1989 that it could no longer go it alone, with almost the entire world set against it. Nelson Mandela was released from his 27 years in captivity on Robben Island in February 1990, leading to South Africa's first one-person-one-vote election in 1994 for a fully inter-racial government and the effective end of centuries of European rule.

These military and political developments are one dimension. A very different one, often more hidden but no less real and no less important in the long run, has been the economic dimension(s) of relations between persons and peoples, within any nation and across the borders of nation-states and continents. Here our world has seen comparably vast and important changes over the twentieth century, whose later stages will vitally condition what can happen in the twenty-first century and possibly beyond.

We can start again with Japan, where the at first unwilling opening of its ports led quickly to a vast hunger for the knowledge and skills of the 'advanced' countries in North America and Europe. The universities of these were soon flooded out with eager Japanese, soaking up every possible skill and process to the point where already by the time of the Second World War Japan had turned itself into a major economic powerhouse. Despite their defeat, the Japanese people and economy bounced back remarkably quickly in the 1950s and were soon the leading nation for the new electronic gadgets and appliances, as for reliable motor cars and other heavy industry. By the end of the century, with many other nations racing to catch up with them, their leading position had become concentrated especially in the electronic field. But woe betide any of us who ever underestimate Japan again.

Germany also recovered remarkably well from a defeat which had left virtually all its cities and factories in ruins, the East doubly hindered by the reparations that had been taken from them by the Russians, the West much helped by the generous Marshall Plan from the USA. By the 1960s Germany had become again the economic giant in Europe, now altogether rid of the political motive to dominate, and for a good ten years willing to finance well beyond its 'fair share' both the European Union and the needs of the poorer nations of the South. The other nations of Western Europe also, of course with many differences in detail, recovered more slowly from the losses of war and grew into relatively rich countries, with well-varied economies and well-educated workforces. Not so in the East. Here the Communist regimes, which had promised so much in terms of equal shares for all, proved to be so dominated by incompetent Russian orders, and so unable to develop the kinds of education that could release a new generation into the skills necessary for the kinds of industries and services common in the West, that in the end the entire Communist control collapsed in late 1989. Much helped by the humanity, open-mindedness and sheer humour of Mikhail Gorbachev, the Russian party leader since 1985, this overthrow in the end grew out of the simple unwillingness of ordinary people, those in the army or police just as much as many others, to obey the rigid orders laid down from 'on high'. A few shots in Bucharest dispatched the Romanian dictator, Nicolae Ceaușescu, but otherwise there was an amazing lack of violence as the Communist regimes of the nine Eastern European states simply vanished, giving way to a period of uncertainty that was soon resolved by free elections, and the beginning of a long struggle for economic growth to match the new political freedom – by no means fully achieved by the end of the century.

Meanwhile, much more needs to be recalled about the economic struggles of the South. Some of these countries have vital mineral resources, not least oil, so that they have been able to sell these to the rich and enjoy the proceeds. Here several of the 'nations' of the Middle East stand out. Saudi Arabia, for example, with its royal family enjoying vast wealth, and its Arab citizens able to take up more or less any opportunity the world holds for them, has been receiving an even bigger population of migrant workers from other lands, who are not allowed to stay for more than a limited time. They are paid enough to send back a good deal to their families at home, whether in India, Indonesia, the Philippines, or Britain, Poland or Argentina. Yet any prospect of their acquiring citizenship is for ever barred.

Many more have certain economic advantages in respect of things they can grow or produce to sell to others, while also gifted with a population growing faster than they can provide for, not least thanks to medical advances that enable a much higher proportion of children to live to maturity than they were accustomed to. So any apparent economic advance can soon 'disappear' because of the ever-growing needs of the growing population. India seemed for many years to be caught in some such trap, while being a country so huge and varied that almost any generalization quickly proves inadequate. In the later years of the century India was being hailed as having found at least some of the means it has long needed to make enough economic growth to outdo the constant population pressure – but at what cost to the equality of livelihood and regard of all sections of the population is much questioned.

At the time of writing, China, still governed by the Communist Party, as it has been since Mao Tse-tung took overall control in 1949, has achieved an astonishing 'success' in relation to economic growth, especially in the cities of the eastern coast. Its low point of the second half of the century, after the political struggles of the 1920s, the Japanese encroachment in the 1930s that led to full-scale war from 1937 on, and then all-out civil war between nationalists and communists as soon as the Japanese were banished in 1945, was in the 'Cultural Revolution' of 1966–76. These are now labelled 'the ten wasted years' – a very mild way of putting it. It all stemmed from Mao's unrealistic hope to get the younger generation to reinvigorate the enthusiasm and commitment that had so driven him in his youth, but which turned into almost total anarchy and irresponsibility, only in the end overcome by the death of Mao and the execution of those who had most closely supported him. Yet within a few years, and under the leadership of Deng Xiaoping, a new policy of 'reform and openness' was introduced which in time has led to a virtually 'capitalist-type' economy, hugely benefiting from foreign investment – at first from overseas Chinese, but by the end of the century from almost every source of wealth around the world.

At the same time, especially in sub-Saharan Africa, there have been, and still are, all too many nations without much by way of 'natural' resources in terms of minerals or unusual plants, but with growing populations, who are finding the conditions of world trade, as of the international organizations 'regulating' it (i.e. the World Bank, the International Monetary Fund and the World Trade Organization) extremely inhibiting. Meanwhile the USA insists on a vast process of 'globalization', not far removed from a new type of imperial economic control, first and foremost through their enormously powerful multinational corporations. More and more of our human lives, in the USA as in most other parts of the world, is subject to processes of information via the television or the Internet, both of them dominated by the USA and its interests. This is hardly the place to go into careful detail, but this wider economic and cultural context is facing the young twenty-first century with massive challenges.

Much could also be said about the effects of modern science, radically altering the ways in which humanity comes to terms with all that surrounds us on the planet – animals, plants, the sky and sea, one another, etc. Or those of modern technology, leading us to all sorts of things humanity can do with ourselves and other parts of the creation, often with scant regard to the long-term effects of such treatment (e.g. the waste from nuclear power stations that no nation has yet discovered how to deal responsibly with). Our whole expectation of communication with different parts of the human race, as of travel between different parts of the planet, let alone of the universe, has grown far beyond what anyone in 1900, apart from a handful of visionaries, could have believed possible.

All this becomes yet more important as we observe how in the last quarter of the twentieth century, people have been moving around the world and – where possible – settling in the big cities of the more affluent countries, and building new lives, while still very much attached to their traditional allegiances and families. In Britain, the Commonwealth provided an effective stepping stone for this, especially in the 1950s when British industries needed many more manual workers than were available in Britain's own population. Since then, comparable numbers and proportions of people from other backgrounds, races, religions and cultures have taken up residence in many of the cities of the world. This has led to a much more serious exploration of what is needed to enable such a variety of human beings to live alongside one another in peace and friendship, all the more since certain cities have had to endure sharp tensions – for example, Bradford and Oldham in England over lack of employment possibilities now that the earlier cotton mills have closed, and New Orleans in the USA when the damage caused by Hurricane Katrina revealed just how sharply it was the Afro-American half of that city's population that were made to carry the personal and other costs. For Christians, and people of other religious traditions, there is a particular importance to the inter-religious dimensions of this search for the best way of living in a multicultural community; we shall return to this in later chapters.

Finally, though by no means least, there is the growth of awareness, very late on in the twentieth century, symbolized first by the United Nations' Rio de Janeiro Conference in 1992, that the way humanity has been treating the natural environment of the planet in recent decades – for example, by the pouring forth from countless aeroplanes directly into the atmosphere of thousands of tons of the carbon dioxide from aircraft fuel – is endangering the very possibility of the environment supporting human and other life for even the forseeable, let alone the long-term, future. Here again, there are innumerable details to be worked through carefully. This cannot be the place to go into these. But it seems to be proven by the early years of the twenty-first century that humanity simply must not, indeed dare not, go on behaving as though there are no serious questions about our own misuse of the environment we live in. This time, it is without doubt the richer peoples of the earth who are causing by far the highest proportion of the damaging trends, so that it is the USA and its Western allies who positively owe to the poorer peoples a vast debt, which it will be extremely difficult to handle in such a way as to enable and provide for human life at the scale we need to in the century ahead.

The story we tell in the following chapters will need to be read against this complex background if it is to be fully understood and appreciated, for the Christian story cannot be separated from the diverse and rich contexts within which the events of that story have been lived out.

1

Christianity becomes a Worldwide Faith

Two illuminating and symbolic episodes

Two entirely real, and deservedly memorable, events at the opposite ends of the twentieth century may stand as symbols of the different contexts then facing Christians: in 1900 the Boxer Rebellion, a strong uprising in China directed specifically at Christians; in 2000 the 'Jubilee 2000 Movement', bringing pressure on the most powerful nations to cancel the unjust debts owed by many of the poorest, giving rise to public manifestations in several continents, the strongest in Africa and Europe, and in which many Christians took part.

In the later years of the nineteenth century, China came under unwelcome pressure from foreign countries, especially Japan, Britain, Germany and France, which concluded with the 'unequal treaties' by which the Chinese authorities were compelled to allow Christian missionaries unimpeded access to most of the Chinese Empire. This gave rise to a wave of anti-foreign feeling which swept across the country. It was particularly threatening for European missionaries who were widely dispersed, but it also threatened very directly those who had welcomed and followed their teachings. 'One more Christian, one less Chinese' was one of the slogans that rang out. This wave became even more threatening when the Dowager Empress issued an imperial decree on 24 June 1900 in support of the violent movement calling itself the 'Righteous Harmony Fists', which encouraged the killing of foreigners. The exact number who died cannot be known. It certainly included hundreds of Catholics, including some missionaries, and at least 188 missionaries among the Protestants (135 adults and 53 children) as well as many more local Christians. In Peking, the capital city, the foreign legations were besieged for 55 days, until a multinational force, including Japanese soldiers, fought its way through and relieved them.

The 'rebellion' was in fact soon over. Hudson Taylor, on behalf of the China Inland Mission, which had suffered more than any other, declined to accept any 'compensation' for the harm done to his colleagues or their followers. Indeed, the first instalment of that compensation sent to the USA was returned, to be used as a fund for the education of young Chinese. These gestures indicated that many missionaries had accepted that they may have been to some extent to blame for behaving in insensitive ways. In fact the mood in China swung hard in the opposite direction, so that in the next years 'scores of Christian schools could record that every single student who had finished the course had been baptized before leaving'.[1]

At the other end of the century there was increasing awareness in many countries of the ever-growing gap between the affluent nations of the North-West and the poorer nations of the South. This only heightened anger in many hearts and minds against the evident unwillingness of the richer nations to take costly and far-reaching steps to enable the poorer to shape their own destinies. So a widely followed movement sprang up, chiefly but by no means only among Christians, that stressed the teaching in Leviticus 25 that in the fiftieth year you are to 'proclaim liberation in the land for all its inhabitants'. Those who have sold themselves into slavery are to be released, those who have lost their land are to have it restored. So why should not the rich nations mark the beginning of the new century in 2000 by cancelling the debts of the poorer? These had in any case often been incurred by greedy and unelected rulers, let alone more or less imposed on the governments of the poor, whether by huge rises in the price of fuel oil, and/or by powerful intergovernmental agencies, especially the World Bank and the International Monetary Fund.

This Jubilee movement achieved considerable success in making its message creditable in many countries, in Africa above all among the impoverished, in Britain and Scandinavia above all among the middle classes, much encouraged by the overwhelming victory in the 1997 general election in the UK of a Labour government.

Yet it must also be recorded that despite what seemed large crowds at its crucial rallies around the leaders of the G8, the eight most powerful nations, in Birmingham, UK, in 1998 and in Cologne, Germany, in 1999, the actual steps taken by the rich governments in response did little more than establish a long-drawn-out and demanding procedure by which the indebted countries could hope to get some release over a span of years. Some relatively small parts of the debt were then released by unilateral action of the UK and Scandinavian governments. But the overall result was deeply disappointing. Despite the imaginative and Christian truth of the campaign, the 'powers of this world' showed themselves to be very far from giving way.

Earlier promise of Christian faith spreading into many new lands

In the early centuries after the death and resurrection of Jesus of Nazareth, the Christian Church spread his good news into many areas around the Eastern Mediterranean – into Egypt and Ethiopia to the south; into the Caucasus to the north – not least into Armenia, the 'first Christian Kingdom'; into Asia Minor and then Europe to the west; and, most startlingly, though little celebrated at the time because all this was outside the Roman Empire and therefore little known, to the east into Mesopotamia, Persia, Kerala in South India, and in 635 even into China where the Persian monk Alopen met a reasonably warm welcome at the imperial court in Chang'An (now Xian). Already in the eighth century, Islamic armies were spreading out to the east and the west of Muhammad's Arabia, conquering most of the Near East as far as India, as well as the whole of North Africa as far as the northern borders of Spain, and through Turkey (though Constantinople did not fall until 1453) up into the Balkans and at one point threatening Vienna. So Europe was the only region where Christian faith was gradually accepted by virtually all the rulers and peoples by the end of the first millennium since Christ, not least with the baptism of Prince Vladimir, the founder of the Russian nation, in 989. With the tragic launching of the Crusades over two hundred years from 1095 on, aimed at the 'repossession' of Jerusalem, but which actually stirred up hatreds, recriminations and antagonisms, not least among different Christian communities, that are by no means wholly reconciled even today, Christian Europe felt for some centuries blocked in by Muslim powers to the east and south. Later chapters on the various regions will briefly mention the early days of Christian faith in each, as the background for developments in the twentieth century.

Within Christian Europe there were two distinctive 'new beginnings' of a 'modern missionary era'. For the Roman Catholics this began with the rise of the Jesuits from 1540 on. Within 50 years they had penetrated into many distant lands, including the Americas and Japan. For the Protestants a comparable new start began among German Pietists at the dawn of the eighteenth century. A particularly striking initiative came from the Moravians. Only a few years after escaping into Germany from intense persecution by the Catholic Counter-Reformation in their own country beyond a line of hills to the south, they sent their first two missionaries in 1732 to live with the slaves from Africa on the Caribbean island of St Thomas. This took place in response to an impassioned appeal from Anthony Ulrich, a freed slave from that island, under Danish rule, who had been brought to Europe to attend the coronation of the King of Denmark, and had had there long conversations with Count Nikolaus von Zinzendorf, who had not long before accepted the Moravians as settlers onto his land in Saxony.

In the eighteenth century, and still more in the nineteenth, many people and groups in the 'Western' churches took up with great enthusiasm the 'missionary cause', at much the same time as European explorers and traders were making their ways into the 'new' lands of Asia and Africa, with the European governments following mostly more slowly and often with highly mixed emotions. Some of these governments exulted in the possibilities of 'empire'; others were much more hesitant. Similarly, some of the missionary pioneers saw their purpose as strongly contrasting with that of the traders and colonists, even as that of opposing them, while others – especially in the later stages – were happy to contribute schools and hospitals to the total western impact on the native inhabitants. North Americans, in large majority Protestants, joined in eagerly during the nineteenth century bringing major new strengths in finances and personnel, as witnessed by the series of ten-yearly 'general missionary conferences' which began with gatherings in New York and London in 1854.

So it was that at the beginning of the twentieth century, both the then leaders of Protestant Christianity, and the 'general public' in the western world, saw huge promise in the sending of yet more hundreds, even thousands, of missionaries into all possible 'mission fields', very often those that had been 'opened up' by their fellow citizens, whether of Britain, France, the Netherlands or Germany. Those from the USA concentrated especially, if by no means only, on China. The vivid and profoundly hope-filled expectations of this movement can be seen in the extract in *SCM Core Reader on World*

Christianity in the Twentieth Century, section 1.1, from John Mott's short volume reporting on his first world tour in the years 1895–97. That tour started with visits in Europe, working up to the foundation, at a conference in Sweden, of the World Student Christian Federation (WSCF) by student leaders from Germany, Britain, USA, Sweden and Norway. His journey continued through the Middle East, Asia (India and Ceylon, then China and Japan) Australia and New Zealand, Hawaii and western Canada, resulting in the foundation of five new national intercollegiate Student Christian Movements eager to join the young WSCF in their turn. His prose shines with the conviction that God is at work through these movements, 'forces for a great forward movement among the races of mankind' that will lead to the 'spiritual conquest of the world'.[2] Today, such language from a westerner sounds dangerously triumphant in the ears of those who are aware just how many 'conquests' of all too many peoples of the world were to be imposed by different forces down the length of the twentieth century. Yet in 1900 it rang clear, fresh and very attractive in western Christian ears.

Despite the tumultuous events of the century, it was nevertheless a time when the Christian faith spread further and faster than any earlier since the very first Christian century. Yet at its end, Mott's prophecy sounded dangerously hollow, although parts of it did indeed become true in ways he could not have anticipated! At that time Orthodox Christians, as the next chapter will discuss, were largely missing from the Student Christian Movements of Western Christianity. Yet they were soon to find their part, as the same John Mott, now General Secretary of the WSCF, was to contrive by holding its 1911 conference in two American colleges in the Hellespont not far from Istanbul/ Constantinople. This was granted the full blessing of the Ecumenical Patri- arch and the active participation of leaders from virtually all the Eastern churches, both those in communion with Constantinople and those of the Oriental, non-Chalcedonian family. One of the undoubted consequences of that productive meeting can be found in *SCM Core Reader*, 1.2, the letter of 1920 from the Ecumenical Patriarchate, at that point liberated from the Otto- man yoke, which first launched the idea of a worldwide 'League (fellowship) of Churches', alongside the 'so-called League of Nations'.[3]

The Roman Catholic Church was also in the nineteenth century busy send- ing out significant numbers of western missionaries into many different nations and areas. They too will often have appeared to the local peoples as typical westerners, often in close relation with the colonizers, if not always. At the turn of the century the Catholic Church as a whole was very strongly constrained by the anti-modernist concern authoritatively set out in the 1907 encyclical *Pascendi* by Pope Pius X. The Vatican's Propaganda Fide, its world mission office, was at that time most unlikely to be taking much interest in what Protestants were getting up to! By the end of the twentieth century, how- ever, the Roman Catholic Church was a very different community.

In the first half of the twentieth century large numbers of 'foreign' mission- aries, both Catholic and Protestant, continued to spread out into many areas in the southern parts of the planet. Of course their individual stories and qualities varied enormously. Books have been filled with the exploits of those gratefully remembered by those they lived among, just as many horror stories have been told about those who made themselves unwelcome! In some areas, the work of the first few generations of missionaries led relatively swiftly to sizeable churches which in due course took over control of their own affairs with no great problem. In others, for instance in the Arab countries, the missionaries at their best offered excellent medical and educational opportunities but had little success in gathering new communities of believing Christians. In some places they were experienced, for good or ill, as close allies of the colonial power; in others, as useful critics of that power.

Some large generalizations can be risked about their effectiveness, for example that their message was on the whole more welcome among peoples still living in their local aboriginal traditions than among those living in a highly 'developed' culture with a proud record of accomplishment and a distinct social structure of its own. But these do not take us far into the invariably complex realities of the hundreds of specific situations and the millions of specific personal relationships that formed the 'stuff' of the life and witness of these missionaries from elsewhere. What must, however, be said, if also of course with room for many complexities and exceptions, is that the astonishing spread of Christian faith during the twentieth century has been in almost every case the work of local Christians, sharing with their neighbours and fellow citizens in their own languages and cultures the good news they had begun to experience and believe in from the foreigners.

Within the 50 pages of but one of the chapters of his magisterial *The Church in Africa 1450–1950*, Adrian Hastings tells the stories of a number of local evangelists whose names will ring down the memories of Christians in their countries far longer than those of any missionaries: William Wade Harris, chief actor in 'the most effective evangelical crusade in modern African history', in 1914 in the Ivory Coast and western Gold Coast; Garrick Braide in Sierra Leone in 1915; John Swatson in 1915 in the Gold Coast; the Anglican Apolo Kivebulaya in Uganda and the eastern Congo/Zaire in the 1920s; and the Catholic Yohana Kitagana, apostle of the mountainous area of Kigezi in western Uganda for more than ten years from 1911 on.[4] There are also many areas where no particular evangelist is named, yet where the community 'converted themselves' in a mass movement 'sparked off' by 'the already existent commitment of a very small minority'.[5]

There are of course many other areas where the growth of the Christian community has been far from as notable as in those examples. Above all in majority Muslim areas, while among, for example, the Coptic Christians in Egypt there have been remarkable renewal and revival movements in the twentieth century, one can seldom point to anything approaching 'conquest'. It is all too easy to imagine the depth and consequences of the communal tensions any such 'victory' would give rise to. Yet in Indonesia relatively strong churches have arisen in areas with a clear Islamic heritage, and there are many areas, for instance in India, where villages have moved their loyalty between Christianity and Islam, depending on who looks after them best in a given period.

In China, whose ancient traditional culture was shaped by the social but hardly 'religious' teachings of Confucius and other sages, and where Christianity first arrived at much the same time as Buddhism and Islam, the

Christian faith failed in its first two attempts to make a widely successful impact. Only in the later years of the twentieth century, as people breathed a new freedom after the tragically wasted and destructive years of the 'Cultural Revolution' and alongside the amazing economic and social rush into western-style modernity, has the faith experienced rapid and remarkable growth. This has been taking place both in underprivileged rural areas and among highly educated university students and teachers who have as good as no direct contact with any church. There are then the former Communist countries, not least Russia and its neighbour nations formerly within the Soviet Union. Since the days of Mikhail Gorbachev, who came to power in 1985, Russian Orthodoxy is experiencing a strong, though hardly yet massive renewal of its 'traditional' position, while Armenia and Georgia likewise remain proud of their long-held Christian traditions. The age-old Muslim peoples of Central Asia are struggling with some revival of that loyalty and practice, yet the majority of today's inhabitants in that vast area have probably never experienced anything 'religious' as a personal or family priority. The future, in religious or any other terms, remains largely uncertain.

Overall, however, there can be no doubt that by the end of the twentieth century the Christianity that was at the beginning so definitely identified with the colonizing powers of Europe and North America has been widened and recast into a genuinely worldwide community. No doubt with a huge complexity of distinct sub-units and internal differences, even quarrels. Yet Christians today may still realistically hold out the hope of being able in the future to bring together the many races and cultures of the one human species into one world community under the God whom they believe is responsible for creating all that is in the first place.

A sidestep to the question of numbers

At this point, not least to offer the available evidence of figures even if some people find them questionable, we look into the matter of counting the 'total' numbers of Christians, and of other religious groupings. A good way to explore this area is to look up on the Internet either www.adherents.com or Wikipedia on 'religions'. You will find in both – they clearly work with each other – summary tables, offering the total number of adherents of the main 'religions' of today's world, and then breakdowns of the larger ones into whatever subdivisions they have. You can also find careful discussions of how these sorts of figures are brought together, with reference to some particularly impressive or useful books from which they have drawn most of their material. Both these websites, Wikipedia by a long way the more recently updated, give the totals as:

- Christians: 2.1 billion, equalling 33 per cent of the world's population
- Muslims: 1.3 billion, i.e. 21 per cent
- Non-religious: 1.1 billion, i.e. 20 per cent (deliberately grouping many different sorts of 'labels')
- Hindus: 900 million, i.e. 14 per cent

- Buddhists: 376 million, i.e. 6 per cent
- Chinese traditional religion: 394 million, i.e. 6 per cent too
- 'Primal indigenous' (certainly including many Africans): 6 per cent again
- Sikhs: 23 million, i.e. 0.36 per cent
- Judaism: 14 million, i.e. 0.22 per cent
- Baha'is: 7 million
- Jains: 412,000 – these last two too small to be given a percentage.

Within the overall figure for Christians, one can find:

- Catholics: 1.1 billion
- Independents: 386 million (grouping at least Pentecostals, African Independents and others)
- Protestants: 342 million (Lutheran, Reformed, Methodists, Baptists)
- Orthodox: 240 million
- Anglicans: 80 million

Without doubt, any such figures are somewhere in the correct ball-park. But the more you look into the details and the discussions, the more the website admits that it often has to deal in approximate rather than exact figures. It is also relatively quickly clear that these sites are using not only encyclopaedias and other books or journals published in North America, but still more that they are rooted in a characteristically North American world-view of wanting to be absolutely 'neutral', whether about which groups can be accepted into their lists, about quoting sources in the fuller lists of suggested sub-figures ('Religions by location', 'Religion in alphabetical order' etc.) or about the many references they have had sent in over (in the case of adherents.com) 30 or more years. One does not feel very much the wiser for spending an hour or two browsing in all this lot!

For it in no way answers the more basic question of how one can 'count' people in regard to such things as belief and behaviour. In any individual life these can come and go, can slide between certainty and doubt, between self-confidence and self-loathing. As for church attendances, there may be an average of 50 people worshipping in a given church each Sunday, but that may involve up to 100 or 150 people over a 3-month span, each and all with many distinct attitudes and convictions that are by no means all identical. 'Counting' religious allegiance is hardly the most important way to define or interpret it.

Still more tricky is the question, 'Why count?' What are we hoping to demonstrate? At the world level, counting can be – especially for Christians who often think of themselves as the largest single group – a way of boasting that 'we' are 'better' than 'they'. That is not an attitude Jesus would have encouraged! Yet even at the level of a single congregation, while figures for average Sunday attendance are no doubt necessary for certain financial and other administrative purposes, the reasons why some people come and some do not, why the congregation may have grown in one year and diminished in another, are full of uncertainties. The basic reasons for someone becoming a Christian are always at their deepest to do with God and the Holy Spirit.

From outside, the observer can only handle much more superficial, and at points misleading, pieces of evidence.

A third set of questions arises from the remark of Professor Jesse Mugambi of Kenya: 'It's one thing to try to investigate the *quantity* of Christians in a given area. It is quite another, and far more important, if no less difficult, matter to investigate the *quality* of their lives and their witness.' We hope this book as a whole will contribute to our readers' appropriate awareness of what that answer opens up.

The crucial questions of quality and obedience

In order to try and help Christians come to terms with the many diversities that face any of us looking at different churches in different cultures, the World Council of Churches undertook, in the middle of the twentieth century, a project by which book-length studies were written about 15 churches in different parts of the world. Each was written by someone from outside that area, who could bring both theological and sociological insights and questions to bear.[6] The task of reading all these, and thus of coming to some conclusion as to what the whole set could teach the Church at large, was entrusted to a small group of experienced mission theologians. In 1969 they published a relatively short report, *Can Churches Be Compared?*.[7] Its conclusions are expressed in a set of deliberately brief theses, to be found in *SCM Core Reader*, 1.9. The second of these insists: 'The basic diversity in the Church is a diversity in self-awareness in relation to surrounding culture, and this self-awareness is constantly changing.' In other words, to understand a particular church from inside you need to understand how they behave towards their neighbours and others within the specific cultural circumstances and opportunities of that particular context. Generalizations about what the Church 'always does' or what 'Christians believe' have at best a slender hold on the actual depths and complexities of what is going on in each group and each place.

Yet it is by the way they live and behave and speak that Christians, like anyone else, are known and judged by their neighbours. So what factors can be seen to have been at work during the twentieth century to encourage so many more of the world's people to see fit to join the Christian community? Of course the chief reason lies with the Holy Spirit – in our different ways we virtually all believe that we are called by God the Holy Spirit to ask for baptism and to serve him in Christ's Church. Nonetheless there are also some more identifiable human factors at work.

One of these has to do with the awareness that all human beings live in a single world. The majority of the human race have until the last few generations lived in 'their own' territories, by 'their own' loyalties and expectations. Already the larger empires had given many of their citizens some sense of a bigger whole to their context than their immediate village or province. Earlier religious traditions had spoken of a creator of all things, yet it seems that the Jewish people were the first to know themselves chosen by the one God who had created all things, and who had called Abraham, Isaac and Jacob, not just for 'their own' sake or advantage, but to serve as witnesses to 'all the peoples on earth [who] will wish to be blessed as you are blessed' (Genesis 12.2). This sense, of a particular people being called by the one God to serve his universal purposes, has been inherited from the Jews, by Christians through Jesus and by Muslims through Muhammad.

This probably helps explain why so many peoples were glad to accept the faith of the conquering Muslim armies as these swept through the Middle East and North Africa in the early years of Islam. This was a faith that gave them a role in the suddenly much bigger and grander world. Certainly this new awareness was a key factor when missionaries from outside Africa or Asia or the Pacific islands arrived. Sometimes they arrived after, yet often also before, other persons or groups from the western colonial powers. These latter would certainly bring a consciousness of a bigger and grander, if also all too often more cruel and more demanding, world 'out there', to which the local people found themselves suddenly expected in some sense to belong. In the twentieth century, those who were called the 'younger churches' in the colonial era have swiftly grown up into full partners with minds of their own, able to seize opportunities and create new relationships in ways that are fully theirs, often very different to what their first missionaries, let alone colonizers, would have thought of or expected.

In mid-century the creation of the United Nations reflected to all humanity this same universal sense of belonging and calling, even if at different times there are exceedingly awkward complexities and tensions involved in working out how to translate that universal loyalty into action. In turn, the UN has offered a focus for three other aspects of distinctively Christian behaviour and obedience: a concern for peace despite whatever wars and tensions are happening; a concern for human rights that belong to every person and people; and a concern for the welfare of the poorer peoples, in spite of whatever economic purposes and processes are being pursued by the more powerful nations and their multinational corporations. These three are all at heart essentially Christian emphases which go on arising freshly in the face of many different situations, and to which the growing 'younger' churches of the twenty-first-century world witness often more actively than their elder siblings.

The concern for peace rather than war had a hard time in the first half of the century when the two world wars were raging, with all too many losses and cruelties. In the first, many Christian leaders in the opposing nations tried to call on God to support their 'side', yet with less than adequately convincing effect (SCM Core Reader, 12.3). In the second, the outright self-righteousness of Hitler's Nazi creed, while at the time it was supported by a dismayingly large majority of German Christians and their leaders, also provoked into being an impressive minority, the Protestant 'Confessing Church', whose foundation document, the Barmen Declaration, based on a draft by the Swiss Karl Barth, is to be found in SCM Core Reader, 1.4. After the end of the war, it was the 'Stuttgart declaration' by a group of Confessing Church leaders to a visiting group from the nascent World Council of Churches (SCM Core Reader, 13.2) that enabled the mutual acceptance between Christians in the previously warring nations, and which foretold the remarkable way in which the German people as a whole (of course with exceptions) have shown since 1945 a determined calling to serve the cause of peace.

The concern for human rights, resoundingly voiced by the *Universal Declaration on Human Rights* agreed by the UNO in 1948, has also continued to prove a shared talisman, even if often pushed aside by the pressures of the immediate intentions and energies of those in power. The process of freeing previously colonized nations, from 1947 (India and Pakistan) onwards, was certainly full of tensions, even outright wars in, for instance, Algeria, Vietnam, Angola and Mozambique, but was in the end completed within 50 years, when the first ever vote open to every single South African citizen of whatever race took place amid great rejoicing in 1994. That gave a memorable climax to the century.

The concern for the poorer peoples was also provoked not least by the world wars, for instance in the foundation of the Oxford Committee for Famine Relief in 1942. Especially in the later years of the century, there have been many causes for wide public appeals in the richer countries for the raising of funds that can be sent to less fortunate and poorer areas, with significant – if never wholly satisfying – amounts of money being so transferred. Still more, as illustrated to some extent above in the story of Jubilee 2000, the governments of the rich nations have at least begun to recognize their responsibility to help the poorer peoples 'develop' their economies and livelihoods in such a way as to be able to share in the total world's discovery of how we can all live together in a reasonable degree of mutual understanding and respect. The text in *SCM Core Reader*, 1.7 illustrates how the World Council of Churches, in its first large 'Church and Society' conference in 1966, was beginning to reach deeply into the depths and dilemmas of this huge area of concern.

What has not yet adequately begun to happen is for the major multinational corporations, the huge money-making powers by which the rich continue to make themselves ever richer, to recognize the cruelty and injustice of their ways. The most important struggles for real criteria of justice to come into effect through the World Trade Organization, as for real commitment to justice and equality in the way the now rapidly dwindling resources of the planet can be responsibly shared out between all peoples, are still ahead. These are perhaps the most crucial issues now facing the UN and the many non-governmental organizations (NGOs). One day it will become apparent by which criteria the peoples of the world, led by their statesmen and -women entrusted with the responsibility to reach decisions, may have been able to win through to an acceptable situation. Christians cannot but profoundly hope that the central criterion will be the love of God as demonstrated in Jesus that comes to be seen as the basic model for how all persons, communities and nations can best live together.

The documents in Chapter 1 of the *SCM Core Reader* include several that illustrate how outstanding Christians spoke on themes such as the significance of a truly worldwide fellowship of Christians (Archbishop William Temple in his enthronement sermon, 1.4), of the importance of non-violence (Martin Luther King, 1.6), of the need for a truly and fairly secular state (M. M. Thomas of India, himself almost certainly the main drafter of both 1.5 and 1.7), and of the true meaning of Christ's call to reconciliation (Archbishop Desmond Tutu, writing out of his searing experience of chairing the South African Truth and Reconciliation Commission in the late 1990s, 1.10). These will provide quick snapshots of the kinds of clarity that has been both needed and aroused. Here we emphasize simply that it is in the practice of their faith in these sorts of contexts, as persons, as communities and as citizens of nations, that Christians in the twentieth century have often proved, and will in future years prove again and again, to be at best convincingly able – as indeed at worst unconvincingly unable – to live out a heart-warming faith, and to put into actual practice the lasting commitments that they attribute at the deepest level to what they have learned of God and of his priorities and purposes in the good news lived out by Jesus Christ of Nazareth.

The pattern of this volume, which also determines the pattern of the *SCM Core Reader*, is deliberately straightforward. We begin with separate chapters on the four main 'families' or 'traditions' of Christians, explaining something of the history and theology of each and how they have at least begun to regard each other positively as 'companions on the way'. Then there are a set of seven chapters, each devoted to one 'region' of the world. These cannot possibly touch on every nation or culture, but should give a fuller sense of how Christian faith has become indigenous to each region and how the Christians of each may be able to contribute to the whole. Finally, we offer four chapters on major themes that Christians have had to struggle with in the twentieth century. Again, these cannot either cover the four themes as fully as they deserve, let alone touch on many others that have been crucial in particular settings. But we hope they can give some sense of how even large and complex quandaries can be analysed and positively resolved. For now, we end this introductory chapter with a sketch of the approach which, we believe, best holds the entire Christian adventure together.

The century of the ecumenical movement

Bishop Lesslie Newbigin (1909–98) was an English missionary who spent many years in India and contributed not a little to the reunion of three separate churches, Presbyterian/Congregationalist, Methodist and Anglican, into the Church of South India. Indeed it was in the founding services of inauguration and consecration for that new church in Madras on 27 September 1947 that he was consecrated bishop. He often pointed out that the twentieth century was probably the first since Constantine became emperor in which Christians devoted more time and energy to reuniting Christians into a single community than to dividing them up into mutually exclusive and hostile camps.

To put it more theologically, God's Holy Spirit has been able in the past century to lead many Christians into a striving for the unity and integrity of the entire company of Christ's followers throughout the world in their central purpose of serving the unity and integrity of humanity as a whole. This is what 'the ecumenical movement' means to those aware of it as God's key to our total future. It provides threads that will run through our chapters. Meanwhile some of the basic purposes and discernments of what is meant by this movement are illustrated in the parallel chapter to this in the *SCM Core Reader* by the texts from Constantinople (1.2), setting out the original invitation to form a League of churches; from two of the Assemblies of the World Council of Churches in 1961 and 1991, struggling to express precisely what Christians intend when they speak of 'unity in Christ' (1.8); and then from the still far too little known *Can Churches be Compared?* (1.9) to answer as best as may be its own leading question.

This whole 'movement', now involving many different sorts of groups and projects that can contribute to the central aim, is undoubtedly one of the twentieth century's outstanding legacies to humanity. Here we offer a schematic way of looking at the history of the movement at the world level. We leave it to readers to explore for yourselves what has accompanied and filled out this movement at national and local levels, as well as what each of you can do to serve its forward movement in your own situation.

There are perhaps three main chapters to the story at world level so far. First, the forebears. Of these, three deserve particular mention. First, the Moravians, already mentioned, under the leadership of Count Nikolaus von Zinzendorf,[8] for their pioneering and worldwide mission activities. Second, the English Baptist William Carey,[9] whose youthful vision of God's call to worldwide mission in his 'Enquiry' of 1792, and then his astonishing service from the Danish colony of Serampore in Bengal, alike in publishing translations of the Bible, in whole or in part, in 39 languages and in suggesting that a world conference of missionaries be called in 1806 at the Cape of Good Hope, remain high points in the total history of the faith. Third, the young men, assistants in grocers' shops in London, who in 1844 started a Young Men's Christian Association,[10] which in its first international conference in Paris in 1855 agreed a distinctive 'Basis' pointing to 'Jesus Christ as God and Saviour according to the Holy Scriptures', phrases that were to become the essential starting points for the World Council of Churches in the next century.

It was then John Mott's work in and through the World Student Christian Federation that gave the crucial start to this distinctive contribution of the twentieth century to Christian history. For it was he, in his early years a staff member of the student YMCA in the USA and then as WSCF General Secretary, who chaired both the preparatory committee for the World Missionary Conference in Edinburgh in 1910 and then that conference itself. This meeting has long been hailed as the essential breakthrough, when missionaries of many different churches – if all from churches of the Reformation – realized how much they could learn from each other's experience, and agreed to form a 'Continuation Committee' (which in due course turned itself into the International Missionary Council) to put their shared vision and commitments into lasting practice.

Out of a dream at that Edinburgh conference came the idea of a comparable world gathering to explore possibilities for divided churches to work together on the sensitive questions of faith and of church order that had been and remain at the root of their divisions. The first such gathering eventually took place at Lausanne, Switzerland, in 1927. Meanwhile, the Archbishop of Uppsala in Sweden, Nathan Söderblom, had called a third type of worldwide conference, this one on the 'Life and Work' of the churches, with a central concern for their commitment and contribution to peace. This took place in Stockholm in 1925, now with the full participation of many of the Orthodox churches in communion with the Patriarch of Constantinople, from whose colleagues the letter of 1920 had been issued (*SCM Core Reader*, 1.2).

These three concerns – world mission, the uniting of divided churches, and the search for a common vision of the churches' social commitment – were from the outset seen by many as belonging in the long run together, even if it was more practical at first to pursue them separately. The International Missionary Council convened a second worldwide missionary conference in Jerusalem in 1928 – remembered above all for a remarkable 'Message' outlining the heart of the one Gospel in ways all participants could accept, written in candlelight by William Temple, soon to become Archbishop of York. Already by the time the other two were ready for their second rounds in the summer of 1937 (Life and Work meeting in Oxford, and Faith and Order in Edinburgh), these were each invited to vote on the desirability of forming an overall World Council of Churches. Both approved it. So a Provisional Committee for that new Council met in Utrecht in 1938, months before the third International Missionary Conference took place in Tambaram, near Madras, India, and just a year before the outbreak of the Second World War. This meant that the WCC could not be formally brought into existence until it was at last able to hold its first Assembly, in Amsterdam in 1948.

The second chapter at the world level consists of the considerable expansion and indeed 'success' of the WCC over the first 40 years of its existence. Welcomed by both the majority of the Orthodox churches, even if those in nations under Communist rule could only officially join in 1961, and virtually all the major Protestant and Anglican churches, it pursued ideas and activities in at least six main areas: church unity, peace, witness, social responsibility, inter-church aid (to which was soon added: refugee and world service, not least in emergencies) and laity (including the specific contribution of women to the Church's life and service in society). By the time of its third Assembly, in New Delhi in 1961, both the International Missionary Council and the remaining Orthodox churches were ready formally to join the Council, so its range of activities and concerns grew wider still. It was at the fourth Assembly, in Uppsala in 1968, the year of the student 'revolts' in Tokyo, Paris and elsewhere, that the WCC faced resolutely out into the world and established commissions for Inter-Faith Relations, for the Churches' Participation in Development, and for an active Programme to Combat Racism.

Things continued apace, with West German funding – thanks to a post-war arrangement for relatively high church taxes in that by now economically highly successful country – largely taking over from the earlier generous funding from the USA. A significant moment came when Philip Potter, from the Caribbean island of Dominica, was elected as the third General Secretary in 1972, a clear indication of the growing significance of the churches of the South. Already in 1969 the new Programme to Combat Racism had aroused strong objections by making financial grants to independence movements in southern Africa that had been driven into active combat. This set off a damaging and long-lasting flurry of argument and vilification in the richer parts of the world, which badly damaged the Council's reputation in the public eye, if not so strongly in well-informed church circles. In the 1980s and 90s there were several successive financial crises, when the number of staff and projects had to be reduced. These cuts did not in fact seriously damage the reputation of the Council among those committed to its purposes, but they gave the impression in quarters less directly involved of a cause that might be fading away. So that as the end of the century approached, there were often voices suggesting that the WCC formula was no longer the 'crest of the wave'.

Meanwhile, however, the Roman Catholic Church had adopted in its Second Vatican Council of 1962–65 a strong and lasting commitment to the one ecumenical movement, with many of its members throwing themselves passionately into joint activities, perhaps most noticeably in Europe. Not that that Church joined the World Council – though the precise reasons for the breaking off of conversations towards that end in 1972 were never made very clear. Yet a high and often very important degree of shared commitment, perhaps especially in the delicate field of interfaith relations, grew up into a new and much wider partnership. There were also the beginnings of contacts with Pentecostal churches, even if relations with the more deliberately 'conservative' evangelical churches, such as the Southern Baptist Convention in the USA, remained very difficult.

So at the turn of the twenty-first century, in a third chapter in its pilgrimage, the World Council of Churches itself is searching and experimenting towards a new sort of 'ecumenical space',[11] which can be considerably more open and tentative than the highly organized structure it has developed for itself. This will allow for a far wider and more hesitant group of churches to enter into conversations in which new relationships and commitments can grow. With the prospect of many more of the independent, Pentecostal-type, self-initiated churches of peoples of the South being able to take more than an occasional interest, what is at present being called the 'Global Christian Forum' promises to allow at one level a much looser sort of life and programme, yet without limiting or damaging the existing projects and purposes of the WCC. Time alone will tell, but if the Christians of the twenty-first century can remain as committed as their previous generations in the twentieth to discovering what the Holy Spirit intends and is opening up for the hitherto all too divided and inflexible older churches, the new century will be remembered all the more kindly in the longer future.

Yet the last word surely needs to be one of sharp warning, such as that with which Adrian Hastings greeted the new century in the pages of the *Tablet* (*SCM Core Reader*, 1.11), as likely to prove 'the very hardest of times'. For despite what can be hailed as significant advances in the twentieth century, for instance in scientific knowledge, or in relations between divided churches, the planet entrusted by God in creation to the care of humanity remains dangerously threatened. Two of the severest threats are hostilities constantly cropping up between different interests and groupings, and the prospect of global warming that is already starting to devastate humanity's inherited patterns of food and of 'civilization'. Both these huge threats arise from the newer expectations of human life that we have somehow – often unconsciously – devised and imposed on one another. Can tomorrow's Christians rise to the challenge of finding ways by which the world as a whole can turn aside these and other threats, and so bring us all nearer to the Kingdom of which Christ spoke? Or will we simply be swept along by the 'ways of the world' into one or more of the disasters which seem to be so alarmingly lurking ahead?

Further reading

World history

This chapter presupposes in the reader an adequate understanding of the overall history of the twentieth century throughout the world. It would be invidious to pick out any particular volumes from among so many already in circulation, and which will undoubtedly be joined by many more as the new century progresses. But one volume which will be of major – and relatively quick – help, not least to those who think of themselves as total beginners: *The Times Atlas of World History* (2000), London: Times Books.

Another book that helpfully presents a masterly account of the history of the century:
J. M. Roberts (1999), *Twentieth Century*, London: Penguin.

History of Christianity

Here again there is a vast choice, though not so large of books that deliberately try to cover the entire globe:
A. Hastings (ed.) (1999), *A World History of Christianity*, London: Cassell, succeeds remarkably well, though it cannot possibly be encyclopaedic, and the majority of its chapters are written by Europeans.
S. Neill (1986; originally 1964, updated by Owen Chadwick), *A History of Christian Missions*, Harmondsworth: Penguin Books, and New York: Viking Penguin, is more nearly encyclopaedic, though with less coverage of Europe.
Both these books have very full bibliographies.

Focusing on the worldwide ecumenical movement are three successive volumes:
R. Rouse and S. Neill (eds) (1954), *A History of the Ecumenical Movement 1517–1948*, Geneva: WCC Publications.
H. E. Fey (ed.) (1970), *The Ecumenical Advance: A History of the Ecumenical Movement: Volume Two 1948–1968*, Geneva: WCC Publications.
J. Briggs, M. Oduyoye and G. Tstetsis (eds) (2004), *A History of the Ecumenical Movement: Volume Three 1968–2000*, Geneva: WCC Publications.
Again, these all have full bibliographies to each chapter, which will be invaluable on specific areas and topics.

Notes

1 From S. Neill (1986), *A History of Christian Missions*, Harmondsworth and New York: Penguin Books.
2 From J. R. Mott (1897), *Strategic Points in the World's Conquest: The Universities and Colleges as Related to the Progress of Christianity*, London: James Nisbet, p. 23.
3 The letter 'Unto the Churches of Christ everywhere' is reproduced in full in Appendix I of W. A. Visser 't Hooft (1982), *The Genesis and Formation of the World Council of Churches*, Geneva: WCC Publications, pp. 94–7.

4 A. Hastings (1994), *The Church in Africa 1450–1950*, Oxford: Clarendon Press, pp. 443–72.

5 Hastings, *Church in Africa*, p. 453. For a vivid picture of comparable local witnesses fanning out across the Pacific Ocean from the 1820s onwards, see A. Hastings (ed.) (1999), *A World History of Christianity*, London: Cassell, p. 515.

6 The full list of these 15 book-length studies (with three shorter ones on India in the same volume) is to be found in S. G. Mackie (ed.) (1970), *Can Churches be Compared?*, Geneva: WCC Publications and New York: Friendship Press, pp. 25f. The first two, both by the late Bishop John V. Taylor, were published by the SCM Press, London and Friendship Press, NY, in 1958 and 1961. All the later ones, from 1965 to 1970, were published by Lutterworth Press (London) and Friendship Press (New York).

7 S. G. Mackie (ed.) (1969), Geneva: WCC Publications and New York: Friendship Press.

8 On whom, see a long-treasured study by A. J. Lewis (1962), *Zinzendorf, the Ecumenical Pioneer: A Study in the Moravian Contribution to Christian Mission and Unity*, London: SCM Press.

9 A useful, older biography is that by S. Pearce Carey (1924), *William Carey*, London.

10 Of which the fullest study is by C. P. Shedd (1955), *History of the World Alliance of YMCAs*, London: SPCK.

11 A key phrase from the report to the 1998 Eighth Assembly, in Harare, Zimbabwe, by the then General Secretary, Konrad Raiser, pp. 81–102, in D. Kessler (ed.) (1999), *Together on the Way: Official Report of the Eighth Assembly of the World Council of Churches*, Geneva: WCC Publications.

2

The Orthodox Churches

The original churches

The central pride and joy of today's many and various Orthodox churches
is that they stand in and actively maintain the living tradition of the earliest
Christian Church. Apart from Rome, seen by them as a non-Orthodox/west-
ern church, all the early churches mentioned in the New Testament, from the
one that will have sprung from the high official of Queen Candace of Ethiopia
(more likely Nubia), baptized by Philip on the road from Jerusalem to Gaza
as told in Acts 8, via the church in Antioch, where 'the disciples first got the
name of Christians' (Acts 11.26) and the churches in Greece, whether Philippi
(Acts 16.12), Thessaloniki (17.1ff.), Athens (17.15ff.) or Corinth (18.1–18), to the
many churches mentioned in Syria and Asia Minor, for instance the seven
addressed directly by St John the Divine in his Revelation (where they still
exist, despite all the difficulties and chances of history since then) were, have
been and still are churches of the Orthodox family. They never tire of remind-
ing their fellow Christians of the western family (or families!) that the unity
Christ prayed for his disciples to live and exemplify in John 17.20ff. must be
as much a unity across all the distances and boundaries in time as of those
in space – and in time looking backward as well as forward! Bishop Kallistos
(formerly Timothy) Ware's presentation of the meaning of tradition for the
Orthodox (*SCM Core Reader on World Christianity in the Twentieth Century*, 2.1)
remains a crucial, indeed essential part of the good news in Jesus for every
community in every century.

That said, these Orthodox churches have nevertheless had to bear a painful record of internal divisions among Christians, as well as an apparently
never-ending succession of cruel pressures and persecutions from outside
their ranks. This is not the place for any adequately detailed history, but the
essential elements of this double history must at least be recorded, for the sake
of understanding those who have been directly involved.

The first set of divisions that have determined much in the shape and the
lives of these churches ever since found a central point in the Council of
Chalcedon in the year 451. This has been counted as the 'third ecumenical
Council', at least by those who have agreed with its findings. But at the time
it was yet another called only a couple of years after an earlier one, by successive emperors on the Byzantine throne of the Roman Empire, in order to
try to reach some conclusion on the endlessly complex disputes caused by a
series of different teachers, each of whom had some of the major church leaders around the Mediterranean, and, still more, some of the leading advisers to

the different emperors, rooting for him rather than the others. At Chalcedon, to which at least three of the major churches of the time (Armenian, Ethiopian and Assyrian) were simply not invited because they were entirely outside the then Roman Empire, the Pope of Rome weighed in with an impressive *Tomos* (letter) which the emperor accepted as 'solving the problem' of how best to speak of the 'two natures' – divine and human – of Jesus Christ. So he simply insisted that the Council accept this word from Rome, and they obediently did. But this procedure so riled the representatives of the Syrian and Egyptian Christians of the Patriarchates of Antioch and Alexandria – at the time cities at least as great and glorious as Rome (which was already being threatened by the waves of barbarians who were to sack it not many years later) – that they refused to agree with the Council's findings. This not so much because they actually disagreed with what that letter said, but because they fiercely resisted the apparent claim of the Patriarch of Rome to force such a decision on the Council, with as good as no respect for his equal colleagues in the other historic centres of authority in the Church.

And so the tragic and long-lasting division erupted between the churches who call themselves 'Eastern' Orthodox, all in communion with the Patriarchs of Constantinople, and those who call themselves (in today's English) 'Oriental' Orthodox. All too often, unfortunately, many – though never all – of both groups have been quick to dismiss and excommunicate the others, so that, if anything, this division has grown increasingly damaging and tragic as the centuries have passed.

Today we need to be aware that there are at least six groupings in the 'Oriental' family: (a) the Copts of Egypt (the word 'Copt' means simply 'Egyptian'); (b) the Syrian Orthodox, worshipping in Syriac (the language nearest to the Aramaic Jesus spoke), led by the Syrian Patriarch of Antioch (one of four leaders who hold this title), often called 'Jacobites' and who are perhaps most accurately spoken of as the West Syrians; (c) the Armenians, under two Catholicoses, of Echmiadzin in Armenia itself, and 'Cilicia' now centred on a suburb of Beirut called Antelias, in the Lebanon; (d) the Ethiopian Orthodox Church in the highlands of the horn of Africa; (e) the Assyrians, better perhaps termed the East Syrians, whose ancient central see was in Ctesiphon/Babylon (now in Iraq) and who in the early Middle Ages were the most widespread church in Christendom, with bishops across the vast area of Persia, Turkestan/Central Asia, India and China, and with a missionary approach that was 'one of the most enlightened chapters in Christian history, society and scholarship' but were then 'drowned in the surging sea of Islam'[1] even before they were almost annihilated by the Mongol hordes sweeping over central Asia and the Middle East – now a small number with communities in India and Iraq but with their Patriarch in Chicago; and (f) important sections of the 'Christians of St Thomas' in India, originally in the SE Province of Kerala where St Thomas is remembered as arriving in the first century, though the total community of Christians there is sadly at present divided into at least eight different churches.

The 'Eastern' family is also diverse. As well as those who are led by the Patriarch of Constantinople in the city we know as Istanbul in Turkey, who has a relatively small flock of Greek-speaking people directly under him, it counts those who belong to the Patriarchs of Antioch (Greek- and Arabic-speaking in the Middle East and beyond) and Alexandria (Greek- and English-speaking, as well as worshipping in their own languages, many more by now in different parts of Africa than in Egypt itself) and those who belong to the Patriarchate of Jerusalem, established in 451 (Greek- and Arabic-speaking in the historic Palestine – now Jordan, the West Bank and Israel – and some of the Arab states in the Gulf). Beyond these ancient groupings there are the national churches of Greece, Russia, Romania, Bulgaria, Serbia, Georgia and Cyprus, together with the smaller, minority churches of the Czech and Slovak lands, of today's Poland, of Albania and the originally 'mission' Orthodox churches of Finland, Korea and Japan – and then the extraordinary spread of large numbers of Orthodox Christians of both 'families', but not least of the 'Eastern' communities, in the course of the twentieth century into both parts of America, especially the USA, as into Australia and New Zealand, western Europe and almost any other available area.

The second major division that was grievously to affect and determine the life of the Orthodox Christians and their churches was of course the estrangement between the leaders in Rome and Constantinople that grew in the second half of the first millennium and broke out into the open with the ex-communication of the Eastern Patriarch by the Exarch Humbert sent by Rome for this purpose in the year 1054. To which the then Patriarch of Constantinople, itself at the time an endlessly more impressive city than the long-ruined Rome, retaliated by promptly issuing a comparable deed of excommunication of the Pope of Rome. These gestures were all too soon followed by the tragic Crusades by western Christians with military purposes and weapons that were directed to repulsing the Muslim conquest of the Holy Land. Yet they eventually involved also the sacking of Constantinople and a major degree of underestimating, indeed all too often despising, the local Christians in the Middle East, who had long since had to learn to come to terms, if hardly to agree with, their Muslim overlords. Ever since then, in countless episodes, the degree of mutual understanding between Orthodox and 'western' Christians has been at best tentative, at worst disastrous (almost always especially to the easterners concerned), until – as will be chronicled below – the later part of the twentieth century has, at last, brought an amazing series of gestures and advances that promise a very much better future.

After the Crusades, another 'fruit' of this second major division has been the more or less constant determination of leading Roman Catholics, including many if not all the popes of Rome, to 'win back' at least some leaders and sections of the Orthodox to allegiance to the Roman Catholic Church of Rome. This urge can perhaps be said to start with the contacts made by the Crusaders with the Maronite Christians of the Lebanon, a sizeable grouping of Syrians who had taken themselves into isolation from successive Persian and Muslim invaders in the hidden valleys of Mount Lebanon, but who welcomed the western armies and gladly recognized themselves as having never renounced the allegiance to the Pope of Rome which was of such importance to these new friends. So they were allowed to keep their Syriac liturgy and their age-old customs and pattern of leadership, in a mode that has proven acceptable time and time again since then. This is that known as 'Uniate', that is, of communities with an Orthodox background who have decided to give their allegiance to Rome, and who continue virtually all their once Orthodox liturgical and other patterns of life, with no more than minor alterations to be sure that they are in no way believing or acting *against* Rome.

This pattern became of major importance in the Counter-Reformation when by a 'treaty' of Brest-Litovsk, on the border between Russia and Poland, the many Orthodox of that part of the Russian lands that had now fallen into Polish hands could be accepted into the Roman allegiance without making major changes in their faith and worship – but which was felt by the Russian leadership, at the time and since, as an underhand and unwelcome trick to steal thousands of believers from them. Over the centuries since, almost every Orthodox Church has had to suffer significant parts of their flocks as it were 'disappearing' into a new Rome-centred allegiance, for many different immediate causes, often that of direct political pressures, such as were imposed by the Portuguese who conquered much of Kerala in India in the seventeenth century, or of a quarrel in their own ranks. So one must now be ready to speak of the Catholic Coptic (or Catholic Armenian, Catholic Syrian, Catholic Ethiopian, etc.) churches, along with those who have a name of their own such as the Melkite (i.e. Catholic Arabic) or Chaldean (Catholic Assyrian) Church.

With the arrival of Protestant missionaries, almost all from the USA or Britain in the first instance, in Orthodox lands in the nineteenth century, there were undoubtedly fears that something similar would happen because of them. And indeed, over the years, especially because of the quality of the educational and health institutions they often set up, some seepage into their ranks and some relatively small 'Evangelical Armenian' (and other such) churches have emerged. But these have never gained the scale of their Catholic counterparts. Moreover, since both these Protestants and the historic Orthodox churches are committed to membership in ecumenical bodies at regional and international levels, relationships in the twentieth century have usually been more open and less ingrained with hostility than many of those between Uniates and Orthodox.

The sufferings of the centuries

As if earlier centuries, with their all too many tragic stories of Persian invasions, of the Arab Muslim conquest, of successive rulers making life difficult for the earlier inhabitants, had not done damage enough, the century to which this book is mainly devoted has unfortunately brought yet more acute sufferings to many of the Orthodox churches.

As it dawned, the majority of them were still, as for many years earlier, held fast within either the Ottoman Empire ruled from Istanbul, or the Russian Empire ruled from Moscow. In both cases this involved relatively strict patterns of control by the state authorities.

In Russia the Orthodox Church, although by a long way the biggest and most outwardly impressive of them all, was in fact ruled since Peter the Great in the mid-eighteenth century by an official appointed by the emperor, so that the Patriarch and bishops were the equivalents of the staff of a department of the Imperial government. Under the last Ottoman Sultans, after the Greeks had successfully broken away in the 1820s, both Romania and Bulgaria had been allowed to take a fair degree of independence as people and as churches, but the atmosphere around any Orthodox still under the rule of the Turks was growingly precarious.

To start with these last, the outbreak of the First World War, with the Turks allied to the Germans and Austro-Hungarians, was lethal for both the Armenians and the Assyrians. In both cases, Turkish troops were clearly ordered to massacre as many of the men of these communities as they could, and to transport – usually in wholly inhumane ways – the women and children into exile wherever this could be found on the borders of the empire, many of them into the desert Arab territories in the north of the Middle East. Millions died in horrific circumstances. These deserve to be remembered as the first holocausts of the twentieth century, even if those that were to follow later were no less terrible. In practice they also gave huge impetus for the emigration of people of these and indeed other Orthodox churches towards western Europe and North America. The Turks continued in a similar way in the 1920s, if not with quite the same quantity of deaths, by massacring thousands of Greeks who had gathered around the coastal town of Smyrna when Greek troops had in vain invaded Turkey from there. The later agreement to exchange any remaining population of Greeks in Turkey with the Turks in northern Greece was also far from comfortable, but at least involved rather less sheer loss of life.

Meanwhile in Russia, the 1917 revolutions against Imperial rule had no sooner brought a most welcome and eagerly accepted opportunity for the Russian church to hold a genuine Council and appoint its own leader in the person of Patriarch Tikhon, previously a bishop in North America, than the Bolshevik rulers brought the curtain down on all that. They consigned Tikhon to jail and only released him when he was prepared to issue a grovelling public statement of total loyalty to them. He died in 1925, and Bishop Sergei, chosen to as it were follow him, though by the Soviet rulers rather than the Church, was put through precisely the same pattern of lengthy imprisonment followed by a statement of utter loyalty which lost him the confidence of large parts of his 'flock'. In fact Stalin was already by then busy with the near total destruction of the Orthodox Church throughout his lands, with only the Georgians and the Armenians (perhaps because he was himself a man of the Caucasus?) being to some extent spared the depth and thoroughness of the assault in Russia itself.

By the time the Second World War broke out, it is now estimated that there were probably as few as four Russian Orthodox bishops at liberty, and with at best a few hundred of the sixty or seventy thousand earlier parish churches remaining open for worship. Curiously enough, it was this ghastly war which was to open the future for a church that Stalin no doubt considered to all intents and purposes already 'finished'. For on the one hand Stalin discovered that he urgently needed a totally new degree of confidence from 'his' people if Russia was to win through. At the same time it was clear from the way the Orthodox Church had sprung into life again behind the lines of the German invasion (until the Germans themselves needed to rein it in!) that there was a latent energy in the people brought out by the church in a way that was simply not to be found in the rest of Russia. So Metropolitan Sergei and his few bishops were given back both the title of Patriarch and a certain freedom to restart church activities. This did indeed help the Russian people to find the loyalty and energy to fight back and eventually – if also with a quantity of human losses and waste such as no western nation had to experience – win out against the very much better armed and trained German forces.

This real but still highly controlled version of church life continued after the end of the war, if not without Stalin trying to use it for some of his own propaganda purposes. Yet in the late 1950s, his successor, Nikita Krushchev for no evident reason undertook a hardly less thorough and abusive drive to reduce the activities of the Orthodox Church (as of its Protestant counterparts, though they were and are much smaller) which by 1964 had obliterated most of the monasteries and closed more than half the open churches, while also sending countless bishops and priests into the labour camps. No wonder that as the possibility of a more real freedom was sensed ahead in the 1970s some would-be reformers were seeking to reach any available sympathizers in other countries, as witness the letter from Yakunin and Regelson to Dr Philip Potter, General Secretary of the World Council of Churches (*SCM Core Reader*, 2.5) which Krushchev had allowed the Russian Church to join in 1961, almost certainly with the intent to make that gesture hide what he was doing to the Church inside the country. The advent of Gorbachev, with his promises of glasnost (openness) and perestroika (reform), brought a more genuine promise of freedom, even if it was to prove excessively complex to bring about any major renewal. Still, at the time of writing, it is often remarked that the Russian Orthodox Church is the only institution in Russia that has not known a major overthrow of its leading personalities and policies since 1989!

Over the same post-war years, the Orthodox churches in other nations dominated by Communist rule (Bulgaria, Romania, Albania, Poland – and Serbia, if to a lesser extent because of Marshal Tito's relative liberality) also found themselves in very rough waters, with a significant number of imprisonments and many restrictions on what they might have wished to do and say. In both Georgia and Bulgaria these years seem to have left the churches with such a degree of internal dissension on their hands that they have been finding it almost impossible as the century ended to emerge into the new era of freedom that their people more generally are beginning to enjoy. So also in Serbia, the eruption of the local wars around Slobodan Milosevic in the 1980s and 90s was supported by significant sections of the Orthodox Church, to such a degree that no real reconciliation with others in the former Yugoslavia is yet in sight. The Polish Orthodox Church, on the other hand, has found itself gifted in the last years of the century with an active youth movement which has produced several outstanding leaders, on the model of the Orthodox Youth Movement in the Patriarchate of Antioch in the 1950s and 60s. Something of the story of Albania will be told at the end of this chapter.

The new achievements and promise of recent years

At the same time, there is also much to report of wholly new, unexpected and very promising developments in the Orthodox churches during this twentieth century, especially in its later years. These can perhaps be grouped under three major headings and focused in one remarkable personality.

Theological renewal in the diaspora

First, the Eastern Orthodox churches can – and do – rejoice in the remarkable renewal of their life, especially of their teaching in specialist theological institutions, enabled by those who went into 'exile'. The first to emerge was that of St Sergius in Paris in the 1920s, to which teachers from the Russian homeland such as Georges Florovsky, Vladimir Lossky, Sergius Bulgakov and Paul Evdokimov brought a remarkably profound and widely appreciated interpretation of the Orthodox tradition. After the Second World War a similarly exciting and widely appreciated seminary named after St Vladimir with its publishing house was developed in the New York area, with outstanding teachers in Jean Meyendorff and Alexander Schmemann. These and other such colleges had admirable results in training generations of Orthodox every bit as truly Orthodox in faith, worship and obedience as their counterparts in the 'homelands', while also appreciating and using to excellent effect the whole range of the freedoms their new context offered. Another major personality, without whom the life and witness of the British churches would have been immeasurably weaker, was Metropolitan Anthony (Bloom, of Sourozh) who led the relatively small but growing Russian Orthodox Church in the British Isles, gave frequent broadcasts in English as well as in Russian, and became in the eyes of many in the 1970s the most attractive evangelist in the United Kingdom. This whole phenomenon has been of great service also to the majority churches in these countries in deepening the awareness of the spiritual tradition of the East, in making the ancient liturgies of the Orthodox world understandable and attractive to Western Christians, and above all in revealing the quality of what it means for a living Orthodox faith to confess in Jesus Christ the summit of all humanity, no less open to whoever are neighbours as to the creator God.

This is not to say that understanding between Catholic or Protestant Christians and the Orthodox is by now invariably easier and better than ever before. There are still many things which other Christians come across in Orthodox churches that they find difficult, even incomprehensible – for instance the way the Ethiopian Church still worships in an ancient language that nobody in the country uses as their own, and only allows to share in the bread and wine of the Eucharist elderly women (too old to be involved in sexual relations with a man) or children under the age of three (too young to be able to sin). At the same time, there are things in the Catholic or Protestant churches that most Orthodox will find equally difficult or incomprehensible (leadership of services without holy communion entrusted to lay members, or the apparent readiness of many to join in various activities of an ecumenical nature with Christians of other churches yet apparently without any interest or desire to move into a closer degree of unity with those). And yet, thanks to the theologians of exile, their books, their colleges and all that they have enabled, the availability of some of the best traditions of Orthodoxy, well interpreted and open to debate and experience, has surely brought renewal also to many people and churches in the countries of the diaspora far beyond what could have been hoped from occasional visits and exchanges with the ancient homelands.

From a very different background, there has also come a notable theological renewal and excitement from the Oriental Orthodox churches as these have seized opportunities open to them. This began in the middle of the twentieth century with the Indians of Kerala. Despite their internal difficulties and splits, the 'Thomas Christians' have contributed enormously, alike at an international level as in India – for example to the far-reaching debate on the properly secular/religiously neutral character of the Indian state and government, with major contributions from Dr M. M. Thomas, among others, from the 1940s onwards, alongside his many other outstanding services in the area of social responsibility and interfaith relations (see *SCM Core Reader*, 1.5). Several other Keralans, such as Bishop Paulos Gregorios, C. I. Itty and Ninan Koshy have also played important roles in the life and witness of the World Council of Churches since 1948. In the later years of the century the world has learned to expect much from the Coptic Church in Egypt and beyond, through the witness of their Pope Shenouda III, but also that of bishops such as Samuel (killed by the same bullets that killed President Sadat), Makarios who, with others, has worked so creatively with the African Instituted Churches, and Angaelos, working with younger people in the London area.

These stand out, but they remain wholly part of the larger and total Orthodox tradition, whose value to the entire Church of Christ has become a much more apparent reality to many open-minded Christians in the other churches than could have been hoped a century ago.

The lasting effects of partnership in the ecumenical movement

As mentioned above, it was from the Ecumenical Patriarchate that the idea of a 'League of Churches' was first mooted (*SCM Core Reader*, 1.2) and so certain Orthodox churches, mainly of the Greek family, took a full part in the early conferences between the wars that took forward the growing conviction that Christians of all backgrounds could and should be working together alike in search of their true unity in Christ, as of their true witness to the surrounding world. At the time of the founding of the World Council of Churches in 1948 the Russian Orthodox Church stood aside, no doubt as required by its state partner, and even held a separate conference at the same time to which other Orthodox churches under Communist rule were invited. But the majority of both Eastern and Oriental Orthodox churches joined the WCC, and have known many benefits from this, in practical and social terms as well as in more specific theological contexts. The Russians, Romanians and Bulgarians could then join the Council in 1961 at its third Assembly, since when the whole Orthodox family has been part, and a very active part, of the total striving of the Christian churches for their common obedience and service.

This has of course not been without awkward passages and experiences, on all sides, as is the case for any of the major families of churches. Yet as one looks back over the first 60 years of the WCC it is surely overwhelmingly clear that the Orthodox churches have both contributed greatly and learned not a little, at local and national levels, as well as in international settings. For an insider's view, see *SCM Core Reader*, 2.8, the passage on 'Learning from One Another' with which Timothy Ware, later Bishop Kallistos, finished his 1963 book. For another, here are two paragraphs by Bishop K. Sarkissian, later Catholicos Karekin II of Cilicia, then of Echmiadzin:[2]

> We must not overlook the great contribution of the ecumenical encounter. An open encounter, a true dialogue, a sincere conversation are not only the key to the discovery of the other, but also of oneself. The great blessing of the ecumenical challenge is self-discovery that casts new light on the existence and vocation of the persons and the communities involved ... The dialogue is an intellectual and spiritual mirror in which one does not see the other alone, but finds in it the reflection of one's own being. And this is the first step towards purification and renewal that is so desperately needed not only by individuals but also by communities.

> The world is one. It is God's world, for God is its creator ... The Church does not stand over against this world, but, on the contrary, at its very centre. Christ's Kingdom is 'not of this world' as Jesus himself proclaimed. Yet it is not also *out* of this world. It is *in* this world, and is there to make it truly, fully, *God's* Kingdom ... Therefore the Church is to be present in education, in family, industry, technology, science, social work, politics, cultural disciplines and whatever affects human life, without interfering *as an institution* in the autonomy of any of these disciplines and areas of life. She has to work in all these spheres as a transforming power. For the Church is the world in transfiguration ... The Church has to bear witness to God's presence, both to his love and judgment. This is why the Church, in order to fulfil this tremendous task, has to be the Church of Christ in unity and obedience.

A rather different field for ecumenical 'progress', namely between the Orthodox churches and the Roman Catholic Church, has also taken major steps in the second half of the twentieth century. The most outstanding moment in this was surely the meeting between Pope Paul VI and Patriarch Athenagoras I of Constantinople in Jerusalem in 1965, when they were both able alike to 'regret the offensive words ... and the reprehensible gestures which marked the sad events' of 1054, and to 'consign them to oblivion' by lifting the double excommunication of each church by the other (*SCM Core Reader*, 2.3). The dialogue to which that led directly has stuttered over the years since, with particular difficulties arising when the Roman Catholic Church, principally through its Polish members, took the initiative to establish itself in the 1990s as a 'local' church also on the territory of Russia. But Rome has pursued an active policy of rapprochement with several other Orthodox churches. In 1986 Pope John Paul II and Patriarch Ignatius Zakka of Antioch, for the Syrian Orthodox family, were able to sign a 'Joint Statement of Faith' in which the long-standing dispute about the incarnation, as laid down by the Council of Chalcedon, was recognized to have been overcome. In later years Pope John Paul was able also to sign comparable joint statements with both Pope Shenouda of the Coptic Church and Patriarch Mar Dinkha of the Assyrian Church of the East. Indeed, in this latter case, there has been considerable follow-up in meetings between the 'original' Assyrian Church and the 'uniate' Chaldean Church which in recent centuries has been the larger of the two. In 2001 the Vatican published guidelines for eucharistic sharing between both communities, with an explicit acceptance of the eucharistic prayer used since the outset by the Assyrians as fully valid. Full union cannot be far away, though one hears that since the comparable situation between 'Orthodox' and 'Uniates' in the Ukraine is very far indeed from any such reconciliation, the Vatican will find it hard to agree to the two ancient churches uniting across what is for others such a difficult barrier.

Such 'top-level' agreements invariably need not a little energy and commitment to be followed through at more local levels, which is not always easily aroused. But they give strong hope for a much more peaceful and peacemaking future.

At the turn of the century, and in response to a considerable disquiet, voiced most sharply by the representatives of the Russian Orthodox Church at its fiftieth anniversary Assembly in 1998 at Harare, Zimbabwe, while shared by many other member churches of different families, the World Council of Churches established a 'Special Commission', consisting of one representative from each of the Orthodox member churches and the same quantity from across the spectrum of its other members. This undertook what looked likely to be an extremely difficult task of reaching shared conclusions about the various areas of difficulty – spiritual, sacramental, political and ethical – and yet did so within the space of four years and with a set of recommendations that were passed, not without controversy, yet with overwhelming majorities and the expression of 'deep appreciation for its work', by the Central Committee in 2002. Members have spoken eloquently of the need for prolonged and sustained mutual listening as the key component in its achievement. Some details can be found in the SCM Core Reader (2.7), and the whole report in The Ecumenical Review (vol. 55/1, January 2003). It was overwhelmingly apparent in the succeeding Assembly, in Porto Alegre in 2006, just how much better the mutual trust and understanding between the Orthodox churches and between them as a whole family and the wider membership of the Council had become. So it can be expected and hoped also in this respect with good reason that the future relationships between Orthodox and other Christians now have the chance to flower that they have so long deserved but so seldom achieved.

A welcome expansion of evangelistic effect

A third area of advance, in some ways perhaps the most surprising, has been the wide range of new areas in which the Orthodox Church has been gathering new members around the world. Much of this is of course due to the emigration of Orthodox from their 'original' home areas into quite different continents in the aftermath of the two World Wars and the other pressures they have come under. Latin America and Australasia, for instance, are two areas where Orthodox churches are now flourishing, not in every township but widely enough not to deserve to be overlooked. Alaska was already an important mission field for the Russian Orthodox Church in the nineteenth century, as was the area of NE China around the city of Harbin, along with Korea and Japan. In all these cases, small Orthodox churches have survived until now, though somewhat swamped by the arrival of much more numerous churches of other backgrounds. Oriental Orthodox from Kerala are at present to be found in countless centres in the Arabian Gulf, among many other foreign workers, often bringing Christian worship to the area for the first time in centuries. And at recent WCC meetings Orthodox priests have taken part from such 'unlikely' countries as Ghana and Indonesia. Maybe the particular persons have had histories of education in different parts of the world, but still the long-term effects of their work and life will surely enlarge the linguistic, cultural and evangelistic horizons of Orthodoxy as a whole, and so of its role and contribution in the common striving for both the faithfulness and the wholeness of the entire Church of Christ in the years ahead. The 1989 initiative of His All-Holiness Dimitrios I, Ecumenical Patriarch of Constantinople in regard to the protection and preservation of the environment (see *SCM Core Reader*, 2.6), which has been no less imaginatively and energetically followed up by his successor, Patriarch Bartholomew, is also a profoundly encouraging gesture for the entire Church of Christ in the new century.

A case study: a most remarkable man

All three of these 'areas' of renewal, as also many of the more traditional values of Orthodoxy, are to be discerned and delighted in through the story of one outstanding Orthodox leader of the present time – the nearest, one might say, that Europe has produced to a Desmond Tutu, if of course very different in every possible detail except for their shared sense of humour.

This is Archbishop Anastasios (Yannoulatos) of Tirana and All Albania. Born in 1929 in Piraeus, near Athens, he grew up amidst the violence and tensions of the Second World War in Greece which were only over in the late 1940s after the intervention of the USA on the side of the democratic forces. Very good at school at mathematics, he eventually decided to study theology – 'What a waste, many of my friends and teachers thought'! – and founded in 1959 a bilingual magazine (Greek and English) called *Porefthendes* ('Go Ye') devoted to the study of the history, theology, methods and spirit of Orthodox world mission. One could almost say that he has single-handedly in his lifetime restored the reality and the horizons of world mission to the Greek churches. This brought him into close involvement with Syndesmos, the international association of Orthodox Youth Movements, which in turn brought him into contact with the World Council of Churches, just as it was uniting with the International Missionary Council, in whose first major conference after that union, in Mexico City, he participated as one of the first Orthodox to appear in that company. Indeed, having asked the conference organizers to arrange for him to share in some effort of pioneer missionary work in that area, he found himself sharing a long trip in the boat in which a missionary of the Wycliffe Bible Translators was to travel into the jungle in Yucatan and explore how the Bible might begin to be translated into the language of one of the not yet contacted indigenous peoples! Ordained as a priest in 1964 he flew directly to Uganda for long-term service there, but soon fell gravely ill with the malaria of the Great Lakes, and was advised to return to Europe. After pursuing postgraduate studies in the University of Hamburg, he spent three years on the WCC world mission staff in Geneva as the first ever 'Secretary for Research and Relations with the Orthodox Churches', before returning to Athens in 1972 to teach in the Theology Faculty as Professor of the History of Religions, which he did until 1991.

Throughout these years he continued to travel, write and look after other significant pieces of work as his own, including nearly ten years as 'acting Archbishop of East Africa' for the still young Orthodox Church there, serving as Moderator of the WCC's Commission for Mission and Evangelism and chairing its ten-yearly conference at San Antonio in Texas in 1989, as well as being the general director of Apostoliki Diakonia, the social welfare organization of the Church of Greece, with the title of Bishop of Androussa.

Then in 1991 the Ecumenical Patriarch invited him to move to Albania, the country which had suffered probably more than any other from its Communist rulers since 1944 and where all religion had been strictly forbidden for some fifty years, in order to take up the leadership of whatever could be rediscovered and renewed of the Orthodox Church there. A demanding vocation if ever there has been one, not least since there was no house for an archbishop, and the temporary cathedral – the real one having been demolished years before – was in a devastated condition with a large hole in its roof. He had to live for his first few months in a hotel and then a small flat, with no certainty that he would be allowed to stay permanently, since the new regime was hardly in favour of close contact with their southern neighbour.

Yet within a year of first setting foot in Albania he had been solemnly elected as Head of the Church in Albania by the Synod of the Ecumenical Patriarchate. In his fourth year a motion put to the Albanian people, in a referendum on the proposed new constitution, which would have forced any non-Albanian religious leader to leave the country, was turned down by popular vote. And within 10 years he had an astonishing record of having been responsible for the building of 80 new churches, 70 others restored from ruin, more than 140 repaired and 5 monasteries restored to effective life, along with 'more than twenty large buildings erected or renovated to house a theological academy, the office of the archdiocese, several diocesan centres and bishops' houses, a diagnostic centre, dispensaries, guest houses and schools, along with one housing a candle factory, printing house, icon atelier, restoration workshop and other church facilities'![3]

In and under all this has been not only the continuation of much of his lifelong international service, now for instance to the Conference of European Churches, and from 2006 as one of the eight Presidents of the World Council, but still more a totally devoted and open-minded commitment to the people and development of Albania, splendidly epitomized in the nickname given him – Archbishop of Tirana and all Atheists! Indeed not only to Albania as if it could live in continuing isolation. For when the Kosovo conflict broke out, leading to thousands of Albanian speakers fleeing over the mountains into Albania, the Archbishop appeared in the seminary and took the students off with him into the hills to discover how best they could help those refugees and alleviate the emergency situation. Some of the students, he recalls,

> were initially afraid, worried some of the refugees might be hostile to Orthodox Christians, even if they were there to help. I said we must go into the middle of the crisis and see the face of Christ in those who suffer. There was one student who asked 'But will the cross I am wearing provoke some?' I said to him that it was enough to wear the cross in his heart. More important than speeches about Orthodoxy are Orthodox actions. Obey the God of love, and don't be afraid.

Later on, when a delegation from the Conference of European Churches had come to Tirana to discuss the political prospects with the Albanian government, there came a moment of such difficulty that the Albanian team leader said: 'We are not going to get any further by ourselves. There is only one thing to do – we'll go and put it all to Archbishop Anastasios. He's the only man who will be able to see a way ahead!' So they went over to the Archbishop's house – and he was!

Underneath all this is of course a wholly admirable spirit, such that a conversation with the Archbishop is almost always full of memorable and inspiring phrases. Jim Forest records many of these. For instance on prayer:

> The experience of St Paul in his apostolic endeavours remains a basic refuge and inspiration, while my prayer for my people and me culminates in his prayer in Ephesians 3.14–21. There is a special music in the Greek text that I don't hear in translations, but the meaning is always clear. Our life is to be a ray of the Holy Spirit, to be used by the Spirit. It is not our own activity that is important, but what God does through us. Prayer summarizes a longing. The problem is that so often we become ego-centred, lacking humility. Thus it is good to pray, 'Oh Lord, deliver me from myself and give me to Yourself'! – a cry of the heart. It is similar to the prayer, 'Lord I believe, please help my unbelief.' … Often in prayer we have no time to think what each word means. But prayer is not an analytical activity. It is in our intention, in our longing. You know you are far away from the ideal and you reach out in prayer. God does not need a detailed report about our efforts. Sometimes the only prayer that is possible is the prayer of silence, silence and the cries of the heart asking the Holy Spirit to dwell in us.[4]

The day Forest left Albania, he reminded the Archbishop that he had been reluctant at first to make his home in Albania. This made him laugh:

> People look at the difficulties of life here and say to me 'How can you stand it? It is so ugly!' But for me it is so beautiful! It is God's blessing to be here

– not the blessing I imagined, but the one I received. My origins are not with the humble people, but I learn from them to become more simple, more true, more honest, more ready to forgive and let go of past injuries. Humility is not an achievement but a development, a contiguous dynamism in our life. So often you meet here in Albania persons who absorb every word, every gesture. Their faces are like a thirsty land ready to absorb every single drop of rain. It is a surprising providence to be sent to serve such people, people you never knew, never expected to meet and yet who receive you with such confidence. Thank God I was sent to live among such people, to be helped by them. People sometimes ask me about my expectations, but I don't know about the future! You can only do your job with love and humility. I am not the saviour of Albania, only a candle in front of the icon of the Saviour.[5]

Further reading

T. Ware (1963), *The Orthodox Church*, first edn, London: Penguin Books, is an excellent introduction to the history and theology of the Eastern Orthodox Church, and has useful bibliographies of by now somewhat older books.

B. J. and J. M. Bailey (2003), *Who are the Christians in the Middle East?*, Grand Rapids MI and Cambridge UK: Wm B. Eerdmans, is an up-to-date and most useful factual survey, including the whole range of churches, Orthodox, Catholic and Protestant, together with a short but well-chosen bibliography. It does not of course include Greece, nor any other European Orthodox church.

A. Schmemann (1963), *For the Life of the World*, New York: National Student Christian Federation (new expanded edn, New York: St Vladimir's Seminary Press, 1997), was an excellent challenge for student communities in the 1960s and still well worth reading.

J. D. Zizioulas (1985), *Being as Communion: Studies in Personhood and the Church*, New York: St Vladimir's Seminary Press, stands out as *the* book on Orthodox theology of the later twentieth century; not easy but well worth reading at least twice over! Many other works are mentioned in footnotes.

J. Forest (2002), *The Resurrection of the Church in Albania*, Geneva: WCC Publications, is a heart-warming, impressionistic account of some months the author spent in Albania talking to various people, above all the Archbishop.

Archbishop Anastasios (Yannoulatos) (2003), *Facing the World: Orthodox Christian Essays on Global Concerns*, Geneva: WCC Publications and New York: St Vladimir's Seminary Press, is a collection of several major essays on related themes of the world scene at the outset of the twenty-first century. Not all that easy, if less technical than some of Bishop Zizioulas' chapters, but well worth taking the time for.

Notes

1 Quotations from A. S. Atiya (1968), *A History of Eastern Christianity*, London: Methuen, pp. 240f.

2 K. Sarkissian, Bishop (later Catholicos, first of Cilicia then of Etchmiadzin) (1970; first edn 1968), *The Witness of the Oriental Orthodox Churches: Recovery, Rediscovery, Renewal*, second edn, Antelias, Lebanon: The Armenian Catholico-sate of Cilicia, pp. 44 and 47–8.

3 J. Forest (2002), *The Resurrection of the Church in Albania*, Geneva: WCC Publications, p. 110.

4 Forest, *Albania*, pp. 123–4.

5 Forest, *Albania*, p. 126.

3

The Roman Catholic Church

Introduction

Any review of the Roman Catholic Church during the twentieth century will call to mind a number of well-known personalities who have borne courageous witness to the Christian faith. Pope John XXIII and Pope John Paul II transformed the Church through their papacies. Archbishop Oscar Romero was martyred at the altar in San Salvador for taking sides with the poor. Archbishop Helder Camara was accused of being a communist merely because he insisted on asking why the poor in Brazil had no bread. Archbishop Denis Hurley will be remembered for his courageous witness against apartheid in South Africa. Mother Teresa (and her Sisters of Mercy) will be celebrated for her commitment to the poor and destitute in Calcutta.

The Roman Catholic Church is the largest single church within contemporary Christianity.[1] It differs from all the other traditions whose story is told in this book in that it is one, universal and worldwide church, that is, a catholic church. Whereas the other traditions are made up of largely autonomous churches and denominations within various countries and nations, the Roman Catholic Church is one single worldwide entity. At the head of the church is the pope, who, as Bishop of Rome, is recognized as the successor of the apostle St Peter. The pope heads a hierarchical ecclesial structure which includes a college of cardinals, and archbishops and bishops exercising authority and leadership (under the authority of pope and cardinals) in dioceses around the world.

However, its ecclesial pattern recognizes both this universality and its identity as the Church within particular local contexts. Go to Italy or Ireland, Portugal or Poland, Spain or El Salvador, the Philippines or Brazil and there may be found the Roman Catholic Church in considerable strength. It will display diversity of culture, language, tradition and social and political witness, while also reflecting a shared faith, a common liturgical pattern, a shared pattern of ministry and decision-making and a common recognition of the pope as the successor of Peter and Head of the Church.

Foundations

The foundational thinking and theology of the Roman Catholic Church may be found primarily within papal encyclicals in which the popes have sought to present the mind of the church on particular topics and challenges.[2] Much of this chapter will, therefore, focus on some of the key encyclicals issued during the period under consideration here. But it must be recognized, of course, that whereas these represent the official positions of the church, there may well be considerable diversity in the ways in which they are received, interpreted and lived out in the day-to-day life of the faithful in diverse contexts around the world. This chapter cannot provide detailed information about this diversity, but the regional chapters, as well as those on thematic topics, provide more information about the way the Roman Catholic family – and the other Christian traditions – has responded to perspectives and positions which have been centrally proclaimed.

The Church of the early Christian centuries saw a division between 'East' and 'West' in the Great Schism of 1054 (see Chapter 2). This schism resulted in a Roman Catholic Church, centred on Rome, which reflected the Western tradition of the first ten Christian centuries and what are now known as Orthodox and Oriental Orthodox churches which inherited the Eastern traditions of the early centuries. Both Roman Catholic and Orthodox traditions, then, trace their origins directly to the early years of the Christian Church and seek to reflect that confessional identity in their life, liturgy and doctrine. In the sixteenth century, the Reformation, initiated by Martin Luther, John Calvin and Ulrich Zwingli from within the Roman Catholic Church, led to the formation of, largely national, Protestant churches (sometimes described as Reformed or Evangelical churches). So from the sixteenth century onwards there have been three very separate streams within Christianity, the Catholic, the Orthodox and the Protestant.

The primary philosophical foundation of Catholic doctrine and ethics up to and during the twentieth century was the philosophical and theological work of St Thomas Aquinas (1224–73). In his *Summa Theologica*, Aquinas seeks, as the name suggests, to sum up the foundations and essence of Catholic Christian doctrine, belief and morality. Aquinas provided the basis for the scholastic approach that became foundational in subsequent centuries, and for the neo-scholasticism that was reaffirmed by the First Vatican Council (1870) (*SCM Core Reader on World Christianity in the Twentieth Century*, 3.1). He laid the essential foundations for what Pope John Paul II called 'the close harmony which exists between faith and reason'[3] that has shaped Catholic doctrine throughout subsequent centuries and has continued to be foundational up to the present time. John Paul II quotes what his predecessor, Pope Paul VI, wrote on the seven hundredth anniversary of the death of Aquinas ('the Angelic Doctor') in 1974:

> He passed into the history of Christian thought as a pioneer of the new path of philosophy and universal culture. The key point and almost the kernel of the solution which, with all the brilliance of his prophetic intuition, he gave to the new encounter of faith and reason was a reconciliation between the secularity of the world and the radicality of the Gospel, thus avoiding the unnatural tendency to negate the world and its values while at the same time keeping faith with the supreme and inexorable demands of the supernatural order.[4]

There is a particularly important point here, not just for the Roman Catholic Church but for all churches and traditions, namely, his understanding of the necessary interweaving of the secularity of the world and the radicality of the Gospel. In his praise of Aquinas, Pope John Paul II reaffirms the historical and contemporary importance of Aquinas' approach to faith and reason and the philosophical and theological continuities between the exposition in his *Summa Theologica* and the contemporary doctrinal and moral teaching of the Church in the latter years of the twentieth century.

The nineteenth-century heritage

The First Vatican Council (1870) issued a number of decrees that became foundational for the church in subsequent years. Among the most important was the *Decree on the Doctrine of Papal Infallibility*:

> We [i.e. Pope Pius IX], adhering faithfully to the tradition received from the beginning of the Christian faith ... teach and define as dogma divinely revealed: That the Roman Pontiff, when he speaks *ex cathedra* ... is endowed with infallibility ... in defining doctrine concerning faith or morals ... If any one shall presume (which God forbid!) to contradict this our definition; let him be anathema.[5]

The Pope also promulgated another highly significant and controversial decree that arose from the Council, namely, *The Dogmatic Constitution on the Church of Christ*, which included a statement on the status and role of the Bishop of Rome (*SCM Core Reader*, 3.2)

> The primacy of the Pope of Rome is no mere precedence of honour. On the contrary, the pope possesses the primacy of regularly constituted power over all other Churches, and the true, direct, episcopal power of jurisdiction, in respect to which the clergy and faithful of every rite and rank are bound to true obedience.

These two doctrines of infallibility and primacy have raised, and continue to raise, deep questions, particularly in terms of ecumenical relationships with both Orthodox and Protestant churches (but see below).

Another key issue at this time was the Church's understanding of the Bible and of the methods of biblical interpretation. During the latter half of the nineteenth century, biblical criticism – employing methods of literary criticism – was increasingly used, mainly among Protestant biblical scholars, as a tool for biblical interpretation. In 1893, Pope Leo XIII issued an encyclical which condemned biblical criticism in an uncompromising way:

> They deny that there is any such thing as revelation or inspiration, or Holy Scripture at all; they see, instead, only the forgeries and the falsehoods of men; they set down the Scripture narratives as stupid fables and lying stories ... and the Apostolic Gospels and writings are not the work of the

Apostles at all. These [are] detestable as the peremptory pronouncements of a certain newly invented 'free science'.[6]

There were contrary voices, such as Alfred Firmin Loisy (1857–1940), a French Roman Catholic modernist biblical scholar, within the Catholic Church, even at this time. However, he was forced to resign his lectureship at the École Pratique des Hautes Études in Paris in 1904 and his priesthood in 1907 on the publication of Pope Pius X's condemnation of modernism.[7]

Half a century later, however, in 1943, while praising this encyclical for warning against the extremes of radical criticism of the biblical text at the end of the nineteenth century, Pope Pius XII, in his encyclical, *Divino Afflante Spiritu*, recognized the important contribution of critical biblical scholarship in enabling a fuller and more authoritative understanding of the text of Scripture. The encyclical affirms that the original text of Scripture can more easily be explained by making use of 'a real skill in literary criticism of the ... text':

> In the present day indeed this art, which is called textual criticism and which is used with great and praiseworthy results in the editions of profane writings, is also quite rightly employed in the case of the Sacred Books ... [for] its very purpose is to insure that the sacred text be restored, as perfectly as possible, be purified from the corruptions due to the carelessness of the copyists and be freed, as far as may be done, from glosses and omissions, from the interchange and repetition of words and from all other kinds of mistakes, which are wont to make their way gradually into writings handed down through many centuries.[8]

This encyclical marked a dramatic change in the approach of the church to biblical interpretation and biblical studies, over a period of 50 years. It brought Catholic, Protestant and Orthodox scholars into closer partnership and collaboration with each other in relation to biblical text, providing a growing interpretative and hermeneutical consensus in this key area of Christian scholarship.

In contrast to this emerging consensus, however, a quarter of a century after the First Vatican Council, in 1896, Pope Leo XIII was instrumental in issuing a statement that has had particularly divisive consequences, especially on ecumenical relationships with the Anglican Communion, during the twentieth century. *Apostolicae curae* addressed the question of Anglican orders of ministry. In a substantial text that examines biblical and historical evidence, the conclusion is reached:

> the sacrament of ordination [which ordains to priesthood and ministry] and the true Christian priesthood has been utterly cast out of the Anglican rite ... no priesthood is conferred, so no episcopacy can be truly or rightly conferred. With this deep-seated defect of form is joined a defect of intention which is equally necessary for the performance of the sacrament ... And so ... we pronounce and declare that ordinations performed according to the Anglican rite are utterly invalid and altogether void.[9]

This declaration that Anglican orders are null and void is still in place, and although there have been substantial bilateral dialogues between the Roman Catholic Church and the Anglican Communion, through the Anglican–Roman Catholic International Commission, it remains a significant hindrance, to say the least, on the way to fuller unity and union not only with Anglicans but with the whole constituency of Protestant and Pentecostal churches.

The early twentieth century

The story of the Roman Catholic Church in the twentieth century begins, then, with a recognition of a number of fundamental doctrinal positions that had been proclaimed or restated during the latter decades of the nineteenth century, and which would play significant roles in dialogues and relationships with other churches and communions initiated during the coming century. These were: the centrality of a scholastic understanding of the relationship between faith and reason; the doctrine of papal infallibility; the decree on the primacy of the Bishop of Rome; a conservative approach to biblical scholarship; and the decree on Anglican orders. These marked efforts by the church to defend the traditional Catholic teaching over against modernism and to reaffirm its identity as the Church of Rome.

As the century took its course, the growing significance of the worldwide ecumenical movement – especially following the Edinburgh World Missionary Conference in 1910 and the developments that sprang from that event – raised severe questions for the Roman Catholic Church. The encyclical *Mortalium Animos* on religious unity, issued by Pius XI in 1928, was a fundamental condemnation of these ecumenical trends.[10] He describes ecumenical trends during the early decades of the century as 'a most grave error, by which the foundations of the Catholic faith are completely destroyed'.[11] It claims that some see the diversity of Christian families and traditions as a sign that 'the Church in itself ... is divided into sections; that is to say, that it is made up of several churches or distinct communities', and seek to bring these several churches into unity and union so as to set aside differences and divisions. Furthermore, it notes that some would 'treat with the Church of Rome ... on equal terms, that is as equals with an equal'.[12] Catholics are forbidden to share in such efforts:

[T]he Apostolic See cannot on any terms take part in their assemblies, nor is it anyway lawful for Catholics either to support or to work for such enterprises; for if they do so they will be giving countenance to a false Christianity, quite alien to the one Church of Christ.

In contrast to the developing perspective within the Ecumenical Movement, not least as set out by the first World Conference on Faith and Order (Lausanne, 1927, i.e. one year before this encyclical), it offers its own understanding of Christian unity:

[T]he union of Christians can only be promoted by promoting the return to the one true Church of Christ [i.e. the Roman Catholic Church] of those who human person as this dignity is known through the revealed word of God and by reason itself. This right of the human person to religious freedom is to be recognized in the constitutional law whereby society is governed and thus it is to become a civil right ...

Religious communities also have the right not to be hindered in their public teaching and witness to their faith, whether by the spoken or by the written word. However, in spreading religious faith and in introducing religious practices everyone ought at all times to refrain from any manner of action which might seem to carry a hint of coercion or of a kind of persuasion that would be dishonorable or unworthy, especially when dealing with poor or uneducated people. Such a manner of action would have to be considered an abuse of one's right and a violation of the right of others.[20]

The Pastoral Constitution on the Church in the Modern World (Gaudiem et Spes)

The Reader extract (*SCM Core Reader*, 3.5) sets out the church's understanding of its relationship to and responsibility for the modern world. It 'gladly holds in high esteem' (para. 40) all that is done by other Christian churches and communities in serving the needs of the world. In approaching its responsibilities in relation to the modern world, the Pastoral Constitution encourages dialogue with the world, emphasizes the importance of being prepared to read the signs of the times, offers the concept of 'the common good, which is the sum total of social conditions which allow people, either as groups or as individuals, to reach their fulfilment more fully and easily' (para, 26), as an overarching concept for its witness within society, rejects 'all social and cultural discrimination in basic personal rights on the grounds of sex, race, colour, social conditions, language or religion' (para. 29) and 'demands that we strive for fairer and more humane conditions'. It also calls, particularly in the light of the proliferation of nuclear weapons, for 'a completely fresh appraisal of war' and states that 'Every act of war directed to the indiscriminate destruction of whole cities or vast areas with their inhabitants is a crime against God and humanity, which merits firm and unequivocal condemnation' (para. 80).[21]

Bettenson and Maunder suggest that this was 'arguably the most radical document of the Council'[22] and stands in a strong tradition of modern Catholic social teaching dating from the 1891 encyclical *Rerum Novarum*. Certainly, it laid the foundation for the church's engagement with the modern world which has had at its heart a commitment to service and to stand for justice for all. In particular, the concept of 'the common good' became foundational for much subsequent Catholic and ecumenical social thought.

Reflections on the Second Vatican Council

Our brief review of these four statements[23] gives some indication of the transformational influence of the Council within the life of the Roman Catholic Church and in the wider Christian community. Their redefinition of the church's self-

are separated from it, for in the past they have unhappily left it. To the one true Church of Christ, we say, which is visible to all, and which is to remain, according to the will of its Author, exactly the same as He instituted it.[13]

So it ends with an appeal for all 'separated children' to 'draw nigh to the Apostolic See' and come to 'recognize the one true Church of Jesus Christ'.

Mortalium Animos was issued in 1928. But it was not the only voice within the Church at that time. One outstanding voice was that of Yves Congar (1904–95). In 1936, he began the publication of a series, *Unam Sanctam*, on a topic in which he had a deep interest, ecclesiology and ecumenism. The first article in the series was his own *Chrétiens désunis*, setting out his understanding of the 'principles for Catholic ecumenism'[14] in the light of the different understandings of unity among the other Christian families. The next 20 years were difficult for him since the church hierarchy found his writing, teaching and approaches to other traditions unacceptable. However, when Pope John XXIII set up a preparatory commission for the Second Vatican Council (which would be convened in 1962), Congar was appointed as a theological consultant, and had considerable influence on the agenda and final documents of the Council. In 1994, at the age of 91, he was created a cardinal. His biblical and theological scholarship, over a period of more than half a century, marked a fundamental shift in the church's self-understanding and in its recognition of and relationship to other Christian traditions. Indeed, his was probably one of the most significant contributions to shaping that transformation in the middle years of the twentieth century.

The Second Vatican Council (1962–65)

The history of the Roman Catholic Church during the twentieth century is marked by the watershed of the Second Vatican Council. It transformed the church and revolutionized its relationships not only with other churches and traditions but also with other world faiths. It was convened by Pope John XXIII, elected Pope in 1958, when he was already 77, on the death of Pius XII. He was expected to be no more than a transitional pope. However, at the end of the Octave of Prayer for Christian Unity in January 1959, without any prior warning or consultation, he announced his intention of convening what he called an Ecumenical Council for the Universal Church. His original vision of the Council as focusing on the reunion of the separated Christian communities was gradually changed to one of the renewal of the Roman Catholic Church, or an occasion for what he came to call 'a new Pentecost'.

In 1960, John XXIII established the Secretariat for the Promotion of Christian Unity, which amongst other early initiatives, arranged the first meeting between a pope and the head of another Christian communion (in this case, with Geoffrey Fisher, Archbishop of Canterbury) since the Reformation. In another most significant initiative, and in contrast to his predecessor who refused to appoint any participants in World Council of Churches Assemblies on behalf of the Roman Catholic Church, John XXIII approved the Secretariat's delegation to the New Delhi Assembly (1961) and invited observers from the other Christian world communions to attend the Second Vatican Council. In his assessment of Pope John XXIII, Tom Stransky writes:

> [H]e had already [i.e. before he opened the Council] won the affection of Catholics and non-Catholics alike. He did so by doing what he did best: being himself. Transparently wide-hearted and affable, humble about his own gifts and limitations, he diminished the cult of the aloof pontifical personality, self-imprisoned within the Vatican. [His] principal contribution to Vatican II ... was its spirit and conduct ... a contagious confidence that the Roman Catholic Church needed serious *aggiornamento* (updating) in order to be faithful, an optimism about the action of God in the world ... and a conviction that the church should 'use the medicine of mercy rather than severity'.[15]

The Second Vatican Council was formally opened in the Vatican in Rome on 11 October 1962. Stransky notes that 'wishes and desires' invited from bishops, superiors general and Catholic theological faculties, produced '9,300 proposals, 9,520 pages in 15 volumes' which were shaped by 11 commissions into 115 booklets, which were then reduced to 20 projects by the time the Council was opened.[16] Between 2,100 and 2,540 bishops met (the number varied between each session) during four long autumn sessions in each of the four years 1962 to 1965. Just over half of the bishops were from Latin America, Asia, Africa and Oceania. The voices of Europe and North America no longer dominated.

John XXIII died on 3 June 1963, at the age of 83, after presiding at only one session of the Council. It was reconvened in the autumn of that year by his successor, Pope Paul VI (1963–78). After considerable deliberation, extensive debate and much drafting and redrafting of documents, sixteen statements were produced on a range of key issues addressed by the Council, including divine revelation, the nature of the Church, the liturgy, the role of the laity, relationships with the Eastern Catholic churches, the Church in the modern world, ecumenical relationships, non-Christian religions and religious freedom. It is impossible to detail the content and significance of all the Council's statements in this chapter.[17] We can only offer a brief analysis of some of the key texts.

The Dogmatic Constitution on the Church (Lumen Gentium)

This sets out the church's self-understanding. The *Reader* extract (*SCM Core Reader*, 3.3) emphasizes, first, the catholicity (i.e. the universality) of the church, but most significantly recognizes that this catholicity is to be found not only within the Roman Catholic Church, but rather embraces all Christians:

> All the faithful, scattered though they be throughout the world, are in communion with each other in the Holy Spirit ... This [is] a characteristic of universality which adorns the people of God ... The Church recognizes that in many ways she is linked with those who, being baptized, are honoured with the name of Christian, though they do not profess the faith in its entirety or do not preserve unity of communion with the successor or Peter.[18]

It further recognizes that 'those who have not yet received the Gospel are related in various ways to the people of God'.[19] In the light of previous (and, indeed, some very recent) statements on the church, *Lumen Gentium* represented a major change in theological perspective.

The Decree on Ecumenism (Unitatis redintegratio)

This was the most significant document with regard to the church's relationships with other Christian communions. It led to Roman Catholic participation and involvement in ecumenical relationships at local, national, regional and international level (though not to membership of the major global ecumenical body, the World Council of Churches, and to bilateral dialogues between the church and other Christian families and traditions (see below)). The Reader extract (*SCM Core Reader*, 3.4) sets out key Catholic principles of ecumenism. These include the recognition that the search for unity is a response to the prayer of Jesus 'that they may be one' (*ut unum sint*), for Jesus is the principle of unity. It recognizes also that the Roman Catholic Church is in real though imperfect communion with those it calls 'separated brethren'. Moreover, it is prepared to affirm that many of the fundamental marks and gifts of the Church – such as the Bible, a genuine life of Christian discipleship, the gifts of the Holy Spirit – exist outside the Roman Catholic Church, and these churches too have been used by God to bring people to salvation, although it states also that salvation in all its fullness comes only through the Catholic Church. Particularly significantly, not least in view of *Mortalium Animos* (1928), it recognizes the importance of the modern ecumenical movement as an instrument to promote deeper Christian unity. It does affirm also, in a phrase that has been the subject of considerable debate and interpretation, that this unity 'subsists' within the Roman Catholic Church, such that it can never be lost but that 'the fullness of catholicity proper to [the Church]' cannot be properly attained while divisions within the Church remain.

The Declaration on Religious Liberty (Dignitatis Humanae)

This declaration also marked a turning point for the church. In 1864 *A Syllabus of Errors* set out the rights of the church with respect to any threats to its sovereignty, powers and jurisdictions and the church's opposition to any call for toleration for error and liberal views and attitudes within society. *Dignitatis Humanae* encourages a very different approach, in some sense matching the UN Declaration on Human Rights (1948), as is illustrated by the following extract:

> This Vatican Council declares that the human person has a right to religious freedom. This freedom means that all men are to be immune from coercion on the part of individuals or of social groups and of any human power, in such wise that no one is to be forced to act in a manner contrary to his own beliefs, whether privately or publicly, whether alone or in association with others, within due limits ... The council further declares that the right to religious freedom has its foundation in the very dignity of the

are separated from it, for in the past they have unhappily left it. To the one true Church of Christ, we say, which is visible to all, and which is to remain, according to the will of its Author, exactly the same as He instituted it.[13]

So it ends with an appeal for all 'separated children' to 'draw nigh to the Apostolic See' and come to 'recognize the one true Church of Jesus Christ'.

Mortalium Animos was issued in 1928. But it was not the only voice within the Church at that time. One outstanding voice was that of Yves Congar (1904–95). In 1936, he began the publication of a series, *Unam Sanctam*, on a topic in which he had a deep interest, ecclesiology and ecumenism. The first article in the series was his own *Chrétiens désunis*, setting out his understanding of the 'principles for Catholic ecumenism'[14] in the light of the different understandings of unity among the other Christian families. The next 20 years were difficult for him since the church hierarchy found his writing, teaching and approaches to other traditions unacceptable. However, when Pope John XXIII set up a preparatory commission for the Second Vatican Council (which would be convened in 1962), Congar was appointed as a theological consultant, and had considerable influence on the agenda and final documents of the Council. In 1994, at the age of 91, he was created a cardinal. His biblical and theological scholarship, over a period of more than half a century, marked a fundamental shift in the church's self-understanding and in its recognition of and relationship to other Christian traditions. Indeed, his was probably one of the most significant contributions to shaping that transformation in the middle years of the twentieth century.

The Second Vatican Council (1962–65)

The history of the Roman Catholic Church during the twentieth century is marked by the watershed of the Second Vatican Council. It transformed the church and revolutionized its relationships not only with other churches and traditions but also with other world faiths. It was convened by Pope John XXIII, elected Pope in 1958, when he was already 77, on the death of Pius XII. He was expected to be no more than a transitional pope. However, at the end of the Octave of Prayer for Christian Unity in January 1959, without any prior warning or consultation, he announced his intention of convening what he called an Ecumenical Council for the Universal Church. His original vision of the Council as focusing on the reunion of the separated Christian communities was gradually changed to one of the renewal of the Roman Catholic Church, or an occasion for what he came to call 'a new Pentecost'.

In 1960, John XXIII established the Secretariat for the Promotion of Christian Unity, which amongst other early initiatives, arranged the first meeting between a pope and the head of another Christian communion (in this case, with Geoffrey Fisher, Archbishop of Canterbury) since the Reformation. In another most significant initiative, and in contrast to his predecessor who refused to appoint any participants in World Council of Churches Assemblies on behalf of the Roman Catholic Church, John XXIII approved the Secretariat's delegation to the New Delhi Assembly (1961) and invited observers from the other Christian world communions to attend the Second Vatican Council. In his assessment of Pope John XXIII, Tom Stransky writes:

> [H]e had already [i.e. before he opened the Council] won the affection of Catholics and non-Catholics alike. He did so by doing what he did best: being himself. Transparently wide-hearted and affable, humble about his own gifts and limitations, he diminished the cult of the aloof pontifical personality, self-imprisoned within the Vatican. [His] principal contribution to Vatican II ... was its spirit and conduct ... a contagious confidence that the Roman Catholic Church needed serious *aggiornamento* (updating) in order to be faithful, an optimism about the action of God in the world ... and a conviction that the church should 'use the medicine of mercy rather than severity'.[15]

The Second Vatican Council was formally opened in the Vatican in Rome on 11 October 1962. Stransky notes that 'wishes and desires' invited from bishops, superiors general and Catholic theological faculties, produced '9,300 proposals, 9,520 pages in 15 volumes' which were shaped by 11 commissions into 115 booklets, which were then reduced to 20 projects by the time the Council was opened.[16] Between 2,100 and 2,540 bishops met (the number varied between each session) during four long autumn sessions in each of the four years 1962 to 1965. Just over half of the bishops were from Latin America, Asia, Africa and Oceania. The voices of Europe and North America no longer dominated.

John XXIII died on 3 June 1963, at the age of 83, after presiding at only one session of the Council. It was reconvened in the autumn of that year by his successor, Pope Paul VI (1963–78). After considerable deliberation, extensive debate and much drafting and redrafting of documents, sixteen statements were produced on a range of key issues addressed by the Council, including divine revelation, the nature of the Church, the liturgy, the role of the laity, relationships with the Eastern Catholic churches, the Church in the modern world, ecumenical relationships, non-Christian religions and religious freedom. It is impossible to detail the content and significance of all the Council's statements in this chapter.[17] We can only offer a brief analysis of some of the key texts.

The Dogmatic Constitution on the Church (Lumen Gentium)

This sets out the church's self-understanding. The *Reader* extract (*SCM Core Reader*, 3.3) emphasizes, first, the catholicity (i.e. the universality) of the church, but most significantly recognizes that this catholicity is to be found not only within the Roman Catholic Church, but rather embraces all Christians:

> All the faithful, scattered though they be throughout the world, are in communion with each other in the Holy Spirit ... This [is] a characteristic of universality which adorns the people of God ... The Church recognizes that in many ways she is linked with those who, being baptized, are honoured with the name of Christian, though they do not profess the faith in its entirety or do not preserve unity of communion with the successor or Peter.[18]

It further recognizes that 'those who have not yet received the Gospel are related in various ways to the people of God'.[19] In the light of previous (and, indeed, some very recent) statements on the church, *Lumen Gentium* represented a major change in theological perspective.

The Decree on Ecumenism (Unitatis redintegratio)

This was the most significant document with regard to the church's relationships with other Christian communions. It led to Roman Catholic participation and involvement in ecumenical relationships at local, national, regional and international level (though not to membership of the major global ecumenical body, the World Council of Churches, and to bilateral dialogues between the church and other Christian families and traditions (see below)). The Reader extract (*SCM Core Reader*, 3.4) sets out key Catholic principles of ecumenism. These include the recognition that the search for unity is a response to the prayer of Jesus 'that they may be one' (*ut unum sint*), for Jesus is the principle of unity. It recognizes also that the Roman Catholic Church is in real though imperfect communion with those it calls 'separated brethren'. Moreover, it is prepared to affirm that many of the fundamental marks and gifts of the Church – such as the Bible, a genuine life of Christian discipleship, the gifts of the Holy Spirit – exist outside the Roman Catholic Church, and these churches too have been used by God to bring people to salvation, although it states also that salvation in all its fullness comes only through the Catholic Church. Particularly significantly, not least in view of *Mortalium Animos* (1928), it recognizes the importance of the modern ecumenical movement as an instrument to promote deeper Christian unity. It does affirm also, in a phrase that has been the subject of considerable debate and interpretation, that this unity 'subsists' within the Roman Catholic Church, such that it can never be lost but that 'the fullness of catholicity proper to [the Church]' cannot be properly attained while divisions within the Church remain.

The Declaration on Religious Liberty (Dignitatis Humanae)

This declaration also marked a turning point for the church. In 1864 *A Syllabus of Errors* set out the rights of the church with respect to any threats to its sovereignty, powers and jurisdictions and the church's opposition to any call for toleration for error and liberal views and attitudes within society. *Dignitatis Humanae* encourages a very different approach, in some sense matching the UN Declaration on Human Rights (1948), as is illustrated by the following extract:

> This Vatican Council declares that the human person has a right to religious freedom. This freedom means that all men are to be immune from coercion on the part of individuals or of social groups and of any human power, in such wise that no one is to be forced to act in a manner contrary to his own beliefs, whether privately or publicly, whether alone or in association with others, within due limits ... The council further declares that the right to religious freedom has its foundation in the very dignity of the

human person as this dignity is known through the revealed word of God and by reason itself. This right of the human person to religious freedom is to be recognized in the constitutional law whereby society is governed and thus it is to become a civil right ...

Religious communities also have the right not to be hindered in their public teaching and witness to their faith, whether by the spoken or by the written word. However, in spreading religious faith and in introducing religious practices everyone ought at all times to refrain from any manner of action which might seem to carry a hint of coercion or of a kind of persuasion that would be dishonorable or unworthy, especially when dealing with poor or uneducated people. Such a manner of action would have to be considered an abuse of one's right and a violation of the right of others.[20]

The Pastoral Constitution on the Church in the Modern World (Gaudiem et Spes)

The Reader extract (*SCM Core Reader*, 3.5) sets out the church's understanding of its relationship to and responsibility for the modern world. It 'gladly holds in high esteem' (para. 40) all that is done by other Christian churches and communities in serving the needs of the world. In approaching its responsibilities in relation to the modern world, the Pastoral Constitution encourages dialogue with the world, emphasizes the importance of being prepared to read the signs of the times, offers the concept of 'the common good, which is the sum total of social conditions which allow people, either as groups or as individuals, to reach their fulfilment more fully and easily' (para. 26), as an overarching concept for its witness within society, rejects 'all social and cultural discrimination in basic personal rights on the grounds of sex, race, colour, social conditions, language or religion' (para. 29) and 'demands that we strive for fairer and more humane conditions'. It also calls, particularly in the light of the proliferation of nuclear weapons, for 'a completely fresh appraisal of war' and states that 'Every act of war directed to the indiscriminate destruction of whole cities or vast areas with their inhabitants is a crime against God and humanity, which merits firm and unequivocal condemnation' (para. 80).[21]

Bettenson and Maunder suggest that this was 'arguably the most radical document of the Council'[22] and stands in a strong tradition of modern Catholic social teaching dating from the 1891 encyclical *Rerum Novarum*. Certainly, it laid the foundation for the church's engagement with the modern world which has had at its heart a commitment to service and to stand for justice for all. In particular, the concept of 'the common good' became foundational for much subsequent Catholic and ecumenical social thought.

Reflections on the Second Vatican Council

Our brief review of these four statements[23] gives some indication of the transformational influence of the Council within the life of the Roman Catholic Church and in the wider Christian community. Their redefinition of the church's self-understanding and ecclesial identity, their recognition of the call to Christian unity and to partnership with other Christian churches and communities in promoting that unity, their openness to dialogue with people of other faiths, and the emphasis on the centrality of basic human and religious rights, as well as the need for the churches to strive for greater justice and for the common good, together amount to an agenda for change and renewal which is unprecedented within the life of the modern Roman Catholic Church.

But there were other aspects also that led to renewal and change. Liturgical changes encouraged greater use of vernacular in the mass, brought the homily into greater prominence and enabled much greater lay participation. There was special emphasis on the need for indigenization, rooting the life and worship of the church within local culture, language and tradition. Collegiality between pope, cardinals, archbishops and bishops was re-emphasized. The pontiff's authority and power within the whole church was seen as being essentially collegial. Alongside this collegial emphasis, greater prominence was given to the role of the laity not only in the liturgy but in the life of the church as a whole.

It is impossible to over-estimate the revolution and renewal that the Second Vatican Council brought about within the church and, indeed, indirectly within all the churches. Stransky summarizes its contribution as follows:

> Without taking account of the debates and resolutions of Vatican II, it is impossible to understand the modern [Roman Catholic Church]. The church's current consensus and dissents – its confidence and its hesitations in theology, pastoral and missionary activities, social and political involvements, ecumenical and inter-religious concerns, and understanding of its own structures – are a result of the Vatican II deliberations and of the subsequent debates about what they meant and intended.[24]

Hans Küng, who was a theological consultant to the Council, offers a similar evaluation:

> For the Catholic Church, this council represented an irrevocable turning point. With the Second Vatican Council, the Catholic Church – despite all the difficulties and hindrances posed by the medieval Roman system – attempted to implement two paradigm changes at once: it integrated fundamental features of both the Reformation paradigm [the need for constant reform] and the paradigm of the Enlightenment and modernity [a positive attitude to modern progress and to the secular world].[25]

Bilateral dialogues

One of the significant consequences of Vatican II was that the Roman Catholic Church initiated a series of bilateral dialogues with other Christian communions and families. These included Roman Catholic–Anglican, Roman Catholic–Disciples, Roman Catholic–Lutheran, Roman Catholic–Methodist, Roman Catholic–Orthodox, Roman Catholic–Pentecostal and Roman Catholic–Reformed dialogues. Two large volumes tell the story of these dialogues and the growing consensus on doctrinal issues that has emerged from them.[26] Some of the most important dialogues were with the Orthodox family. The most significant of these are highlighted in Chapter 2 and readers are referred to that chapter for an examination of the results of these conversations. It is impossible to summarize here even the main themes explored in this wide range of ecumenical conversations, far less the content of the emerging consensus and continuing areas of dispute in any detail, but some key aspects may be highlighted.

First, some topics appear regularly in Roman Catholic conversations with the broad diversity of churches and traditions that have been involved. Ecclesiology (that is, issues around the nature of the church), and the closely related issues of ministry and ecclesial authority have been widely explored. More specifically, the primacy of the pope (that is, the understanding of the pope as the symbolic and, in relation to matters of doctrine and morality, authoritative head not only of the Catholic Church but of the whole Church of God), has been, as can be imagined, a matter of very energetic debate. Similarly, the nature and meaning of sacraments, and most especially, the Eucharist, one of the areas of fundamental theological disagreements, has been the subject of a number of theological dialogues. Another key topic has been the nature and role of the Bible. The appropriate approach to biblical interpretation, the role of the Bible as the locus of authority for doctrine and morality and the role of tradition and the pope and college of cardinals and bishops in the process of biblical interpretation has been a particularly sharp issue for debate, especially in conversations with churches of the Reformation. In some conversations specific issues raised within a particular tradition have taken centre stage, such as the nature and work of the Holy Spirit in the Pentecostal dialogue, and, particularly significantly, the meaning of the key Reformation doctrine of justification by faith in the dialogue with Lutherans (see below).

A second reality is that areas of consensus have emerged among the theologians engaged in many of these dialogues. Two examples from among many may be given here. Mary Tanner[27] suggests that 'the biblical concept of *koinonia*, understood as the fundamental reality of the church', is an overarching theme in many of the dialogues. The Methodist–Roman Catholic dialogue, for example, interprets *koinonia* (communion, fellowship) as including 'participation in God through God in the Spirit', through which members become 'members of the body of Christ sharing in the same Spirit' and 'deep fellowship among participants, a fellowship which is both visible and invisible, finding expression in faith and order, in prayer and sacrament, in mission and service'.[28]

Similarly, the Anglican–Roman Catholic International Commission (ARCIC) report (1990) on *Church as Communion*,[29] explores in considerable depth the significance of communion both with a view to understanding what it means to affirm that Anglicans and Roman Catholics 'are already in a real though as yet imperfect communion' and to explore, in the light of communion, 'the outstanding difficulties that remain between us' so as to help the churches 'to grow into a more profound communion'. The emerging consensus between the theologians of both traditions is not seen as a definitive agreement between the two churches. Rather it states that 'the document is ... not an authoritative declaration by the Roman Catholic Church or the Anglican Communion'. It elaborates the shared understanding of communion in terms of four theological emphases, namely: communion unfolded in Scripture; sacramentality and the Church; apostolicity, catholicity and holiness; and unity and ecclesial communion.[30] Mary Tanner summarizes the shared understanding of the constitutive elements of communion in the report as follows:

> [T]he common confession of the apostolic faith, revealed in scripture and set forth in the Catholic Creeds, with the acceptance of the same moral values, the same vision of humanity and hope in the consummation of all things; a common baptism; celebration of one Eucharist; the leadership of the apostolic ministry with oversight entrusted to the episcopate, which holds the local church in communion with all the local churches; and a ministry of oversight having collegial and primatial expressions and open to the communities' participation in discovering God's will.[31]

A similar consensus is summarized in the Disciples–Roman Catholic dialogue as follows:

> Participation in this communion begins through baptism and is sustained in continuing eucharistic fellowship. The Holy Spirit uses the church as the servant by which the word of God is kept alive and constantly preached, the sacraments are celebrated, the people of God are served by the ministers with responsibility for oversight, and the authentic evangelical life is manifested through the life of holy and committed members of Christ. That is why Disciples and Roman Catholics agree that the church is the company of all the baptized, the community through which they are constantly kept in the memory of the apostolic witness and nourished by the eucharist.[32]

In view of the historical disagreement, not to say conflict, between, in particular, the Roman Catholic and Lutheran and Reformed traditions on the meaning of salvation, one of the major breakthroughs owed to the bilateral dialogues was that on the doctrine of justification by faith (*SCM Core Reader*, 3.6).[33] This was a highly significant theological consensus among leading theologians from both traditions. Paragraphs 15–16 of this report offer a summary of the common understanding between the two traditions on this crucial doctrine:

> In faith we together hold the conviction that justification is the work of the triune God. The Father sent his Son into the world to save sinners. The foundation and presupposition of justification is the incarnation, death and resurrection of Christ. Justification thus means that Christ himself is our righteousness, in which we share through the Holy Spirit in accord with the will of the Father. Together we confess: By grace alone, in faith in Christ's saving work and not because of any merit on our part, we are accepted by God and receive the Holy Spirit, who renews our hearts while equipping and calling us to good works.
> All people are called by God to salvation in Christ. Through Christ alone are we justified, when we receive this salvation in faith. Faith is itself God's gift through the Holy Spirit who works through word and sacrament in the

community of believers and who, at the same time, leads believers into that renewal of life which God will bring to completion in eternal life.[34]

On the basis of this theological consensus a joint statement by the Lutheran World Federation and the Roman Catholic Church underlines the historic significance of the agreement reached: 'The understanding of the doctrine of justification set forth in this Declaration shows that a consensus in basic truths of the doctrine of justification exists between Lutherans and Catholics', and on this basis they declare together that '[t]he teaching of the Lutheran churches presented in the declaration does not fall under the condemnations from the Council of Trent. The condemnations in the Lutheran confessions do not apply to the teaching of the Roman Catholic Church presented in this declaration.'[35]

These are important areas of agreement. But however significant may be the growing consensus among those involved in these dialogues, an even more challenging issue, for all the churches, has been that of reception, that is, the ability and willingness of the churches and traditions engaged in any particular dialogue to accept the consensus reached on any particular issue of doctrine or morality as the official and authoritative understanding of the church. It is one thing for theologians to reach agreement (laudable as that may be). It is quite another for the church to absorb that agreement into its own doctrinal and catechetical position. Mary Tanner expresses the importance of this challenge as follows: it is now a matter of 'moving from theological conversation to changed relations. Unless there is continuing progress in the process of reception in changed lives and relationships, the theological conversations will remain the preserve of only a few and have little or no effect on the unity or mission of the churches.'[36]

Relationships with ecumenical organizations

The setting up of the Secretariat for the Promotion of Christian Unity (SPCU) by Pope John XXIII in 1960 and the Second Vatican Council's Decree on Ecumenism led to a radical change in the Catholic Church's relationships with other churches. Immediately after its establishment the Pope accepted the SPCU's nominations for observers to attend the WCC Assembly in New Delhi. This marked the beginning of a close fraternal and working relationship between the Catholic Church and the WCC. Catholic observers have attended every Assembly since then and fraternal delegates (with no voting rights) have attended meetings of the WCC Central Committee. Pope Paul VI and Pope John Paul II visited the WCC headquarters in Geneva and WCC general secretaries have visited the pope at the Vatican. The church has been a full member of one of the key commissions of the WCC, the Commission on Faith and Order, and has collaborated closely with the WCC in other aspects of its programme.

In January 1965, a Joint Working Group (JWG) between the Roman Catholic Church and the World Council of Churches was set up as the official forum for exploring common questions and initiating and sustaining shared activities and programmes. The Seventh Report (1998) describes the JWG's task as follows:

> It undertakes its spiritual and pastoral tasks in a spirit of prayerful conviction that God through Christ in the Spirit is guiding the one ecumenical movement. The group tries to discern the will of God in contemporary situations, and to stimulate the search for visible unity and common witness, in particular through collaboration at world, regional, national and local levels between the RCC, the WCC, and the WCC member churches. This means giving attentive support and encouragement to whatever contributes to ecumenical progress.[37]

Over the years, it has undertaken studies in a number of key areas of common concern, including: Catholicity and Apostolicity (1968); Common Witness and Proselytism (1970 and 1980); the Church: Local and Universal (1990). The priorities that are highlighted in the Seventh Report of JWG as having been recommended to the Canberra Assembly of the WCC (1991) are in many ways representative of the main thrust of the Group's work throughout its 40-year history. They were: the unity of the Church: goal, steps and ecclesiological implications; ecumenical formation and education; ethical issues as new sources of division; common witness in missionary endeavours; social thought and action.[38]

One of the main continuing questions during the latter decades of the century was whether the Roman Catholic Church should and could become a full member of the World Council of Churches. There was growing energy behind this question as the church became increasingly committed to ecumenical partnership at regional, national and local levels throughout the world. For example, the Roman Catholic Church is a full member of the regional conference of churches in the Pacific and in the Caribbean, among others. The Eighth Report of the Joint Working Group (2006) estimated that the Roman Catholic Church was a full member of around 70 regional and national councils of churches.[39] In the UK, for example, the Roman Catholic Church is a full member of around 80 per cent of local churches together groups and councils of churches. The question that has been asked, therefore, is: if this level of committed ecumenical partnership is possible at these levels should not the church be a member of the WCC, the main instrument of global ecumenical relationships?

This question was first raised at the fourth meeting of the Joint Working Group (JWG) in 1966, and considered at the fourth WCC Assembly (Uppsala 1968). There were further discussions of the issue at meetings of the JWG in 1969 and 1970. The final resolution of the meeting of the Secretariat for the Promotion of Christian Unity in November 1970 warned against 'raising expectations prematurely' and encouraged 'sincere and generous cooperation with the World Council'.[40] However this resolution is interpreted, no application for membership of the WCC was made and the matter went into abeyance.[41]

The question was raised again from time to time in subsequent years. During the final decade of the twentieth century, the World Council of Churches inaugurated a process of reflection, 'Towards a Common Vision and Understanding of the WCC'. The Policy Statement adopted by the Central Committee in 1997 included the following paragraph:

> The Roman Catholic Church has been, since the Second Vatican Council, an active participant in the ecumenical movement and a valued partner in numerous ways with the World Council of Churches ... It is inconceivable that either the WCC or the Roman Catholic Church could pursue its ecumenical calling without the collaboration of the other ... While membership in the WCC is by no means the only way for the churches to work together on a worldwide level, some member churches of the WCC which maintain bilateral relations with the Roman Catholic Church believe that the fellowship of the WCC is impoverished by the absence of the Roman Catholic Church from this circle of churches.[42]

This paragraph is significant for three reasons. In the first place, it recognizes the centrality of the ecumenical vision, calling and partnership for both the WCC and its member churches and for the Roman Catholic Church, and a wish for that partnership to be deepened. But, second, it also recognizes that membership of the WCC is not the only way by which the Roman Catholic Church (and other non-member churches) 'can work together on a worldwide level', and, third, notes that some member churches feel that 'the fellowship of the WCC is impoverished by the absence of the Roman Catholic Church from this circle of churches'.

The WCC Assembly in Porto Alegre in 2006 received the Eighth Report of the Joint Working Group between the Roman Catholic Church and the World Council of Churches (1999–2005), which concluded with a helpful reflection on 'Prospects for the Future' of ecumenical collaboration involving the Roman Catholic Church (*SCM Core Reader*, 3.9). The 2006 Assembly also recognized that the nature of the question of membership had changed and that any deeper relationship would require what the World Council called a 'reconfiguration' of ecumenical structures and relationships, a new ecumenical space, that would, among other things, encourage 'an even more organic relationship [than currently exists] with the Roman Catholic Church in the quest towards the visible unity of the Church'.[43]

Continuing issues of debate

These deepening ecumenical relationships are, of course, to be welcomed. But there are continuing areas of major disagreement. We can only give two examples here. Encyclicals on the potentially church-dividing issues of approaches to human sexuality and the ministry of universal primacy were at the centre of debate during the last decades of the twentieth century.

It was in 1968, three years after the end of Vatican II, that Pope Paul VI issued *Humanae Vitae* (*SCM Core Reader*, 3.7). This was seen by many Catholics, including priests (as well as by Christians from other traditions) as very conservative, not least in view of the growth of the global population during this period and the changing attitudes towards issues of sexuality. It caused considerable controversy at the time and it is likely that many of the Catholic faithful did not, and do not, adhere to its demands. This was, and is, a reminder that questions of morals and ethical behaviour can be as potentially church-dividing, both within any particular tradition and between the Christian traditions, as the faith and order questions that have been, on the whole, more central to ecumenical relationships and dialogues. ARCIC and the Roman Catholic Church–WCC Joint Working Group have offered significant insights into approaches to consensus on some of these questions. But these tensions remain.

In 1995, Pope John Paul II, in his encyclical, *Ut unum sint* (*SCM Core Reader*, 3.8), invited the churches to study the issue of universal primacy with a view to reaching a shared understanding.[44] The concept – which had already featured in some of the bilateral dialogues – was being offered, at the time, as potentially unifying, but it was seen by many outside the Roman Catholic Church as a hindrance rather than a constructive proposal towards deeper Christian unity. Such a proposal takes us to the heart of the fundamental distinctions between the Roman Catholic, Orthodox and Protestant understandings of the essence and nature of the Church of Christ and is likely to be a matter of considerable debate for the foreseeable future.

What of the future of the Church?

Hans Küng[45] suggests that there are 'four conditions [that] need to be met' as the Church faces the future. First, 'it must not turn backwards ... [to] the Middle Ages or the time of the Reformation or the Enlightenment'. Second, 'it must not be patriarchal ... but be a church of partnership, [accepting] women in all ministries'. Third, 'it must not ... succumb to confessional exclusiveness ... but be an ecumenically open church ... [and practise] mutual recognition of ministries and complete eucharistic fellowship'. Finally, 'it must not be Eurocentric or put forward any exclusive Christian claims'.

These are clearly fundamental issues. Indeed, these may well be not only essential requirements for the future of the Roman Catholic Church in the twenty-first century, but key factors in the future of Christianity as a whole. Openness to reformation, commitment to inclusive partnership, the search for an ecumenically open church and the development of a global *ecumene* are challenges that will emerge throughout our survey of Christianity in the twentieth century.

But one key question emerges from our study of the Roman Catholic Church during the twentieth century, namely, whether it is true to say, as David Ford has suggested, that 'the Second Vatican Council has probably been the single most important ecclesial event of the twentieth century, with implications far beyond the Roman Catholic Church'.[46] It is beyond doubt that there was a dramatic contrast between the pre-conciliar and the post-conciliar church. In its renewed understanding of the nature of the church, its internal structures and patterns of decision-making, in matters of liturgical and spiritual life, in ecumenical relationships, in approaches to other world faiths, in matters of social

and international liberty and justice, the Council opened up unimagined possibilities for reform and change. In these and other areas of the church's life
the Council did contribute in crucial ways to the transformation of the church.
From the perspective of Christianity as a whole, the most notable of these may
well have been the impact of the Decree on Ecumenism (*Redintegratio Unitatis*)
on the church's relationships with other Christians and churches at global,
regional, national and local levels. Ecumenical relationships generally have
been dramatically changed as a direct result of the Second Vatican Council
and the church's commitment to implementing its ecumenical challenge. In
particular, the bilateral dialogues in which the church has been involved have
led to an unprecedented degree of consensus on many theological and ethical
issues, though, of course, many remain unresolved.

However, it may be that the more significant issue in measuring the long-
term impact of the Second Vatican Council is not the changed attitudes and
the greater consensus but the degree to which these have led to actual change
both in the inner consciousness of the church and in its commitment to enabling a real transformation within the church. Many of the Vatican Council's
challenges still cause controversy and even conflict within the church as in its
relationships with other Christian churches. Among these are major 'internal'
ecclesial issues (e.g. around the ministry of women) as well as 'external', moral (e.g. around homosexuality, abortion and contraception) and socio-political
issues (e.g. about the church's role in social transformation).

It may, therefore, be fair to conclude that whereas the Second Vatican Council may have been *one of* 'the most important ecclesial event[s] of the twentieth
century' many of its most significant transformative perspectives and decrees
have yet to achieve their full impact within the Roman Catholic Church and
the worldwide family. Indeed, it may be that one of the major challenges of
the early years of the twenty-first century is for the Roman Catholic Church
to allow the Council to achieve more fully its reforming and transforming
purpose and potential.

However, perhaps the most crucial question will not be the continuing inheritance from the Second Vatican Council, but the way in which the Roman
Catholic Church struggles with the many conflicts and controversies that currently face it under the leadership of John Paul II's successor, Pope Benedict
XVI. Time will tell how the Roman Catholic Church will ultimately respond
to the many crises caused by the decline in religious and priestly vocations
in many parts of the world, the accusations of child abuse against a small but
significant minority of its priests, sharp criticism of the Catholic Church for its
refusal – against the better judgement of some leaders even within the church
itself – to sanction the use of condoms even in regions such as Africa and
Asia, where the AIDS pandemic is causing such suffering, and signs of a more
conservative and reactionary approach both to other Christian traditions and
to other faith communities. It may well be, as Küng has suggested, that a third
Vatican council will be felt to be needed in order to lead the Catholic Church
'from Roman Catholicism to an authentic Catholicity'.[47]

Further reading

H. Küng (2001), *The Catholic Church*, London: Phoenix Press, offers a comprehensive, informed, stimulating and, at times, controversial account of
the history of the Catholic Church from the beginning until the end of the
twentieth century.

A. Hastings (1991), *Modern Catholicism: Vatican II and after*, London: SPCK,
gathers a wide range of essays by Catholic scholars on the Catholic Church
since Vatican II. Hastings' own chapter on 'Catholic History from Vatican I
to John Paul II' is itself a very valuable and perceptive account of much of
the period covered in this chapter.

E. Stourton (1998), *Absolute Truth: The Catholic Church Today*, London: Penguin,
offers an account of the church 'at the beginning of the third millennium'
by a Catholic journalist who writes with honesty and perception, and tells
its stories inspiringly.

K. Kilby (2007), *Karl Rahner: A Brief Introduction*, London: SPCK, provides a
useful introduction to one of the key theologians of the Catholic Church
during the century.

Catechism of the Catholic Church (1994), London: Geoffrey Chapman, is an authoritative statement of the church's faith and teaching. Anyone who wishes to
discover what the church teaches and believes both in matters of doctrine
and morality will find in the *Catechism* what Pope John Paul II called, on the
back cover of the English version, 'a sure and authentic reference text for
teaching Catholic doctrine ... [that] is offered to any individual who wants
to know what the Catholic Church believes'.

Pope John XXIII's autobiography (1965), *The Journey of a Soul*, New York: Mc-
Graw-Hill, gives a personal insight into the faith and mind of the pope
whose vision the Second Vatican Council was and so contributed in a
unique way to what the church has become during the last decades of the
twentieth century.

Two recent publications, written by scholars from Korea and Zimbabwe respectively, offer perspectives on the history and development of the Roman Catholic
Church in Africa and Asia, which balance the other volumes listed here:

P. H. Gundani (2001), *Changing Patterns of Authority and Leadership: Developments in the Roman Catholic Church in Zimbabwe after Vatican II*, Harare: University of Zimbabwe.

Jai-Keung Choi (2006), *The Origin of the Roman Catholic Church in Korea*,
Chelernham PA: The Hermit Kingdom Press.

Notes

1 The Roman Catholic Church is not the only church to use the title 'Catholic' in
its name. The Old Catholic Church has its origins in post-Reformation Netherlands. There are Old Catholic communities in a number of European countries
as well as in the USA and Canada. Old Catholics have a fundamental ecumenical commitment and have established a number of ecumenical dialogues

with other churches and communions, including Anglican and Orthodox. The Eastern Catholic Churches are in full communion with the Roman Catholic Church, focused on the pope, but retain many of the liturgical rites and traditions of the Eastern (Orthodox) churches. But they show considerable diversity in different settings. Their very existence has been a cause of conflict between the Roman Catholic and Orthodox churches, both historically and during the twentieth century. For further information, see Chapter 2.

2 For a very helpful collection of papal encyclicals and other key Catholic documents, see http://www.papalencyclicals.net

3 John Paul II (1998), Encyclical Letter *Fides et Ratio* of the Supreme Pontiff John Paul II to the Bishops of the Catholic Church on the Relationship between Faith and Reason, Vatican City: Libreria Editrice Vaticana, p. 65.

4 Quoted in *Fides et Ratio*, p. 66.

5 Vatican Council, Session IV, cap. 4. *Collectio Lacensis*.

6 *Providentissimus Deus*, Encyclical of Pope Leo XIII on the Study of Holy Scripture, taken from http://www.vatican.va/holy_father/leo_xiii/encyclicals/documents/hf_l-xiii_enc_18111893_providentissimus-deus_en.html, para 10 (13 Sept. 07).

7 For a resumé of his life and work, and a helpful bibliography, see F. L. Cross and E. A. Livingstone (eds) (1997), *The Oxford Dictionary of the Christian Church*, third edn, Oxford: Oxford University Press, p. 993.

8 Pope Pius XII (1943), in *Divino Afflante Spiritu*, paras 16–19, taken from http://www.papalencyclicals.net/Pius12/P12DIVI.HTM (13 Sept. 07).

9 Quoted in Henry Bettensen and Chris Maunder (1999), *Documents of the Christian Church*, Oxford: Oxford University Press, p. 290.

10 Pope Pius XI (1928), *Mortalium Animos* on Religious Unity, taken from http://www.papalencyclicals.net/Pius11/P11MORTA.HTM

11 *Mortalium Animos*, para. 4.

12 *Mortalium Animos*, paras 7–8.

13 *Mortalium Animos*, paras 10–12.

14 Cross and Livingstone (eds), *Dictionary*, pp. 397–8.

15 T. Stransky (1995), 'John XXIII 1881–1963', in I. Bria and D. Heller (eds), *Ecumenical Pilgrims: Profiles of Pioneers in Christian Reconciliation*, Geneva: WCC Publications, p. 116.

16 T. Stransky (1991), 'Vatican Councils I & II', in N. Lossky (ed.), *Dictionary of the Ecumenical Movement*, Geneva: WCC Publications, p. 1054.

17 For the full text of each statement, see A. Flannery (ed.) (1975), *Vatican II: The Conciliar and Post-Conciliar Documents*, Collegeville, MN: Liturgical Press, and for a penetrating account and evaluation of the Council, see Adrian Hastings (1990), *The Second Vatican Council and Its Influence across 25 Years*, London: SPCK.

18 *Lumen Gentium*, paras 13 and 15.

19 *Lumen Gentium*, para. 16.

20 *Dignitatis Humanae*, para. 4, taken from http://www.vatican.va/archive/hist_councils/ii_vatican_council/documents/vat-ii_decl_19651207_dignitatis-humanae_en.html (14 Sept. 07).

21 These quotations taken from http://www.vatican.va/archive/hist_councils/ii_vatican_council/documents/vat-ii_cons_19651207_gaudium-et-spes_en.html

22 Bettensen and Maunder, *Documents of the Christian Church*, p. 366.

23 For information about another key document, *Nostra Aetate*, The Declaration

on the Relation of the Church to Non-Christian Religions, see *SCM Core Reader*, 16.3.

24 Stransky, 'Vatican Councils I and II', p. 1054.

25 H. Küng (2001), *The Catholic Church*, London: Phoenix Press, p. 192.

26 H. Meyer and L. Vischer (1984), *Growth in Agreement I, Reports and Agreed Statements of Ecumenical Conversations on a World Level, 1971–1982*, Geneva: WCC Publications; H. Meyer, J. Gros and W. Rusch (2000), *Growth in Agreement II, Reports and Agreed Statements of Ecumenical Conversations on a World Level, 1982–1998*, Geneva: WCC Publications. For a comprehensive bibliography of the dialogues involving the Roman Catholic Church and the topics covered, see the Centro pro Unione website, http://www.prounione.urbe.it

27 M. Tanner, 'Ecumenical Theology', in D. Ford with R. Muers (eds) (2005), *The Modern Theologians*, Oxford: Blackwell, p. 564.

28 'Towards a Statement on the Church' (1986), in Meyer, Gros and Rusch (eds), *Growth in Agreement II*, p. 587.

29 'Church as Communion' (1990), in Meyer, Gros and Rusch (eds), *Growth in Agreement II*, p. 329.

30 'Church as Communion' (1990), in Meyer, Gros and Rusch (eds), *Growth in Agreement II*, pp. 330–40.

31 M. Tanner in Ford and Muers (eds), *The Modern Theologians*, pp. 564–5.

32 'The Church as Communion in Christ' (1992), in Meyer, Gros and Rusch (eds), *Growth in Agreement II*, p. 396.

33 'Joint Declaration on the Doctrine of Justification' (1999), in Meyer, Gros and Rusch (eds), *Growth in Agreement II*, pp. 566–82.

34 'Joint Declaration on the Doctrine of Justification' (1999), in Meyer, Gros and Rusch (eds), *Growth in Agreement II*, pp. 568–9.

35 'Joint Declaration on the Doctrine of Justification' (1999), in Meyer, Gros and Rusch (eds), *Growth in Agreement II*, p. 579.

36 M. Tanner in Ford and Muers (eds), *The Modern Theologians*, p. 568.

37 Seventh Report of the RCC–WCC Joint Working Group (1998), para. 3.1, taken from http://www.oikoumene.org/ en/resources/documents/wcc-commissions/joint-working-group-between-the-roman-catholic-church-and-the-wcc/98-seventh-report-of-the-joint-working-group.html#c11985

38 Seventh Report (1998), para. 6.

39 For a more detailed analysis, see Eighth Report of the Joint Working Group (2006), Geneva: WCC Publications, pp. 115–17.

40 J. Grootaers (1997), 'An Unfinished Agenda', *The Ecumenical Review*, July, p. 312.

41 See T. Stransky, in Appendix B, Eighth Report (2006), and Grootaers, 'An Unfinished Agenda', p. 316.

42 Policy Statement on 'Towards a Common Understanding and Vision of the WCC', September 1997, para. 4.11, taken from http://www.oikoumene.org/?id=1561

43 Report of the Policy Reference Committee, adopted by the WCC Assembly (2006), taken from http://www.oikoumene.org/en/resources/documents/assembly/porto-alegre-2006/1-statements-documents-adopted/institutional-issues/report-of-the-policy-reference-committee/report-as-adopted.html

44 Pope John Paul II (1995), *Ut unum sint*, London: Catholic Truth Society.

45 Küng, *The Catholic Church*, p. 213.

46 D. F. Ford (1997), *The Modern Theologians*, second edn, Oxford: Blackwell, p. 103.

47 Küng, *The Catholic Church*, p. 211.

4

The historic Protestant churches

By 'historic Protestant churches' are meant those now centuries-old churches which inherit their distinctive teachings and practices from the complex events of the 'Reformation' in Europe in the sixteenth century. Many other churches have sprung up with a broadly 'Protestant' character in later centuries. Indeed the far-reaching families of 'Evangelical' and 'Pentecostal' churches could hardly have taken the forms they have in the nineteenth and twentieth centuries without the background of the Reformation and their older sister churches categorized as 'Protestant' – for which see the following chapter. Here we concentrate on the rise of the Lutheran, Reformed, Anglican, Baptist, Moravian and Methodist families of churches during the last five hundred years, and on what has become of them and their distinctive contribution to the whole Church of Christ in the twentieth century.

'The Reformation' is often dated from 31 October 1517, when the Augustinian monk, recently appointed professor, Martin Luther fixed to the door of Wittenberg Cathedral in central Germany, as the announcement of the agenda for the next public debate in the theology faculty, his 95 Theses. They dealt with the then 'hot' subjects of repentance, the sacrament of penance, and the selling – authorized by the pope – of indulgences by which people could buy the shortening of their time in 'purgatory' after their death. This gesture, and the content of the theses, did indeed set loose, and in a public way, a whole mass of questioning and eventual reformulation of central Christian doctrines, let alone of splits between Christians and the reshaping of substantial parts of the total (as then understood) Catholic Church no longer in communion with the Roman pope.

Yet the origins of this sort of teaching go much further back into other episodes in the church in Europe, which significantly shaped the emphases and arguments of the Reformation. Three of the figures who took a lead in these earlier episodes are Peter Waldo, John Wycliffe and Jan Huss.

Peter Waldo

Peter Waldo, a rich citizen of the French city of Lyons, already in the early 1170s declared himself 'converted' to what Jesus of Nazareth had really expected of his followers, gave most of his wealth away to the poor, and lived on what others would give him by way of alms. He spent his time travelling and preaching the Good News that Jesus had brought. He was excommunicated for 'unofficial preaching', expelled from Lyons, and condemned as a 'heretic'. But he had gathered considerable groups of followers, not least in northern

Italy, many of whom took refuge in isolated and readily defensible villages in the Alps, so that they continued in the obedience he had taught them, long after his death. In modern times they have become the 'Chiesa Evangelica Valdese' (Waldensian Evangelical Church, in English) which was first given civil rights in Piedmont-Savoy in 1848!

John Wycliffe

Nearly two hundred years after Waldo, an English clergyman, John Wycliffe, a noted teacher in Oxford already in the 1360s, laid much emphasis on a distinctively personal search for and grasp of the Christian faith – rather than an unthinking following of inherited custom and practice. He insisted on the Bible as the only true criterion of Christian doctrine, which did not provide any satisfactory authority for the kind of papal rule that had grown up, and took issue with many of the religious practices and institutions of the time. He too had many followers, known as 'Lollards', among the ordinary people of England, and although he was expelled from Oxford in 1381, and died not long after, his teachings had spread very fast throughout much of Europe.

Jan Huss

In particular, Wycliffe's teachings had a major impact on Jan (John) Huss, a priest in the Bohemian capital city of Prague, who was ordained in 1400 and soon became a well-known and loved preacher in the Bethlehem Chapel there. His often impassioned sermons, some of them about the moral failings of many of his fellow clergy, attracted much support, not least from both the King of Bohemia and the famous University of Prague, which made him its Rector. But the local archbishop persuaded the pope to excommunicate him. He appealed to a General Council of the Church and was given a 'safe conduct' to the Council of Konstanz, in the South of Germany, in 1415. There the assembled bishops condemned him and had him immediately burnt at the stake. This gave rise to 'Hussite Wars' in Bohemia in the 1420s and 30s, and to a community of 'Czech Brethren' which was still relatively strong when the Reformation happened a century later. That part of this community which by the early eighteenth century had had to take refuge in caves in the hills of Moravia, after ferocious persecutions by the then Catholic rulers, was invited by the young Count Nikolaus von Zinzendorf to take refuge on his estate at Herrnhut in SE Saxony in the 1720s. They became the 'Moravian Church' to which so much of the best in the worldwide missionary movement of the nineteenth and twentieth centuries is owed.

So Luther was to some extent thundering at an open door in many areas of Europe. He, too, above all else, emphasized the importance of the teachings of the Bible, and thus of the 'justification by faith' (rather than works, let alone payments!) on which St Paul had insisted in the Epistle to the Romans. His essay 'On Christian Liberty' (SCM *Core Reader on World Christianity in the Twentieth Century*, 4.1), written in 1520, illustrates how directly, even simply, he challenged many of the complexities and 'traditional' practices that had come to dominate Christian thinking and spirituality over the Middle Ages.

His teachings were quickly caught up into a long-drawn-out process of major meetings and councils, in which the political rulers found themselves playing at least as vital parts as the church leaders. The term 'Protestant', for instance, arose from a 'protestatio' against the majority presented by five reforming princes and fourteen self-governing cities at a 'Diet' in the Rhineland city of Speyer in 1529. The Augsburg Confession, for further instance, long regarded as the main 'standard of faith' for the Lutheran churches, was written for a council in the south German city of that name in 1530, presided over by the 'Holy Roman Emperor', Charles V, in whom the Spanish and Austrian imperial successions came together.

So from very early on the Reformation took shape as a force dividing not only the Church but also the then rulers of different parts of Europe and of different political allegiances, together with their peoples. The story of the Polish city of Torun (*SCM Core Reader*, 4.4) provides a vivid illustration of the local difficulties. In turn these divisions played an active role throughout the continent and beyond, in a series of struggles and wars that culminated in the hugely damaging Thirty Years War of 1618–48. That was finally brought to an exhausted close by negotiations in the city of Münster in northwest Germany, with their key phrase *cuius regio, eius religio* (the one who rules is the one whose religion will be followed there) – i.e. a nakedly political 'solution'.

Not long after Luther set one whole barrage of arguments loose in the German-speaking areas (though quickly picked up also elsewhere), a French lawyer and theologian, Jean Calvin, took refuge in the Swiss city of Basel from the forces of the then French king seeking to destroy reforming movements in his country. There he wrote a first edition of his great *Institutio Religionis Christianae* (*Institutes of the Christian Religion*). He was invited to go to the free city of Geneva but was eased out in 1538 when the city council preferred the teachings of the Zürich Reformer, Ulrich Zwingli, to those of Calvin. Yet they invited him back in 1541, and he then dominated the scene in the city, with teachings that spread out widely beyond it, until his death in 1564. In particular, it was his teachings, rather than Luther's – though the differences are relatively minor – that won hearts and minds in peoples as far apart as the Low Countries and Scotland to the west, and Hungarians, Bohemians and Poles to the east, as well as the Waldensians much nearer in the Italian Alps (*SCM Core Reader*, 4.2).

A more radical strain of the Reformation arose very early with the Anabaptists, on which see the *SCM Core Reader*, 4.3. This calmed down (in most cases was rapidly suppressed by the rulers) almost as quickly as it had shot up, but not without frightening the rulers, as did the Peasants' Wars in Germany, where Luther disappointed his rural and lower-class followers by taking the side of the princes and estate owners. Yet the Mennonite tradition, which maintained parts of this radical witness in the Netherlands, has never been lost and has reappeared in the later twentieth century as a significant influence in the ecumenical movement, especially through one of its leaders in the USA, John Yoder. The Baptist tradition, strong in Britain since the early

1600s and through that also from very early on in the USA, is perhaps best seen as a slightly less radical counterpart of the same wing.

Another whole 'tradition' that owes its origin as a separate entity to the Reformation is the 'Anglican'. In England, where many educated people, not least the theological teachers in Oxford and Cambridge, were eagerly following developments on the Continent, the decisive initiative was nevertheless taken by the King, Henry VIII. Despairing of ever being able to father a son by his Spanish wife, Catherine of Aragon, and finding the pope – no doubt strongly influenced from the Spanish court – hostile to any idea of a divorce (on the grounds of her having been Henry's brother's wife first!), the King decided in 1533 to break with the pope and set himself up as the temporal ruler of the English church. He handed the succession to the archbishopric of Canterbury which fell conveniently vacant to Thomas Cranmer of Cambridge, whose Book of Common Prayer of 1549/1552 has ever since profoundly shaped Anglican spirituality. Thus the Church of England found itself combining a loyalty to the (previously) 'Catholic' order in regard to the shape and equipment of churches, as to the responsibilities of bishops, priests and deacons, while the doctrine and spirituality of the now no longer Rome-linked 'Church of England' became much more like that of the continental Protestants. Many Anglicans have ever since found it difficult to think of themselves as either Protestants or Catholics because they feel they are 'both'.

The Methodist Church also had its origin in England, two hundred years later, when an Anglican priest, John Wesley, found his heart 'strangely warmed' by a Moravian preacher in 1738 soon after Wesley had returned from an unhappy attempt to fulfil a calling as a missionary in North America. Within a short time he set out with a new vocation to preach to those across the British Isles who had never heard the Good News from the existing parish churches. Soon he had become the most effective evangelist the British have ever known, drawing into Christian fellowship very significant numbers and leaders from the rural areas and newly urban working classes that the largely upper-class and land-owning Anglicans had sadly neglected. One striking example of Wesley's liturgical imagination is the central prayer, said by all present, of the annual 'Covenant Service', which he provided for all Methodist congregations to use at least once a year (SCM Core Reader, 4.5).

After the Thirty Years War, Europe 'settled down' into a pattern that has lasted, more or less, until now. In the north and west there are 'state churches' – Lutherans in Finland, Sweden, Norway, Denmark and Iceland, also in much of northern Germany and the Baltic territories of Estonia and Latvia, with Reformed/Calvinists in the Netherlands, Scotland and as a minority church in France, Anglicans in England, Wales and Ireland – though with many 'free churches' arising in Wales over the eighteenth and nineteenth centuries, and the bulk of the Irish population, as opposed to the English landlords and the workers they brought in from Scotland, remaining Roman Catholics. The Catholic Church had strong and faithful leaders in the rulers in Spain and Portugal, France, much of southern Germany, the Austro-Hungarian Empire and Poland (until this was divided between Prussia, the Austro-Hungarian Empire and Russia from 1773 onwards). Italy has been until very recently an almost entirely Catholic country. Under the Ottoman (and thus largely

Muslim) Empire until 1918, the Greek, Romanian and Bulgarian populations remained almost entirely Orthodox. So did the Russians in their empire, with the Georgian and Armenian peoples having their own branches of Orthodoxy.

There were no few changes and developments over the centuries, not least as the political situations moved on. Several of the Protestant churches knew internal splits for largely secondary reasons, and relations with the governments and rulers were always proving tricky in one or other place. New churches also sprung up from time to time – in one of London's poorest areas, William Booth, for example, a rebel Methodist leader, broke away in 1865 to form his own 'Salvation Army'. This soon developed its distinctive style alike of Christian fellowship, of music for worship and of evangelism on the streets, as of social help for those in need. Both these ministries have made notable contributions to the overall witness of 'historic Protestantism'.

In the twentieth century

From these various, often difficult and complex beginnings, how have the historic Protestant churches developed? What are their typical elements and distinguishing signs in the life of today? Here are five, always discussable, always particular to the communities concerned, yet which will be found almost always where a church, at local or national level, considers itself characterized by the term 'Protestant'.

- *Centrality of the Bible.*
  Protestants are people who read and rely on the Bible as the key and indispensable record of the purposes of God through the ages, including today. The texts in the *SCM Core Reader*, 4.6 and 4.7, demonstrate this rather fully, with the many twists and turns by which Protestant Christians have been significantly enriched in their reading of the Bible over the centuries.
- *Participation in worship by everybody, especially in singing.*
  Protestant worship, whether of a congregation in church on a Sunday, or of a group in a house during the week, is invariably an occasion in which everyone present is expected – and will expect – to play an active and definite part. Singing has long been a principal expression of this. Most Protestant denominations will have their own favourite and best-known hymns, often written by their own authors and musicians, like the hymns Luther wrote in German, or those in English of John Wesley's ever-fluent brother Charles. In modern times, many Christian churches, especially but by no means only Protestants, are increasingly happy to sing hymns written in and for people of a different tradition, but Protestant churches are outstanding for their quantity and variety of eminently singable hymns from every period of their life.
- *A vital role entrusted to ordained ministers, but never total authority.*
  Protestants are in this distinguished alike from the Roman Catholic Church, which entrusts a supreme and in the most important cases 'infallible' authority to the pope of Rome, as from Pentecostals who recognize the authority

and outpouring of God's Holy Spirit wherever they find this happening. All Protestant traditions rely on their ordained ministers for teaching and leadership, and place high importance on extensive programmes of training such ministers, almost always in part in the best available universities. But they do not entrust such people with authority to take vital decisions on their own. Many Protestant churches promote senior ministers to the rank of bishop, but do not expect a wholly different quality or level of teaching or decision-making from these. Ministers are expected to be reliable and competent teachers, leaders of worship and pastoral counsellors, but not to take decisions in isolation.

- *Decisions are taken with equal weight given to lay and ministerial voices.*
  Both at the local level and at any higher levels, Protestant churches are characterized by their insistence that there shall be at least as many lay Christians as ordained ministers involved in church meetings and synods from which important decisions are to be expected. The exact forms and disciplines of these will vary from church to church, but the fact of the lay votes being at least as many as the ministerial is a key feature of Protestantism.
- *The worldwide Church of Christ is seen as composed of particular, mostly national, units.*
  As we shall see, Protestantism has become no less worldwide than Catholicism, but is always organized in units that correspond to the overall shape and size of the particular people(s) they are serving. This can on occasion involve a definite political decision: Scots have their own Presbyterian (= Reformed or Calvinist) Church of Scotland that is to be unmistakably distinguished from the (Anglican) Church of England, on national lines. In many other situations national gatherings have simply been the most convenient pattern to bring local congregations and area synods together for whatever overall discussions and decisions have proved to be necessary. In the later part of the twentieth century, Protestants have discovered the value of their specific world-level meeting points (Lutheran World Federation, Baptist World Alliance, Anglican Communion, World Methodist Council, World Alliance of Reformed Churches among them), but have been cautious to endow any of these with responsibility for binding decisions.

So what share are these churches presently taking in facing up to the promises and challenges facing Christian faith in the twenty-first century? It is always dangerous to generalize, not least when even the story of how these historic churches came into being over the last five hundred years is so many-sided. But there are at least three wide fields in which the Protestant churches have made, and are still making, a contribution without which the total Christian scene would be very much weaker.

1 Spreading out into every possible new land and culture

Already in the seventeenth century, British and Dutch Protestants were moving out, for instance into North America and South Africa, of course for political and economic reasons at least as much as for the sake of anything religious, but still starting what has since become one of the most striking marks of Protestant history. North America came first, with the different colonies that later became the USA, each with a different religious colouring – Virginia for the Anglicans, New England for the stricter Puritans, Pennsylvania for the Quakers. Of course there was also the tricky matter of how the local people there would receive the Europeans (on this, see Chapter 11 on North America). There were also the French-speaking Roman Catholics who took possession of Quebec, and the Spanish Catholic missions pushing northwards from Mexico into what later became California and Texas. Yet, overall, by the late eighteenth century North America had become as much an 'established' Protestant area, even if the young USA wrote the total separation of church and state into its Constitution, as Latin America had become a Catholic continent under the Spanish and Portuguese. Later on, large numbers of Latin American Catholics would immigrate in their turn into the USA, just as in the mid-to-late twentieth century Latin America would experience a huge growth of Protestant, particularly Pentecostal, churches.

South Africa was by no means the same sort of story, not least because the Dutch presence took a long time to grow beyond an outpost. But again, looking at the twentieth century realities, it became a country with a strong majority of Protestant Christians in a wide variety of churches, and where Christian faith, for so long a principal feature of the harsh divisions between the peoples there, was in the end able to contribute signally to its emancipation from the divisive, apartheid policies of the cruel whites-only party that ruled from the 1940s until 1994.

German Protestants took the lead in bringing Christian faith to areas of India and Africa not yet reached by either the early Orthodox or the Catholics under Portuguese or Spanish rule. Moravians and Baptists pioneered the Christian faith among the slaves in the Caribbean who were to rise up and achieve their own nations, starting with Toussaint L'Ouverture in Haiti in the 1790s. David Livingstone, a Scottish Presbyterian, was the first man known to have walked the whole way across the middle of Africa, preaching the gospel while also struggling to counter the effects of the slave trade. As ocean-going Europeans arrived in the various parts of the world, the majority of them from Protestant nations (Dutch and British) in the eighteenth and nineteenth centuries, when the dominance of Spanish and Portuguese military forces had died away, Protestant churches of different types sprang up around them. Later chapters will tell more fully about each different area, with the roles played there by the different churches. The main 'result' is that by the later twentieth century the 'original homelands' in Europe are by no means any longer the countries where the largest Protestant populations are to be found. As later chapters will show, it has been in most cases active evangelism by the early Christians of the local culture and language that effectively ensured the long-term significance of these churches!

Precisely what these churches have contributed to their new homes varies enormously – again, any generalizations are impossibly dangerous. But one thing is sure: the first Protestants who arrived in wholly new countries either already knew in theory or soon learned in reality that the 'new' church there was called to stand on its own feet, was not simply to copy what the newcomers had brought with them, and was in time to become an independent and self-supporting church which would in its own way discover what God was intending them to contribute to the future of humanity as a whole. There was no single overlord for the missionaries. As Protestants they brought the Bible in their own languages with them as the essential resource for the new faith. However, as soon as the Bible could be translated into the language(s) of the local people, that which had arrived as the historic European Protestant faith was set to become the faith of people in each of many other countries and cultures in ways that no one from outside could limit or determine (see *SCM Core Reader*, 7.2 for an African discussion of this).

So European Protestants' missionary endeavours have now led to a deeply vital and significant reality by which people of very different languages and cultures are living out the Christian faith in their own ways within their own particular contexts. Of course the Orthodox churches have already known this in comparable ways in their home areas many centuries earlier, if with a rather stronger connection, not least in liturgical terms, to the 'mother' church. And European Catholics, especially the Jesuits, came onto the same trail in some areas two or three generations earlier than any Protestant – though with a particularly strong sense of working in obedience to the teachings of the pope in Rome. The point here is not to compare these three histories, let alone to judge any one of them by the others. It is to point out that the historic Protestant churches, for all their lack of central direction – indeed to some extent all the more effectively because they have been such a set of 'loose cannons' – have contributed greatly in this out-reaching way. Their contribution is by no means over yet.

Looking forward from the early years of the twenty-first century, China and (South) Korea are two of the countries presently experiencing this 'Protestant' growth and outreach very strongly. Hundreds of Korean Protestants are serving as missionaries in Siberia, and many Chinese 'Christians' (in China that is used as the term for Protestants in counterpart to Catholics) have their eyes and hearts fixed on the phrase 'back to Jerusalem' as something their churches will be able to contribute to in the years ahead. There are no longer so many parts of the world for which any sort of 'Christian colonialism' would be appropriate now, let alone a 'Protestant' one. But we can be hopeful that as Christians in the South take ever more seriously their responsibility to work for the Kingdom of God throughout the planet and not only in their 'own patch' there will be many cases of these newer Christians helping people in Europe (see Chapter 12 below for a careful analysis of the 'decline' of Christian faith there) to rediscover the distinctive meaning and depth of God's initiative in Jesus of Nazareth which so many in the one-time 'Christendom' have by now abandoned.

At one level we can expect Protestants, here very much including Pentecostals, to press on their Orthodox and Catholic fellow citizens a fuller appreciation of the value of the freedom patterned in the life of Jesus, for instance in relation to the equality of women and men in church life and leadership. Also at an even deeper and wider level, as can already be seen in the explorations of the World Council of Churches, there are many Protestant thinkers and leaders of the churches of the South who are praying and working for the peoples of Europe and North America to discover the humility and love by which to throw off the greed and selfishness of their consumerist societies, dominated by the competitive outlook of the 'free markets', and so recover a goal of living for and with one's neighbours in much more simple, outgoing and sharing lifestyles.

2 Exploring and resolving many major intellectual challenges

The centuries since the Reformation have brought many challenges of different sorts for Protestant Christians. Perhaps because they were in one sense 'starting anew' at the Reformation (even if Luther, Calvin and many others insisted it was the *re-formation* of the existing church they were promoting, not the starting of a totally new one) it was from the first the teaching function and the intellectual challenges that they needed to confront and pursue with special intensity and eagerness. Protestant churches are probably far better known for their professors than for their saints, though they have had no shortage of the latter.

In particular, while the hostile ideas of the 'enlightenment' in the later eighteenth century stemmed above all from Catholic France, it has been in Germany that this challenge to Christian faith has been most intensely felt and met, with a long series of leading theologians, say from Friedrich Schleiermacher to Karl Barth and Jürgen Moltmann. Their books and lectures have circulated around the world and have shown that the truth of God and of his revelation of himself in Jesus of Nazareth need not fear even what the most intelligent and penetrating of modern thinkers may come up with, in the sciences, in medicine, in technology, communications or any other worthwhile spheres of intellectual curiosity. Not that all the discussions and arguments have come to an end with a definitive proof, no more than the arguments with Greek philosophers in the early centuries, or those with Jewish leaders at the time of the resurrection. But those mentioned just now, and many other Protestant teachers, even more than the most respected and loved of popes, have been outstanding in accepting the intellectual challenges of 'modernity' and in showing, to all who will take the trouble to read and think carefully, that there is no shortage of evidences of God's love and care, even in the times of the most ghastly tragedies that human beings have inflicted on one another. Protestants, for all their numerous differences with one another, have all along preached and argued that God's action in Jesus, as we know it from the Bible, deserves unstinting response by way of loving, reconciling living and true, life-enriching worship.

The *SCM Core Reader* (4.6 and 4.7) offers two examples of ongoing explorations into understanding the Bible that have undergirded all such discussions during the twentieth century. The earlier is by a teacher who spent his life as a scholar of the New Testament and a member of the Congregational Union, C. H. Dodd. Here he discusses the sort of authority that Christians can and do recognize, respect and indeed obey in that complex of ancient books. The later one gives a compressed but reasonably full list of several distinct 'approaches' or ways of reading the Bible, in the kind of careful study that deserves the term 'criticism'. Both show just how the whole business of exploring, disentangling, doubting and yet also reaffirming what human beings can receive from that book of books, has become enormously enriching. At the same time each of us is encouraged to work her or his own specific way through the complex story of salvation as experienced in the long history of Israel and then, supremely, in the life, teachings, death and rising of Jesus of Nazareth two thousand years ago, as these are conveyed to us in the Bible as a whole.

Again, it is no part of this chapter to claim that Protestants have always been right and the other churches wrong! Already in Chapter 1 we have mentioned how the various families of churches began to reconcile in the twentieth century some of the major quarrels and debates of the times of mutual rejection and division. It is not too far from the truth to record that up until very recently the Orthodox churches have on the whole stuck faithfully to the teachings of the Fathers of the early centuries, without being known for participating in the arguments around, say, modern science. So also the Roman Catholic Church has all along had its teaching ministry entrusted to each successive pope. Pope John Paul II has been in the late twentieth century a most significant teacher in almost any field, but not so many of his predecessors are remembered for what they got right in the ever-widening arguments about modern challenges to the faith. Again and again, the most demanding and sensitive of theological explorations arising from the many questions and new areas of human experience, brought about by the changes and developments in learning and in society over the nineteenth and twentieth centuries, have been pursued and wrestled with by Protestant theologians and teachers. By no means always with outstanding success! But the need to accept such challenges and work through to generally satisfactory new understandings and behaviours is one that Protestants have all along known to be of the highest importance to all Christians. The degree to which the Vatican Council in the 1960s was at last able to accept, for all Catholics, what Protestants had characteristically said about the Bible and the use of local languages for Christian worship, became signs of what Christians are able to receive from one another, even when still severely divided.

Looking forward, it is as ever impossible to be sure just what new questions and debates will mark the twenty-first century. There are clearly several under way at the time of writing, for example the challenge the G8 leaders set themselves in 2000 to reach high levels of advance towards (if in no case the total figures in) the Millennium Development Goals throughout the world, or the possibilities of avoiding, or at least weakening, the huge threats of climate change brought on by humanity's reckless emissions of carbon into the atmosphere for the last hundred years. It is hardly difficult to imagine that the whole business of genetic manipulation, of vegetables, of animal meats, let alone of human embryos and babies, may throw up vastly tricky and difficult questions for our children and grandchildren. Whatever the challenges may turn out to be, one has good reason to believe that Protestant theologians and leaders will be among those Christians giving imagination and energy to resolving them, alike in thought and in action, in ways that can foreshadow God's purposes as known in Jesus.

3 The energies behind the contemporary ecumenical movement

A third area where it has been mainly Protestants who have contributed much that will remain crucial as Christian faith advances through the twenty-first century is that of the contemporary ecumenical movement. As is recalled in the last pages of Chapter 1 above, this search for the unity God in Christ intends for his whole Church has flowered in the twentieth century in a way that no earlier century since the first has known. This movement towards Christian unity has been for many people the single most hopeful aspect of their experience of 'church' and yet will need in the twenty-first century no less commitment by many different church organizations and leading individuals than it has been granted in the twentieth.

So while there is no monopoly for or by any type of church in this movement so far, it is worth stressing that the majority of the commitment given to it all has come, certainly up until the Second Vatican Council in the 1960s, from Protestant Christians and from the historic Protestant churches. This is not to deny that it was the Ecumenical Patriarchate of the Orthodox churches that first proposed a 'League of Churches' as early as 1920, nor that the Roman Catholic Church entered in a remarkably dynamic and promising way into this same movement at the Second Vatican Council. Yet the hard grind of it all has been undertaken throughout the history sketched in Chapter 1 by people and leaders of the historic Protestant churches. One vivid sign of this is that the first six general secretaries of the totally new World Council of Churches, since it was brought into existence in the late 1930s, have all been Protestants, if of widely differing backgrounds: Willem Visser 't Hooft (Reformed, Dutch), Eugene Carson Blake (Presbyterian, USA), Philip Potter (Methodist, Caribbean), Emilio Castro (Methodist, Uruguay), Konrad Raiser (Lutheran, Germany) and Samuel Kobia (Methodist, Kenya).

There has not exactly been a rush to reunite the hitherto separate churches, though a great deal of discussion in many different countries towards such unity has taken place. At one level there have been a number of significant movements to bring together into effective unity the different groups into which Protestants of the same background had split – for instance the forming of the reunited Church of Scotland in the 1920s, as of the total Methodist Church in England, Scotland and Wales in the 1930s, with the two Dutch Reformed Churches in the Netherlands and their Lutheran fellow Christians joining into the 'Protestant Church of the Netherlands' in the 1990s.

A second, relatively frequent process has seen churches that are not so severely divided from one another meeting to work out how they can recognize each other more fully and work together more effectively for the sake of the gospel. One particularly striking example of this has been the process involving Lutheran and Reformed Churches on the continent of Europe. This reached a high point in the signing of the Leuenberg Agreement in 1973, by which the churches recognized generally the validity of each others' sacraments and ministries. For a further step in this direction, see *SCM Core Reader*, 4.9. A second high point came in 2003 when these churches agreed to call themselves the 'Community of Protestant Churches in Europe', not as an end point to their movement into unity, but as a sign that they intended to work together even more closely at the level of Europe and in relating to the European Union. In all these, and many other comparable processes, much is made of Christian unity consisting in 'reconciled diversity' – that is, once-divided churches agreeing to share the gifts God has given them, yet without forcing each other into a single mould which would disown their previous histories.

More important still has been the breakthrough beyond at least one major confessional barrier in the Protestant churches in the Indian subcontinent in the mid-twentieth century, with the Anglicans joining the Methodists, Congregational and Presbyterian churches (all of British missionary background) in the united Church of South India, whose model was (in great part) followed some years later in North India – there with Baptists also involved – as also in Pakistan and in Bangladesh. These by no means involved all the churches in each area, but the movement has led to the formation of the Communion of Churches in India (Church of South India, Church of North India, and the Mar Thoma Church) as a foretaste of an eventually fuller union.

Chapter 11 on North America tells of several examples of comparable discussions and advances towards Christian unity in Canada and the USA. These have had to face many different questions in the course of their by now long history, by no means least that of racial equality and mutual recognition, but have advanced further, with notable patience, than many had thought likely.

Nonetheless, in the early years of the twenty-first century, it seems clear that the dynamism for the ecumenical movement, spanning the entire life, witness and worship of the churches, is now to be found more urgently and energetically among Christians of the South than among those of the more comfortable and economically 'successful' North and West. The earlier commitment in these latter areas has apparently worn off, perhaps on the one hand because their churches have been very slow and foot-dragging about losing themselves into the new unities that God has been offering them, on another because the highly 'consumerist' attitudes and expectations of the culture(s) now ruling the roost in these lands give little attention to ideas and activities that are for the worldwide totality of God's people rather than for the peoples of the North and West in their own safe and familiar little world(s).

That again is a horribly brief and dangerous generalization. There are still many 'historic Protestants' in the North and West who are doing their best to help the ecumenical movement to advance. But it is undeniable that it has to some degree lost the interest, let alone the decision-making hearts, of those who lead public opinion in the northern and western world, while it is among the more needy and yearning worlds of the South that Christian hope and commitment and imagination, in regard to Christian unity, along with other long-lasting and stubbornly difficult concerns, can gain the followers it deserves. And this because at least three newer challenges are already requiring on very different canvases many of the sensitivities and commitments that Christians have learned in and from the inter-church ecumenical movement.

One is starting to be explored through the early, tentative meetings of what is being called a 'Global Christian Forum', in which representatives from any and every possible sort of Christian church or grouping can be encouraged to meet and share what God, as known in Jesus, means to them. This is what the

World Council of Churches came into being to be. Yet the degree of mutual commitment to fellow members that has grown up relatively quickly among its members over its first 50 years has led to decisions and patterns of organization that have in effect made it difficult for other families of churches to become full members of the Council – Roman Catholics because of their own regulations and expectations, most Pentecostal and independent churches because so much more is expected of WCC membership than they can readily rise to. So there is under way a movement to explore how significantly wider and looser gatherings can be enabled to take up the age-old, yet always new, challenge to discover the unity which Jesus promised for all his disciples in John 17.

The second is the whole new possibility of interfaith dialogue and interfaith co-operation between persons and groups from within the major world faiths with enough humility and long-term courage to explore in this field. Chapter 16 sets out briefly how far Christians have advanced into this area.

The third is the vast field of the need for far deeper intercultural contacts and mutual learning between the previously dominant culture(s) of the economically richer West and those of the poorer South, if together we are to ensure a hopeful future for humanity as a whole. This has already been touched on above.

In respect of none of these three is there need for any suggestion of pre-eminence for Protestants. But it may surely be claimed that the experience in the twentieth century of the ecumenical movement, which has owed a great deal to Protestants, deserves to be studied and followed in a good many respects, if by no means all, in these comparatively new and sensitive fields.

One hopes that those taking up this whole cause in the century ahead, in all its manifold expressions and outworkings, will be able to learn from the best experiences of their forebears, many of them Protestants, in the twentieth. The list of names to honour could stretch from Nikolaus von Zinzendorf (Moravian, of the eighteenth century), through William Carey (Baptist, of the nineteenth) to John R. Mott (Methodist, of the early twentieth), and on in the twentieth to Dietrich Bonhoeffer (Evangelical, of Germany; from whom see two profound poems in SCM Core Reader, 4.8), José Míguez Bonino (Methodist, of Argentina; see SCM Core Reader, 10.8), Kosuke Koyama (United, of Japan; see SCM Core Reader, 9.4), and Desmond Tutu (Anglican, of South Africa; see SCM Core Reader, 1.10). All of these are only and always among hundreds and thousands of others, some well known but most very little so, yet all working and praying together that God's will be done and God's Kingdom come in the way he wishes and at the time he sets. There is no shortage of Christians in the Orthodox, Catholic and Pentecostal families of churches who are praying no less fervently for God's will to be known and done, yet many of these, especially those who follow the story of the ecumenical movement, will be among the first to thank God for what their 'historic Protestant' neighbours and colleagues have been able to initiate.

Further reading

In relation to the history and 'outcomes' of the Reformation, there are three recent books, covering many different stories from many different nations in Europe and beyond, the first concentrating on the central theological questions, the second more on the social and political contexts in the 1500s, and the third on the longer-term results around the world:

D. MacCulloch (2003), *Reformation: Europe's House Divided, 1490–1700*, London: Allen Lane (Penguin Books, 2004).

R. Po-Chia Hsia (ed.) (2004), *A Companion to the Reformation World*, Oxford: Blackwell.

A. E. McGrath (2007), *Christianity's Dangerous Idea: The Protestant Revolution – A History from the Sixteenth Century to the Twenty-First*, London: SPCK.

The reading suggestions appended to other chapters of this volume, both those dealing with different continents and those on particular areas of concern, will suggest many significant Protestant authors. Among those mentioned there, for other books, are three outstanding Protestants who combine their theological interests with active involvement in the current life of the world around them:

D. Tutu (1999), *No Future Without Forgiveness*, London: Rider, in which he reflects theologically on the experience of the South African Truth and Reconciliation Commission.

K. Koyama (1974), *Water Buffalo Theology*, London: SCM Press, written out of his experience of serving as a missionary in the deeply Buddhist society of Thailand.

José Míguez Bonino (1995), *Faces of Latin American Protestantism*, Grand Rapids MI and Cambridge UK: Wm B. Eerdmans, a series of lectures to academic audiences in the USA.

In the German-speaking world, which, since Luther's time, has been such an important source of Protestant theology, the outstanding figure of the later twentieth century has been Jürgen Moltmann. His major books are hardly easy reading, and rather long, though always enriching. A shorter one, with an 'extended introduction', by David Jenkins, the former Bishop of Durham, is *Theology and Joy*, London: SCM Press, 1973.

5

Pentecostalism

Pentecostalism grew from a small sect at the beginning of the twentieth century to a worldwide movement at its end, from a faith that, in Harvey Cox's words, 'brought hope to losers and rejects to a movement many of whose leaders are ostentatiously rich ... from seeing signs and wonders as harbingers of God's new day to being obsessed with the techniques of rapture'.[1] This phenomenal growth in Pentecostal churches throughout the world was one of the most significant aspects of Christianity in the twentieth century. Few regions have been left untouched by this development.

This chapter will examine this trend. It will explore possible definitions, seek to trace the origins and development of these aspects of contemporary Christianity and explain the diverse features of Pentecostalism as a global phenomenon. It will conclude by examining the ways in which Pentecostals have related to other Christians and by assessing Pentecostalism at the end of the century. In focusing on the Pentecostal family, we seek to highlight its importance as a 'new' phenomenon having its origins within the twentieth century.

A distinctive evangelical understanding of Christianity has been a prominent mark of many Protestant churches since the eighteenth century and here too there has been considerable numerical growth. Its direct origins go further back into previous centuries than those of Pentecostalism and its contemporary developments are, in some ways, more diverse than in the case of Pentecostalism. Consequently, we will attempt no more in this chapter than to define Evangelical Christianity and trace its early beginnings. Its developments will be exemplified in chapters on the various world regions.

Towards definitions

The term 'evangelical' derives from the Greek word *euaggelion* (good news or gospel).[2] However, definitions that adequately describe the diversities within these global Christian phenomena are always going to be ultimately unsatisfactory and insufficiently comprehensive. For example, many Christians within all the worldwide traditions would regard themselves, as individuals and within their churches, as being shaped by the gospel. They would, therefore, see themselves as 'evangelical' Christians but would not understand themselves as being within what we might call 'the Evangelical camp'. In a European context 'evangelical' has been and is still used for churches that have their origins in the Protestant Reformation of the sixteenth century (for example, the Evangelical Church in Germany [EKD]) and would not usually bear the connotations of the term as used in this chapter. Martin Luther (1483–1546) used the term 'evangelical' to describe all Christians who accepted the doctrine of *sola gratia* (by grace alone), which he saw as the heart of the Christian faith. Nevertheless, despite these ambiguities, an attempt at a definition is necessary at this point.

McGrath offers the following:

> Evangelicals … find their identity in relation to a series of central themes and concerns, including the following:
> 1. The identification of Scripture as the ultimate authority in matters of spirituality, doctrine and ethics.
> 2. A focus on the saving death of Jesus Christ on the cross as the only source of redemption and hope.
> 3. An emphasis upon conversion or 'a new birth' as a life-changing religious experience.
> 4. A concern for sharing the Christian faith, especially through evangelism.[3]

These points closely reflect Bebbington's fourfold definition in terms of 'biblicism, conversionism, crucicentrism [focusing on the cross of Christ] and activism'.[4]

Most Christians who regard themselves as Pentecostal would affirm these typical evangelical characteristics – scriptural authority, emphasis on the saving power of the cross of Christ, conversion as a mark of discipleship and a commitment to evangelism – as being central to their understanding of Christian faith and life. What would mark them out as Pentecostals, however, would be an additional emphasis on baptism by the Holy Spirit, following conversion, a personal experience of the Holy Spirit and its expression, most particularly, in worship and devotion. 'Pentecostalist Christianity manifests religious phenomena which, so its adherents believe, reproduce or reintroduce the miraculous charismata [gifts] of the New Testament, being infused with the power of the Holy Spirit.'[5] For many Pentecostals, the foremost expressions of such charismata are speaking in tongues (*glossolalia*) and divine healing. But Walker suggests that adventist hope as a revivalist sign of the end-time is also a key characteristic.[6]

A. H. Anderson (drawing on R. M. Anderson[7]) defines Pentecostalism as 'a movement concerned with the *experience* of the Holy Spirit and the *practice* of spiritual gifts'.[8]

We should note here that charismatic Christians, who share many of these characteristics, may be found within Pentecostal churches as well as in the traditional churches. It would be fair to say, however, that the Charismatic Movement was not always at ease with classical Pentecostalism. New popular songs and choruses, excitement and intensity in worship (including dancing and movement), as well as speaking in tongues and miracles of healing are features of what has been a growing Charismatic phenomenon, described as a renewal movement, within many of the denominations during the latter half of the twentieth century.

From the perspective of world Christianity as such, it should also be noted that whereas these are common features of these movements, there is considerable diversity also from continent to continent and from country to country. As we shall discover, local culture and traditions, as well as Christian heritage, have shaped local expressions.

There was diversity also in relation to the Bible. Whereas all Evangelical, Pentecostal and Charismatic Christians affirmed what McGrath calls the 'identification of Scripture as the ultimate authority in matters of spirituality, doctrine and ethics', some would go further to take a fundamentalist stance. In its earliest form in the eighteenth- and nineteenth-century evangelical revivals, fundamentalism affirmed the centrality of the fundamentals of the faith, including the Bible as the inspired and inerrant Word of God, the deity of Christ and his atoning death, his resurrection and ascension, and his return in judgement. In this form, it became a test of Christian 'orthodoxy' over against modernist tendencies. However, in the twentieth century, fundamentalism focused increasingly on the literal inerrancy and accuracy of Scripture. In all matters of faith (such as creation) and behaviour, the inerrant word of the Bible was definitive and final. Such fundamentalism became an increasingly formative as well as divisive factor within these movements and within the churches generally during the century (see Chapter 11, and *SCM Core Reader on World Christianity in the Twentieth Century*, 11.5 and 11.6, for further information about Christian fundamentalism).

Origins

The beginnings of modern evangelicalism may be found in the eighteenth-century revivals in Europe and North America. The revival in England, led by John Wesley (1703–91) and Charles Wesley (1707–88) and also by George Whitfield (1714–70), is described as 'the evangelical revival'. Remaining within the Anglican Church of England, they began a renewal movement, largely as a result of their itinerant preaching ministry, that was to have a lasting influence on Christianity worldwide in subsequent centuries, leading in due course to the formation of the Methodist Church. A parallel movement in Wales, focused on Howell Harris (1714–73) and Daniel Rowland (1713–90), who were also Anglicans, led to an evangelical revival based on a Calvinist theology. Both of these movements – although they developed in different theological directions – were influenced by the Pietist movement, especially among the Moravian Brethren in Germany. Pietism emphasized inner religious experience and personal devotion and commitment, focused on prayer, Bible study and a strong belief in the work of the Holy Spirit in the human heart. It also stressed Christian philanthropy and service to those in need within the community, as well as missionary activity and evangelism.

During the same period, Jonathan Edwards (1703–58), who had been nurtured in the piety of New England and its Puritan tradition, began his ministry at the Congregational Church in Northampton, Massachusetts, where he was ordained in 1727 and which he left in 1750 after a dispute with the congregation. During his ministry, the congregation experienced a series of revivals and awakenings and, in due course, he emerged as the most influential figure in Evangelical religion in America and its colonies. His extensive writings meant that he was a key figure not only in encouraging and fostering evangelical revival but also in providing a theological foundation for American evangelicalism in his own and subsequent centuries. He was an intellectual, a revivalist, a promoter of holiness and a Christian thinker.[9]

During the next one hundred and fifty years, the holiness movement which sprang from these beginnings, with its revivalist and evangelical features, grew and spread, especially in the USA, not least through journals such as *Guide to Christian Perfection* (1839–45), which became the *Guide to Holiness* (1846–1901). Experiences of Spirit baptism among many of these groups sowed the seed for the germination and phenomenal growth of Pentecostalism during the twentieth century.

Pentecostalism began at the Apostolic Faith Gospel Mission in Azusa Street, Los Angeles. In 1906, William J. Seymour, a black preacher, ministered to the mixed-race congregation of Azusa Street. As a result of his ministry the congregation began to experience the Holy Spirit and to display spiritual gifts such as speaking in tongues, healing and ecstatic worship. Brought up within the Catholic and Baptist traditions, Seymour was converted through his connection with a holiness group and soon began preaching. He was deeply influenced by Lucy Farrow (a former slave and niece of the abolitionist, Frederick Douglass), who was in turn influenced by Charles Fox Parham. She testified to her baptism by the Holy Spirit and practised spiritual gifts, including speaking in tongues. Seymour longed to share that experience, but as a black man he was excluded from services and classes held by Parham and others. However, he came deeply under Parham's influence and began preaching.

In February 1906 he moved from Houston, Texas, to Los Angeles. Initially excluded from the church to which he was invited, because he had not been 'baptized in the Holy Spirit' – and had been preaching about an experience he had not shared personally – in April of the same year he did receive his baptism in the Spirit. The prayer meetings in a private house soon outgrew the accommodation, and they moved to 312 Azusa Street, a redundant African Methodist Episcopal church. Reports of the first service led by Seymour at the new premises spread around the United States and worldwide. One of the key features of these prayer meetings was the diversity of the congregation: they brought together men, women and children, black and white, Hispanic and Asian, rich and poor, illiterate and educated, a social and racial diversity and an ecstatic spirituality that drew sharp criticism from some quarters locally. Within months Azusa Street Mission became the largest congregation in Los Angeles (see *SCM Core Reader*, 5.2 and 5.3).

Seymour's influence continued and he travelled widely within the United States, preaching and speaking against racism. His stance for racial integration led to his being rejected by some within the newly developing movement, but there can be no doubt that he was one of the key influences – some would claim *the* key – in the founding of Pentecostalism. Later in this chapter, we will need to consider whether Seymour's legacy of the unity of racially and socially diverse groups survived the tests of the twentieth-century growth of Pentecostalism. But for the moment we note Cox's description of early Pentecostalism as 'bringing hope to losers and rejects' and recognize that this was due in no small measure to Seymour's powerful ministry.

Pentecostalism – a global phenomenon

During the subsequent century, Pentecostalism became a global phenomenon that embraced a wide variety of movements. One estimate[10] suggests that there were 524 million Pentecostal and Charismatic Christians in the world by the year 2000, out of a total of 2,000 million Christians. Other figures[11] estimate a similar total number of Christians worldwide (1,928 million in 1995) but give the number of Pentecostal Christians as 105 million, with a further 110 million being categorized as African Indigenous sects (and largely Pentecostal in belief and practice). As has been noted in Chapter 1, such figures (and the definitions and descriptions upon which they are based) must always be regarded with considerable caution, but they do indicate that there was an important and significant growth within Pentecostalism during the twentieth century, a growth that is one of the key phenomena in world Christianity during that century.

Some Pentecostal churches are white and middle-class 'mega-churches' in the developed world. Others are indigenous movements in developing countries, rooted in local cultural and religious contexts. Whereas it has its origins in the USA, the majority of those who would describe themselves as Pentecostal are now in Asia, Africa and Latin America. This change in focus has inevitably, as we shall see, meant changes in self-understanding and practice, as well as in the interpretation of the gospel faith. But we must start our overview by asking why Pentecostalism has seen such growth in the developing nations.

Walter Hollenweger ascribes this to

> its roots in the spirituality of the 19th century African American slave religion: an oral liturgy, a narrative theology and witness, the maximum participation of the whole community in worship and service, the inclusion of vision and dreams into public worship and an understanding of the relationship between the body and the mind manifested by healing through prayer.[12]

In many countries around the world, although not in all, it is a grass-roots movement that attracts the disadvantaged and underprivileged. It should be noted, however, that the growth of Pentecostalism has not been confined to the poor and marginalized, and in both the developed and developing world it has appealed in powerful ways to the more prosperous 'middle-class' populations in these countries. South Korea is one striking example. This is a reminder that we are dealing with a diverse phenomenon and that no one description or explanation can do adequate justice to world Pentecostalism during the century.

We may illustrate this global phenomenon by examining the growth of Pentecostalism in Latin America. Wolffe, writing in 2002, estimates that there were 'probably 30–35 million' (based on Freston) for the whole of Latin America (including Central America).[13] This would have been about two-thirds of a total Evangelical/Protestant (terms that are synonymous in Latin America) population of around 45 million, which is itself about 10 per cent of the total population. This means that the Roman Catholic Church is still nominally dominant, but David Martin estimates[14] that 'perhaps less than 20 per cent' of the population are actively Catholic. Wolffe concludes that 'the balance between committed Pentecostal and Catholic religious practitioners may be less radically unequal than at first appears'.[15] He further notes that the distribution of Pentecostal Christians in the various Latin American countries shows considerable variation. For example, in Brazil, the largest Latin American country, 15 per cent of the population were Protestant in 1998 (of which about 60 per cent were Pentecostal). In Guatemala, 22.5 per cent of the population were Pentecostal in 2002, while in Costa Rica, El Salvador and Nicaragua Protestants represented 10–15 per cent of the population (assuming similar proportions of Pentecostals, this would represent between 7.5 per cent and 11 per cent of the population).

Wolffe quotes Martin to explain this phenomenon:

The Pentecostals speak the language of the people ... They propose a restoration of scarred and fractured relationships, a repudiation of corruption, a discipline of life, an affirmation of personal worth, a cancellation of guilt, a chance to speak and to participate, sisterhoods and brotherhoods of mutual support in sickness and health, and a way to attain *Sanidad Divina* [divine healing] ... [T]heir conversion is a matter of being literally 'shaken' by a total re-orientation of the heart and the will in order to join the ultimate fiesta.[16]

Some key conclusions may be drawn. First, the Pentecostal emphasis on experience provides a new sense of meaning to those who have been hitherto rejected. Second, the oral, rather than the literary, culture of Pentecostalism is clearly attractive to people who are illiterate or semi-literate. It is also empowering, as Wolffe notes, when combined with an experience of encounter with God. Third, the Pentecostal emphasis on healing and on release from 'dark' forces (which Wolffe describes in terms of 'the cosmic struggle with the powers of evil')[17] resonates with the spiritual world of many, especially among the poorer communities, in Latin America. Indeed, some scholars see echoes of folk Catholicism in this aspect of Pentecostalism. Fourth, many scholars have noted that women have played an increasingly significant role within Pentecostalism in the continent, in contrast to the inevitably male-dominant leadership within the Roman Catholic Church (although it should be noted that Hollenweger has been critical of 'the deplorable waning in the role of women' generally within Pentecostalism).[18] Finally, the caution noted above is applicable in Latin America, namely, that although its broadest appeal has been among the urban poor, Pentecostalism has also appealed to more prosperous groups within society, originally under the influence of US missions. The Brazilian Church of the Four-Square Gospel (originally a US import, but an independent church since 1988) is an example of this. The 'prosperity gospel' has, therefore, played its part in the growth of Pentecostalism in Latin America, as it has done worldwide. (See *SCM Core Reader*, 5.5, 10.5, 10.6 and 10.7, for extracts that illustrate the growth and development of Pentecostalism in Latin America.)

Key issues for Pentecostals

The global growth of Pentecostalism suggests a number of key issues that need to be explored.

Living with diversity

We have already noted that the growth and development of Pentecostalism in different situations around the world has not been a uniform process. The way it has taken root in different cultural, economic and religious contexts has led to a diverse movement, ranging from mega-churches in prosperous cities to indigenous churches in Africa, Asia and Latin America. This diversity is seen by some to be a threat to traditional Pentecostal orthodoxy and by others as a source of enrichment.[19] There are, of course, common features that are gathered around the defining centrality of the experience of baptism in the Spirit and the outworking of that experience in gifts of the Spirit such as speaking in tongues, healings and signs and wonders. But since the heart of Pentecostalism is in its oral tradition rather than in an overarching theology as defined, for instance, in agreed confessions of faith, there is considerable diversity of belief. Similarly, there will be a variety of patterns of worship, but all, in various ways, will enable believers to experience and celebrate the gifts of the Spirit in every member. Worship in whatever context will be marked by exuberant liveliness, energetic music and singing, powerful proclamation, an intensity of prayer, signs of healing and wonders, and a longing for and expectation of God. This shared experience gives this diverse movement its fragile coherence.

The Bible and believing

What place does the Bible have as the authority in matters of faith and morality and as a bond of unity between Pentecostals? Naturally, in one sense it holds the central place. In the absence of Pentecostal credal formulae and a commonly agreed theology and liturgy, the Bible is recognized by all Pentecostals as (in McGrath's words above) 'the ultimate authority in matters of spirituality, doctrine and ethics'. It is at the heart of worship, its teaching is the source of preaching and evangelism, and the signs and wonders that the Bible describes are the promise that the Holy Spirit will continue to work in and through Pentecostal Christians today. But Hollenweger raises fundamental questions about the correct interpretation of Scripture within modern Pentecostalism. If there is no 'given', authorized understanding of Scripture and every believer is free 'to decide the correct interpretation, because Scripture is clear in itself',[20] how can the diversity of understandings of Scripture be accounted for? Hollenweger rightly asserts that all Christians read Scripture selectively, each through his or her own spectacles, and that it is impossible to claim that any one person or church holds 'the pure gospel'. This happens within traditions, Pentecostalism included, as much as between traditions, and calls for an 'internal dialogue' within Pentecostalism as much as a dialogue between the traditions, such as the study on hermeneutics (the development of principles and paradigms for the interpretation of text) inaugurated in recent years by the World Council of Churches.

Can the same be said about what Pentecostals believe? If there is no commonly held interpretation of the Bible, is there a commonly held and agreed faith? Anderson claims[21] that the 'fundamental proposition' is the experience of the Holy Spirit at work and the gifts that follow. Specifically, he defines three key claims that characterize modern global Pentecostalism, claims, incidentally, that have their roots firmly within the early Church as presented in Scripture. The claims are that Jesus Christ, first, saves from sin, second, heals from sickness, and, third, delivers from the power of Satan. This represents an all-embracing understanding of salvation that addresses the troubles of human life in all their aspects, including socio-economic as well as individual and personal troubles. This seems to be in tune with the gospel narrative. It resonates with the inherited religious culture and inherent spirituality (rooted in a dualistic understanding) of many indigenous Pentecostal Christians around the world. It may also resonate with the social and personal challenges that confront Pentecostal Christians, in more affluent contexts, who are more deeply influenced by western cultural norms. Within a diversity of Pentecostal belief, this may represent something of the heart of their understanding of the truth of the gospel.

The challenge of mission

Throughout the century a Pentecostal understanding of mission has had at its heart 'the conviction that the Holy Spirit is the motivating power behind all mission activity'. [22] Pentecostal understanding of mission was heavily influenced by an Anglican missionary, Roland Allen (1868–1947), who spent ten years, from 1893 to 1903, serving the North China Mission with the (Anglican) Society for the Propagation of the Gospel. Through his later writings he became formative in missionary theory in the early decades of the century. He was critical of contemporary missions for imposing foreign financial and policy control on local churches and commended a return to a New Testament understanding of the Church as local and indigenous, trusting in the Holy Spirit to equip believers with all the gifts necessary for the Church's life and witness (see *SCM Core Reader*, 5.4).[23]

The tension between the missionary enterprise, largely from the USA and Europe, with its temptation to exercise leadership over the local church, and the indirect influence of Allen's writings pressing for local and indigenous leadership within the new churches, was a feature of Pentecostalism for much of the twentieth century. The globalization of Pentecostalism threatens to reinforce what José Míguez Bonino calls 'a transnational mentality ... [that is] foreign to a deeper indigenization. It has been too limited by some current theological formulations adopted from the Anglo-Saxon Evangelical circles.'[24] There has been continuing debate about the degree to which Pentecostal expansion, in Latin America, for example, has been the product of funding and missionary effort from the USA or whether it is predominantly indigenous in character. Certainly, indigenization has occurred in diverse contexts such as Chile, western Ghana, Indonesia and China, which have been deeply dependent on local Christians as leaders and evangelists. Wolffe quotes an unnamed scholar

> who began his research on Latin American Protestantism with the assumption that its expansion was primarily a factor of influences and money from the USA, [but] eventually concluded that 'Latin Protestants explode in growth because they are an autochthonous [indigenous] movement, coming primarily from the poor'.[25]

There can be little doubt that one of the predominant reasons for the success of Pentecostal mission has been acculturation (i.e. the degree to which it has been shaped by and rooted in particular local, indigenous cultures). In his analysis of Latin American Pentecostalism, Wolffe concludes: 'Latin American Pentecostals are not merely adapting to the secular cultural background of their adherents, but are engaged in a reshaping of their outlooks in a manner which remains culturally accessible but has a distinctive radical appeal.'[26]

There are clearly questions of political and cultural influence and power at stake here intermingled with the missionary drive. Martin[27] explores this question from two perspectives. One section asks about 'The Americanization of Latin American religion?' and another about 'The Latin Americanization of American religion?' At the end of the former section he concludes that the success of US missionary enterprise in Latin America indicates both the strength of US cultural influence and the desire of many Latin Americans to have whatever the USA offers for their day-to-day life. In the latter section, Martin concludes that one of the key reasons for the success of Pentecostalism in the continent has been its ability to be immersed in the local culture, leading to what he describes as 'total autonomy'. He does maintain, however, that Protestantism has been less able (in his words) to 'go native' than Catholicism (see *SCM Core Reader*, 5.5).

The gift of healing

For Pentecostals, the gift of healing is one of the key fruits of the work of the Spirit. One of the greatest influences in this aspect of Pentecostal life was W. M. Branham (1909–65). He had considerable gifts of diagnosis but, according to Hollenweger, was less skilful in terms of 'healing prognosis'.[28] The fundamental conviction of faith evangelists is that faith in the power of the Spirit – the faith of the sufferer but also occasionally the faith of others – brings health, a conviction that springs, to some extent at least, from the New Testament, from the ministry of Jesus and the mission of the first apostles. Hollenweger notes that the extravagant lifestyle of many Pentecostal healers has been the subject of considerable criticism. Their mission continues, however, and Hollenweger comments that they go on 'selling the same product under the new trading label of "The Third Wave" – and this in spite of the severe criticism by the great majority of North American Pentecostals'.[29]

These healing ministries are usually rooted in a dualistic understanding of the world, where there is a cosmic struggle between God and Satan, between the forces of good and evil, between healing and wholeness and disease and fracture. 'Everything is either divine or cosmic.'[30]

There is a growing debate within Pentecostalism itself about this theological framework and the place and nature of healing within a theological understanding of the gospel and in the practice of evangelism. Hollenweger quotes an article by Robert A. Guerlich in the Pentecostal journal *Pneuma*, referring to Gerd Theissen's claim that 'Exorcism is not a sign of faith. There is no spiritual war in Scripture between the faithful and the demons ... The battle was won already (Barth). *That* is what we confess.'[31] Hollenweger also draws attention to the criticism made by some Pentecostal theologians of the narrowly individualistic understanding of evil and the need to understand 'the geography of evil – the sinful and evil structures of society ... They must see that the texture of social living makes no easy distinctions between the personal and the social.'[32]

These are key issues for Pentecostals but they must be seen within the broader context of a valid Christian healing ministry not only within Pentecostalism but within the worldwide Church as a whole. But it must also be recognized, as we have already noted, that one of the reasons for the growth of Pentecostalism has been its ability, not least in relation to its healing ministry, to tune into the 'pre-Christian' culture and spirituality of indigenous communities. There is clearly a fundamental theological task here that needs further exploration within Pentecostal dialogues with other Christian traditions.

A WCC consultation on Faith, Healing and Mission held in Accra, Ghana, in 2002 focused precisely on this issue. Its aim was 'to deepen dialogue on faith and healing as essential elements of the church's mission'.[33] The report affirms a number of 'common convictions', including the following: healing comes from God; prayer for healing is an essential part of mission; healing must be understood in individual and social terms and in terms of the well-being of creation. It also addressed the question of the failure of prayer for healing and recognized that 'Healing is a journey into perfection of the final hope, but this perfection is not always fully realized in the present.' The report also notes a number of areas for further debate including the need to address issues of 'unethical manipulations and practices [that] are taking place in the name of faith healing', in order to 'bring sanity into the phenomenon of faith healing'. Significantly, it highlighted the need for theological reflection on the place of spirits and demons: 'Do spirits and demons really exist or are they only a metaphor for explaining suffering, possession and sickness?' Finally, it called for further reflection on whether all healing comes from God.

These are crucial questions not just for relationships between Pentecostals and other Christian traditions but also within Pentecostalism itself where there would be a wide diversity of views on these matters.

Social transformation

The origins of Pentecostalism in the Azusa Street Mission in Los Angeles gave to early Pentecostals a strong sense of social inclusiveness. As an African-

American preacher, Seymour represented in his own person Pentecostalism's roots in that tradition, but also its openness to people of other social groups and ethnic origins. His own difficulty in gaining access to Pentecostal meetings led by Parham, for example, and the racist opposition he experienced early in his own ministry in Azusa Street, indicate that social inclusiveness and racial segregation were in tension within early Pentecostalism. R. M. Anderson claims that early Pentecostalism was 'an oblique expression of social protest ... born of radical social discontent'.[34]

There is general agreement among scholars that there is ambiguity within Pentecostalism around the issue of social transformation. On the one hand, the prosperity gospel[35] still plays a key role in Pentecostal evangelism and lifestyle: true gospel faith promises prosperity. The rapid growth of Pentecostalism among middle-class communities around the world is adequate proof of the attractiveness of this claim. In such communities, it is likely that embracing the capitalistic ideal is higher up the agenda than social transformation. On the other hand, as we have already seen, these mega-churches not withstanding, Pentecostalism is predominantly a grass-roots movement among the poor and marginalized. In these communities, social transformation would be a key priority since they would see in the gospel a promise of the justice, equality and freedom of God's Kingdom in Jesus Christ

Thus analysts have drawn attention to Pentecostalism as 'a powerful movement of the poor', which as such is 'pregnant with potential for the transformation of society'.[36] In his analysis, Anderson[37] notes the South African experience and the formation of 'Relevant Pentecostal Witness', whose patron was Frank Chikane, a pastor and theologian within one of the African Instituted Churches and former General Secretary of the South African Council of Churches, the national ecumenical council that was at the heart of the South African and international opposition to apartheid during the latter half of the twentieth century. This is a powerful reminder of the possibility of a radical Pentecostalism that is at the forefront of social liberation and transformation. Similarly, José Míguez Bonino, himself a Methodist liberation theologian in Argentina, recognizes within Latin American Pentecostalism 'a vision of society that takes account of the structural aspects of human life ... and sees in them an arena for the work of the Spirit'.[38] These examples are illustrative of a powerful strand within contemporary Pentecostalism that is prepared to understand the struggle with the forces of evil not just in individual terms but also in socio-economic and socio-political terms. Such developments become increasingly significant in a global context where the growth of Pentecostalism has occurred within the more prosperous (and therefore more economically influential) communities as well as within the poorer, grass-roots (and therefore generally marginalized and less economically influential) communities. These trends may well contribute to a broader understanding of mission within the context of the Kingdom of God in the coming period and may also be a key factor in developing collaborative partnerships and theological dialogues with other Christian traditions.

Dialogues and relationships

During the latter decades of the twentieth century, the Pentecostal movement was increasingly engaged in developing relationships and mutual
understanding with other Christian traditions. We cannot review all such
dialogues and developments in this chapter. Two such dialogues illustrate
this aspect of twentieth-century Pentecostalism, namely, relationships with
the World Council of Churches and the dialogue with the World Alliance of
Reformed Churches.

Relationships with the World Council of Churches[39]

Following an initiative from the Seventh Assembly of the WCC in Canberra
(1991), a consultation was held in 1994 in Lima, Peru. Papers presented included
the following: 'Our Pentecostal Identity', 'Pentecostalism in the Power of the
Spirit', 'A Pentecostal Perspective of Evangelization', 'Our Vision of Unity and
Ecumenism' and 'Living in the Unity of the Spirit'. Similar meetings were
held in Leeds, England, in 1995 (where the focus was on the Black-majority
Pentecostal churches in the UK), in Nigeria in 1996 (focusing on the African
Instituted Churches) and in Costa Rica in the same year where, significantly,
the WCC report on *Baptism, Eucharist and Ministry* (1982) was discussed, as
well as the approaches of Pentecostal spirituality to issues of justice and to
the use of Scripture.

The Joint Consultative Group between Pentecostals and the WCC was established following the Eighth Assembly of the WCC in 1998. The first meeting
was held in the Abbey of Hautecombe, France, in the year 2000, and subsequent meetings were held in Quito, Ecuador (2001), Seoul, South Korea (2002),
Cleveland, USA (2003), Johannesburg, South Africa (2004) and Cairo, Egypt
(2005). For the purposes of this volume on Christianity in the twentieth century, these consultations, although they were held during the early years
of the twenty-first century, enable us to assess the ways in which the Pentecostal movement developed its commitment to ecumenical dialogue and
participation.

In its report to the Ninth Assembly of the WCC (February 2006), the
Joint Consultation set out a number of key affirmations[40] (see *SCM Core
Reader*, 5.7):

- They enjoyed a genuine sense of community
- They recognized that each shared a deep devotion to God and manifests a
  desire to act according to the will of God
- They recognized that they have much more in common than they first
  thought
- In their prayer and bible study they recognized the presence of the Holy
  Spirit and have found in Scripture an unparalleled authority for the on-
  going life of the church
- They were touched by the richness of the diversity among them
- They were agreed that they were to proclaim the good news of the gospel
  to the world

- The present divisions hinder the work of this witness
- The question of how the Spirit is discerned has emerged.

Equally significantly, the Group also identified a number of challenges that needed to be addressed,[41] which are listed as follows: inadequate understandings of one another; tensions about understandings of mission and evangelism (including proselytism, an issue which has been a topic of major worldwide ecumenical debate during recent years); understanding the gifts of the Spirit; the role (and theological understanding) of the sacraments in the life of the Church; different ways of interpreting and understanding Scripture and the ways in which the work of the Spirit is discerned. (For an example of Pentecostal thinking at this WCC Assembly, see *SCM Core Reader*, 5.7.)

The overarching question that emerged from the series of consultations was: To what extent do the member churches of the WCC see each other as 'churches' and on what basis is such a question answered? This can be unpacked in terms of a number of interrelated questions:

- What is the nature of the church?
- Who are the members of the church?
- What is church and what is not?
- What or who is the ultimate authority in the church?
- What are the criteria by which an individual church recognizes another as church?

It is intended that these conversations will continue in the coming years at global, regional, national and local level.

Reformed-Pentecostal International Dialogue (1996-2000)[42]

A series of official meetings between representatives of the World Alliance of Reformed Churches (WARC) and representatives of the Pentecostal movement from around the world identified and explored four key themes: Spirituality and the challenges of today (1996); The Role of the Holy Spirit in the Church (1997); The Holy Spirit and Mission in Eschatological Perspective (1998); The Holy Spirit, Charisma and the Kingdom of God (1999).

The final report was published as *Word and Spirit, Church and World* (see *SCM Core Reader*, 5.8).[43] The report shows that there are points of joint affirmation. First, both stand in communion with the Nicene-Constantinopolitan Creed in their belief that the Holy Spirit is the Lord and Giver of Life and, together with the Father and the Son, is to be worshipped and glorified (15). Second, the Holy Spirit is present and active , not only in the Christian Church, but also in human history and in various cultures. 'The work of the Spirit is broader than we think' (19). Third, together they stress the mutual bond between the Word and the Spirit. Through the Holy Spirit, the Bible speaks the Word of God (22). The Bible is an instrument of the Spirit (35).

Four affirmations shape the remainder of the report. First, the Church is the creature of the Word and the Spirit. Second, the Church is the community of the Holy Spirit's leading. Third, the Church is the community of the Spirit's gifts. And, finally, the Church is *in* but not *of* the world. 'In each of these areas of common conviction, Reformed and Pentecostal emphases are often different. These differences are sometimes complementary, sometimes divergent' (36, and elucidated in 37–95).

Within each of these sections, in addition to an impressive range of shared affirmations, key divergencies are noted:

- First, whereas 'Reformed Christians tend to use the language of "covenant" to describe the initiative of God and the formation of God's people … Pentecostals tend to use the language of "the outpouring of the Spirit" [for this work of God]' (38–39).
- Second, whereas 'Reformed Christians affirm that the Spirit leads the Church as a community in ongoing confession of Christian faith … in each time and place … Pentecostals frequently manifest their beliefs through personal testimony in … life and worship' (43–45).
- Third, whereas 'Reformed Christians affirm that the Spirit's gifts are experienced in the congregational life of Reformed churches … leading [them] in faithfulness … Pentecostals affirm that spiritual gifts – such as healing, prophesying, casting out demons, speaking in tongues – enhance the faith of persons and the life of the community of faith' (51–53).
- Finally, whereas from time to time 'Reformed Christians have been involved in prophetic acts for altering oppressive situations in society … Pentecostals focus more on individuals than on structures, viewing persons as individuals … [recognizing that] programs of personal renewal … have had far-reaching implications for social transformation' (61–62).

As we conclude this review of the phenomenal growth of Pentecostalism in the twentieth century, three key questions must inform our further thinking. First, what do Pentecostal Christians bring to the larger Christian family? Our review has highlighted a number of key aspects. Above all, Pentecostal Christians bring into our understanding of Christian discipleship an experience of the Holy Spirit (see below) and the practice of spiritual gifts. Pentecostal Christianity cannot (and does not) claim that these are exclusive to their approach to Christianity. After all, other traditions, from the ancient Orthodox traditions through to the more recent experience of the Salvation Army, would make similar claims about the key role of the Spirit in the life of the Church. What is distinctive about these aspects of discipleship as found in the Pentecostal movement is that there is a deliberate attempt to reflect within the contemporary Christian life something of the liveliness and energy of early Christianity as found in the Acts of the Apostles and elsewhere in the New Testament, in ways that have to a lesser or a greater degree become less prominent within many of the other traditions.

Another key aspect that has emerged from our review has been the ability of the Pentecostal approach to Christian discipleship to adapt itself in response to different social, cultural and religious contexts. Whereas there are key features that mark most, if not all, Pentecostals, there is also great diversity in the ways that these features are lived out and celebrated in different settings. In this way, Pentecostalism in the USA is very different from

Pentecostalism in Africa, and this in turn will be very different from Pente-costalism in Latin America. This ability to be responsive to different needs and contexts is clearly a strength of the movement and has contributed, as we have seen, to its phenomenal growth during the century.

The other key feature of Pentecostal Christianity that we have noted is the approach to theology and theological discourse. This is a difficult matter to evaluate adequately, but there is a clear distinction between the approach of the major historic traditions of Christianity to theology and the approach of Pentecostalism. This is not to say, in any way, that theology is not important within the movement. It is to say, however, that personal belief and experi-ence, gifts of the Spirit, and Spirit-filled worship have a higher priority for a Pentecostal Christian than any attempt to express this faith and practice in theological or creedal language or to systematize their beliefs within some kind of theological framework. Clearly, there are theologians and academics within the movement, some of whom have contributed to our study, and they have played a key role in interpreting faith and experience both within the movement and for other members of the Christian family. But theology may well play a less significant role in Pentecostal life than it does in other tradi-tions. There are two implications of this observation that may be important. First, there is always a danger that Christian experience and practice is too far and too easily removed from its theological grounding, in the mistaken belief that personal faith and experience are all. One of the continuing debates of twentieth-century Christianity was whether an overemphasis on Christian experience was as much of a threat to an authentic Christianity as an over-emphasis on an intellectualism that threatened to remove the essentials of the faith from the grasp of the majority of Christians. Second, however, an overemphasis on *personal* experience and belief may undermine the tradition of the Church (in the sense of the essentials of the faith as formed and handed down through the centuries of the history of the Church) and so rob Christ-ianity of its essence. Pentecostal Christianity challenges the Christian family to reflect on this issue and so makes an important contribution to the shaping of Christianity for the twenty-first century.

Second, what can the traditional churches learn from Pentecostals about the gifts of the Holy Spirit? From the beginning, Christians have recognized that the life and witness of the Church is a working out of the presence and power of the Spirit through the lives of individuals and the Christian com-munity. All the traditions have emphasized this Spirit-formed and Spirit-led understanding of the Church, in varying ways and to different degrees. For some, the Church as such is the communion (koinonia) of the Holy Spirit, the fellowship within which the Spirit is at work. This ecclesiologically focused understanding of the Spirit is in marked contrast with other perspectives which see the Spirit at work not only within the Church but also throughout human community, including other faith communities, and in the whole of creation, empowering personal renewal and social transformation. The Pente-costal understanding of the Spirit brings a further dimension into view. Its emphasis on a personal experience of the Spirit, on the exercise of the gifts of the Spirit, in worship, witness, prophecy and healing, and on the necessity of a second 'baptism in the Spirit' as a prerequisite of true conversion and conviction, brings into the larger Christian family a more personal and active understanding of the work and power of the Holy Spirit.

Finally, what should be the aim of ecumenical/bilateral dialogues with Pentecostals: unity or union, partnership, mutual understanding, collaboration or mutual tolerance? In his examination of the relationship between Pentecostalism and the ecumenical movement, Hunter claims that the Pentecostal movement at large has not come to judge ecumenical relationships as an important work of the Spirit.[44] Indeed, in some contexts there has been antagonism towards an ecumenical movement that is perceived as being in conflict with some of the key aspects of the Pentecostal tradition.

Recent developments within the ecumenical networks have increasingly recognized the diversity of ecumenical relationships, locally, nationally and internationally. The commitment of the Ninth Assembly of the WCC (2006) to support the move towards a Global Christian Forum that would gather together as widely diverse a range of Christians as possible, argues against a narrow and exclusivist understanding of 'ecumenism'. At the same time, there are Christian churches and traditions, as well as many individuals within churches and traditions, many Pentecostal Christians among them, who fear that pushing at the boundaries of plurality towards a greater universalism could lead to an unacceptable syncretism.

Hunter concludes his analysis as follows:

[T]he rate at which the world 'decreases in size' demands that all traditions devote attention to living out their shared identity in Christ. Since the Pentecostal movement is global and significant, it cannot shrink from its responsibilities. It must interact with other Christians, other religions and the whole of creation.[45]

From an ecumenical perspective, there is real hope here. It is unlikely that growing ecumenical relationships will lead to a search for deeper structural unity between Pentecostal churches and others. But it is likely that the priority of these relationships, certainly in the immediate future, will continue to be growing partnership in Christian witness and service, a search for deeper mutual understanding that may lead to an enrichment of faith and worship for all concerned, and certainly a growing mutual trust and tolerance that will be a prerequisite for these developments. Above all, they will bring into the ecumenical family an enriched understanding of the work of the Holy Spirit in renewing persons, churches and communities, globally, regionally and locally.

Further reading

Three books offer an understanding of Pentecostalism 'from the inside':

A. H. Anderson (2004), *An Introduction to Pentecostalism: Global Charismatic Christianity*, Cambridge: Cambridge University Press.

A. H. Anderson (2007), *Spreading Fires: The Missionary Nature of Early Pentecostalism*, London: SCM Press.

A. H. Anderson and W. J. Hollenweger (eds) (1999), *Pentecostals after a Century: Global Perspectives on a Movement in Transition*, Sheffield: Sheffield Academic Press.

Other authoritative studies of Pentecostalism include the following:

H. Cox (1996), *Fire from Heaven: The Rise of Pentecostal Spirituality and the Re-shaping of Religion in the Twenty-first Century*, London: Cassell.

W. J. Hollenweger (1972), *The Pentecostals*, London: SCM Press.

W. J. Hollenweger (1997), *Pentecostalism: Origins and Developments Worldwide*, Peabody MA: Hendrickson.

W. Kay and A. Dyer (eds) (2004), *Pentecostal and Charismatic Studies: A Reader*, London: SCM Press.

D. Martin (1990), *Tongues of Fire: The Explosion of Protestantism in Latin America*, Oxford: Blackwell.

A. Walker (1989), *Restoring the Kingdom: The Radical Christianity of the House Church Movement*, London: Hodder & Stoughton.

J. Wolffe (ed.) (2002), *Global Religious Movements in Regional Context*, Aldershot: Ashgate, which includes a chapter on the origins of the movement and on its expansion in Latin America.

Notes

1 H. Cox (1996), *Fire from Heaven: The Rise of Pentecostalism and the Re-shaping of Religion in the Twenty-first Century*, London: Mowbray, pp. 16f.

2 See for example, Mark 1.14: 'Jesus came ... proclaiming the gospel (*euaggelion*) of God ...'

3 A. E. McGrath (1997), *An Introduction to Christianity*, Oxford: Blackwell, p. 331.

4 D. W. Bebbington (1989), *Evangelicalism in Modern Britain: A History from the 1730s to the 1980s*, London: Routledge, pp. 1–19.

5 A. Walker (1993), 'Pentecostalism and Charismatic Christianity', in A. E. McGrath (ed.), *The Blackwell Encyclopedia of Modern Christian Thought*, Oxford: Blackwell, p. 428.

6 A. Walker (1997), 'Thoroughly Modern: Sociological Reflections on the Charismatic Movement', in S. Hunt, M. Hamilton and T. Walter (eds), *Charismatic Christianity: Sociological Perspectives*, Basingstoke and London: Macmillan; reprinted in J. Wolffe (ed.) (2002), *Global Religious Movements in Regional Context*, Aldershot: Ashgate and Milton Keynes: Open University, pp. 203–4.

7 R. M. Anderson (1979), *Vision of the Disinherited: The Making of American Pentecostalism*, Peabody MA: Hendrickson, p. 4.

8 A. H. Anderson (1999), 'Introduction: Pentecostals at a Crossroads', in A. H. Anderson and W. Hollenweger (eds), *Pentecostals after a Century: Global Perspectives on a Movement in Transition*, Sheffield: Continuum, p. 20.

9 For a list of Edwards' writings, see M. A. Noll (1993), 'Jonathan Edwards', in McGrath (ed.), *Encyclopedia*.

10 D. B. Barrett and T. M. Johnson (2000), *International Bulletin of Missionary Research*.

11 Taken from www.adherents.com (9 Jan. 06).

12 Quoted in A. H. Anderson (1999), 'Global Pentecostalism in Transition', in Anderson and Hollenweger (eds.), *Pentecostals after a Century*, p. 23.

13 J. Wolffe (ed.) (2002), *Global Religious Movements in Regional Context*, Aldershot: Ashgate in association with The Open University, p. 69.

14 D. Martin (1990), *Tongues of Fire: The Explosion of Protestantism in Latin America*, Oxford: Blackwell, p. 58.

15 Wolffe, *Global Religious Movements*, p. 70.

16 Martin, *Tongues of Fire*, p. 83, in Wolffe, *Global Religious Movements*, p. 72.

17 Martin, *Tongues of Fire*, p. 83, in Wolffe, *Global Religious Movements*, p. 74

18 W. Hollenweger (1999), 'Critical Issues for Pentecostals', in Anderson and Hollenweger (eds), *Pentecostals after a Century*, p. 185.

19 Hollenweger, 'Critical Issues', p. 177.

20 Hollenweger, 'Critical Issues', p. 185.

21 A. H. Anderson (1999), 'Pentecostalism in the New Millennium', in Anderson and Hollenweger (eds.), *Pentecostals after a Century*, pp. 214f.

22 Anderson, 'Pentecostalism in the New Millennium', p. 220.

23 R. Allen (1927), *The Spontaneous Expansion of the Church and the Causes which Hinder It*, London: World Dominion Press.

24 J. Míguez Bonino (1994), 'Pentecostal mission is more than what it claims', *Pneuma* 16, pp. 285f.

25 Wolffe, *Global Religious Movements*, p. 77.

26 Wolffe, *Global Religious Movements*, p. 86.

27 Martin, *Tongues of Fire*, pp. 271–95.

28 Hollenweger, 'Critical Issues', p. 179.

29 Hollenweger, 'Critical Issues', p. 179.

30 Hollenweger, 'Critical Issues', p. 180.

31 R. A. Guerlich (1991), 'Spiritual Warfare: Jesus, Paul and Peretti', *Pneuma* 13, pp. 33ff., quoted in Hollenweger, 'Critical Issues', p. 180.

32 E. Villafañe (1993), *The Liberating Spirit: Towards an Hispanic American Social Ethic*, Grand Rapids MI: Wm B. Eerdmans, p. 201, quoted in Hollenweger, 'Critical Issues', p. 181.

33 See Report of the WCC Consultation on Faith, Healing and Mission, December 2002, *International Review of Mission*, July/October 2004, nos. 370 and 371, Geneva: WCC Publications, pp. 325–555.

34 Anderson, *Vision*, p. 229.

35 That is, the belief that true faith in the gospel's promises brings to the believer social and economic prosperity.

36 C. B. Johns (1993), *Pentecostal Formation: A Pedagogy among the Oppressed*, Sheffield: Sheffield Academic Press, p. 78.

37 Anderson, 'Pentecostalism in the New Millennium', p. 213.

38 J. Míguez Bonino (1997), *Faces of Latin American Protestantism*, Grand Rapids MI: Wm B. Eerdmans, pp. 66f.

39 See the Pentecostal Charismatic Theological Inquiry International website at www.pctii.org/wcc/, for this and a wide range of other valuable resources relating to this chapter.

40 Programme Book for the Ninth Assembly, Porto Alegre, February 2006, Geneva: WCC Publications, pp. 169–73

41 Programme Book, pp. 171f.

42 See *Cyberjournal* for Pentecostal-Charismatic Research, *Cyberjournal* 8, September 2000.

43 References in brackets are to paragraph numbers in the text as it appeared in the *Cyberjournal*.
44 H. Hunter, 'Two Movements of the Holy Spirit in the 20th Century? A Closer Look at Global Pentecostalism and Ecumenism' at www.epcra.ch/papers/hamburg99/hunter.htm (23 Feb. 06).
45 Hunter, 'Two Movements', final paragraph.

6

Middle East

Introduction

The intertwining origins of Judaism, Christianity and Islam – all having their
roots in the region we now know as the Middle East – have given these monotheistic faiths a degree of common history and common belief (despite the
deep differences that are their marks of identification and distinctiveness).
They share a faith in the one and only God. They recognize Abraham as their
common ancestor. Jews, as the people of God, recognize him as their patriarch.
Christians recognize him as one from whom Jesus Christ was descended.
Muslims see him as the original Muslim who, with his son Ishmael, restored
monotheistic worship in Mecca and with whose monotheistic faith Muhammad established a spiritual link, through his insights into prayer and worship.
All this means that the contemporary history of Christianity in the region (or
indeed worldwide) cannot ultimately be understood without a recognition of
the bonds as well as the conflicts which these common beginnings represent.

For the purposes of this chapter, the Middle East is defined as the region
between the eastern shores of the Mediterranean Sea in the west and the eastern border of Iran in the east, and from Armenia in the north to the tip of the
Arabian peninsular in the south, while also including Egypt in North Africa.
Three of the ancient Christian centres of authority and evangelization are
found in the region, namely, Jerusalem, Antioch and Alexandria. Orthodox,
Oriental Orthodox, Latin Catholic, Uniate Catholic and Protestant traditions
(including Anglican, Lutheran and Presbyterian) are represented. Within this
region, Christian communities may be found in Cyprus, Egypt, Iran, Iraq,
Israel/Palestine, Lebanon and Syria. These Christian communities include
ancient churches that can trace their history back to the very beginnings of
Christianity, through whose evangelizing efforts, directly or indirectly, the
whole of Christendom has grown. Ancient roots, an enriching diversity of
traditions and, for many, a sense of being the living stones in the Holy Land
and its surrounding region, and a constantly changing community, create a
significant Christian presence – even if that community has been severely
affected by emigration during the recent period.

In most of the countries of the region, with the exception of Israel/Palestine
and Cyprus, Muslims are in the majority and Christians are in the minority,
the largest minority being in Lebanon.

In such a region, where ancient roots and identities play such a key role in
the contemporary life of the Christian churches, the relationships between the
churches are crucial. The traditions these churches represent make ecumenical

relations challenging. But the twentieth century contributed in fundamental ways to forging new partnerships, despite – and, at times, because of – the deep political conflicts in the region during this period.

A brief historical overview

The history of Christianity in the region has had to do with persecution and movement as much as with ancient roots and traditions, with ecclesial centres, for example, having to be transferred from one location to another because of harassment, division within traditions, and inter-religious conflict – a pattern that, in many ways, still continues amidst the continuing turmoil and tension of the region.

The Crusades

Of all the events that have shaped the history and, especially, the religious history, of the Middle East, the medieval Crusades were of particular significance. They need to be set in context. In the centuries immediately following Muhammad's death in 632 CE Islam made attempts to invade the countries of Christendom in the Middle East. The earliest assault, during the seventh century, saw the defeat of Byzantium in Syria, followed by the conquest of northern Syria, Iraq and Egypt, peoples who shared a largely common ethnic and cultural identity. The later wave of attacks was against the Turkish East and the Latin West, peoples of a very different cultural and ethnic identity. These assaults represented real threats against Christians in the region, even if they were not always perceived as such at the time!

The military expeditions between 1095 CE (led by Pope Urban II) and 1204 CE were undertaken, partly in response to previous attacks, in the name of Christianity, in order to recapture the Holy Land from what was perceived to be Muslim dominance and to set up crusader States within the region, States which turned out to be relatively short-lived. They were waged on the basis of an extended understanding of the Augustinian 'just war' doctrine (see Chapter 13), apparently in defence of churches in the Middle East.

The objective of these expeditions was the holy city of Jerusalem. The association of the city with the military campaigns led to their being seen in terms of pilgrimages, thus taking on a spirituality of their own that raised them above merely military campaigns and giving those who engaged in them a spiritual status as Christian knights. Johns (*SCM Core Reader on World Christianity in the Twentieth Century*, 6.1) notes that the 'lure of booty, of an adventure shared with comrades in arms, and of the mysterious Orient ... all played their part among the heady mixture of religious and worldly motives which drew the Christian knights of Europe into battle with Islam'.[1] Johns evaluates the historical significance of these campaigns in the following terms:

[I]f the crusades never constituted a serious threat to Islam's military control of the Near and Middle East, the very existence of the crusader States caused grave offence to Islam. The profanation of the Holy City, the reduction of the Muslim population of Syria ... to the status of inferior subjects, the interference with the hajj [the annual Muslim pilgrimage to Mecca which is one of the five pillars of Islam] and other religious obligations, all amounted to an unforgivable affront to the collective dignity of Islam. So also did the ultimate defeat and expulsion of the crusades from the East constitute a lasting and bitter humiliation to Christian pride.[2]

Whatever judgement history may make about the justification and justice of these Crusades and their 'successes' and 'failures', there is little doubt that this period has contributed in fundamental ways to deep-seated suspicion and destructive conflict in the region in subsequent centuries, which continued to be significant ingredients in the religious memory of the twentieth century. They were, in Johns' words, 'old wounds' which the events of the nineteenth and twentieth centuries were to reopen.

The rule of empires

The changes and transformations of the crusader centuries (eleventh to the thirteenth centuries) were followed, not many years later, by rule over the countries of the region by various political powers. Prominent among these, of course, was the Ottoman Empire (thirteenth century to 1924), an extensive Muslim empire. For example, it ruled what we now know as Israel/Palestine, as well as Lebanon and Syria, until the early years of the twentieth century. From the end of the First World War (1914–18) and the fall of the Ottoman Empire, Syria and Lebanon were ruled by France until shortly after the Second World War (1939–45). Cyprus was governed in turn by French, Venetian, Turkish and British rule from the period of the Crusades until 1960, when it gained its independence. This complex political history, which is illustrated above by only a few examples, inevitably contributed to the turbulent political and religious situation in the region during the twentieth century.

The establishment of the State of Israel

The establishment of the State of Israel in hitherto Arab Palestine was one of the most significant events in the recent history of the region. Theodor Herzl (1860–1904), the founder of modern political Zionism, travelled widely visiting state leaders in order to press upon them the urgent need to support the Zionist cause. After the First World War, the Balfour Declaration, issued on behalf of the British Government in 1917, and signed by A. J. Balfour, British Foreign Secretary at the time, offered support to the Zionist cause of setting up in Palestine a home for the Jews in a way that did not jeopardize the rights and privileges of those who already lived in that land or the rights of Jews living in other parts of the world.

These and other efforts led to the setting up of the State of Israel in 1948. The Declaration for the establishment of Israel (*SCM Core Reader*, 6.2) was approved at a session of the People's Council, comprised of representatives of the Jewish community in Palestine and the Zionist Federation, on Friday 14 May 1948, several hours before the British Mandate for Palestine came to an end.

The Declaration asserted the natural right of the Jewish people to be like all other peoples, exercising self-determination in their sovereign state, and proclaimed the establishment of a Jewish state in Eretz Israel, named 'the State of Israel'. It went on to establish governing structures and institutions and, significantly, to call for 'peace and cooperation with the Arabs of Israel, the neighboring countries and their peoples, the Jewish people throughout the Diaspora, and the United Nations Organization'.[3] Whatever the justice of the establishment of the State of Israel, which many Christians throughout the world would wish to affirm, it clearly also had a negative impact on relationships in the region. Jean Corbon[4] claims that it became a 'bridgehead' for US influence and that this led to many Arab countries looking for (and securing) support from the Soviet Union.

Thus began the powerful significance of the existence of Israel for East–West international relationships during the second half of the twentieth century. Corbon justifiably claims that 'Israel was perceived by many Islamic states as a powerful, Western, settler, colonial entity'. All this signifies a web of influences that had a fundamental effect not only on the politics of the region but also on its religious, including its Christian, communities.

Recent wars and conflicts

Another key factor in its recent history were the many wars and conflicts that affected the region during the second half of the century, some of them, at least, directly or indirectly, the consequence of the establishment of the State of Israel. In addition to the two World Wars and the Suez crisis (1956), one of the most significant conflicts was the Six-Day War of 1967. Israel attacked Syria, Jordan and Egypt in the belief that these three Arab states were about to launch a massive attack on Israel. The air forces of Egypt, Jordan, Syria and Iraq were decimated, Egyptian tanks were destroyed, Israel's army reached as far as the Suez Canal, and the West Bank (of the Jordan River) and the Golan Heights were captured from Jordanian and Syrian forces respectively.

This conflict left a lasting legacy on the political and religious landscape of the Middle East. UN resolution 242, passed in the aftermath of the 1967 war, affirmed that the establishment of a just and lasting peace in the Middle East was paramount and that the achievement of such a peace would be dependent upon Israeli withdrawal from territories (not 'the' territories) occupied in the conflict and the recognition of the sovereignty of every state in the region and their right 'to live in peace within secure and recognized boundaries'.

The struggle to achieve such a settlement, which has often erupted into violent conflict, continued throughout the remainder of the century, with Israel (often backed by the major western powers) and the Palestinians (and their Arab supporters) constantly failing to reach an adequate and lasting settlement. So further conflicts involving Israel resulted during the remainder of the century, including the Yom Kippur war (1973) and the Intifada (the Palestinian uprisings in 1988 and again in 2001). In the wider region, the wars that devastated Lebanon (1975–90), the Iran–Iraq war (1980–88), the first Gulf war (1991), the wars in Afghanistan on the fringes of the region and the more recent Iraq war (2003), toppling Saddam Hussein, who was in due course executed for war crimes, all also had significant impacts not only on internal relationships within the region but also on the perceptions and impacts of the region within the broader global community.

In reflecting on the significance of these wars, Jean Corbon writes:

> In these wars, the lives and welfare of the people of the Middle East are not taken with the same seriousness as economic and political advantage. The failure to do so, which is criminal in terms of the law, and above all of the Christian faith, generates state terrorism directed against the people of the region who resist by using the feeble means at their disposal, sometimes including desperate acts of violence. The deep underlying cause of these conflicts is essentially injustice inflicted on these peoples, from which they are condemned never to break free.[5]

The Christian churches during the twentieth century

As we have already seen, the Orthodox, Oriental Orthodox, Latin Catholic, Catholic Uniate and Protestant traditions all have a significant presence in the region, albeit, except in Cyprus, now as minority religious communities. (For further information on these traditions, see Chapters 2, 3 and 4 respectively.) In this section, we can provide only a brief factual review of the diversity of these Christian communities as they have developed during the twentieth century. (The 'Further reading' section at the end of the chapter will guide interested readers to more detailed information.) This review is based on an alphabetical list of countries where there is a significant Christian presence. Key issues with regard to Christianity in the region as a whole will be considered in a later section.

Such a factual overview, however, misses aspects of the reality and experience of Christians in the Middle East during this period, and especially during the latter decades of the century. For one thing, in many of the Middle Eastern states, since Christians have been in a minority (often a small minority), they have had to cope with the inevitable pressures and tensions of living alongside a Muslim (or, in the case of Israel, a Jewish) majority. As we shall see, this has often meant a struggle to maintain a Christian identity and to offer an authentic Christian witness. Another factor that has shaped Middle Eastern Christianity during this period has been emigration. The suffering and persecution of Christians in some contexts, and the general political, economic and social situation, have placed considerable pressures on the Christian community. Consequently, a large number of Christians have been forced out or have emigrated to other Middle Eastern countries, to North America and Europe (and elsewhere) in order to provide better opportunities and circumstances for themselves and their families. This trend has continued into the twenty-first century, marking the life of the churches in the region in significant ways.

Cyprus

Cyprus is the only country in the region to have a Christian majority, estimated in the WCC's *A Handbook of Churches and Councils* (2006) at 82 per cent. Orthodox form the largest community, with Protestants (including Anglicans) and Catholics being small minority communities. According to Christian tradition, Cyprus was evangelized by Barnabas (see Acts 13) in the first Christian century and the church was fully established by the fourth century. The (Orthodox) Church of Cyprus has always played a key role in the political life of the island and, indeed, it led the struggle for liberation from British rule that began in 1955. Archbishop Makarios III, having led the liberation struggle, became the first President of Cyprus when it gained independence in 1960. A Greek-led coup d'état in 1974, and the subsequent invasion by Turkey, led to the division of the island into Turkish and Greek communities, a division that the Church of Cyprus has always opposed. In subsequent years, it established two new bishoprics, in Limassol and Morphou, and developed an extensive social action and education programme within the island.

Egypt

Egypt, like all the other countries of the region, with the exception of Israel/Palestine, is predominantly Muslim, with no more than about 15 per cent of the population being Christian. Egypt was also Christianized from the first century CE, according to tradition through St Mark the evangelist. Alexandria became one of the chief centres of the early Church. St Athanasius (regarded by the Coptic Church as the Pope of Alexandria from 327 to 373 CE) was formative in the process of developing and safeguarding, in particular, the christological doctrines during the fourth centuries. The Coptic Orthodox Church and the Greek Orthodox Church split following the Council of Chalcedon in the fourth century. The Coptic Church of Egypt was founded among descendants of the ancient Egyptians. It uses mainly the Coptic language and its worship is based on the Liturgies of Saints Basil, Gregory and Cyril. By the end of the twentieth century there were nearly 10 million Coptic Christians in Egypt (in a population of around 57 million). Monasticism had its origins in Egypt (through St Anthony in the third century). By the end of the twentieth century, however, only 20 monasteries and 7 convents remained. The election of Pope Shenouda III as the one hundred and seventeenth Pope of Alexandria in 1971 led to a period of renewal and growth, especially among youth. His weekly Bible studies in the Cathedral of St Mark in Cairo attracted over 7,000 people. His meeting, in 1973, with Pope Paul VI, led to their signing a common declaration on the issue of Christology and to the establishment of joint commissions for dialogue on unity. From 1991 to 1998, Pope Shenouda was one of the presidents of the World Council of Churches.

The Greek Orthodox Patriarchate of Alexandria and All Africa (which has around 500,000 members) is the second ranking Orthodox see after Constantinople and has jurisdiction over all Orthodox communities in Africa. It too traces its origins to St Mark the evangelist and during the twentieth century in particular engaged in extensive missionary activity throughout Africa. In the

WCC *Handbook*, the Church describes itself as 'striving to be a truly African Orthodox Church, struggling to find ways and means to support itself and to build on the foundations of the original work of the Apostle Mark, Evangelist of Africa'.[6]

There are also a number of small Evangelical churches in Egypt, including the Evangelical Presbyterian Church of Egypt, Synod of the Nile, which was founded in 1854 by American missionaries and became autonomous in 1926. It has around 250,000 members in over 300 congregations. It administers a number of educational establishments, as well as hospitals, orphanages, youth centres and one of Egypt's largest development agencies. It participates in dialogue with Anglicans and Lutherans and seeks to be a voice for ecumenism and interfaith dialogue within Egypt.

Iran

In Iran, no more than 3 per cent of the population was Christian by the end of the twentieth century, consisting predominantly of the Armenian Apostolic Church, having around 135,000 members and coming under the jurisdiction of the Holy See of Cilicia (see below). Small Catholic and Protestant (including Anglican) churches were established in the nineteenth century. The Catholic community includes Catholics of both the Latin and Eastern (Uniate) rites. The 1978 Islamic revolution led to some degree of persecution, the closure of some churches and the banning of some church institutions and organizations.

Iraq

The situation was similar in Iraq. The Christian community was very small at the end of the twentieth century (although it had been considerably larger in previous centuries) and consisted predominantly of Syrian Orthodox and Chaldean Catholic Christians, together with small Evangelical and Pentecostal communities. Some estimates give the number of Christians as 1 million at the turn of the century but this is likely to be an exaggeration. During the Saddam years, in the final decades of the twentieth century, there were Christians in prominent positions within his government but his attacks on Kurdish areas in northern Iraq led also to the deaths of many Christians and the destruction of churches. The early years of the twenty-first century have seen continued violence against these small Christian communities and a high level of emigration.

Israel/Palestine

The Christian churches here, naturally, have a deep significance for Christians worldwide, since they represent the Christian presence in the land where Jesus fulfilled his ministry, and where he was crucified and raised. Latourette notes that during the years following the First World War 'age-long emotional and social barriers and racial conflicts prevented Christianity from achieving major advances'.[7] Each of the four families of Christians was represented in the Holy Land during the twentieth century. The (Eastern) Greek Orthodox

Church, with a membership of around 400,000, is the largest church in Israel/ Palestine. It dates back to the time of the apostles in Jerusalem and has a Patriarch in Jerusalem and acts as one of the guardians of the holy places of Christianity. The Oriental family includes the Armenian, Coptic, Ethiopian and Syrian Orthodox Churches. There is an Armenian Patriarch of Jerusalem, and Syrian, Ethiopian and Coptic Archbishops of Jerusalem. There are also Orthodox churches that have come into communion with Rome, having Eastern origins and practices (including liturgical practice) but being in communion with Rome. One example is the Greek Catholic Church (Melkite). It is the second largest church in the Holy Land and has a Greek Catholic Patriarchal Exarch in Jerusalem. The Maronite Church is also a church in the Eastern tradition which is in communion with Rome. The Latin or Roman Catholic Church in Palestine has at the present time a Palestinian Patriarch who is seen as the leader of the Catholic community. Along with the Greek Orthodox Church, it has custody of the holy places. The Anglican and Lutheran communities are the result of missionary activity during the nineteenth century. During the twentieth century, both churches came under Arab rather than English or German leadership. There are also other small Protestant communities, largely the result of twentieth-century missionary activity, many of them Evangelical or Pentecostal churches.[8]

Lebanon

The Christian community in Lebanon is the largest minority in the region. It is estimated that almost 40 per cent of the population was Christian at the end of the twentieth century. Lebanon became independent in 1944, following the termination of the French mandate in 1943. Power was then distributed between Christians, Muslims and Druze, a Muslim group that split away from Islam in the eleventh century. The main Christian presence is the Maronite Church, a church in the Catholic tradition, which has been in communion with Rome since the twelfth century and which traces its history to the fourth century. There are also smaller Catholic communities, including the Melkites and the Chaldeans. The Orthodox Patriarchate of Antioch (see below under 'Syria') has a strong presence in Lebanon. The Armenian Apostolic Church (a church in the Oriental Orthodox family founded, according to tradition, by the apostles Thaddaeus and Bartholomew) has a presence and a jurisdiction throughout the Middle East, in Greece, Europe and America. During the First World War the Armenians suffered a horrific massacre at the hands of Turkey when 1.5 million Armenians were killed. Those who survived emigrated from Armenia to the Middle East and elsewhere. In 1930 the Catholicosate (the head of the church is called a Catholicos) of Cilicia was established in Antelias in Lebanon. The present Catholicos, Aram I, was Moderator of the Central Committee of the World Council of Churches from 1991 until 2006. This has brought the church to prominence within the global ecumenical movement.

Two relatively small communities of Evangelical churches also play a significant role in Lebanon, and more widely. The National Evangelical Synod of Syria and Lebanon traces its history and development during that early period to Protestant missionaries from North America and Britain. It is an

Arab-speaking synod, formed in 1920. In subsequent years, it has seen both growth and emigration. The war years (1975–90) led to damage and destruction of many of its buildings. It shares in ecumenical partnership both in Lebanon and in the Middle East as a whole. The other Evangelical community is the Union of Armenian Evangelical Churches in the Near East which has churches throughout the region. It began in the nineteenth century as a reform movement within the Armenian Apostolic Church. It was established in Lebanon as well as Syria after the Armenian massacre and became independent in 1948. It describes itself as having a modified congregationalist polity. It works with the other churches in the region, especially in education and health care. Both the Synod and the Union have a presence in Syria also.

Syria

Syria obtained independence from France in 1946. It is the only officially secular state in the Arab world (although Muslims form over 90 per cent of the population). The largest Christian communities – only around 5 per cent of the population are Christian – are the Greek Orthodox Patriarchate of Antioch and All the East, the Syrian Orthodox Patriarchate of Antioch and All the East (both of which have a presence throughout the Middle East and worldwide) and Uniate Catholic communities that belong to a number of Eastern rites. The Armenian Apostolic Church is also present. The Greek Orthodox Patriarchate is Arab-speaking. Since the First World War its numbers have declined because of emigration but it still has deep concern for the whole of the Middle East and for the Church and its witness in a complex multifaith society. The Syrian Orthodox Patriarchate is an Oriental Orthodox church that uses Syriac-Aramaic. At the beginning of the century it suffered persecution under the Ottoman Empire and many of its members were killed. In 1964 the Catholicosate was re-established, initially in India, and is now located in Damascus. Both the Greek Orthodox Patriarchate of Antioch and the Syrian Orthodox Patriarchate of Antioch have been members of the WCC and the Middle East Council of Churches.

Ecumenical relationships in the region

The efforts towards ecumenical collaboration and partnership began in the early years of the twentieth century. In 1914, Near East Relief was set up, largely through Protestant mission agencies, to respond primarily to the suffering of Armenians in the tragic massacre at the hands of the Ottoman Empire. In 1917, the Roman Catholic Church established the Congregation for Oriental Churches, as a focus for a more comprehensive approach to Catholic communities in the region. In 1919, the United Missionary Council of Syria and Palestine had been formed by Protestant missionary societies working in the region. In 1924, the (Protestant) Near East Christian Council was formed, according to Corbon, 'under the aegis of the IMC [International Missionary Council], [by] the Protestant communities which sprang from the proselytism of the Western missionary societies'.[9] In 1961, it became the Near East Council of Churches.

Informal contacts between Protestant and Orthodox churches, begun in the 1930s, led to the beginning of formal dialogue in 1964. This dialogue led to establishing the Middle East Council of Churches (MECC) in 1974, at its first Assembly in Nicosia (Cyprus). There were three families of Christian churches in membership, Orthodox, Oriental Orthodox and Protestant (or Evangelical). In 1990, the Catholic churches of both Latin and Oriental rites joined the MECC.

Corbon ascribes the ecumenical developments of the 1960s to four immediate events: the Second Vatican Council (1962–65), the first Pan-Orthodox conference in Rhodes (1959), formation of the (Vatican) Secretariat for the Promotion of Christian Unity and membership of Orthodox churches of the region in the WCC, some from the beginning in 1948 and others in the New Delhi Assembly (1961).[10] But he also recognizes that behind these immediate influences is a period which he describes as 'clandestine effervescence'.[11] This process had been at work within the Orthodox and Oriental Orthodox churches since 1902 when Joachim III, Ecumenical Patriarch of Constantinople, launched the first ecumenical appeal of the twentieth century to all Orthodox churches 'to search for common grounds with other churches'.[12] It was followed, in 1920, by the call to all the churches of Christ to form a 'communion of churches' (see Chapter 2 on Orthodoxy and *SCM Core Reader*, 1.2, which is the text of the letter from the Ecumenical Patriarchate suggesting the formation of a world league of churches). So from the beginning, through the Ecumenical Patriarchate, the Orthodox Patriarchates of Alexandria, Antioch and Jerusalem, the Coptic Church of Egypt, the Union of Armenian Evangelical Churches and the Evangelical Church of Lebanon and Syria, there was a strong Middle Eastern presence within the World Council of Churches.

The MECC remains a key ecumenical instrument in the region itself (and within the wider global ecumenical family). At the end of the century, it had '27 member churches in 12 countries representing 14 million Christians'.[13] It developed four priority objectives: the continuity of the Christian presence in the region; the renewal of the spiritual quality of church life (which included overcoming the confessional mentality); the pursuit of Christian unity among the churches of the Middle East; and enabling the common witness of the churches.[14] A more recent account of its guiding principles highlights fellowship and mutual support among the churches, developing understanding between Christians and people of other faiths, nurturing a spirit of service and being a mediator between Christians in the Middle East and those within the worldwide community.[15]

Corbon evaluates the significance of the MECC in the following terms:

> Every church is autonomous in its decisions, but these decisions cannot be expressed other than in co-responsibility with the other churches. These two exigencies are inseparable. The problem of the plural Middle East is such today that every church cannot exist, henceforth, without the others, nor operate without co-operating.[16]

At the Sixth General Assembly of the MECC in 1994, Gabriel Habib (General Secretary from 1974 until 1994) offered a perceptive evaluation of the Council over its 20-year history (*SCM Core Reader*, 6.3).[17] He expressed a concern that there was 'a turning to some kind of political "pragmatism" based on personal interest, and leading to greater fragmentation'. He believed that the rise of 'ethnic' nationalism meant that religion had become 'a source of conflict' rather than an instrument of 'unity and peace'. He drew particular attention, therefore, to the churches' role within a multifaith context:

> The continuity of the Christian presence in the region is contingent upon two interconnected forms of the Christians belonging to it. The first is their belonging to the land in which Christ was born, lived and died and rose again; and was sanctified afterwards by the blood of Apostles and Holy Martyrs. The second is their spiritual affiliation to the Divine revelation that God gave to Abraham, the one father they share with people from other religions … [Now] they are invited … to define their belonging to the cultural and spiritual climate of the monotheistic religions without compromising the essential role of Jesus Christ in their faith.

He concluded by affirming that

> the main importance of the Council for the Christians of the Middle East lies in that it expresses the will of the Churches to remain in the region and to continue to be present in it, not by discrimination or domination, but by seeking to achieve unity and by witnessing to their God through service and through reaching out to others with the love conducive to reconciliation and peace.[18]

A grouping of Evangelical churches was also formed in the region during the century. The Fellowship of Middle East Evangelical Churches is an association of Evangelical (Protestant) churches. The Fellowship, which grew out of the missionary councils and the Near East Christian Council, has continued in existence alongside the newly formed MECC from 1974 onwards. Most of its members are also members of the MECC. Indeed, these churches were instrumental in enabling and encouraging the closer ecumenical relationships that led to the latter's formation. They continue to pursue the goal of fuller unity. In 1997 the Fellowship's 'Proposal for the Unity of the Evangelical Churches in the Middle East' was not accepted by all its members. A new proposal for a formal agreement between the Reformed and Lutheran churches was launched in 2005.

Theological dividing issues in church relationships

Three issues may be highlighted here, which are crucial for relationships not only between churches in the Middle East but also between churches in other regions. First, there was the issue of *the person and nature of Christ*. This theological dispute has been at the heart of the divisions between the Eastern Orthodox family and the Oriental Orthodox (see Chapter 2 on the Orthodox churches). The Eastern Orthodox churches accepted the Christology of the Council of Chalcedon in 451 which affirmed the two natures of Christ as both human and divine (one person *in* two natures). The Oriental Orthodox churches rejected this view in favour of the Cyrillian understanding that affirmed the person of Christ as fully human and fully divine (one person *'from* two natures').

Ecumenical relationships during the twentieth century, not least in the Middle East, led to dialogue among the ancient churches on this issue. At a meeting at Chambesy in 1990 there was an Accord on christological faith between the Orthodox and Oriental Orthodox churches that sought to put an end to the dissensions of the fifth century. It had its origins in a Christological Declaration agreed by Pope Shenouda III and Pope Paul VI in 1973.

The 1990 Accord (*SCM Core Reader*, 2.4), was the culmination of a process begun in meetings of theologians of both traditions and was based on an agreed statement on the nature of Christ issued in 1989, which stated:

> The four adverbs used to qualify the mystery of the hypostatic union belong to our common tradition – without comingling (or confusion) ... without change ... without separation ... and without division ... Those among us who speak of two natures in Christ, do not thereby deny their inseparable, indivisible union; those among us who speak of one united divine–human nature in Christ do not thereby deny the continuing dynamic presence in Christ of the divine and the human, without change, without confusion.[19]

The consequence of this theological agreement was the lifting of the anathema that had resulted from the ancient dissensions. So in 1993, it was agreed that 'we have understood that both families have loyally maintained the authentic Orthodox Christological doctrine and the unbroken continuity of the apostolic tradition, though they may have used Christological terms in different ways'. On this basis, the lifting of the anathemas meant that 'the restoration of full communion for both sides [was] to be immediately implemented'.[20] Clearly, for the Middle East, as for other regions, this was a most significant agreement that was to change in fundamental ways relationships between the Orthodox and Oriental Orthodox churches. Corbon offers this evaluation:

> All the churches can today profess in their direct languages the same faith in the Lord Christ, true God and true Man. The Christian Middle East appears as the microcosm of universal ecumenism: there where the greatest diversity had abounded in division, the grace of communion in unity has over-abounded.[21]

The second dividing issue was *the history of tension between the Roman Catholic Church and the Orthodox family in relation to the Eastern rites Catholic churches*. As the previous section has indicated, the Eastern rite Catholic churches have a considerable and diverse presence in the Middle East. In 1993, an agreed statement on this question was issued by the Joint International Commission for the Theological Dialogue between the Roman Catholic Church and the Orthodox Churches. This Balamand statement was entitled: 'Uniatism, method of union of the past, and the present search for full communion' (*SCM Core Reader*, 6.5). Given the history of tensions around this issue within the region, this agreement was particularly significant.

One of its key paragraphs reads:

> [T]he Catholic Churches and the Orthodox Churches recognize each other as Sister Churches, responsible together for maintaining the Church of God in fidelity to the divine purpose, most especially in what concerns unity. According to the words of Pope John Paul II, the ecumenical endeavor of the Sister Churches of East and West, grounded in dialogue and prayer, is the search for perfect and total communion which is neither absorption nor fusion but a meeting in truth and love (cf. *Slavorum Apostoli*, n. 27).[22]

On this basis, it was recommended that 'these [Eastern rite] Churches ... should be inserted, on both local and universal levels, into the dialogue of love, in mutual respect and reciprocal trust found once again'. The admission, in 1990, of the Catholic churches in the Middle East as the fourth family of member churches of the MECC was a sign that this dialogue was already a reality, even before the final agreement had been reached.

Finally, there is the question of *evangelism, proselytism and the Protestant identity*. There is a fundamental ambiguity here. The Protestant churches in the Middle East came into being as a result of missionary activity from the USA and Europe. In some cases, this missionary activity was intended as a means of renewing the 'indigenous' churches in the region. But it often resulted, not in the renewal of these churches, but in the creation of new Christian communities in which those who had been touched by the missionary activity felt more at home. Members of the indigenous Orthodox churches left these churches to form new 'evangelical or Protestant churches'. The consequence of this was accusations of proselytism (which may be defined as deliberately encouraging Christians to leave the indigenous church in order to form a new implanted church community). Inevitably, this led to suspicion and mistrust and, occasionally, to conflict.

While it was a major issue throughout much of the century – and was referred to in the call to unity issued by the Ecumenical Patriarch of Constantinople in 1920 – it became a particularly crucial question in the last decades of the century, not only within the Middle East but globally. From 1961, the WCC devoted much time and energy to seeking agreement on patterns of Christian mission and witness that respected the indigenous communities. The WCC joint statement on common witness, agreed in 1997, 'Towards common witness: a call to adopt responsible relationships in mission and to renounce proselytism' (*SCM Core Reader*, 6.4), was a significant contribution towards an ecumenical consensus on this difficult issue. It concludes:

> [W]e decry the practice of those who carry out their endeavours in mission and evangelism in ways which destroy the unity of the body of Christ, human dignity and the very lives and cultures of those being evangelized; we call on them to confess their participation in and to renounce proselytism.

Key issues that had an impact on the whole region

So far, our review of Christianity in the Middle East has focused on historical, political, ecclesial and ecumenical aspects. These impinged on the various countries and churches of the region in different ways. But there were a
number of issues that had an impact on the whole region and contributed in
significant ways to the shaping of Christianity in the Middle East during the
century. This final section will briefly examine some of these common issues.

Relations with Judaism

Jews and Christians have lived together in the Middle East from the earliest
beginnings of Christianity and both have lived with Islam since the seventh
century. Their shared Abrahamic origins, and their recognition of one another as 'people of the book' meant at least a mutual toleration as ethnic and religious communities. The establishment of the State of Israel in 1948 changed
this situation. Relationships between Christians and Jews, as religious communities, were increasingly 'overshadowed by the political dynamic and its
injustices'.[23] Yet there are a number of encouraging and hopeful projects aimed
specifically at fostering, with mutual respect and understanding, dialogue
and collaboration in social witness and service among Jews and Christians.

Relations with Islam

In many ways, the same questions arose in relation to Islam. The key issue was:
how do Christians and Muslims live together as religious communities in a
context where the political questions are dominant and where conflict often
occurs across religious boundaries? Considerable efforts have been made, not
least by the Middle East Council of Churches, to foster mutual understanding,
particularly in the context of social and personal relationships, among Christians and Muslims in several countries of the region. *Courrier Oecuménique*, one
of the periodicals of the MECC, published regular reports of consultations on
issues of common concern, throughout the latter decades of the century. A
number of centres for Christian–Islamic studies have been set up. There are
five such institutes in Lebanon alone. Corbon comments that the important
goal is 'to move from co-existence to community'.[24]

Religious extremism

Extremism, not least in the form of fundamentalism among Christians, a radical Islamic approach among some Muslims and ultra-orthodoxy and fanatical
Zionism among Jews, fuelled the tensions between the religious communities
throughout the region during the period. Such extremism frequently translated itself into political radicalism of various kinds. Not infrequently, among
communities throughout the region, a perceived – and often real – injustice
created extremist reactions that led to conflict, violence and war. In many
cases, these responses had common causes and roots. Corbon identifies the
following among some of the main influences: 'a deep rooted fear of threat

to their identity, revolt against injustice and humiliation, anger against leaders of their community and, lastly, the refusal to co-exist with those who are "other" and hence their exclusion'.[25]

In an Afterword to her magisterial study of fundamentalism in Judaism, Christianity and Islam, *The Battle for God*, Karen Armstrong offers the following evaluation, that may be applied to these extremist positions, though it is not specifically focused on the Middle East:

> [All fundamentalists] have neglected the more tolerant, inclusive, and compassionate teachings and have cultivated theologies of rage, resentment and revenge. On occasion this has led a small minority to pervert religion by using it to sanction murder. Even the vast majority of fundamentalists, who are opposed to such acts of terror, tend to be exclusive and condemnatory of those who do not share their views ... [These] theologies and ideologies are rooted in fear ... It is [also] important to recognize that these movements are not an archaic throwback to the past; they are modern, innovative and modernizing ... Religious Zionists and fundamentalist Christians and Muslims all insisted on the need for dynamism and revolutionary transformation in keeping with the forward thrust and pragmatic drive of modern society.[26]

The role and understanding of Jerusalem

Jerusalem is a holy city for Jews, Christians and Muslims. As such, it has long been a place of pilgrimage as well as a focus for eschatological hope. The historical and contemporary struggles over the status and future of Jerusalem, during the Middle Ages as well as in the twentieth century, have shaped relationships over the centuries. An international agreement on the status of Jerusalem, acceptable to Jews, Christians and Muslims within the city and the region, would be an essential prerequisite of peace in the Middle East. For the Christians of the region, Jerusalem is also a meeting point for all the traditions, Orthodox, Catholic and Protestant.

The Statement agreed by the Eighth Assembly of the World Council of Churches in 1998 (see *SCM Core Reader*, 6.6), seeks to represent a common Christian understanding in relation to Jerusalem. It includes the following affirmations (or rather 'reaffirmations' from previous WCC statements):

> Jerusalem is a holy city for three monotheistic religions ... who share responsibility to co-operate to ensure Jerusalem be a city open to adherents of all three religions, a place where they can meet and live together ... The question of Jerusalem is not only a matter of protection of holy places but is also organically linked with the people who live there, their living faiths and communities. The holy shrines should not become merely monuments of visitation, but should serve as living places of worship integrated and responsive to all communities who continue to maintain their life and roots within the city ... The future status of Jerusalem is to be seen as part of a general settlement of the wider Middle East conflict as related to the destinies of the Israeli and Palestinian peoples alike.[27]

Echoing a joint memorandum issued by Christian leaders and heads of churches in Jerusalem (1994), the statement calls on all parties 'to go beyond exclusivist visions and actions, and without discrimination, to consider the religious and national aspirations of others, in order to give back to Jerusalem its true universal character and to make of the city a Holy Place of reconciliation for humankind'.

The Palestinian question

This is one of the most crucial and difficult issues that faced the Middle East during much of the twentieth century, and continues to offer challenges into the twenty-first century. A number of fundamental ideological and political issues have been at the heart of the conflict. They include a failure by some leading Palestinians and Middle Eastern states to recognize the State of Israel's right to exist, a denial of the reality of Palestinian identity and history, an extension of Israeli occupation, and security measures (such as the Wall built during the early years of the twenty-first century) that have failed to accord full justice to Palestinans.

This is not the place to trace the history of this conflict or to reach a consensus on what would be a just solution to a conflict that marked the latter half of the twentieth century. However, some key aspects of the situation need to be noted. First, war and conflict created a large number of Palestinian refugees both within Israel/Palestine itself and in the bordering states. Refugee camps became places of patent suffering and injustice and consequently, by general consensus, became breeding grounds for extremist and violent responses to injustice and oppression. The international community (for example, through the UN) have recognized a responsibility to ensure an appropriate humanitarian response to the suffering and to oppose violent responses, but have been generally very slow in responding to these challenges.

Nor is there any dispute, secondly, that Israeli Jews suffered as a result of Palestinian attacks on the Jewish population, particularly during the decades following the 1967 war, and that Palestinians have suffered poverty, persecution and violence as a result of Israeli policy and actions, not least the continuing development of Israeli settlements.

Third, notwithstanding the pre-twentieth-century history of the region, the reality and legitimacy of the State of Israel were recognized by some states within the international community though certainly not by all, and certainly not by all states in the Middle East. On the basis of such agreements as there were, international responses and negotiations were, therefore, based on the premise that both the Jewish people of Israel and the Palestinians (both Christian and Muslim) had legitimate claims that would have to be fundamental to any ultimate agreement. The establishment of a Palestinian Authority for Gaza and the West Bank has certainly been an important step towards a settlement, but questions remain about its powers, its freedom to govern its people, its attitude towards the State of Israel and the attitude of Israel towards it.

The Sixth Assembly of the World Council of Churches (Vancouver, Canada, 1983) resolution on the Middle East stated:

The Israeli settlement policy on the West Bank has resulted in a de facto annexation giving final touches to a discriminatory policy of development of peoples that flagrantly violates the basic rights of the Palestinian people. There are fears of relocation of the inhabitants on the West Bank and their expulsion. A large number of Palestinians are under detention in the prisons on the West Bank and in camps in Lebanon. There is escalation of tension in the Occupied Territories. The consensus among the Arab nations appears to have been lost. External and internal pressures have caused a serious rift within the Palestinian movement. In many situations there are increasing violations of human rights, especially of minorities, and religious fanaticism is a bane of many communities. [28]

The Christian communities both within the Middle East and internationally, have strongly supported peace initiatives, recognized the legitimacy of claims for a Palestinian as well as an Israeli state, and have provided advocacy and humanitarian assistance to Palestinian refugees and others who suffered as a result of the conflict.

One of the Christian responses to these issues was the setting up of Sabeel, the Ecumenical Liberation Theology Center, which has its headquarters in Jerusalem. It is a Christian movement rooted in the Bible and seeking to reflect the suffering and hopes of the Palestinian people. It has sought to apply the insights of liberation theology, born within the Latin American context, to the realities of the situation in Israel/Palestine. It has also enabled theological reflection on some key issues such as the nature of God, the implications of being a chosen people, the centrality of land and issues of nationalism and self-determination. Opponents of its work, such as the David Project Center for Jewish Leadership, claim that it fosters, through its theological and socio-political initiatives, a distorted understanding of the Palestinian cause and the legitimacy of Israel's right to exist. Nevertheless, it has made a very significant contribution in enabling Palestinian Christians to reflect theologically on the issues that face them on a daily basis.

Any political and ecumenical consensus in the Middle East during the present century will have to grapple with the key issues we have examined, including relationships between the faith communities, the approach to extremism in all its forms, the place of Jerusalem, and issues raised by the Palestinian question. All these have been complex, deep-rooted but in the end unavoidable issues. They have contributed so much both to the specific problems facing Israel and Palestine and to the tensions that have dominated the region, especially during the second half of the twentieth century.

Final reflections

This survey of Christianity in the Middle East during the last century has highlighted a number of key insights. First, in this region – as indeed in any other region – it has been impossible to separate religious aspects of the situation from the socio-political context. Relationships between the Christian traditions in this cradle of Christianity are dependent, both within the individual states and across the region as a whole, not only on agreement on theological and ecclesial issues but also on the social and political realities.

Second, Christianity in the Middle East region cannot be understood in isolation from the global community. During the twentieth century, it was largely the international community that determined where boundaries were drawn after the First and Second World Wars and, therefore, contributed in substantial ways to creating the political landscape of the nation-states of the region. Similarly, the global Christian community, in the form, primarily, of the Catholic and Orthodox families as well as the ecumenical agencies, has had a crucial influence on relationships between the churches in the region. The world Church was also crucially dependent on the realities and perspectives of the churches within the Middle East as it reached judgements on the developing political, humanitarian and ecclesial situations.

Third, mutual understanding and relationships between the Christians of the region cannot be separated from interfaith relationships. At key points throughout the century, Christian leaders and agencies emphasized the need to develop dialogue and relationships of mutual respect and understanding between Jews, Muslims and Christians. Nowhere was this dialogue more crucial than in the Middle East.

Finally, as the birthplace of the three monotheistic religions, the Middle East has been in many ways determinative in terms of the relationships between these religions worldwide. The future of religion in the region cannot be separated from the future of religion and religious relationships in the whole global community. Establishing peace and justice, as well as deepening Christian unity, in the Middle East, will be one of the fundamental prerequisites for global peace, justice and unity.

Further reading

H. Badr (ed.) (2005), *Christianity: A History in the Middle East*, Beirut: MECC, is a key text. It is a comprehensive survey of Christianity over the centuries. Chapters 29, 30 and 31 are written by specialists on aspects of Christianity in the twentieth century.

J. Corbon (2004), 'The Middle East', in J. Briggs, M. Oduyoye and G. Tstetsis (eds), *The History of the Ecumenical Movement: Volume Three 1968–2000*, Geneva: WCC Publications, specifically surveys ecumenical aspects, including the formative years of the Middle East Council of Churches.

J. Johns (1992), 'Christianity and Islam', in J. McManners (ed.), *The Oxford Illustrated History of Christianity*, Oxford: Oxford University Press, pp. 163ff., provides an excellent analysis of the history of relationships between Christians and Muslims from the seventh to the twentieth century.

K. S. Latourette (1971), *A History of the Expansion of Christianity, Volume 7: Advance through Storm, 1914 and after*, Exeter: The Paternoster Press, pp. 262ff., offers an authoritative brief summary of developments in the first half of the century.

H. van Beek (ed.) (2006), *A Handbook of Churches and Councils: Profiles of Ecu-*

menical Relationships, Geneva: WCC Publications, pp. 523ff., offers a comprehensive summary of the current situation of ecumenical agencies and member churches of the World Council of Churches in the region.

Notes

1 Johns (1992), 'Christianity and Islam', in J. McManners (ed.), *The Oxford Illustrated History of Christianity,* Oxford: Oxford University Press, p. 172.
2 Johns, 'Christianity and Islam', p. 174.
3 http://www.jewishvirtuallibrary.org/jsource/History/dectoc.html (accessed 18 May 07).
4 In J. Briggs, M. Oduyoye and G. Tsetsis (eds) (2004), *A History of the Ecumenical Movement: Volume 3, 1968–2000,* Geneva: WCC Publications, p. 592.
5 J. Corbon (2004), 'The Middle East', in Briggs et al. (eds), *A History,* p. 594.
6 H. van Beek (ed.) (2006), *A Handbook of Churches and Councils,* Geneva: WCC Publications, p. 534.
7 K. S. Latourette (1971), *A History of Expansion, Volume VII: Advance through Storm, 1914 and after,* Exeter: Paternoster Press, p. 264.
8 For more detailed information on Christianity in the Holy Land and in the region, see B. J. Bailey and J. M. Bailey (2003), *Who are the Christians in the Middle East?,* Grand Rapids MI: Wm B. Eerdmans.
9 Corbon, 'The Middle East', p. 595.
10 Corbon, 'The Middle East', p. 595.
11 J. Corbon (2005), 'Ecumenism in the Middle East', in H. Badr, *Christianity: A History in the Middle East,* Beirut: MECC, p. 876.
12 Corbon, 'Ecumenism in the Middle East', p. 875.
13 van Beek (ed.), *Handbook,* p. 526.
14 Corbon, 'The Middle East', p. 600.
15 van Beek (ed.), *Handbook,* p. 526.
16 Corbon, 'Ecumenism in the Middle East', p. 880.
17 G. Habib (2005), 'Ecumenism in the Middle East: A Personal Experience', in Badr, *Christianity,* pp. 890ff.
18 Habib, 'Ecumenism in the Middle East', p. 892.
19 Text taken from http://www.monachos.net/library/Texts_of_the_Agreed_Statements_of_the_Joint_Commission (accessed 23 May 07).
20 Text taken from http://www.monachos.net/library/Texts_of_the_Agreed_Statements_of_the_Joint_Commission (accessed 23 May 07).
21 Corbon, 'Ecumenism in the Middle East', p. 882.
22 *Eastern Churches Journal,* vol. 1, no. 1, Winter 1993/94, para. 14, p. 18.
23 Corbon, 'The Middle East', p. 604.
24 Corbon, 'The Middle East', p. 604.
25 Corbon, 'The Middle East', p. 605.
26 K. Armstrong (2001), *The Battle for God,* London: HarperCollins, pp. 366ff.
27 http://www.wcc-coe.org/wcc/what/international/palestine/state20.html (accessed 6 June 07).
28 D. Gill (ed.) (1983), *Gathered for Life: The Official Report of the Sixth Assembly of the World Council of Churches,* Geneva: WCC Publications, where the whole statement appears on pp. 147–51.

7

Africa

The twentieth century's great success story?

The beginnings

Africa may well have been the first continent where the Christian faith took hold. St Matthew's Gospel records that Joseph took Mary and the baby Jesus down to Egypt as refugees from Herod within days of his birth. We have no evidence of any direct follow-through in Egypt. Nor do we know what the Ethopian eunuch, a 'high official of the Kandake or queen' (Acts 8.27) may have later made of his baptism on the road through the desert, though we can be sure that it was of high importance to him. Already before that, the Synoptic Gospels record that a man called Simon, from Cyrene, on the coast of what is now Libya, carried Jesus' cross for him to Calvary. Luke records in Acts 2.9 that there were people from 'the districts of Libya around Cyrene', almost certainly Jews, present in Jerusalem at Pentecost who heard the apostles' first efforts at witnessing to the resurrection. It is then hardly surprising that 'men from Cyrene' were among those who brought the Good News to Jews and Gentiles alike in Antioch even before Barnabas was sent there (Acts 11.19ff.) and that Lucius of Cyrene was among those who ordained Barnabas and Saul for their first mission (13.1–4). Apollos of Alexandria, presumably a Greek-speaker (Acts 18.24; 1 Corinthians 1.12; 3.4–6; 4.6) also clearly became an influential witness alongside Paul.

We cannot directly trace what became of these initial beginnings. But it is certain that Christian faith spread early and quickly through Egypt and from there westwards across North Africa and southwards into Nubia. The Coptic Church in Africa looks back to St Mark as its founder, and still today is widely regarded, inside its own ranks but also in many other parts of Africa where it has sent priests, as the original 'fountainhead' of today's Church in so many different parts of the continent. This is not the place to trace in any detail what happened to those early churches; enough to remind ourselves that three of the greatest figures of Christian witness in the early centuries lived and worked in North Africa: Anthony, the founder of the monastic tradition (c. 285–356); Athanasius, who stood out for the true faith against the Arians in the run-up to the Council of Nicea (296–373); and Augustine of Hippo (354–430) whose writings are still known and honoured, if also often today contested, throughout the worldwide Church.

We also know that the Church took root up the valley of the Nile in Nubia. There is evidence of a Christian King Joel in Dotawo, Upper Nile, still in 1484 with a Bishop of Ibrim named Merki, as of an appeal for help for Christians in Nubia arriving at the Ethiopian court as late as 1520.[1] Yet already in 642, only ten years after the death of Muhammad, the Muslim Arab army had conquered the great city of Alexandria and all Egypt with it. The Coptic Christians played important roles serving the new rulers, and have managed with considerable difficulty to maintain their church down the centuries until today. Yet those Arab forces were to sweep across North Africa and up the Nile valley over the following fifty and more years, so that well before any European Christians opened up the next series of contacts, Muslim rulers were in unchallenged control of the entire continent north of the great forest belt and remain the dominant religious presence throughout that same area (except for Ethiopia) until today.

Christian faith arrived in the mountains of Ethiopia in the early fourth century in what was then the Red Sea kingdom of Axum. A young Syrian from Tyre named Frumentius was among a group of traders captured on their way home from India. Taken into the service of the King of Axum, Ezana, who soon became a Christian, he began to spread Christianity around the kingdom. Encouraged later to go and report on this to the Patriarch of Alexandria, Athanasius, he was consecrated as the first Bishop of Axum, and Abuna (Metropolitan) of the Church of Ethiopia, in around 340. From then on, until late in the twentieth century, the Ethiopian church has relied on their Coptic sister church to supply them with successive Abunas, even at times of severe isolation after the kingdom was reduced to a relatively small area deep in the mountains. Just as Ethiopia treasures its record of never having been colonized, indeed of being the only African nation to defeat an intending European power – the Italians, at the battle of Adwa in 1896 – so they treasure their ancient link with the Jewish people (in legendary form the union of the Queen of Sheba with King Solomon which gave Ethiopia its King Menelik I) together with a profound sense of belonging to the ancient Hebrew race and culture. Hardly surprising that they also treasure their age-long presence through a small monastic community in the Church of the Holy Sepulchre in Jerusalem. By the fifth century, already the whole Bible was translated into Ge'ez, the local language at that time. The Christian King of Axum, active in the politics of the Red Sea region, had a good enough reputation across the water at the time of Muhammad for the prophet in about 615, still in Mecca but under severe threat, to arrange for some of his followers to take refuge there.[2] But in later centuries there have been frequent clashes and wars between Ethiopia and the surrounding Muslim powers.

European initiatives bring new beginnings

A totally different series of beginnings started in the late fifteenth century after Portuguese ships began sailing along the coasts of West Africa. Not least since the strongly Catholic Portuguese would not sell gunpowder or weapons to non-Christians, the early contacts with local rulers often resulted in the king accepting baptism and a European name, yet without any lasting interest save that of profiting from the sale of unwanted tribespeople to the Portuguese as slaves. So in 1482, when the Portuguese began negotiations with a local ruler at the mouth of the river Kongo, such a baptism took place and Christianity became an established cult at the court.[3] At the death of that ruler 'a baptized son defeated his pagan brother and ruled for nearly 40 years (1506–1543)' as Afonso I, 'working actively and assiduously to build a Christian kingdom' with 'a strong Christian cult at court'. One of his sons was sent to Portugal and there ordained as Bishop of Utica and Vicar Apostolic of the Kongo. Kongo was in no way spared the predictable strains of dealing commercially with the Portuguese, as politically with neighbouring tribes and rulers, which were many and often hostile. The Christian kingdom lasted on until the early nineteenth century, with a notable period in the mid-seventeenth century when Italian Capuchin friars were given responsibility for it by the Propaganda in Rome, in succession to the failing Portuguese. Its inland capital was named São Salvador. Later in that century it produced, at a time of rapid disintegration, a local prophetess, an aristocratic nun who believed herself to be possessed by St Anthony of Padua, a Franciscan friar of the thirteenth century. She led a strong attack on fetishes (*nkisi*), but lost the trust of the Capuchins. They persuaded the authorities to arrest her, and she was burnt as a heretic in 1706.

The very 'success' of the slave trade, by which a huge number of West Africans were 'exported' to the Americas between 1500 and the later nineteenth century – figures vary between 9 and 15 million, but probably many more even than these were killed in the fighting between tribes in Africa, as from ill-treatment or disease during captivity and the time at sea – made it more than difficult for the other European seaborne powers, Dutch, French or British, to make any significant religious contact.

One of their earliest lasting missionary adventures was that of a Dutch Moravian, Georg Schmidt. He had responded to an appeal for a 'chaplain' circulating in Holland in the late 1730s from the Dutch settlers at Cape Town. But it didn't take him long to realize that the real needs for Christian service in the area were among the Africans. He walked out of Cape Town, across the Cape Flats and through the first line of mountains until he found a sheltered valley out of sight and contact with the settlers. There he lived for a few years with the Khoikhoi ('Hottentots' to the Europeans), sharing their simple lives. Before he left in 1744 to go back to Europe he planted a pear tree and gave his Dutch New Testament to a young woman, who had learned from him the rudiments of his language and how to read. When other Moravians were next able to go there – in 1792 after the British defeat of the Dutch in the Napoleonic wars – they knew the place by the pear tree, and were received by the old woman still treasuring the Bible. The place was named Genadendaal (valley of grace) and remains until today a major centre for Moravians and for African Christianity at the southern end of the continent.

Yet another, again very different, beginning started from 1787 onwards when Granville Sharp in London, one of the initiators of the anti-slavery movement, 'was persuaded that it would be a real step forward if some of the black people in London, many of whom were penniless and in trouble, could be resettled on the coast of Africa'.[4] This was at first hardly a success, but a larger company of black people in Canada, former British servicemen, many of them enthusiastic Christians of different Protestant churches, were recruited for the same end. They arrived in 'Freetown' in what had become known as Sierra Leone in 1792. Then in 1807 the British Parliament decreed the abolition of the slave trade, after which the British ships stationed off West Africa began to land any Africans seized off slaver vessels back in Freetown. From January 1808 Sierra Leone was a Crown colony. Like the Kingdom of Kongo it has had many rough passages in its history, but from there, as from its later, neighbouring sister settlement, under the jurisdiction of the USA, in Monrovia, Liberia, many 'returned' Africans, having become Christians in their time of exile, have brought the new faith to their original people. Probably the most notable of them was the Yoruba Samuel Crowther, consecrated in 1864 as the first African Bishop of the Anglican Church – though the story of how the young missionaries from the Church Missionary Society (CMS), sent out to Nigeria to support him, in fact patronized him and ruined his efforts is a particularly dark episode in the total story.

With the creation at the outset of the nineteenth century of many missionary societies among European Christians, the numbers of missionaries sent out to Africa became much greater. But the climate was still very difficult, especially along the West African coast, and few of these missions were able to grow at all quickly. Moreover, during the century, the interest of the major European powers was growing and growing, with both the English and the French governments snatching at particular areas. This led into the shameful 'scramble for Africa' in the final 30 years of the century, with Germans, Belgians and Italians also grabbing what they could. European missionaries could not but find themselves playing a significant part in this unpleasant 'scramble', with which the Africans themselves were far from content. There is no space here for details, but let at least two significant missionary figures of the second half of the century be mentioned, for the ways that their contributions, each very different, point forward to the century to come.

John Colenso (1814–83), the gifted son of lower-middle-class parents in Cornwall, had managed to get to Cambridge and shone at mathematics, becoming a fellow of his college. Yet in his early years he needed to work very hard to pay off family debts. In the process of becoming a clergyman he grew beyond the relatively narrow evangelicalism of his youth and learned much from F. D. Maurice. In 1853 his debts were surprisingly settled and he was able to accept the invitation from Robert Gray, Anglican Archbishop of Cape Town, to go to South Africa and serve as Bishop of Natal, with a double ministry – as bishop of the churches for the English settlers who were already occupying half the province, and as chief missionary to the Zulu people who lived on the other half. During his 30 years there Colenso did an immense amount of work:

- on the Zulu language and what it could teach those of other mother tongues;
- on his own theology in the light of questions his Zulu servants and colleagues asked of him, which led to a huge study of the Pentateuch and many of the insights of modern biblical studies;
- on a series of confrontations with the settlers in Natal, with the Archbishop of Cape Town, and with the British colonial authorities; in each case Colenso

worked to understand and represent what he was learning from the Africans and for their long-term interests;

- and then into the political tensions between the settlers and the Zulu kingdom, which grew into a disastrous and full-scale war in 1879, when Colenso's insights and readiness to mediate were brutally overlooked by the British authorities.[5]

Charles Lavigerie was appointed Archbishop of Algiers in 1867, 'hitherto a position of little importance and one concerned with not much more than the chaplaincy of French settlers'.[6] Yet he was to prove the most outstanding Catholic missionary strategist of the nineteenth century. He founded a monastic society, the Missionaries of Our Lady of Africa, almost immediately known better as the White Fathers, because of the plain white, Arab-style dress they were given to wear. A women's order of White Sisters followed on the same path. Lavigerie insisted on a strategy of adaptation in clothes, language and food. But not on any theological adaptation – his men and women were to follow strictly the theological and liturgical rules laid down by Rome.

'He was something of a David Livingstone fan', insisting on having his headquarters in Africa, and taking great pride in discovering new peoples to whom he could send a team of White Fathers. Their record, as instanced in 'Two Outstanding Catholic Missionaries' (SCM Core Reader on World Christianity in the Twentieth Century, 7.1), is one of high excellence. These two, and many more, were 'men and women who struggled for decades, often without any significant break, in single-minded purpose to build up the Catholic Church throughout Sub-Saharan Africa'. It would be impossible to understand the Christian history of the first half of the twentieth century in Africa without a sense of their contributions.

Many of them were outstanding linguists and highly knowledgeable about local customs and history. They lived a good deal nearer to village life than did most other missionaries, and without this commitment to a deep Africanization of their work, learnt from their founder Lavigerie and insisted upon with an almost military discipline, they could not have achieved what they did.

Africa takes off in the twentieth century

Whatever may deserve to be said about the many, very different, missionaries from outside, what really matters is what the local people did with what they received. Here the story of Africa is astonishing in the way so many initiatives in the new century have come from Africans and had such far-reaching effects on thousands and millions of their fellow Africans. The time has not yet come for any long-term evaluation, and space here is horribly short for even a summary account. In the matter of numbers alone (and remembering the cautions about all such calculations discussed briefly in Chapter 1[7]), it seems that in 1900 Africa will have had some 10 million Christians, the majority of them Copts and Ethiopians, while by 1984 there were some 234 million, and every expectation then that by 2000 it would be 394 million (that is, 48 per cent of the total population, slightly more than Islam, counted by a similar source as likely then to be 315 million and 41 per cent).[8]

The wholly unpredictable yet crucial beginning of this new phase took place in Buganda, on the eastern shore of Lake Victoria. Two missionary teams arrived there at almost exactly the same time, Anglicans from the CMS in England and French White Fathers from Algeria, in 1879. They quickly found receptive and intelligent hearers in the circle of young men around the Kabaka of Buganda, Mutesa, who were in no way bothered that they came from different churches and witnessed to some extent against one another – the young men if anything found this 'intriguingly appealing'. Mutesa died in 1884, to be followed by his somewhat unstable son Mwanga. Towards the end of 1885 there was news that an English bishop was travelling through Kenya to take the leadership of the CMS team, and Mwanga, presumably out of fear that to allow such a senior figure into his country would lead to a colonial invasion, ordered that the bishop be killed before he reached the capital. This indeed happened, not without one of the newly baptized younger men being in turn killed for having told the missionaries what had happened to their bishop. In June 1886, for no known reason, Mutesa suddenly ordered a series of deaths, mostly by burning alive, among the new Christians of both churches, probably about a hundred in all. Others of them were able to escape, and indeed to take up the leadership positions for which they had been at the court in the first place, some months later.

The story continues with much further fighting, involving Muslims too, and other complications, not least those of the arrival in 1890 of the British Captain Lugard of the East Africa Company, offering the *Pax Britannica*. What is certain is that those young men, and the women who joined them, had grasped a truth and purpose in Jesus and his Church, no matter whether Protestant or Catholic, which had carried them through martyrdom and its consequences, and which they proceeded to take out into the life of Buganda and its people over the next two generations and beyond.

In a quite separate area, West Africa saw in the years of the First World War the entry on the scene of local prophets who taught and healed and sang in ways that were wholly Christian, in no way in hostility or separation from the existing churches, yet which had an attraction far beyond that of the missionaries. The first and foremost of these was William Wade Harris, a native Liberian, from the Grebo people, aged about 50, who in late 1913 'crossed the frontier into Ivory Coast to begin the most effective evangelical crusade in modern African history'.[9] Brought up a Methodist, and having worked for years as a teacher for the Protestant Episcopal (US Anglican) Church, he could speak and read English. Imprisoned for advocating a revolution to end the black 'independence' of Liberia in favour of rule by the British, he had seen a vision of the Archangel Gabriel, proclaiming him a prophet to prepare the way of Jesus Christ, while commanding him to abandon the European dress he enjoyed, in particular the shoes he had recently ordered from America.

So he appeared in a white gown with black bands, carrying a gourd, a cross, a Bible and a bowl for baptizing. He preached the imminent return of Christ, to be prepared for by a radical conversion of life – the Decalogue and

Sunday to be observed, the authority of the Bible accepted, and the 'fetishes' of traditional local religion burnt. He did not condemn polygamy – indeed he would appear to have had several wives himself. The response to this message in villages all along the Ivory Coast and into the western Gold Coast was amazing. Tens of thousands abandoned and burnt their fetishes and were baptized, promising to live as Christians. Early in 1915 he was arrested by French officials and roughly expelled back into Liberia. He lived another 12 years, yet without ever trying anything of the same sort again. But his followers did indeed pursue the life of a Christian as he had taught them, and still do. Many of them joined the local missionary church, Catholic or Methodist, and where there was none, set one up of their own. His name is still widely hallowed and honoured.

Back to the other side of Africa, two men there had comparably effective and lasting, personal evangelistic ministries among peoples on the edges of Uganda. Apolo Kivebulaya, baptized not long after the young men at the Buganda court, in 1894, served at first in Toro, western Uganda, as a deacon and priest in the Anglican Church. In 1921 he had a vision of Christ in the form of 'a man who stood beside me and said to me "Go and preach in the forest because I am with you".' For over ten years he preached in totally unselfish poverty to the pygmies, an isolated and usually undervalued people in the forest, out of whom has grown what is now the substantial Anglican Church in Eastern Congo, even if it was sadly wounded at the end of the century by the civil wars over control of the local mineral wealth (especially coltran, essential for mobile phones) between the ex-Rwandan Hutus and their opponents in the Rwandan and Ugandan armies.

The second was Yohana Kitagana, baptized in 1896 at the Catholic mission in Kisubi in his mid-30s, a tall, dignified and highly intelligent man with five wives. He had in fact already abandoned all his wives, saying 'God must suffice for me.' In 1901 he received a chiefdom but announced his desire to become a missionary to peoples other than his own and set off for Bunyoro in western Uganda. Some time later, in the more northern kingdom of Bunyaruguru, he found himself caught up among a people revolting against the imposition of Ganda chiefs, and calmly continued his work despite the obvious danger. In 1911 he moved into the mountainous district of Kigezi, and for over ten years, until the arrival of three White Fathers in 1923, he preached and directed the work of other resident catechists. He is remembered as continually moving through the valleys and hills wearing only an animal skin – apart from the white gown he kept for Sundays – teaching about God and Jesus, and calling on people to destroy their fetishes. He was indeed the apostle to Bunyaruguru and Kigezi, and many memorable stories are still told about him.[10]

Independent African churches

In a very different situation, South Africa, already long since strongly affected by the dominance of white foreigners, claiming almost all power and authority for themselves, the year 1911 saw Isaiah Shembe, a Zulu who had worked for a time with the African Native Baptist Church, call together the followers of his prophecies in a new Church of the Nazarites – in Zulu, the Amanazaretha – and to a special place, a here-and-now Jerusalem or Zion in Ekuphakameni, near Durban. For nearly 100 years this has seen each year some of the largest meetings of Christians anywhere in Africa or indeed in the world. As well as showing gifts of healing and prophecy, Isaiah Shembe composed liturgical hymns in Zulu.[11] Still more, for his annual

> July festival at Ekuphakameni and the January Festival on the mountain of Inhlangakazi, in the services of baptism, washing of the feet and healing, he and his people developed a symbolically and emotionally highly charged liturgy which is undoubtedly extraordinarily different from the rather impoverished worship of late 19th century Protestantism.[12]

Different again, this time with a background in a Baptist church, in which he was working as a catechist, Simon Kimbangu, a villager in his early 30s from Nkamba in the Lower Congo, found himself in March 1921 challenged to heal a sick girl as the Jesus he spoke about had done. After a short prayer he laid hands on her in the sort of way Jesus did, and she declared herself healed. That led within days to huge crowds assembling from all around, and a number of further healings. Still more, a group of senior Baptist leaders, all Africans, arrived to examine what was going on and pronounced it to be indeed 'the work of God'. Kimbangu continued to preach fervently, not least about the future in God's hands, making it quite clear that while he had been given dreams and gifts beyond what he had known earlier it was the power of Jesus he was witnessing to, not his own.

Around him there sprang up at the same time quite a number of other 'prophets', with whose teachings Kimbangu and his followers were far from agreed. Both a British Baptist missionary and a Belgian administrator came within a month or two to see for themselves and reported that there was nothing inappropriate or worrying about what Kimbangu was doing. Within another month, however, other prophets were calling for people not to pay their taxes, and abandoning their workplaces, with at least one Catholic chapel being vandalized, so that many Belgian settlers were urging the government to suppress these movements. The administrator returned to arrest Kimbangu, but his friends got him away in the confusion. The next day the village was sacked by Belgian soldiers. In hiding, Kimbangu continued his ministry of preaching and healing for some weeks. But when he returned to Nkamba in September he was arrested. He was put on trial and condemned to death. At the request of the Baptists this was commuted to life imprisonment, and he spent his remaining 30 years in prison at the other end of the Congo without any contact with his family or followers.

When his son was given permission, in 1959, after the announcement of the Belgian withdrawal in a year's time, to gather his father's followers into meetings of the 'Church of Jesus Christ on Earth by the Prophet Simon Kimbangu' he discovered that he was leading over a million people. They were to grow hugely over the years across the entire Congo, later Zaire, and beyond its borders, with outposts in Brussels and London and wherever Congolese gather. More recently, at the end of the century, there have been major problems over the succession to leadership after members of the immediate family have all departed this life. But the church remains a most notable example of Christian witness gathering a new church for Jesus in a way no missionary from Europe ever could.

A third notable beginning took place in Nigeria in the 1920s. Isaac Akinyele, brother of a man who was to become later the Anglican Bishop of Ibadan, slipped out of the Anglican church and briefly joined a small faith-healing church in the area. They came to be called 'Aladura' – praying people. Not long afterwards another loosely attached Anglican, Moses Orimolade, with a history as a 'wandering preacher', found himself healing a young woman, Abiodun Akinsowon, and with her developing a new Society, called the Cherubim and Seraphim. Then in 1930 Joseph Babalola, a young driver of a steamroller for the Public Works department, heard a voice call out his name and tell him to leave his job and preach the gospel. He returned to his home town, naked and covered with ashes, and found himself lodged in the local gaol. But a year later he was baptized in the sea, and in July 1930 started his remarkable preaching.

> Several times a day, armed with Bible and handbell, he called on the people to bring out their idols and juju to be burnt. God alone was sufficient. Never in Yorubaland had there been such a mass movement, never such bonfires of the implements of traditional religion. Suddenly Aladura expanded into one of the major religious groupings of the Yoruba, although many of the converts of the Babalola revival undoubtedly found their way into Anglicanism or Methodism. Here again, religious division between 'independency' and the mission churches was by no means a hard one.[13] ·

Another notable leader was attracted to the revival, and began preaching with it, Josiah Oshitelu. He insisted on several features that the others couldn't accept: he used a number of strange 'holy names', including 'Arrabablalhhubab' for himself; in his healing services he identified people as witches; he permitted polygamy and claimed the right to seven wives for himself. So before long he split off and founded his own Church of the Lord (Aladura), while Akinyele and Babalola turned their main body of Aladura in 1941 into the Christ Apostolic Church. Both remain among the larger groupings of Christians in Nigeria, with Oshitelu's having been the subject of one of the first profound academic studies of an 'African Initiated Church'[14] and having been brought into the fellowship of the World Council of Churches at the end of the century by his second successor, his grandson who also directs a computer firm in Germany.

These paragraphs describe all too inadequately no more than a few of the thousands of 'African Initiated Churches', which of course vary enormously in all sorts of ways. John Mbiti once memorably described their 'movement' as

> an African opportunity to mess up Christianity in our own way. For the past two thousand years, other continents, countries, nations and generations have had their chances to do with Christianity as they wished. And we know that they have not been idle! Now Africa has got its chance at last.[15]

Yet these glimpses, along with the earlier group, may help to bring out two major features of this entire rush of millions of Africans into one or other form of Christian church.[16]

First, they discovered in these (and many other) fellow African preachers an invitation to obey God in a new way, yet a way on which they could – and still do – bring with them many of the most profound and important features of their ancestral traditions and beliefs. Not so much the outer habits and practices: almost all the Christians condemn fetishes and juju, yet the arguments about appropriate initiation ceremonies for new adults and those around polygamy still go on. But the 'new' Christianity allowed them – and it is often said that the same is true in its own way for the Islam which has attracted so many other Africans, especially in West Africa – to bring their own spirituality and religious sensitivity into the wider fellowship of the worldwide Church.[17]

Second, it is clear that the arrival of European and other foreigners in Africa, evidently bringing with them a wholly different range of powers and purposes, was responsible for impelling many Africans into looking for some way ahead that would provide them with a bridge to this 'new world'. Not that they wanted to become exactly like the whites – far from it! But it is as if they have almost unconsciously looked for ways of becoming comparable to the whites, in religion, in education, in commerce and in whatever else was appropriate – and have then added, to the benefit of us all, in the longer run, their own music, their own sensitivities to God, their own abilities to heal and excite through prayer and preaching, and much else. This passage into a new world is by no means at an end. To mention only one particularly tricky area, that of the expected relationships between men and women, African women who have understood contemporary western relationships will insist that there is much their men-folk have yet to learn.[18]

Towards the new century

There is much more that could be said about what happened to African Christians and to their faith during the twentieth century, which was no less tumultuous for them than for other parts of the world. Caught up to some extent in the two World Wars, though continuous major fighting only swept over the largely desert areas of North Africa in the Second, the peoples of Africa then went through the messy processes of achieving independence, with a bitter war in Algeria involving the French, a tragic uprising of Kikuyus in Kenya against the British, long-drawn-out wars in Angola and Mozambique with the Portuguese, and a civil war against the settlers in Rhodesia, now Zimbabwe. Some countries had a relatively straightforward passage to independence – most of the French colonies, and not a few of the British – but again and again Africa has since then known coups and revolutions and new tyrannies. These have undoubtedly tried and tested the faith and obedience of many people – how could it be otherwise? And yet by the end of the century Africa was proud of having so many Christians, and of bringing its own gifts and leaders into the total world community.

If there is one story above all others that communicates this growth into world leadership, it is surely that of the new South Africa, with both its political leader, Nelson Mandela, and its Christian religious leader, Desmond Tutu, standing head and shoulders above most other twentieth-century figures for sheer goodness and integrity.

This is not the place to try and summarize the long and intricate history of the struggles that led to the once-in-a-lifetime day in 1994 when the entire adult population of South Africa went to vote for the first time, and people were happy to stand in queues of black and brown and white and mixed race for hour after hour, thrilled by being at last a single, if also 'rainbow' (Tutu's word) people.

The three successive documents in *SCM Core Reader*, 7.7, 7.8 and 7.9 can convey something of the different flavours of different stages of the later years of that whole struggle.

SCM Core Reader, 7.7 contains most of 'The Freedom Charter', solemnly adopted at the 'Congress of the People', called by the African National Congress and other movements, in 1955, a time when the white government, with the Afrikaaner National Party, having won power in 1948, was in the full flood of implementing its programme of apartheid (= separation). The chairman of the Congress was Chief Albert Luthuli, a devout Congregationalist. It was in no way a specifically Christian gathering, even if Trevor Huddleston was there as a figure known for his stubborn defence of the equal rights of the blacks. The text is crystal clear, alike in what it opposes and in what it demands. Yet at the same time it is in no way bitter or exaggerated; it breathes an integrity and a patience, as if even its opponents will not really be able to resist the strength of its case for ever – which at the time they no doubt thought they could! Taken together with, for example, Alan Paton's novel *Cry the Beloved Country*, with his beautiful study of the long-suffering country parson, it breathes a faith, a purity of belief in what deserves to be believed in, that is wholly other than any political calculation, any manoeuvre of subtle greed, let alone any threat of protest or uprising. There is a deep sense of the sheer truth of what they are asking for, whoever their opponents and whatever resistance they are all too likely to put up to its requests.

SCM Core Reader, 7.8, by contrast, provides an interestingly typical piece from a very different generation, from Steve Biko (1946–77), who for a few dismayingly short years was the figurehead of the movement that was called 'Black Consciousness', in deliberate counterpoint to the voices that only ever spoke of such all-races-together things as equality and democracy and sharing. Steve Biko was in no way against those things, but he well knew how far away from reality they not only already were but would remain as long as apartheid was allowed to flourish. He was no theologian, but a remarkably clear-thinking and articulate man who here, even as a pointedly 'angry young man', speaks truths that all South Africa, and not least the often too compliant older clergy needed to hear and dare to act on.

SCM Core Reader, 7.9 then brings the heart of *Challenge to the Church – The Kairos Document*, one of the key texts that influenced Christian opinion abroad to wake up to the seriousness and urgency of securing a major overthrow of the apartheid regime. In fact it only appeared four years before the decision to release Nelson Mandela from his long captivity, which was the decisive turning point in the struggle. It sets out the crucial distinction between the 'state theology', which had justified apartheid, the 'church theology', which was more concerned to look after the internal concerns of the churches than the crying evils in society, and the 'prophetic theology', which could recognize the Kairos for what God had made it, the opportunity to join all possible hands to overthrow the apartheid regime at long last. This appeal certainly spoke to many friends of South Africa in Europe and North America, who may have tipped some of the important balances in persuading governments to withdraw support, and firms not to invest in or trade with firms in South Africa – the set of political and economic decisions that undoubtedly contributed sharply to the willingness of President de Klerk to open the way to a wholly different South Africa.

It would hardly be true to suggest that Christians were responsible for the overthrow of apartheid, neither internally within South Africa, still less from outside. What is true is that for ten and more years, a strong set of Christian voices from inside – Beyers Naude, Desmond Tutu, Steve Biko, Allan Boesak, Denis Hurley, Smangaliso Mkhatshwa amid many others – spoke and acted in harmony with a growing number of voices from outside, most notably that of the World Council of Churches,[19] with its Cottesloe conference of 1960, its grants to the liberation movements from its Programme to Combat Racism in 1970, and the conferences it held in Harare in 1985 and in Lusaka in 1987, where insiders could meet with their allies outside, in such a way as greatly to undermine the power of apartheid in the first place, and then to help persuade enough of the key politicians and commercial people that there was no future in it, and that South Africa must steer in the opposite direction. On 11 February 1990, the world, through innumerable TV cameras and every other possible channel of communication, shouted for joy when Mandela walked through his prison gate and delivered his speech in Cape Town, as it did again four years later, perhaps a little less rapturously but more prayerfully, as South Africa went to the polls in 1994.

Further reading

As will be clear from the footnotes to the above, this chapter is greatly indebted to the two magisterial survey books by the late Adrian Hastings:

A. Hastings (1979), *A History of African Christianity, 1950–1975*, Cambridge and New York: Cambridge University Press.

A. Hastings (1994), *The Church in Africa, 1450–1950*, Oxford: Clarendon Press and New York: Oxford University Press, which includes 65 pages of Bibliography.

Hastings would himself have insisted that readers outside Africa should consult as much as possible books and articles written by Africans. The documents in the *SCM Core Reader*, Chapter 7, come from books all well worth reading:

K. Bediako (1995), *Christianity in Africa: The Renewal of a Non-Western Religion*, Edinburgh: Edinburgh University Press.

S. Biko (1978), *I Write What I Like: A Selection of His Writings*, A. Stubbs CR (ed.) London: The Bowerdean Press. This book includes a personal memoir by Fr Stubbs which is deeply moving.

M. Kanyoro (2002), *Introducing Feminist Cultural Hermeneutics: An African Perspective*, London: Continuum/Sheffield University Press.

A. Luthuli (1962), *Let My People Go: An Autobiography*, London: Collins.

J. Mbiti (1990), *African Religions and Philosophy*, second edn, Oxford: Heinemann International.

L. Sanneh (1993), *Encountering the West: Christianity and the Global Cultural Process: The African Dimension*, London: Marshall Pickering.

Not to be missed, finally, are the major books – one an autobiography and the other a biography – of the two outstanding South African leaders:

J. Allen, (2006), *Rabble-Rouser for Peace: The Authorised Biography of Desmond Tutu*, London and New York: Random House.

N. Mandela (1994), *Long Walk to Freedom: An Autobiography*, New York and London: Little, Brown and Company.

Notes

1 See A. Hastings (1994), *The Church in Africa 1450–1950*, Oxford: Clarendon Press, p. 68, and his reference on p. 630/1 to Joseph Cuoq (1984), *L' Église d'Afrique du Nord, du 2e au 12e siècle*, Paris, as 'the best complete survey of the evidence for the decline of Christianity in North Africa'.

2 Fred Donner (1999), 'Muhammad and the Caliphate: Political History of the Islamic Empire up to the Mongol Conquest', in John Esposito (ed.), *The Oxford History of Islam*, New York: Oxford University Press, p. 8.

3 K. Ward (1999), 'Africa', in A. Hastings (ed.), *A World History of Christianity*, London: Cassell, p. 201.

4 See Hastings, *The Church in Africa*, pp. 179ff.

5 See J. Guy (1983), *The Heretic: A Study of the Life of John William Colenso, 1814–1883*, Pietermaritzburg: University of Natal Press, and Johannesburg: Ravan Press, a moving study of how this admirable man had to handle in Natal an impossible amount of troubles, while also producing an immense quantity of important intellectual and spiritual work.

6 See the many references to Lavigerie in Hastings, *The Church in Africa*; the quotations in these paragraphs come from pp. 564–5.

7 See pp. 12–14 above.

8 Figures from www.adherents.com quoted from J. Mbiti (1991), *Introduction to African Religion*, Oxford and Portsmouth NH: Heinemann Educational Books.

9 See Hastings, *The Church in Africa*, pp. 343–5.

10 These two short sketches are drawn from Hastings, *The Church in Africa*, pp. 470–1.

11 For an insightful discussion of the effects of being able to handle religious matters in the vernacular, see Lamin Sanneh's document on 'The Vital Importance of Scripture Translations' in *SCM Core Reader*, 7.2.

12 See Hastings, *The Church in Africa*, p. 503.

13 This section owes much to Hastings, *The Church in Africa*, pp. 514–18; the quotation is from p. 576.

14 H. W. Turner (1967), *History of an African Independent Church: The Church of the Lord (Aladura)*, 2 vols, Oxford: Clarendon Press.

15 In his article (1974), 'Faith, Hope and Love in the African Independent Church Movement', in a short-lived journal of the World Council of Churches, *Study Encounter*, vol. 10, no. 3, SE/63, p. 9.

16 See *SCM Core Reader*, 7.5, for Hastings' careful analysis of several of the causes and motivations in the total movement of independent and African Initiated Churches.

17 For fuller discussion of two key aspects of this, see the documents by John Mbiti and Kwame Bediako in *SCM Core Reader*, 7.3 ('Awareness of God') and 7.4 ('Role of Ancestors').

18 Here readers are referred to *SCM Core Reader*, 7.6 and 15.6, where Musimbi Kanyoro expresses both her strong sense of being wholly and unmistakably an African woman, yet also her sharp questions about how this needs to be much more fully explored and worked through, by men as much as by women.

19 The action of the WCC over this whole period is chronicled in P. Webb (1994), *A Long Struggle: The Involvement of the World Council of Churches in South Africa*, Geneva: WCC Publications. See also Nelson Mandela's speech to the WCC Assembly in Harare in 1998, in D. Kessler (ed.) (1999), *Together on the Way: Official Report of the Eighth Assembly of the World Council of Churches*, Geneva: WCC Publications, pp. 227–31.

8

South Asia: Bangladesh, India, Nepal, Pakistan and Sri Lanka

South Asia or the Indian subcontinent, which is the focus of this chapter, saw enormous changes during the twentieth century. It moved from British colonial rule, with its associated oppressive as well as some beneficial influences, at the beginning of the century, through a painful period of considerable conflict and turmoil, to independence in mid-century. This had major repercussions, as we shall see, for the life of the Christian churches.

At the beginning of the century, the region was characterized by considerable poverty and socio-economic inequality. The majority of the population was economically poor and disenfranchised in a society where the upper echelons of society enjoyed considerable wealth, power and influence. Such inequalities inevitably caused considerable suffering and conflict. While the economic situation changed during the century, the poorest in the subcontinent remain among the poorest peoples of the world. At the beginning of the century, the economic situation was exacerbated by colonial rule that meant a complete absence of democratic institutions, with policy decisions being taken by foreign governments that wielded the power and influence.

Independence from colonial rule, and the consequent partition of British India, came in 1947, at considerable cost in human lives, social division and forced estrangement, not least after the British had left. This led to the establishment of a number of independent sovereign nations, namely, the Republic of India, the Islamic Republic of Pakistan, including East Pakistan (which became the People's Republic of Bangladesh in 1971), as well as Ceylon (the island nation off the southern coast of India that was renamed Sri Lanka in 1972). Nepal, a landlocked, mountainous country in the Himalayan mountain range, has continued to be a constitutional monarchy.

This region of Asia gave birth to some of the major religions of the world. Over the centuries (and, of course, throughout the twentieth century and into the present period) the subcontinent has been characterized by religious pluralism, with Buddhism, Hinduism, Islam and Sikhism, as well as animist and other indigenous religions, dominating certain areas of the subcontinent. This has meant that Christianity has always been a small minority religion in all the regions of the subcontinent (except for north-east India, as we shall see).

The history and development of Christianity

There has been considerable debate about the origins of Christianity in Asia generally, and especially in this region. For example, the St Thomas Christians (an Oriental Orthodox family which has been divided into a number of distinct churches over the years) trace their origins back to the first centuries of Christianity and to the missionary enterprise of St Thomas. Koshy[1] draws attention to a 'long-proved tradition of [Asian] Christianity that chose to look neither to Rome nor Constantinople as its centre' and was Asian in its essential identity, an 'eastward movement' in which St Thomas 'was the central figure'.[2]

Catholic priests and missionaries started arriving in India not long after Vasco de Gama touched the western coast of India in 1498. Working out from Goa, which was occupied by the Portuguese, initially this Catholic mission (through such pioneers as the Jesuit, Roberto di Nobili, who reached Madurai in Tamilnadu), made only gradual progress. But over the next few centuries it became a significant influence and led to what is today a major Christian presence in the subcontinent. The Protestant missionary enterprise began in the mid-eighteenth century. It too was a major influence in shaping the Christian presence in the subcontinent.

At the beginning of the twentieth century, Christian architecture and liturgy, denominational structure and patterns of ministry, and even theological emphases, were essentially 'western'. All this was undergirded by an over-dependence on missionary funding and the inevitable 'western' control over church policy and decision-making. Whatever the mutual relationship between the colonial powers and the missionary enterprise (and the nature of the relationship is a matter of considerable debate), there is no doubt that church life was heavily influenced by and reflected these western traditions. Some (such as Koshy; see *SCM Core Reader on World Christianity in the Twentieth Century*, 8.1) would argue strongly, therefore, that this 'westernization' of Christianity in the region had robbed the Christian churches of their essentially Asian identity. Inevitably, then, the story of Christianity in the region during the twentieth century is, at least in part, the story of the unravelling of the negative effects of this connection and the rediscovery of an Asian Christian identity. K. M. Pannikar[3] criticizes the western approach to Asia for three reasons, namely, the political and socio-economic consequences of colonialism, the racist nature of some of the attitudes involved and the effects of western missionary policy. He had no doubt that the missionary enterprise and the colonial domination were closely connected, as indicated by the title of his major work, *Asia and Western Dominance*.

But it was also the case that many of the missionaries were very influential in the process of recovering an Asian Christian identity within the churches in the region. Hans Reudi Weber[4] has described missionaries in the region as 'midwives of the Asian church' and identifies four ways in which they were influential, namely, their personal lives and Christian witness, their role in developing institutions such as the Christian colleges, their willingness to foster missionary collaboration and the key role of Bible translation.

Some Asian leaders at the beginning of the century were prepared to voice their concern in worldwide gatherings. The most notable example was V. S. Azariah (1874–1945), the first Indian to become a bishop of the Anglican Church in India – he was consecrated Bishop of Dornakal in 1912. He addressed the Edinburgh (1910) conference on 'the unequal partnership between Western missionaries and their indigenous colleagues'.[5] He concluded his address:

> Give us friends. The favourite phrases, 'our money', 'our control', must go ... We shall learn to walk only by walking – perchance only by falling and learning from our mistakes, but never by being kept in leading strings until we arrive at maturity.

Azariah himself gave the following assessment of the Edinburgh conference and its significance in relation to the indigenization of the Indian church:

> [Edinburgh 1910 marked a] new era ... in the missionary world when the indigenous Church was ... frankly acknowledged to be the greatest, the most potent, and the most natural factor in the evangelization of the country. It is on the efficiency, purity and missionary activity of this Church that the evangelization of India will depend.[6]

Early ecumenical influences and relationships

Clearly, then, Asian Christian leaders were beginning to play leading roles within the wider ecumenical movement at the beginning of the century. Edinburgh (1910) had crystallized the beginnings of a movement which had its origins in the nineteenth century. Indeed, it was a hundred years earlier that the pioneering Baptist missionary in India, William Carey, had suggested that all the Christian churches of the world should be invited to attend a gathering at the Cape of Good Hope in 1810. This dream did not come to fruition but it indicated that within the missionary enterprise there were those who planted the seeds of ecumenical relationships in the soil of the subcontinent long before the fruit of their vision came to any kind of maturity.

However, the most influential pioneers of ecumenical relationships in the region were the YMCA, YWCA and the World Student Christian Federation (WSCF). The YMCA is one example of the influence of these organizations. The World Alliance of YMCAs was founded at its first world conference in Paris in 1855. The basis of the Alliance was agreed at the Paris conference: 'to unite those young men, who regarding Jesus Christ as their God and Saviour according to holy scriptures desire to be his disciples in their faith and in their life, and to exercise their efforts for the extension of the Kingdom among young men'.[7] Partly under the influence of Luther Wishard, the American YMCA leader, who travelled extensively throughout Asia from 1888 onwards, the India committee of the YMCA became affiliated to the World Alliance in 1891, the first Asian movement to do so. Leaders such as V. S. Azariah gained their ecumenical vision and formation through the YMCA and it became a platform which enabled them to 'express their longing for Christian unity and to manifest it ... The younger churches realized [through these influences] that the divisions imported from the West had to be taken seriously and the denominational differences must be overcome for discovering a full and stable church unity.'[8]

One of the most influential ecumenical leaders in the early years of the twentieth century was John R. Mott (1865–1955), who served the WSCF as General Secretary and later as President for 33 years and chaired the Edinburgh conference (1910). In the period following the Edinburgh conference (during 1912 and 1913), Mott held a series of regional and national conferences in Asian countries, including Ceylon (now Sri Lanka) and India. Their specific intention was to bring together missionaries and indigenous Christian leaders to explore the issues raised at Edinburgh and to enable national leaders increasingly to assume leadership positions. The Indian conference recommended the formation of provincial representative councils of missions and of a national missionary council. This development signalled a significant movement away from the missionary dominance to an increasingly indigenous leadership within the churches of the region.

V. S. Azariah both symbolized and enabled this shift. His book, *India and the Christian Movement*, was a revised version of an earlier book that sought to set out his understanding of the key issues that faced the Indian church at the beginning of the twentieth century. Another major influence within the region was the formation of the International Missionary Council in 1921, chaired by John R. Mott, under the direct influence of Edinburgh (1910). It united in a federation national missionary councils and councils of churches in Asia (and other continents and regions) with the councils of missionary societies in Europe and North America. Its first world conference was held in Jerusalem in 1928, where the matter of the relationship between younger and older churches was one of the most prominent issues. Other central themes of this gathering had important implications for the Christian churches in the subcontinent in the early decades of the century. They included a theological understanding of approaches to 'non-Christian' religions, responding to secularization and the shift from missions-centred to church-centred thinking (that is, from missionary to indigenous responsibility). Koshy quotes from the section of the conference message that reflected on Christ among the nations:

> Our message is Jesus Christ. He is the revelation of what God is and of what man through Him may become. In Him we come face to face with the ultimate reality of the universe ... We hold that through all that happens, in light and darkness, God is working, ruling and over-ruling.[9]

This would prove to be a foundational statement for the developing work and witness of the churches in the region.

The conference also set out its position on the issue of indigenization, highlighting the need for the Christian Church to understand Christ from a local as well as from a universal perspective, 'to share its life with the nation in which it finds itself ... being alert to the problems of the times' and to be kindled with 'missionary ardour'.[10]

This period was formative in the process of progressing from a missionary-dominated Christian presence in the region to a church that was increasingly indigenous in its identity and under national leadership. In *India and the Christian Movement*, Azariah comments:

At a time when the spirit of nationalism sweeps over the land and everything un-Indian is looked upon with suspicion, it is a moral and spiritual obligation upon all missionaries and missionary societies from abroad and from all Churches in India, to seek to do everything they can, to make it possible, both in appearance and in reality, to identify the Christian movement with the indigenous Church and indigenous leadership.[11]

He himself had played a key role in enabling that identification to become a greater reality within the Indian church.

The churches

In this brief chapter, we cannot give a full account of the wide diversity of churches and denominations in the subcontinent, nor trace their development during the century. We offer here a brief summary of the key features of the larger churches and denominations. This account does not examine these churches separately within each nation-state because the historical continuities and discontinuities caused by the partition of India would make such an account over-complicated. We draw attention only to any distinctive features displayed by any one of the traditions in a particular context.

The Mar Thoma Syrian Church of Malabar

Part of the family of St Thomas Christians, as we have seen, this is one of the most ancient church traditions in India (and in the subcontinent as a whole). It is an independent reformed Oriental Orthodox church that traces its origin to the first Christian century and the mission of St Thomas, a tradition that is 'old, strong and an integral part of the self-understanding of the Syrian Christian community'.[12] There is evidence of a Christian community in southwest India from the fourth century onwards and no known evidence against the claim of an ancient origin. The church underwent a process of reform during the eighteenth century, largely under the influence of Anglican evangelical missionaries (although there had also been earlier attempts during the fifteenth century at reforming the church under the influence of Roman Catholic missionaries). The reform brought together, within this ancient church, an evangelical biblical faith and a liturgical and devotional life rooted in the Syrian Orthodox tradition. These two streams, represented by the Orthodox and Reformed traditions, within the life of the church, have given it a unique identity. It has been described as a 'bridge church'. These two streams within the church's life are also in constant dialogue with each other within the church itself.

Many of the key characteristics of the Mar Thoma Syrian Church were developed during the early years of the twentieth century as the implications of the 'reformation' were worked out in the life of the church. It is openly ecumenical and sees itself as 'part of the one apostolic and catholic church', as the preamble to its constitution emphasizes. It is in communion (that is, a relationship which is focused on being able to share fully in each others' eucharistic celebrations) with the Anglican churches around the world through the worldwide Anglican Communion. It is fully involved as a member of the National Council of Churches of India, the Christian Conference of Asia and the World Council of Churches (in which many of its leaders have played a particularly significant role). M. M. Thomas, one of its foremost laymen and theologians, played an enormously influential and formative role in the ecumenical movement nationally, regionally and at a world level (see *SCM Core Reader*, 1.5). One of the ways in which this ecumenical commitment was manifested was through the Joint Council formed in 1978 between the Mar Thoma Church, the Church of South India (CSI) and the Church of North India (CNI).

Its evangelical faith also gives it a strong commitment to evangelism and 'the mission of evangelization of the people of India'. Another prominent aspect of its mission commitment is its engagement in issues of social justice and equality in India (and elsewhere). It has played an important role, as we shall see, among the Dalits (formerly known as the 'untouchables'), the marginalized, low-caste peoples of India.

The Roman Catholic Church

This came to the subcontinent largely as a result of Portugese (but also, to a lesser extent, French and British) occupation following Vasco de Gama's arrival, and its related missionary enterprise, from the fifteenth century onwards (most particularly through St Francis Xavier). In those early centuries, European Catholic influence inevitably dominated and shaped the life and liturgy of the church. By the beginning of the twentieth century, there were just over 1 million Catholics in the subcontinent, largely under the leadership of bishops from Europe. By the beginning of the twenty-first century, this figure had grown to around 20 million. During this period, leadership within the Catholic community has become increasingly indigenous, not least as a result of the changes brought about by Indian partition in 1947.

A number of Catholic Bishops' Conferences have been established in the various nations to co-ordinate and develop the spiritual life and mission of the Catholic faithful. Thus there are Conferences in India, Bangladesh, Pakistan and Sri Lanka, which, together with ten other Conferences in other regions of Asia, constitute the Federation of Asian Bishops' Conferences, formed in 1972 to provide mutual support and to strengthen the church and its witness in Asian society. Among its priorities – shared with the Conferences in the subcontinent – has been the promotion of mutual understanding, co-operation and unity between the Catholic community and other churches and ecclesial communities. But the Conferences have also given priority to what has been described as 'the triple dialogue with Asia's religions, Asia's cultures and Asia's poor'.[13]

Caste was an enduring problem for the Catholic Church in India during the early years of the century (as it had been for other churches). At the end of the nineteenth century, Catholic missionaries from different backgrounds had different attitudes to caste both in society and within the church. Some believed that the caste system should be respected, while others believed that it was the responsibility of the church to oppose it. During the century the Catholic Church, along with the other churches and ecclesial bodies in the subcontinent, struggled with this key issue and the Christian communities in these countries have increasingly reflected their local cultures and traditions as well as, to some extent at least, their ancient religious traditions.

One of the most significant recent developments was the appointment of the first Dalit, Marampudi Joji (who is one of three Dalit bishops in the Conference of Catholic Bishops in India), as Roman Catholic Archbishop of Hyderabad in 2006. This appointment was particularly significant given that 60 per cent of India's Catholics are Dalits.

Another key issue during the early part of the century – which it faced in common with other Christian traditions – was the degree to which the church should free itself from western cultural and theological influences and assume an Asian form. This was a very controversial issue at the time and the Vatican in Rome feared that 'Asianization' could undermine the unity of the church.

By the end of the twentieth century, there were around 17 million Catholics in India, organized in 149 dioceses, and constituting around 1.6 per cent of the total population, making it the largest Christian church in India. There are 11 dioceses in Sri Lanka, with around 1.3 million Catholics, 7 dioceses in Pakistan, also with around 1.3 million Catholics, 6 dioceses in Bangladesh, with around 300,000 members and 1 diocese in Nepal with around 7,000 members.

Baptist churches

Foremost among the pioneers of the Baptist missionary enterprise in India was William Carey (1761–1834). He left England to be a Baptist Missionary Society missionary in India in 1793. He spent his early years in India in Calcutta, learning the language and preaching. He earned his living as manager of an indigo factory. But during this initial period he could not claim one convert. In 1800, he moved to Serampore, where there was a very gradual response to his teaching and preaching. He was one of the founding members of Serampore College, which still plays a key role in accrediting degree schemes for theological colleges and seminaries throughout the subcontinent. One of Carey's main legacies was the translation of the Bible, which he saw as crucial to any missionary enterprise. In 1801 he was appointed Professor of Sanskrit, Bengali and Marathi in Fort William College. He remained in that post for 30 years. He translated the whole Bible into Bengali (1809) and the whole Bible or parts of it into 24 other languages or dialects. He published grammar books and dictionaries in Sanskrit, Marathi, Punjabi and Telugu. But Carey also had a crucial influence on the understanding of the foreign mission of the church. Many would contend that his missionary work was the trigger for the growth and development of mission not just in India but also in other parts of the world. Alongside missionaries from Britain, there were

Baptist missionaries from the USA, Australia and New Zealand. Links with the mother churches and societies generally continued to be strong.

During the twentieth century, the Baptist tradition grew throughout the region. By the end of the century, there were around 1.8 million Baptists in India, a growing – though small – number in Nepal, Bangladesh, Pakistan and Sri Lanka. The Myanmar Baptist convention is the largest Protestant church in the country with around 800,000 members. The Council of Baptist Churches in Northern India joined the united Church of North India in 1970, but the Baptists in the south of India did not join the united Church of South India. Many Baptist churches that did not join the CNI formed the Association of Baptist Churches in North East India.

The Congregational and Presbyterian churches[14]

These were also the fruit of mission from Britain, America and Australia. The Congregational churches were formed as a result of the work of the London Missionary Society with missionaries from Great Britain and Australia, and the American Board of Commissioners of Foreign Missions. The Presbyterian churches were formed through the work of the Church of Scotland Mission, the Dutch Reformed Church in America and the Basel Mission in Switzerland and Germany. They also had connections with the Presbyterian churches in England and Australia. 'However, faced with the challenge of the mission frontier and the necessity of better credibility, the churches themselves began to be increasingly aware of the scandal of disunity and sought ways of overcoming it.' As a result, different kinds of mergers or unions among churches were beginning to take place. In October 1901, a Federal Union took place between the Presbyterian missions in South India, the United Free Church of Scotland Mission, the American Arcot Mission of the American Dutch Reformed Church and the Basel Mission. In 1904, the Congregational churches of the London Missionary Society in South India and the Congregational churches of the American Board Missions in South India and Jaffna came together in a Federal Union. In 1908, these two bodies, the Presbyterian and the Congregational, came together to form the South India United Church. This church would be one of the partners in the negotiations that would lead to the Church of South India.

The Presbyterian Church in India

This church is located mainly in the north-east region of India, separated from the Indian mainland by Bangladesh in the west of the region and bordering Burma to the east. The church was the result of missionary work from the Presbyterian Church of Wales (UK) during the nineteenth century, beginning in the Khasi Jainatia area (Meghalaya) with the arrival of the Revd Thomas Jones and his wife in the Khasi Hills. During the second half of the nineteenth century, the church in the Khasi Hills had been growing. By 1901 there were already over 15,000 Christians, gathered in almost 400 churches and places of worship, and an assembly had been set up.

Mission work began in Mizoram, one of the north-east Indian states, in the last decade of the nineteenth century when missionaries from Wales and the Arthington Mission (through F. W. Savidge and J. H. Lorrain) began an evangelistic campaign.[15] The first Welsh missionary, the Revd D. E. Jones, served there from 1897 to 1926, and according to Lloyd, who served there from 1944 to 1964, 'he it was who left the deepest impression on the Mizo Church during its first and formative years',[16] through his preaching, his Christian story-telling, his schools and classes and his encouragement of hymn-singing (which became and remains a central facet of Mizo spirituality). Initial responses came from among the youth, and the first two converts were baptized two years after missionary efforts began. In the century that followed, the work grew and developed through evangelism, educational, health and social services. There were also several waves of revival. Missionaries gave priority also to enabling and encouraging local Christians to take responsibility for the life of the church, and after the departure of missionaries during the 1960s, Mizo Christians assumed positions of leadership in all areas of the church's life and witness. In a period of half a century, Lloyd claims that Mizoram underwent what was 'tantamount to a complete conversion'. According to 1998 statistics, the Presbyterian Church of India then had a total strength of 1 million members in 2,522 local churches. There are over 600 ordained pastors and more than 1,000 missionaries working in the region itself, in other regions of India and in partner churches around the world. The 1991 census of India quotes figures of 85.73 per cent Christians in Mizoram, although this may be an underestimate. For the north-eastern region generally, the figure is 13.64 per cent, much lower than in Mizoram, but much higher than the rest of India.

In an article on 'Church-mission dynamics in Northeast India', Lalsangkima Pachuau makes three observations about the nature of mission in the region (see *SCM Core Reader*, 8.2).[17] First, he notes the 'localized character of mission activity'. Priority has always been given to mission among local people within the state. He clearly implies that this focus on local witness by the indigenous population is a key factor in the growth of the church. Second, he draws attention to the role of Christianity in what he calls 'modernization'. He focuses particularly on the churches' role in education and the importance of this aspect of the Christian mission as a prelude to evangelistic 'success'. It is significant that the state of Mizoram, which has one of the highest proportions of Christians within the population, also ranks as one of the highest (for many years, *the* highest) in India for adult literacy. Finally, he suggests that the focused approach to evangelism in the region has been an important factor:

> They have understood mission simply as evangelism, and evangelism mainly as verbal proclamation, and all as a battle for Christ to conquer new lands as an extension of God's kingdom ... Conversion and church planting are the dominant goals of the mission enterprise.

When the present author visited Mizoram in 2001 and asked about the reasons for the success story of the church, the spirit of revivalism, especially emanating among the youth of the church (born perhaps from the Welsh revival of 1904–05 which was flourishing in Wales during the early years of the missionary enterprise in the state), was cited as the primary reason for the growth and continued influence of the Christian community in Mizoram. But it was significant also that at the beginning of the new century, and despite the obvious strength and vitality of the church, there was considerable concern about the future and the possible consequences of globalizing influences – such as drugs, alcohol and worldwide communications – on the life and future of the church.

Lloyd comments of the early decades of the Christian presence in the region, that 'it was unquestionably the profound sense and continued recollection of the condition of their past lives that made Mizo Christians passionately eager not only to pray God to send the light, but ready to take it to those who were still in deep darkness'.[18] What was true of the early missionary period, has remained true throughout the life of the church in the region.

The United Evangelical Lutheran Church in India

This has its origin in Danish, Swedish, Norwegian and American missions that date back to 1706. The first synod was held in 1853. The United Lutheran Church has 1.5 million members in 3,000 congregations that are to be found predominantly along the length of the eastern part of India. The 11 Lutheran churches that constitute the United Lutheran Church relate individually to the Lutheran World Federation but are collective members of the WCC and the Christian Conference of Asia.

The Anglican Church

The Anglican Church in the subcontinent has its origins in the seventeenth century. One important influence was the commitment of the East India Company, the foremost and most influential trading company between Britain and India, to appoint chaplains to serve on their ships and later to provide spiritual care for all those in their employ. Their primary concern was the welfare of their employees, but occasionally conversions came in the wake of pastoral care. The company's chaplains came under the jurisdiction of the Bishop of London. The first Anglican church to be established in India, as a consequence of the work of these chaplains, was St Mary's Church, Madras, built towards the end of the seventeenth century.

The first missionaries came to India towards the beginning of the eighteenth century. The early Lutheran missionaries were supported in their work by the Society for the Promotion of Christian Knowledge (SPCK). A century later, the Church Missionary Society and the Society for the Propagation of the Gospel came on the scene, working in Christian support, education and evangelism. At this time, a close inter-relationship was perceived between Christianizing the local population and the commercial and political interests of the East India Company and the British Government. Developing a strong church, it was thought, could strengthen and support the interests of the state.

By 1837, there were three Anglican dioceses in India, established as a result of an Act of Parliament: Calcutta (founded in 1814), Madras (established in 1834) and Bombay (established in 1837), with episcopal authority continuing to be derived from the Church of England and the British state. By the beginning of the twentieth century, a number of additional dioceses had been established, often involving difficult struggles.

The early years of the century saw the beginnings of a real effort to 'Indianize' the Anglican Church in India. A conference held in Calcutta between 30 December 1912 and 5 January 1913 'marked the transition of the movement for self-government from reconnaissance to detailed planning'.[19] A key resolution made a commitment 'to full synodical government ... on the basis of consensual compact'. However, this was not immediately implemented since it would have required a British Act of Parliament. Instead, a provincial council for the whole Anglican Church in the region was established.

In subsequent years, considerable energy and commitment went towards the disestablishment of the Anglican Church in India, so that it became independent of the Church of England and the British Government and became self-governing. The Parliamentary Bills enabling these changes were finally passed towards the end of 1927. On 1 January 1930, the Church of India, Burma and Ceylon was established.

However, a decade before this momentous event, discussions had already begun towards the reunion of the churches in India. The Lambeth Conference of worldwide Anglican bishops, meeting in 1920, encouraged reunion on the basis of the key statement of the requirements for union set out by the Lambeth Conference of 1888, namely, a common understanding of Scripture, the historic creeds, the sacraments and of an ordained ministry within the historic episcopate (a fourfold basis usually known as 'the Lambeth Quadrilateral').

This decision set in motion negotiations between the Anglican Church and the United Church of South India (formed from Congregational and Presbyterian churches) which were later joined by the South Indian Province of the Methodist Church in 1925. Proclaiming the gospel was at the heart of the motivation for these negotiations from the beginning. Winning India for Christ – as the task of evangelism in India was often described at this time – would only be possible when the Indian churches, whose divisions were inherited and were not of their own making, could become one. Both before and after final agreement on the basis of a United Church, recognition of ministry was the most controversial issue. The proposal was accepted that the new church should have two parallel ministries, one episcopal and one non-episcopal. In supporting this position, William Temple, Archbishop of Canterbury at the time, believed that since this was 'attempting what is ... an unprecedented enterprise' it should at least be possible 'that unprecedented expedients may be legitimate and appropriate'.[20] He therefore commended that

> the Church of England would not break communion with the Church of India, Burma and Ceylon if the four dioceses were to join the Church of South India; on the other hand, any subsequent intercommunion between the Church of England and the Church of South India would not at this stage be unrestricted.

When the Anglican bishops voted at the Lambeth Conference in 1948 on the issue of acceptance of the presbyters of the CSI, 134 voted for acceptance, 97 voted against and 100 did not vote.

The formation of the Church of South India left the Anglican Church in Burma and Ceylon (Sri Lanka), both of which became separate provinces and which are still in existence, the northern Indian dioceses and the dioceses in Pakistan which became part of the united Church of North India and the united Church of Pakistan respectively (see below).

The United Churches

These became a notable and pioneering development in the subcontinent during the latter half of the century, following partition. They became symbolic of the possibility of fuller unity, not just within Asia but more widely around the world. However, as this volume indicates, this early promise was not borne out in many other situations. Space prevents a full account of the formation and development of these churches during the century or an adequate assessment of their prospects for the twenty-first century, but it is important to set out here key aspects of these significant expressions of Christian unity and union.

The Church of South India

In South India, after 28 years of negotiation, in which missionaries often played key roles, the (united) Church of South India was formed in 1947. It brought into unity Anglican, Congregationalist, Presbyterian (these last two already united in the South India United Church) and Methodist (British) Christians to form the first united church in Asia. In his opening sermon at the inaugural service, J. S. M. Hooper interpreted the significance of the event: 'God has matched us with His hour; the Church of South India has an unparalleled opportunity. The reconciliation between our divergent elements enables us with a fresh conviction and force to proclaim the Gospel of reconciliation to all the clashing elements in this nation's life.'[21]

Lesslie Newbigin claims that a 'Pledge' by the five Anglican bishops 'completely transformed the situation'.[22] The Pledge stated: 'We agree that all who have the status of Presbyters [that is, serving clergy] in the United Church are capable of performing all the functions assigned to Presbyters in the United Church by the Constitution of that Church in every congregation of the United Church.' It gave confidence to churches that had found it difficult to reach a decision, to vote in favour of union. This union of episcopal and non-episcopal 'marked a momentous breakthrough'.[23]

The services of inauguration and consecration were held in St George's Cathedral, Madras, on 27 September 1947 (see SCM Core Reader, 8.3). Newbigin quotes from a letter he wrote at the time:

> I wish I could convey a sense of the unity of the whole congregation in the whole of the service. It was, after all, something quite new for which there were no precedents, and yet there was never a moment of stumbling or awkwardness ... [H]ere God had taken something lifeless in itself, and breathed into it and it became the vehicle of the working of the Holy Spirit that none of us will forget. It was unthinkably faithless now not to believe that

just in the same way the scheme of union, which had been a paper document for so many years, will become the vehicle of the living Spirit.[24]

By the end of the century, the Church of South India (CSI) had grown numerically. It started with 14 dioceses. The WCC *Handbook*[25] indicates that there were
20 dioceses in 2006 (including the Diocese of Jaffna in Sri Lanka) and a total of
3.5 million members (the largest Protestant church in India today). But Abraham
and Thomas are critical of its achievements over the sixty years of its history:

> [T]here is a general feeling that CSI has failed to live up to expectations ... [It]
> is a denomination like other denominations. Unity has become 'visible' and
> real, but it has not extended to other churches. Dialogues with the Method-
> ist Church of India (American) and the Lutheran churches [see above] have
> not led anywhere. Nor has unity gone beyond denominational cohesion.
> The CSI today is one United church, and that is no small accomplishment;
> but tensions persist because of caste, regional and linguistic differences
> within the body.[26]

The Church of North India

This was established in 1970, after 40 years of negotiation. It brought together
six churches and denominations, namely, the Council of Baptist Churches
in Northern India, the churches of the Brethren, the Disciples of Christ, the
Church of India (Anglican), the Methodist Church (British and Australasian
Conferences) and the United Church of Northern India (Congregational and
Presbyterian). It covers the whole of India, except the 4 southern states and
has 1.5 million members in 26 dioceses.

One of the CNI bishops gave the following evaluation of the church in 1994,
almost a quarter of a century after its inauguration: '[The Church of North
India is a] visible expression of our oneness in Christ ... [and accepts] the
episcopal, presbyterian and congregational elements in church order, as the
means through which the lordship of Christ in his church may be realized.'[27]
But Bishop Joshua is also critical of the church because 'the engagement in the
field of mission and evangelism by the united church seems to be less than the
sum total of what was being done by the various denominations before the
union'. It shares with the CSI the challenge of being a small minority church
in a predominantly Hindu population, 'which is becoming increasingly conscious of its Hindu identity and political power'.[28]

The Church of Pakistan

This was also established in 1970 through the union of Anglican, Lutheran,
Methodist and Scottish Presbyterian traditions. It was set up with 4 dioceses
but at the end of the century it had 500,000 members in 8 dioceses, and as such
is the second largest church in the country after the Roman Catholic Church.
Christians form only 3 per cent of the total population of Pakistan (a figure
that has remained more or less the same throughout our period), 97 per cent
of whom are Muslim. It has recognized that its leaders have faced 'problems

of identity and full participation in the social and political life of the country'.[29] Towards the end of the century, one of the most challenging problems that faced the Christian churches was the blasphemy law, violation of which can be punishable by the death penalty. Christian mission and evangelism, as well as other means of articulating the faith, could place Christians (as well as those of other minority religions) in danger despite the fact that minority religious groups had full legal rights.

The Church of Bangladesh

This was formed in 1971, the year that East Pakistan received its independence from Pakistan. The Diocese of Dhaka of the Church of Pakistan became an autonomous united church, the Church in Bangladesh. It owes its origins to nineteenth-century mission by the Church Missionary Society (Anglican), the Oxford Mission to Calcutta and the English Presbyterian Society. In 2006, it had 15,000 members in 2 dioceses. As in Pakistan, Muslims have formed the vast majority of the population (86 per cent in 2006) with 12 per cent Hindus and only 0.4 per cent Christians. Bangladesh is one of the least developed and most densely populated countries in Asia, and major annual flooding is a constant threat. In this context, the church – the majority of whose members are poor – has had to face a considerable challenge in responding to human need. Like other churches in the region, it has been dependent, during the latter decades of the century, on external funding to finance its social and development programme.

Collaboration

A number of organizations were established in the subcontinent during the twentieth century in order to foster collaboration and unity among Christians. We can do little more here than provide a very brief introduction to two such organizations, the National Councils of Churches and the Evangelical Fellowships.

In each of the countries of this region there has been a National Council of Churches (NCC) that was established to foster mutual understanding and collaboration between the Protestant churches. Although the Roman Catholic Church is a member of national councils in many countries around the world, at the time of writing it is not in membership of any of the councils in the countries of the subcontinent. The NCC in Bangladesh was founded in 1949, and includes 10 member churches and 6 associated member bodies. The NCC in India was formed in 1921 as the National Christian Council of India, Burma and Ceylon and became the National Council of Churches in India in 1979. It includes 29 member churches, 16 regional councils, and a number of Christian organizations and agencies. The NCC in Myanmar was founded in 1949 and has 13 member churches and a number of co-operating bodies. As a very new body (it was founded in 1999) in a country with a very small Christian population, the NCC in Nepal has yet to work out its membership and constitution, but given the history of Christianity in the country during the century its coming into existence at the end of the century was significant in itself. The NCC in Pakistan came into existence in 1948 and has 4 member churches and a number of associate member organizations. The Christian Conference of Asia provides a forum where these councils and their member churches can work in partnership.

Evangelical Fellowships have also been formed to bring evangelical Christians and churches into closer relationship with each other. There has been considerable growth in the number of evangelical Christians in the region during the century. These fellowships, which are affiliated to the World Evangelical Alliance, bring them into closer relationships with the world Church as well as with one another. Each of the countries of the region has an Evangelical Fellowship which is affiliated to the Evangelical Fellowship of Asia. The significance of these fellowships is indicated by the fact that the Indian Fellowship, for example, has almost 150 member bodies and churches. (For an evaluation of the significance of the Lausanne Covenant in the Asian context, see *SCM Core Reader*, 8.4.)

Challenges

A number of issues challenged Christians in the subcontinent during the twentieth century. As a conclusion to this chapter, we will review briefly two of the key issues and outline ways in which Christians have responded.

Pluralism

All the churches in the region (except in north-east India) have existed in a context of religious pluralism. Hinduism, Buddhism and Islam have been the dominant religions in India, Sri Lanka, Pakistan and Bangladesh respectively. Within each country, there has been a substantial minority from another world religion. Consequently, inter-religious tensions have on occasion led to conflict, violence and civil war, such as the conflicts between Hindus and Muslims in Kashmir, between Buddhists and Hindus in Sri Lanka and between Sikhs and Hindus in certain areas of India.

These are often very difficult and challenging contexts for Christian churches. For example, there has been growing evidence, especially towards the end of the twentieth century, that the very small Christian community in Pakistan has found it increasingly difficult, faced with the persecution it has suffered within an Islamic state. In a study of the situation in Pakistan, Patrick Sookhdeo (who is Director of the Institute for the Study of Islam and Christianity), quotes[30] the Church of England Bishop Michael Nazir-Ali (formerly general secretary of the Church Mission Society): 'The life of the Church of Pakistan is lived out today in a context which is becoming more and more difficult. There is cause for concern and even for fear.'[31] In situations such as this, evangelism, Christian witness and dialogue become critical and sometimes conflictive issues.

On the other hand, Christians have sought to explore creative ways of responding to pluralism in the region. A statement by the Third Assembly of the Christian Conference of Asia in 1964 on 'Christian Encounter with People of Other Beliefs' reflects on the nature of dialogue and concludes:

> The dialogical situation within which the Christian encounter takes place is characterized ... by the universality of the gospel as it encompasses all men [sic], the mutuality that is promised when the dialogue takes place in honest and loving openness and the finality of Christ himself who alone is Lord.[32]

In a paper presented to a conference held in 2000, organized by the Council for World Mission and hosted by the University of Cambridge, M. Thomas Thangaraj[33]sets out a number of principles which could shape the Christian response (see *SCM Core Reader*, 8.5). These include:

- The challenge to join a wider circle of engagement, so that Christians draw not only on their own traditions but also upon those of other religions.
- The challenge to redefine boundaries, in view of the effects of globalization on religious communities.
- The challenge to renegotiate catholicity in an unjust and unequal world and in a Church that includes both rich and poor.
- The challenge to formulate a new theology of religions. Christian theology can no longer be defined solely by the Christian tradition and landscape. It must draw on dialogue with the other religions if Christians are to find their place theologically in a plural society.

Wesley Ariarajah, a Sri Lankan theologian, formerly on the staff of the World Council of Churches and now Professor of Theology at Drew University, USA, expresses the same conviction (see *SCM Core Reader*, 8.6):

> In the long run, what Asia needs is a 'wider ecumenism' or 'an ecumenism of religious traditions' that transcend and run parallel to Christian ecumenism – the destiny of the Christian peoples of Asia is no doubt tied up with the destiny of all its people. Building actual relationships across religious communities, which are recognized for who they are, is a necessary process on the road to a wider ecumenism.[34]

There are challenges here not just for the churches of Asia but for world Christianity in the twenty-first century.

Pluralism does not only demand a religious and theological response. Clearly, it has deep social and political consequences in the region. The churches often become engaged, therefore, in the search for socio-political responses. One example is the costly involvement of the Sri Lankan churches, and especially their leaders, in the search for reconciliation and peace in the conflict with the Tamil Tigers in the Jaffna province.

Poverty and marginalization

In all the countries under consideration in this chapter, poverty and marginalization have continued to have their devastating consequences throughout the century. For example, EconomyWatch figures indicate that whereas there was a percentage reduction of people in absolute poverty in India from 51 per cent to 26 per cent between 1977 and 1999, the real numbers of people in poverty are still alarmingly high: 328 million in 1977 and 260 million in 1999. World Bank figures for Bangladesh indicate a similar trend. Whereas there was a percentage reduction between 1991 and 2000 from approximately 60 per cent to 50 per cent, population growth meant that the real figure remained unchanged at 60 million people. The poor have also been in the majority in most of the churches. Inevitably, therefore, considerable effort has been made to channel aid from overseas donors, and the churches have often been at the forefront of radical and transformative funding schemes. However, although overseas aid has played a key role in 'development', of greater long-term significance have been projects aimed at economic and socio-political transformation.

One significant example is the commitment to the Dalit community in India. Dalits are part of India's indigenous community. Formerly known as the untouchables, they have suffered considerable injustice and oppression throughout the century (and indeed throughout the centuries) – a situation that has its origins within their traditional socio-religious status. The term Dalit means 'broken and oppressed people'. Despite efforts to give them proper recognition and status within the communities, they have remained marginalized and poor.

In 1992, the Dalit Solidarity Programme was set up in India to address this continuing injustice. Its stated aims were:

- to bring together the Dalits in solidarity with one another, cutting across their religious, linguistic, regional and ideological differences;
- to work in close association with other indigenous people (Tribals) to be of support in [sic] each other and resolve their common problems;
- to evolve an alternate education system which would direct people at large towards a path of equality and justice, and conscientize the enslaved and margnalized Dalits to realize their worth and power; and
- to internationalize the Dalit issue for total liberation of the marginalized sections across the world.[35]

The WCC's Dalit Solidarity Programme was established 'to support the dalit struggle in India, assist its internal organization and development, and raise awareness of dalit issues within WCC member churches, international fora including the United Nations and the wider international constituency'.

Dalit theology has been developing in India over recent years as a form of liberation theology: '[P]athos and suffering are the essence of dalit existence, and it is the experience of suffering that mediates to dalits their knowledge of God. "We proclaim and affirm ... that Jesus Christ himself was a dalit – despite his being a Jew."'[36]

There has been an Evangelical critique of Dalit theology, partly because it has been consciously influenced by liberation theology, partly because some have maintained that the Dalits' oppression originates to some degree from the acceptance of the caste system by Christian missionaries in the past and partly because they discern in the call for Dalit solidarity an acceptance of the socio-religious status of Dalits in Indian society. One example of an Evangelical voice is that of Vinay Samuel who called for an attempt 'to establish more realistic economic routes to transformation rather than the political solutions of Dalit theology'.[37] (For an account of Dalit theology, see *SCM Core Reader*, 8.7.)

Final reflection

At the beginning of the twenty-first century, our brief survey of Christianity in the subcontinent brings into focus a number of key reflections. First, the growing significance of India as an economic, commercial and political force in the region and worldwide, means that it will inevitably become a key arena for exploring the implications of growing globalization on societies such as those in the subcontinent and the ways in which faith communities (not least the Christian community) respond to these diverse challenges. The fact that the churches in this region exist in situations of frequently stark economic disparity, poverty and persecution will pose key challenges to the paradigm of inevitable globalization. How can the churches contribute to society's struggle with a growing global role in business and financial services, while also tackling the continuing poverty throughout the subcontinent? How can the benefits of globalization for the economic well-being of the nations of the region be shared more equitably? How can the economic divide, between the nouveau riche (especially in India) and those in poverty, be addressed and who should address them? Should these issues be tackled by the individuals themselves, by governments or by international financial institutions? What responsibilities should the national and global Christian communities carry in this regard?

Second, the diversity of Christianity in the region will continue to be both an enrichment and a challenge. As we have seen, the subcontinent has set an example to other world regions in establishing united churches during the last half century. Nevertheless, the challenge of wider and deeper partnership and unity remains. Can these united churches become catalysts for this wider unity within the subcontinent or (as many claim in other regions of the world) are these structured patterns of union no longer the most creative ways of responding to the gospel call to unity and the need for a united Christian witness? In other words, can the united churches in the subcontinent act as uniting (rather than united) churches and be means of drawing other Christian communities into unity and union?

Third, one important aspect of this ecumenical challenge will be to develop new patterns of relationships, partnerships and, hopefully, deeper unity, between those churches already engaged in ecumenical councils and, on the one hand, Evangelical and Pentecostal churches and fellowships and, on the other hand, the Roman Catholic Church. It may be that the minority status of the Christian community may well provide a creative context for such developments in the future, and offer insights for Christians in other regions where Christianity has become or is becoming a minority faith.

Fourth, Christianity is a minority faith in each of the nations of the subcontinent, and as such the churches' response to a pluralism of faiths and religious practice in such settings will be a significant contribution to worldwide Christianity's grappling with the challenge and opportunity of pluralism in other contexts. Thangaraj's analysis (see above, p. 139) provides a foundational paradigm for creative mutual relationships between faith communities and for an enlarging of theological and religious horizons. At the end of his analysis, Thangaraj makes two predictions. He writes:

> Every discipline within the theological curriculum will take into account [aspects] of interreligious conversation and dialogical engagement ... [and will] be pervaded by an ethos of dialogical engagement ...
> I am confident that a time will come, very soon, when it will be seen as vulgar and anachronistic if a Christian theologian, when faced with a theological issue, does not ask himself or herself: what do my Hindu friends or Muslim friends or others have to say about this? That to me is the greatest challenge of religious pluralism today.[38]

Throughout the twentieth century, Christian leaders from the region played highly significant roles in informing and shaping the self-understanding, unity and witness of the world Church. In the new century, global Christianity must continue to learn important lessons from the way Christians in the subcontinent, their churches and leaders, engage with these challenges. The questions of globalization and poverty, Christian unity and diversity, and Christian identity and pluralism are not just challenges for the subcontinent but for Christian churches worldwide.

Further reading

K. C. Abraham and T. K. Thomas, 'Asia' (2004), in J. Briggs, M. Oduyoye and G. Tstetsis (eds), *A History of the Ecumenical Movement Volume Three 1968–2000*, includes helpful assessments of the churches, especially of their ecumenical relationships.

V. S. Azariah (1936), *India and the Christian Movement*, Madras: CLS, provides a valuable insight on Christianity in India from the perspective of an Indian leader in the early decades of the century.

M. Gibbs (1970), *The Anglican Church in India, 1600–1970*, India: SPCK, gives an overview of the Anglican missionary enterprise and the development of the Anglican Church in India.

Anyone with an interest in the unique story of Christianity in north-east India should read the very sympathetic account of the last 150 years or so:

J. M. Lloyd (1991), *History of the Church in Mizoram*, Aizawl: Synod Publications Board.

Four books provide helpful insights on the Indian subcontinent within the context of broader studies of Asia:

N. Koshy (ed.) (2004), *A History of the Ecumenical Movement in India*, vols I and II, Hong Kong: WSCF/YMCA/CCA. This two-volume history of the ecumenical movement in Asia provides a historical survey of Christianity in Asia during the century, with a particular focus on ecumenical developments.

For a critical analysis of the relationship between the western missionary enterprise and Asian Christian identity:

K. M. Pannikar (1953), *Asia and Western Dominance*, London: George Allen and Unwin.

C. Sugden (1997), *Seeking the Asian Face of Jesus*, Oxford: Regnum, provides a very perceptive evangelical perspective on Christianity in Asia.

Notes

1 N. Koshy (ed.) (2004), *A History of the Ecumenical Movement in Asia*, vol. I., Hong Kong: WSCF/YMCA/CCA, p. 8.
2 Koshy (ed.), *A History*, p. 11.
3 K. M. Pannikar (1953), *Asia and Western Dominance*, London: George Allen and Unwin, p. 455.
4 H. R. Weber (1966), *Asia and the Ecumenical Movement*, London: SCM Press.
5 N. Lossky et al. (eds) (1991), *Dictionary of the Ecumenical Movement*, first edn, Geneva: WCC Publications, p. 73.
6 V. S. Azariah (1936), *India and the Christian Movement*, Madras: CLS, p. 81.
7 Koshy (ed.), *A History*, vol. I, p. 41.
8 Koshy (ed.), *A History*, vol. I, p. 49.
9 Koshy (ed.), *A History*, vol. I, p. 69.
10 Weber, *Asia*, p. 162.
11 Azariah, *India*, p. 89.
12 Lossky et al. (eds), *Dictionary*, p. 647.
13 V. Fabella (2004), *The Roman Catholic Church in the Asian Ecumenical Movement*, in Koshy, *A History*, vol. II, p. 118.
14 Information on these churches based on http://michigan.csichurch.com/
15 For an authoritative account of the early history of the mission and the growth of the church, see J. M. Lloyd (1991), *History of the Church in Mizoram*, Aizawl: Synod Publication Board.
16 Lloyd, *Church in Mizoram*, p. 35.
17 L. Pachuau (2003), 'Church-mission Dynamics in Northeast India, *The International Bulletin of Missionary Research*, October.
18 Lloyd, *Church in Mizoram*, pp. 349f.
19 B. Palmer (1999), *Imperial Vineyard: The Anglican Church in India under the Raj from the Mutiny to Partition*, Sussex: The Book Guild, p. 92.
20 Quoted in Palmer, *Imperial Vineyard*, p. 226.
21 from www.indianchristianity.org/ csi
22 L. Newbigin (1985), *Unfinished Agenda: An Autobiography*, Geneva: WCC Publications (through special arrangement with SPCK, London), p. 87.
23 K. C. Abraham and T. K. Thomas (2004), 'Asia', in Briggs et al. (eds), *A History*, vol. III, p. 503.
24 Newbigin, *Unfinished Agenda*, p. 96.
25 H. van Beek (ed.) (2006), *A Handbook of Churches and Councils*, Geneva: WCC Publications, p. 251.

26 Abraham and Thomas, 'Asia', p. 503.
27 In T. F. Best and G. Gassmann (eds) (1994), *On the Way to Fuller Koinonia: Official Report of the Fifth World Conference on Faith and Order*, Geneva: WCC Publications, p. 147.
28 Abraham and Thomas, 'Asia', p. 504.
29 van Beek, *Handbook*, p. 296.
30 P. Sookhdeo (2002), *A People Betrayed: The Impact of Islamization on the Christian Community in Pakistan*, Fearn Ross-shire: Christian Focus Publications and Pewsey Wiltshire: Isaac Publishing, p. 351.
31 M. Nazir-Ali (1987), *Frontiers in Muslim–Christian Encounter*, Oxford: Regnum Books, p. 91.
32 D. J. Elwood (1980), *Asian Christian Theology: Emerging Themes*, Philadelphia: Westminster Press, p. 219.
33 M. T. Thangaraj (2000), 'The Challenge of Religious Plurality', in K. Wickeri et al. (eds), *Plurality, Power and Mission*, London and Hong Kong: CWM/CCA, pp. 200ff.
34 W. Ariarajah (2004), 'Christianity and People of Other Religious Traditions', in Koshy, (ed.), *A History*, vol. II, p. 163.
35 See http://www.oikoumene.org/?id=2643 (September 1998).
36 A. P. Nirmal, quoted by Abraham and Thomas, 'Asia', p. 500.
37 Quoted in C. Sugden (1997), *Seeking the Asian Face of Jesus*, Oxford: Regnum, pp. 445f.
38 Thangaraj, 'Religious Plurality', pp. 211f.

9

East Asia and the Pacific

This chapter has to cover an astonishingly large part of the globe – something like half the ocean space, and over a quarter of the human population! Simply for reasons of space it will need to pass briefly over all too many interesting personalities and episodes. The books listed for further reading at the end will provide more substantial material for those whose interest is kindled.

The Islands of the Pacific – a latter-day Christendom?

In the late 1970s, says Charles Forman,

> the Pacific Islands were in all probability the most solidly Christian part of the world. At the beginning of the century many island peoples had still not heard the Christian message. Seventy-five years later that situation had changed completely. Practically all of the islanders, except for the Indian people in Fiji, were Christians. The people were more devoted in Christian belief and gave to the churches a larger place in their life than did the people of any other region. Christianity was more important here than in Europe, America or Australasia, the lands from which missionaries to the Pacific had first come.[1]

In fact the very first Christian missionaries were Spanish. 'In 1668 the Spanish queen mother and regent, Mariana, sent a Jesuit mission from the Philippines to Guam in the Ladrones (= thieves, in Spanish) Islands, which were renamed in Mariana's honour.'[2] After a first, surprisingly 'successful' year in which 13,000 people were baptized, the missionaries aroused emotions that led to horrific scenes, all too often repeated elsewhere in later years. 'When Guamanians were told that Christianity would call for abandoning the traditional sexual freedom of their "bachelor houses" and the cults of their ancestors, resistance to the mission stiffened.' A lengthy war eventually 'swept both northern and southern islands until the completion of Spanish conquest by 1694. It has been estimated that about 5,000 of a pre-war population of 100,000 survived the violence and accompanying epidemics.'[3]

In the eighteenth century the Spanish were largely supplanted by Dutch, British and French explorers in this vast region. Many of the islands' peoples had long experience of the arrival of ships sailed by white-skinned Europeans before any organized Christian missionary efforts were undertaken. In 1796 the first group sent out, by the non-denominational society that was soon to be known as the London Missionary Society, was to the island of Tahiti. This had been claimed for Britain in 1769 by Captain James Cook, himself killed in Hawaii in 1779 when one of his men drew a gun in an unnecessary quarrel with some indigenous islanders. The missionaries found a remarkably discouraging situation there, with rivalries between different groups to some degree following different 'religious' loyalties. They were soon caught up in a web of such difficulty that half the party took advantage of the next ship to arrive, an American ship, to disappear in search of a better future in Sydney. Yet in the end, not least after long periods of the missionaries being out of contact with London because of the Napoleonic wars, the indigenous 'king' to whom they had attached themselves won out over his adversaries in 1815, was baptized in 1819, and oversaw a period in which the new religion became the 'established' church in a way that hardly pleased the strictly 'non-conformist' ideas of the British party!

Hawaii was then itself the scene of a second 'total beginning' when the American Board of Commissioners for Foreign Missions sent out in 1819, as their first project, an inexperienced and unprepared group of earnest North American Calvinists, accompanied by three young Hawaiians who had spent some years in New England as students. Arriving soon after the unexpected death of the great King Kamehameha, and the suspension by his widow of the whole *kapu* system, 'a supernatural sanctioned web of custom, radiating holiness, and enforced by fear of the spirits' revenge',[4] they gradually found themselves being warmly welcomed by the royal family and within a few years 'leading' a church into which something like half the population was willingly, if hardly articulately, crowding.

These beginnings were followed in a thousand other situations throughout the far-flung islands across the South Pacific over the nineteenth and early twentieth centuries. Each group had their own culture and history, with different rulers and leading personalities, and they received missionaries chiefly from Britain and France, the two European nations claiming most of these island groups as 'their own'. Yet there were also no small numbers of Spanish Catholic missionaries moving in where they could, and with Germans, both Protestant and Catholic, joining vigorously later in the nineteenth century as Germany claimed several important areas, not least the northern side of the eastern half of the 'big island'. Its 'western' half was already claimed by the Dutch, though the British – including again the London Missionary Society – had long since started to work along the southern shore.

It must be emphasized that the stories of each of these island groups are strikingly different in detail. What, however, is relatively true – and importantly distinct from the other areas to be surveyed in this chapter – is that in one way or another, the Christian faith fairly soon became welcome to the rulers and before long to the great majority of the populations of them all, even to those – for instance the hundreds of different tribes in the highlands of New Guinea – who at first seemed determined to reject any outside interruptions to their long-established patterns of life. Even more true is that the carrying of the Good News of Jesus as the revelation of the one and highest God was largely done by fellow islanders. From Tonga, Samoa and Fiji in particular, three of the larger groups and where churches had quickly become hugely popular, many islanders took the initiative to visit other islands as yet unenlightened. They mostly proved to be admirably welcome and effective transmitters of the Good News. (See *SCM Core Reader on World Christianity in the Twentieth Century*, 9. 1 for insight into their way of presenting the gospel.)

The major 'event', which was to transform a scene that had to a large degree settled down into a relatively tranquil 'Christendom' situation, was the Second World War, especially the build-up in Japanese-dominated areas (for example, the Caroline Islands taken over by Japan from Germany at the outset of the First World War) of military preparations for the air attack that destroyed the US fleet in Pearl Harbor, Hawaii, on 7 December 1941, and then the vast, largely air-initiated, Japanese invasions throughout South-East Asia and much of the Pacific that followed swiftly. The fiercest fighting in resistance to the Japanese was in Papua New Guinea, where they never quite succeeded in capturing Port Moresby, the town that the Australians, acting for the British, had made the effective capital. But the fighting did involve the central highland areas, previously entered only by a few handfuls of explorers and missionaries, to the lasting shock of the peoples who lived there without any previous contact with the coastal regions.

In the second phase of the Pacific war, starting from the significant victory of the American air forces over the Japanese in the Midway Islands in June 1942, the long slow advance of the USA and its allies, contested bitterly all the way, brought untold suffering, oppression and deprivation to almost all the peoples of the Pacific.

> They were trapped between armies. The eyes of many survivors were opened to the consequences of involuntary colonial captivity. The great powers, which had once appeared to be sponsors of Christian missions, had brought destruction and death. Protestants had heard and sung the hymn 'Onward Christian soldiers, marching as to war'. Yet the 'warfare' of the 'One, Holy, Catholic and Apostolic Church', which had been born, according to the creed, in a period of military occupation and suffering 'under Pontius Pilate', was understood as never before to be a gospel of peace and good will, vastly differing in its essential central symbol, the Cross, from the motives and conduct of the 'war and rumours of wars' so many Islanders had endured.[5]

The Second World War ended in August 1945 with the horror of the atomic bombs dropped on Hiroshima and Nagasaki. But that was in turn the beginning of another era of fear, oppression and expropriation for the Pacific, if now for small pockets of its peoples, especially in the Marshall Islands, where the USA used Bikini Atoll for a series of atomic and hydrogen bomb tests in the 1940s and 50s (*SCM Core Reader*, 9.2), and in French Polynesia where Moruroa and Fangataufa were used by the French for similar purposes until the early 1990s. Given the continuing use of the Marshalls for long-range missile testing, and the unwillingness of both French and British Governments to abandon their reliance on nuclear arms as a 'last resort', the nuclear threat remains a spectre hanging over the Pacific, as the Pacific Conference of Churches has on many occasions reminded their fellow Christians around the world.

At the same time, the experience of the Second World War was by no means only negative for the Pacific peoples and for the Christians among them. The sheer wealth, brazen power and human bluntness of western military personnel were important new contacts, revealing what the wider world was really like. The fact that so much harsh responsibility in and for the churches had simply fallen for some years to the indigenous leaders meant a sea change in their own spiritual self-confidence under God, so that neither they nor the missionaries could envisage the latter returning to pick up the reins again. Moreover, the necessity of considerably more contact, under war pressures, between indigenous leaders of the different denominations, above all between Protestant and Catholic, led to a vastly better field of understanding and sympathies than any of them had known earlier. For all the uprooting and destruction the war had brought, it was undoubtedly also a maturing experience for the churches, giving them a wider and deeper sense of the calling to be 'church' over against the dominant powers of the 'world', which has greatly helped their leaders to face up to and to meet the challenges of the second half of the twentieth century.

These new challenges have been to a considerable degree the same now for the Pacific as for other parts of our irreversibly one world:

- the need for much better systems of training pastors and church leaders;
- the needs and opportunities to share in nation-building;
- the growing economic and political pressures of powerful multinational firms from outside the area identifying the resources they want and will relentlessly take, whatever the interests of the local people;
- the weakening of the traditional village churches as so many of the younger and educated people go off to the urban areas; and
- the consumerism of smaller but powerful sections of the population enriched by the incoming economic powers, including those of international tourism.

None of these is peculiar to the Pacific. Yet the Pacific churches have given themselves both the will and the means to tackle many of the challenges that arise, for instance in the Pacific Council of Churches, created in a series of meetings from 1961 onwards and which welcomed the Roman Catholic Church into full membership in 1976, the Melanesian Council of Churches gathering the wide variety of churches in Papua New Guinea and the immediately surrounding islands, and in the happy partnership of the Pacific Theological College, in Suva, Fiji, and the Roman Catholic Pacific Regional Seminary built in 1972 within walking distance.

Japan – a radically different culture

Japan is in one sense the 'odd man out' in this chapter, in that the Christian faith, despite three strong periods of growth in different epochs, has – yet – neither lastingly attracted growing numbers of Japanese, nor penetrated the distinctive Japanese cultural tradition as effectively as in the Pacific, Korea or China. Nonetheless, Japan had a tumultuous history throughout the twentieth century, with very 'high' as well as very 'low' moments, and remains a country and a people of the highest importance for the future of humanity. We shall do well to follow what happens to Christian faith there with both attention and prayer.

Christianity first 'arrived' with St Francis Xavier in 1549, in the southern island of Kyushu, where a local civil war was underway. Some of the local rulers were glad of outside support, and so ordered their people to adopt this foreign religion. This initiated a period of considerable 'success', with some 200 local churches within 30 years. Xavier took himself off in 1551 but his Jesuit colleagues moved into other areas and in 1559 one of them was granted an audience with the then Shogun (military ruler). Things became more difficult when Spanish Franciscan missionaries arrived from the Philippines in 1593, still more so when in the early 1600s both Dutch and English traders arrived, with their Protestant convictions, inevitably suggesting that the European powers were looking for some sort of 'conquest'. In 1606, Christianity, despite having gained some 250,000 adherents, was declared illegal – a declaration that was not followed through immediately but which prepared the way for the appalling tragedies of 1637–38 when all missionaries were expelled and the local Christians nearly all exterminated. Shusaku Endo's two novels about those Christians (see 'Further reading' at the end of this chapter) recount key episodes in this, still the most important 'moment' in the history of Christianity in Japan.

A remnant remained in the far south, but for most purposes Christian faith and all other foreign contacts were rigorously excluded from Japan until the 'opening up' by the 'Black Ships' from North America under Commodore Matthew Perry in 1853. That led in turn to the 'Meiji Restoration' (a new imperial dynasty) in 1868 and an all-out rush by thousand upon thousand of Japanese to familiarize themselves with every possible facet of the western civilization that seemed so much more powerful and successful than their own. In 1859 the first Protestant (North American) missionaries arrived, as did a French Catholic priest. At first they found at best a hesitant welcome. Kozaki Hiromichi wrote about the ways his fellow students who became Christians at the time had been treated: 'Some were placed in solitary confinement at home; some were cast out by their families. One mother tried to make her son recant by threatening to commit suicide; another parent confronted his son with a drawn sword.'[6] Yet after the notices proscribing Christianity were lifted in 1873, the missionaries' efforts to interest members of the former 'samurai' (noble) class met with some success, even if the dominant Buddhists were clearly strongly hostile.

By the outset of the twentieth century, the missionaries of both major traditions had taken initiatives to create a network of educational institutions from nurseries to universities that led the way in preparing young Japanese for the 'modern' skills and outlook that were so eagerly sought. Japan was rushing by every conceivable channel into the 'new world' of western modernity, and very successfully so, as was demonstrated by its success in the battles in northeast China of the 1890s and then the epoch-making surprise (to the West!) of its victory over the Russian army in 1904. That led throughout the first half of the twentieth century to an ever-increasing stress on military prowess and a nationalist outlook, which led the majority of Christians to accept successive imperial orders, not least the 'Imperial Rescript on Education' of 1890 which 'enjoined all citizens to loyalty, filial piety and sacrifice for the state to maintain the imperial throne'.

In the same years, the number of Christians was increasing steadily, up to some 300,000 by 1939,[7] one-third of them Catholics and most of them from the class of urban, educated and upper-middle-class people who continued to be aware that their close contact with foreign missionaries was hardly helping their acceptance in the wider society. Indeed, one outstanding interpreter and teacher of the Bible, Uchimura Kanzo, broke away from the denominational churches to form a 'Non-Church Movement' which gathered over two generations a considerable following. However, this new movement was probably even less diverse socially and less engaged in society than the churches. There have more recently been a number of Pentecostal-type indigenous Christian initiatives,[8] yet without any having made a decisive breakthrough in either popularity or quality of witness.

A very different figure, Kagawa Toyohiko, probably the most impressive Japanese Christian of the early twentieth century, threw himself tirelessly, from Christmas Day 1909 onwards, into social and peace projects designed to serve the poor and outcast – of which Japan has a full share, not least the *Ainu*, the indigenous inhabitants of the northern island, Hokkaido (see *SCM Core Reader*, 9. 3), and the *buraku* in the cities, the 'discriminated against' 2 per cent, who are still today shunned and despised by 'proper' society. Kagawa travelled and lectured widely, deeply convinced that Christian faith is concerned with the *whole* of human life, as a trade union leader, a social seer, and idealist for his own and every other country, always above all else a preacher and evangelist. 'He informed the moral conscience of a largely non-Christian nation',[9] but his witness was in the same years increasingly drowned out by the war drums of nationalism. In the second half of the century the worldwide Church has had occasion to notice among Japanese Christians above all Kosuke Koyama, who has spent most of his adult life as a missionary outside his homeland, yet whose *Mount Fuji and Mount Sinai* is one of the most profound, self-critical and impressively Christian studies of an author's own culture and nationality. The *SCM Core Reader* (9.4) provides a memorable example of his teaching.

The drums of nationalism led of course to the spectacular entry of Japan into the Second World War with the attack on Pearl Harbor in December 1941 and the swift, often very cruel occupation of large parts of South-East Asia and the Pacific, to add to the significant parts of China already occupied during the 1930s. Japanese Christians kept their heads down throughout the war, although they bore their share of losses in the horrific costs of the hand-to-hand fighting, the naval battles and above all the vast bombardments of the last months of the war culminating in the bombing of Hiroshima and Nagasaki. One relatively minor episode, yet of major importance to Protestant Christians, was the 'union' forced on all Protestant denominations in 1941 by the military leadership into the 'Kyodan' (united church), yet from which a large half of them, if by no means all, split away again as normal church life restarted after 1945. This episode, with its often unspoken decisions about the relative priorities of nationalism and Christian universalism, remains a profoundly sensitive and troubling heritage for Japanese Christians.

As the worst damage of the war receded, Christian faith knew a third period of relatively swift growth, as people looked into a different, and no longer militarily dominated future. In 1947 a Christian, Katayama Tetsu, became Prime Minister, with as many as six fellow Christians in his Cabinet. Yet the period of relative popularity died away in the early 1950s. Christians shared to the full in the astonishing economic triumphs of Japan, both in the automobile industry, as in the wealth that flowed into Japan from the Korean and Vietnam wars. By the turn of the millennium a fresh lead in wealth-creation had long since been taken by the computer industry and the electronics that flow from it. Japan has now known itself for well over a generation once more as a wealthy, successful, democratic society, yet with renewed worries in some quarters about the growing popularity and indeed formal state/national character being given to visits to the Shinto imperial Yasukuni Shrine – and certainly with a marked downturn in the growth of the churches. This last feature contrasts vividly with the enormous growth of the many 'new religions' based loosely on Shinto and Buddhist traditions, most notably the more political Soka Gakkai and the more peace-oriented Rissho Kosei-kai, both with many thousands of active members.

The churches appear to have stuck for years now at a figure of less than 1 per cent of the population,[10] and have been for too long experiencing a dwindling recruitment of pastors and priests. Both major traditions, wrote James Phillips in 1980, 'are so enervated at such a crucial time', while already in the late 1960s Robert Lee summed up his analysis: 'a variety of American patterns of church organization, evangelism, leadership etc. have been transplanted to Japan with only minor adaptation. Consequently, the Christian Church lacks an indigenous identity and remains essentially the Stranger in the land – at times welcomed, at times feared and distrusted.'[11]

One startling exception to these gloomy analyses is the popularity of western-style, and thus Christian, weddings, including the highly publicized church weddings of TV personalities and film stars!

A 1991 survey discovered that the percentage of Christian and church-related weddings was 35.9 in one region and 23.8 in another. ... At the very least the fact that scores of younger Japanese are choosing Christian weddings indicates that the present environment is more open to Christianity and that much of the social stigma attached to the Christian faith has declined during the postwar period.[12]

Precisely what the Holy Spirit sees, intends and will one day bring about is no doubt quite different. Watch this space!

Korea – growth following on oppression

The first Christian known to arrive in the 'Hermit Kingdom' of Korea was a Jesuit who in 1594 came – and went again – with an invading force from

Japan. Many of the Koreans who were seized by that force and taken into slavery in Japan later became Christians there, and were probably martyred with many others in the persecution of the 1600s. It is also known that several of the early Christians in China hoped to visit Korea, then officially in more or less vassal relationship with the Chinese Empire, but never managed it. Yet the first Christians in and of Korea were a group of scholars who in 1777 met at a Buddhist temple to study tracts that had been written and published by Jesuits in China. This group in time became the first Korean Catholic Church, although they and their successors were made to face a cruel series of persecutions by their rulers from 1786 on, the most severe from 1866 to 1871 when at least 8,000, approximately half the believing Christians, together with 9 French priests, were executed. No wonder the Catholic Church by the beginning of the twentieth century had more or less shut itself away in ghetto conditions in mountainous districts in the south.

The first Protestants to touch Korea came by sea: Karl Gutzlaff came exploring along the west coast in 1832. He is known to have made contact with some Catholics and given them Bibles in Chinese. So also a Scottish missionary, Robert J. Thomas, took sail in 1866 on a US trading ship bound for the capital Pyongyang, and died when it was wrecked by the captain's carelessness. More important, another Scot, the Revd Dr John Ross (1842–1915) of the United Presbyterian Church, settled in China near the strictly closed border with Korea and was able through contacts and friendship with Koreans to produce between 1874 and 1887 a first primer about the Korean language, a history of Korea in English, and the entire New Testament in Korean. By this time, however, Japan had imposed on the weak Korean monarchy a first treaty to open up the shut-away country, with the USA and the British and German Empires quick to follow suit. So the first North American Protestant missionaries – both Presbyterians and Methodists – arrived in 1885 and soon started an impressive programme of schools and hospitals. By 1900 they had made good progress. They enjoyed the tacit support of the king and had not had to face any organized opposition – indeed many young progressives were delighted to follow the promise they brought of western-style development. The capital city hosted a 'Great Revival' in 1907, whose effects spread into the whole Korean peninsula and parts of Manchuria, so that by 1910 Korean Protestants already counted for more than 1 per cent of the entire population – a percentage never yet reached in Japan.

But this was precisely when Korea was forced into submission by Japan. A 'triangular struggle' for influence over Korea between Japan, China and Russia had led to Japanese victories in China and then in the Russo-Japanese war. Japan quickly established a 'Residency' in Pyongyang, declared Korea a 'Protectorate' in 1907, and forcibly annexed it to the Japanese Empire in 1910. Immediate outcomes included the confiscation of much land, the imposition of laws for business and economic life that favoured Japanese interests and a decree that all schools must teach only in the Japanese language – to which last the missionaries and their followers only adhered with the greatest of reluctance. No wonder that already in 1919 there was an act of protest by a public declaration, of whose 33 signatories 15 were Christians. They insisted on a non-violent approach, but were brutally treated by the Japanese, with many churches burnt down and many Christians killed. The occupying force's insistence also on the paying of homage at a national Shinto shrine for Korea was long resisted, again with the price of no few deaths. This entire period to 1945 was deeply unhappy for the Korean people. Resentments and arguments over who had and who had not obeyed Japanese laws continued for some time after the occupation finished with the end of the Second World War.

During these same years there grew up a marked division among Korean Protestants between those believing that their faith required of them action on social concerns and an open, exploring mode of theological enquiry, and those who saw their prime obedience in 'church growth' and who in matters theological held firm to a traditional, often relatively literal, reading of the Bible. This split has continued to shape the history of the Christian faith in Korea, despite considerable diversity of understandings and actions in both groups.

The Second World War had hardly dwindled into history when the tensions between the northern part of the country, ruled since 1945 by the Soviet Union, and the southern part ruled initially by the USA, burst in June 1950 into an all-out war. At first, an offensive from the North swept over much of the South, only to be met by a rapidly assembled force under the United Nations which gradually pushed the North Korean troops, by now joined by the Chinese, back almost to the Chinese border. It eventually ended in a 'truce' in 1953 with a border along the original line that has remained – despite a very small number of recent contacts – the most tightly closed in the world. Among many other painful and distressing episodes, this war saw a large-scale flight of Christians from North to South, such that the remaining churches of the North, under the tight-fisted rule of the 'Communist' Party, have ever since hardly been able to be visited, let alone to give their own witness in the wider world.

The war was disastrous also for the Korean people in the South. Yet, as the years passed, the country recovered. Frustrations with the long-serving President Syngman Rhee, although a prominent Christian, resulted in a student-led revolution in 1960 which drove Rhee from office. But he was hardly gone when the military stepped in and initiated a period of military rule which was to last over 18 years. But these were also years of growth, not least for the churches, including now the Catholic Church, several of whose leaders took a strong part in the eventual movements that restored fully democratic and civilian rule in 1987/88.

Since 1945 there have been no limits imposed within South Korea either on incoming missionaries or on the founding of new churches. While Presbyterians remain a major 'type' there are some 87 different factions within it. Many other denominations have come in, and not a few have been created from within. These have included the 'Holy Spirit Association for the Unification of World Christianity', otherwise known as the Moonies after its founder Sun-Myung Moon, which by the end of the century had lost all credibility as a Christian community. On a pattern also well known in the USA, Korea has seen the rise of many 'mega-churches' counting their members in thousands, and now boasts the largest single church building anywhere in the world to house a congregation that is numbered in tens of thousands.

The Protestant churches are also known to be among the most 'productive' around the world in sending out missionaries to other areas. At one time there were said to be 3,000 Korean missionaries in Siberia. There is unfortunately also – not for the first or only time – evidence that they repeat the mistakes of their forerunners from other backgrounds. But with the founding of 293 secondary schools and 40 universities on Christian foundations, and the overall number of Protestant Christians having risen from 6 per cent of the population in 1970 to 25 per cent by the end of the century, with the Catholics also making strong advances, it is hardly surprising if Christians in South Korea see themselves becoming before long a majority in an Asian country, for the first time since the Spanish conquest of the Philippines.

One distinctive movement in theological exploration that has arisen in South Korea is that of minjung theology, taking seriously, indeed as its starting point, the actual experience of the 'ordinary people' who have had to suffer the undersides of history even in those periods which the 'top people' may have considered successful. *SCM Core Reader*, 9.5, by the well-known academic, Professor Kim Yong-Bok, provides one quick example of this. As in other countries, the Second Vatican Council opened hearts and minds to the possibilities for Roman Catholics to work together with other churches. This has made a big difference also in South Korea, though the dominance of more 'conservative evangelical' views among the Protestants means that the National Council of Churches has had to struggle for even small steps towards any overall Christian unity.

At the turn of the century, there seemed to be some chance for the long-hoped-for reunion between the two Koreas, with visits of the respective heads of government in both directions. This has been probably for over 60 years now the single most ardently desired change among the people of both states. It remains something of a mirage. Yet when it comes Christians from both 'sides' will deserve a significant part of the credit for their constant care, hope and prayer about it.

Australia and New Zealand – a very different set of clashes between 'old' and 'new'

Aborigines reckon they have been living in Australia for something like 40,000 years. The Maori look back to their ancestors arriving from Hawaiki in the Pacific in 11 canoes, each carrying a different tribe, around a thousand years ago. But Christian faith first arrived in both Australia and New Zealand in the aftermath of European adventurers, the Dutchman Abel Tasman in 1642, and the Englishman Captain James Cook in 1770. It was a grim omen that on each of those two arrivals both European and indigenous men were killed on the beach because some sort of quarrel broke out between groups who totally failed to understand one another.

British ships carrying passengers arrived not so very long after Captain Cook, in 1788 in the bay that is now Sydney Harbour, in order to establish a prison settlement there for particularly unwanted and socially outcast criminals from the British Isles. A generation later, in 1814, the Revd Samuel Marsden, chaplain since 1790 to the Australian settlement, sailed with a group of missionaries into a bay in what was to become the city of Auckland, towards the tip of the North Island of what the Maori know as Aotearoa and the British call New Zealand. There he preached the first Christian sermon, presumably to the small congregation who had come with him, perhaps with a few curious Maori looking on. In both cases it took some time for significant numbers of other British to arrive in order to settle in this distant part of the globe, but when they did they almost all came in order to make a new life and to be able to explore and expand over the beauties and fertility of these new lands, that is, with hopes and expectations to which any Christian faith they had was relatively tangential, and which in no way took into account any people already living there.

In the case of Australia, the early contacts between Europeans and Aborigines proved almost totally unhelpful all round. There was as good as no mutual understanding, no expectation of friendship or mutual support, no experience of being able to learn the others' language(s) or of positively benefiting from what the other was doing or wanting to do. Already the early chaplains to the prison settlement gave up on any idea of active evangelization – indeed it was probably because Marsden had heard from some traveller that the 'natives' in New Zealand were somewhat easier to approach that he took leave from his duties in Sydney and went over to New Zealand in the hope of starting a more effective missionary project there. Within a few years he was joined by other Anglican clergy, as by friendly Methodist ministers who based themselves on the other side of the island, and not so long after by less friendly Roman Catholic clergy, from France.

By 1845 it could be reckoned that of some 110,000 Maori on the North Island, at least 60,000 of them regularly attended services of one of these groups of Christians. In particular the Christian emphasis on peace was proving of considerable value in resolving long-standing enmities between different tribes, so that there was a definite atmosphere of Maori acceptance, indeed of their creative inculturation of the new faith into their own spirituality and architecture. As always, it was as Maori Christians witnessed to their own relatives and neighbours that the missionaries could see that their initial work was earning the hoped-for reward. One signal outcome of this early 'success' of the missionaries was an initiative taken by the Anglican priests. As soon as they heard that the British Government was sending a 'Governor' for the new colony, they invited both him and the Maori chiefs to sign, in February 1840, the Treaty of Waitangi by which the chiefs agreed to hand over to the great Queen Victoria of England the 'sovereignty'/'Kawanatanga' of their lands and accepted her governor's promise to respect and 'guarantee' the 'entire supremacy of the Chiefs and all the people of New Zealand of their lands, their settlements and their personal property'.[13]

Nothing of this happened among the Aborigines in Australia. As the numbers of new settlers grew and grew, so the Aborigines found themselves increasingly pushed out of the more fertile areas onto the edges of what was rather quickly to become the ring of coastal settlements down the east coast and round the south-east and south-west corners of the enormous, but already then largely desert territory. Missionaries did later indeed arrive and started schools and medical stations to 'help' the Aborigines, but almost always with a paternalism and a lack of the ability to establish real mutual understanding, let alone friendship – if admittedly with people of perhaps the most unusual cultural background that had ever faced newly arriving Christians – yet which was to last far too long! Also in Aotearoa/New Zealand the substantial numbers of settlers arriving from the British Isles in the second half of the nineteenth century took very little notice of the Maori, even after their self-regarding land-grabbing had led to not a little fighting and loss of life in several areas.

Within a couple of generations, the sheer quantity of European settlers, in both lands far beyond that of the indigenous, soon drove the latter into almost totally dependent and secondary positions, leaving the Europeans virtually total power to develop the kind of societies they had been hoping for. In many fields, not least that of 'religion', this meant following, often rather conservatively, the familiar practice of the homeland. So the 'Christian history' of these two newly established nations is – to a European mind – extraordinarily similar to that of their homelands. English arguing with Scots over Calvinism, Irish defending Roman Catholicism over against a British tendency to secularism, and many other familiar headline-filling awkwardnesses can be found down the years. Partly for this reason, no doubt, both countries have very largely known in the twentieth century, the long, slow, ebbing-away of Christian faith, typical of relatively wealthy, post-Christian Europe (see Chapter 12 below), in favour of a high degree of individualism coupled with an increasingly consumerist society where what you possess and how you spend your money is of far 'higher' importance than any belief in God. One significant exception to this has been the formation in 1977 of the 'Uniting Church of Australia' from out of the earlier Congregationalists, Methodists and a large part, but not all, of the Presbyterians. This has flourished well in many regards, not least in initiating, in partnership with the Anglicans and Roman Catholics, a formal public apology in 1996 to the Aboriginal people for co-operating with the government policy of assimilation which had separated so many parents from their children in order to take these latter into white society.

Yet in the later years of the twentieth century it is from among the 'first' peoples (the favourite term in Canada) that measures of a new challenge, and indeed of a new force of Christian faith, have arisen in surprising yet undoubtedly positive ways. On the occasion of the one hundred and fiftieth anniversary of the Treaty of Waitangi, when the Queen of England visited Waitangi for a Christian service of remembrance, the Maori Anglican Bishop of Aotearoa, Whakahuihui Vercoe, declared in his address:

Since the signing of the treaty 150 years ago I want to remind our partners that you have marginalized us. You have not honoured the treaty. We have not honoured each other in the promises we made on this sacred ground.

This reminded the nation that

while there are some who would like a compliant church that says its prayers and baptizes the status quo, there are others for whom direct political action is the outcome of their faith. ... The tensions between the prophetic and political roles of the church, which have a long and noble tradition, and its pastoral ministry, which equally has a rich and worthy history, remain very much alive.[14]

See *SCM Core Reader* (9.6) for a prophetic, if at the time somewhat idealistic, set of suggestions from a Conference on Christian Order in New Zealand of 1945 which have been having their effect in the following generation.

Meanwhile in Australia, where already in the 1960s the Australian Council of Churches set out a new approach, rejecting assimilation and advocating allowing Aborigines to develop in their own way on their own lands, there were by the 1980s a growing number of ordained Aborigines in most of the mainline churches, including the Roman Catholic. 'In 1985 the Revd Djinyini Gondarra was installed in Darwin as the first Uniting Church Moderator of its Northern Synod ... and Arthur Malcolm was consecrated in Townsville, Queensland, as the first Aboriginal Anglican Bishop.' Still more, the presence in 1980 of church leaders

alongside the Yungngara people protesting at oil drilling on the land at Noonkambah in northwest Western Australia ... indicated their acceptance of Aboriginal spirituality ... Christian corroborees, called 'Jesus purlapa', first performed by the Warlpiri people of Yuendumu in the Northern Territory, have widely spread through Aboriginal communities across northern and central Australia. They use 'traditional body paint, dance motions and melodies', but the subject matter is Christian, such as the Easter story.[15]

It can be hoped that now that there are evangelists among the Aboriginal peoples, able to integrate significant aspects of the age-old indigenous spirituality into their presentation of the Good News of God's Kingdom as revealed in the life, death and rising of Jesus, the immigrant peoples too may one day be able to discover anew the meaning of the 'traditional' faith of their 'homelands' that they are mostly at present so ready to forget about.

China – the biggest surprise of all

China's contacts with Christians go back much further than those we have mentioned in this chapter so far. Already in the year 635 CE a Persian monk named Alopen arrived, with a group from the Church of the East, based in Mesopotamia, in the then capital of the Chinese Empire, Chang'An (now Xian). They were welcomed and allowed to set up a monastery in the city.[16] We know little about what subsequently happened to their witness. It was officially ended by Emperor Wu Zong's 'attack on all foreign religions, Buddhist, Manichean and Christian' in 840.[17] We know that the faith lived on in small groups, probably mostly of a cultural 'Nestorian' minority that linked up later with the Mongols, but it was for practical purposes lost to China.

The next two approaches came from within the Roman Catholic Church. Following up on the two visits by Marco Polo in the 1260s and 70s, Pope

Nicholas IV sent a Franciscan mission led by John of Montecorvino that arrived in Khanbaliq[18] in 1294 and was in turn welcomed by the Mongol Emperor Timur. This flourished for a couple of generations, in some sensitive rivalry with the Nestorians. But in the far-reaching upheavals caused by the overthrow of the Mongol rulers and the seizure of power by the peasant-led Ming dynasty in 1369, all Christians were again expelled from the empire.

The third beginning was one of the most impressive missionary ventures in Christian history, when two Jesuits, Matteo Ricci and Michele Ruggieri were allowed to follow through on Francis Xavier's dying hope that he could visit China, and 'penetrate even to the Emperor himself'.[19] Ricci's story cannot be retold in any detail here. By the end of his 27 years in China, the final 10 spent in Beijing with some contact with the household of the Wanli Emperor, and much more with scholars of the imperial court, Ricci was able to point to his witness having led to more than 2,000 Chinese becoming Christians. These included many scholars, including one of the country's 'outstanding Confucian scholars, Xu Guangqi, from Shanghai'.[20] The Jesuit mission flourished for a further century, if not without serious opposition among Chinese scholar-officials,[21] and with ever-increasing rivalry from other Catholic monastic orders, including the Dominicans and the Franciscans. These followed other priorities and policies than the Jesuits, particularly concerning the traditional Chinese family rites which Pope Clement I was persuaded by them to condemn in a Papal Bull of 1715. It was only – and after endless discussions – countermanded in 1939! In turn the Emperor Kangxi [22] issued an Edict in 1721 banning Christianity, which led to the closure of all churches, with instructions that all Christians, except the Jesuits in Beijing, be compelled to renounce their faith.

The fourth approach was initiated by Protestants, in the first place by Robert Morrison of the London Missionary Society. He took an interpreter's job with the British East India Company, so as to be able to live from 1807 onwards on Chinese soil, though only in the heavily isolated foreign enclave for traders using the southern port of Guangzhou (formerly Canton). There he worked on the translation of the Bible into Mandarin, which was completed in 1819. Not many years later, western traders started bringing opium to sell along the south China coast, which led to the First Opium War against the imperial forces of 1840, and that in turn to the infamous 'Unequal Treaties' from 1843 on, especially those signed with France, the self-appointed 'protector of Catholic missions' in 1858 and 1860. By these the empire reluctantly agreed to accept foreign influences, not least Christianity. They opened the floodgates by which all too often unprepared missionaries of many different churches and nationalities flooded into China. No wonder the slogan 'One more Christian, one less Chinese' was to dog the entire mission thrust for nearly 100 years.

The most startling effect of this fourth thrust into China was kindled in fact by the apocalyptic yearnings of a young man, Hong Xiuquan. After repeated failures to pass the imperial examinations for a job in the civil service, he met one of Morrison's helpers in 1836 and was given a Christian tract. That led him to a dangerously excitable understanding of the book of Revelation, out of which he came to call himself 'God's Chinese son'. [23] From a distant rural hideout in the southern mountains, he launched with a handful of friends in 1849 what became 'the Taiping Rebellion'. This all too nearly overthrew the empire and was suppressed not least with the help of troops provided by the otherwise hated foreigners, some of them under the fervent Christian, and later General, Major Charles Gordon. Given the deep resentment of the imperial 'system' by so many of the less favoured classes of Chinese society at the time, it is no wonder that hatred of the foreigners, not least of the missionaries, became such a dominant feature of Chinese society – as has been mentioned in Chapter 1 in regard to the Boxer Rebellion of 1900.

In fact the early years of the new century, once the Boxer episode had been laid to rest, saw many shifts in public opinion and much favourable growth in the Christian cause. By 1914 the number of Christians was reckoned to be about 500,000,[24] rather more than half of them Catholics. This comparative 'success' was signalled most startlingly in the fact that the man who was nominated as President of the Provisional Republican Government in December 1911, Dr Sun Yat-sen, was a much-travelled Christian and founder of the Chinese Nationalist Party, the Guomindang. He was never able to rule over more than a fraction of the enormous landmass that is 'China', but his years of political striving – he died in March 1925 in the midst of horrific civil conflict – resulted in him still today being revered as the Father of Modern China.

Space cannot here allow any adequate account of the early part of the century. From 1910 onwards China was in the throes not only of internal strife – from the mid-1920s, above all between the Guomindang under Chiang Kai-shek and the Communist Party under Mao Tse-tung – but soon also of an all-out war with Japan which seized the wealthy industrial provinces of the north-east in 1931 and then in 1937 conquered the key ports of Shanghai and Guangzhou, together with large areas of eastern China. No sooner had the Japanese been at last defeated in 1945 than the civil war between Guomindang and the Communists broke out more fiercely than ever. It does not take too much imagination to understand the profound horror most Chinese in these years came to feel about the 'anarchy' of lawless violence and the heartfelt relief with which the 'final' victory of the Communists in 1949 was greeted.

Under these conditions, what Chinese Christians longed for above all was a church they could themselves both shape and lead. See *SCM Core Reader*, 9.8, for the speech by the then young Cheng Ching-Yi to the Edinburgh 1910 World Mission Conference, with its passionate, if polite, insistence on the 'three-self' policy, agreed a generation earlier by two missionary leaders in Britain and the USA, but at the time all too rarely implemented by the missionaries. Over the 1920s and 30s Chinese Christians and their missionaries – from many different nations, though with a large majority of US citizens – found themselves desperate for any promise of stable government and of a different future, yet unable to bring any decisive contribution to bear. Protestants were able to ordain significant numbers of indigenous ministers, even bishops, while the Catholics were much slower over this, only managing to make a decisive start thanks to Fr Vincent Lebbe, who rejected the customary 'protection' by the French embassy and persuaded Pope Benedict XV in 1919 to signal his intention to inaugurate a Chinese hierarchy.

This relatively lengthy background is essential for the evaluation of what was to happen from the moment when on 1 October 1949 Mao Tse-tung proclaimed from the balcony of the former Imperial Palace in Beijing 'The Chinese people have stood up'.

Many different factors were at work as Christians wondered and struggled with their consciences about how to respond to this new regime. Not least differences between the different denominations (with Catholics and Protestants long since considered two entirely different religions), and between them and many of the 'independent Chinese churches' such as the Little Flock and the Jesus Family, let alone Pastor Wang Mingdao, the 'man of iron', a staunch fundamentalist in Beijing who had charge of no more than a single congregation but whose publications and stern teachings were widely followed. But also differences between those who wanted above all to preserve the Church in enough freedom to pursue its own cause, and those who believed God had chosen Christians to serve the whole people of China, especially as a distinctively 'new China' was being born. Professor T. C. Chao, China's leading Christian theologian, honoured the year before by being chosen as one of the six Presidents of the new World Council of Churches at its founding Assembly in Amsterdam, may stand as a symbol for those 'torn between two worlds; in his own person he was to suffer the agony of a spiritual darkness induced by his refusal to separate theology from life,'[25] and who died in November 1979, just as churches were reopening, after 30 years of uncertainty about the most fundamental questions of truth and obedience.

The new government had many more important things to think about than relationships with Christians, but before many months had passed a line of policy became relatively clear. As can be seen in *SCM Core Reader*, 9.9, Prime Minister Zhou Enlai left no doubt that there were severe disagreements, but that the Communists were wholly committed to 'religious freedom'. A clause in the new Constitution laid this out, briefly, and as the policy became clear for a 'United Front', in which government would work together with groups of somewhat different convictions, leaders of those other groups could begin to shape their reactions.

In the Catholic community, Bishop Gong Pinmei of Shanghai, descendant of on old Catholic family, stood out for the heat and weight of his refusal to bend an inch to the new government, strongly proclaiming his total obedience to the pope in Rome (who was strictly refusing to 'recognize' the Communist government – as is still the case in 2007 – and whose nuncio was eventually appointed to the Republic of China in Taiwan in 1966!).

On the Protestant side, leadership was taken by a prominent layman, chairman of the National YMCA, Professor Y. T. Wu, well known also in the circles of the Student Christian Movement. In May 1950 he led a group of 19 church leaders to meet with Zhou Enlai for what became a series of four meetings. Out of these emerged, drafted by the Christians – if not without a close awareness of the likely government reaction – the 'Manifesto' which can be found in *SCM Core Reader*, 9.10, and which was to shape the 'official' response of the Protestant churches from then on. They engaged themselves to cast off their links with all foreign imperialism, especially that stemming from the USA – a point the Korean War, about to break out, was to underline massively; also to re-examine self-critically the extent of the self-support, self-government and self-propagation they had so far achieved; and to devote themselves to unity and reform across the denominations. This was the launch pad for the slimming down of the all-too-many church buildings and congregations as the new, Communist-dominated era got under way, as for the pattern of working loyally with the new government even while continuing to teach and preach the true and lasting Christian gospel.

The Korean War was then the trigger for the Protestant missionaries, most of them now 'enemy aliens', to take themselves away. On the Catholic side, the order from Rome was for all priests to stay at their posts! All too many found themselves, often for quite trivial reasons, suspected of criminal intent and even imprisoned. The later Bishop of Shanghai, Jin Luxian, was sent to prison for what became 27 years, for having encouraged one of the ordinands in the seminary to escape to Hong Kong and pursue his studies there. Meanwhile, on the Protestant side, the Three-Self Patriotic Movement had come into being as the uniting and in the end authoritative organ of the total Protestant community, accepted into the 'United Front' as an appropriate partner for the government. It took considerably longer for a comparable body to be formed by and for the Catholics – only in 1958 did the Chinese Catholic Patriotic Association come into being, under lay leadership.

And so the basic situation for the next 40 years took shape, of 'open' churches, registered with the government and obeying whatever current regulations the government chose to lay down – such as worship only in approved buildings and conducted by approved leaders. *SCM Core Reader*, 9.11, is a representative statement, written in 1957, by Chao Fu-san, a Protestant, earlier Anglican, leader, expressing a real sense of repentance on the part of Christians that they had not challenged the imperialism of the West, of which so many missionaries had been part, nor recognized the evils of the economic and social systems of the old China. Alongside the 'open' churches, there grew up another network (or, in later years, several – at least among Protestants), consisting of unregistered, 'unofficial' churches pursuing their own policies under their own chosen leaders. The word 'underground' is often used for these latter, not least by themselves. But it is misleading in as much as the Public Security (= police) have often been even more interested in the latter network(s), for obvious reasons, so that the possibility of doing things without being watched and known about was, even from early on, more than a little unrealistic.

But life was much more complicated than just this. There was the moment for 'one hundred flowers to bloom' in May 1957, which lasted for six weeks, immediately followed by the severe 'Anti-Rightist Movement' in which many outspoken critics were jailed. In 1958 came the 'great leap forward', when every village was encouraged to work together to create small steel mills in the backyards, and when – as we now know – millions died of starvation. The confusions caused by all these, let alone by all the variations that local leaders around the huge country could imagine, must have been unbearable for local churches to live with. And then came the 'Cultural Revolution' when Mao, chiefly – as we now know – in order to sideline some of his closest colleagues, incited large groups of 'red guards', consisting of keen teenagers, to go out and call in question any and every 'established' custom, team, habit and expectation. This inaugurated a ten-year period of reckless anarchy that is now tellingly remembered as 'the ten wasted years'. Here again, religious people or institutions were by no means the main targets, or even significantly picked out in the documents. Yet every church was closed, every pastor or monk sent off with his peers to be shut away in pigsties or other unpleasant 'residences' – from which proximity many close friendships between Christian clergy and Buddhist monks originated! Even to have a Bible in one's house could produce death threats. The great majority of Bibles were dug into the soil of gardens or otherwise 'disappeared' for the duration. Some people 'escaped' with much lighter burdens than others, yet almost anybody with a public reputation, let alone office, will have endured intolerable pressures that could only still further sap motivation and horrifically reduce the nation's capacity to function normally. The sheer degree of stupidity and waste beggars description.[26]

Yet, by no means for the first time in Christian history, it has been out of the depths of these sufferings that wholly new and unexpected developments have grown. Bishop K. H. Ting, Chairman of the China Christian Council from 1980, preaching in 1982 in the chapel of Lambeth Palace, as leader of the first delegation of Chinese Christians to visit Britain since 1949 (*SCM Core Reader*, 9.12), can only use the word 'resurrection' for what has happened to the Church since Mao's death and all the changes brought about in the late 1970s as Deng Xiaoping took over the helm of government. Not that all has been fair sailing – far from it, as any mention of the Tiananmen Square incident of 4 June 1989 will poignantly indicate. But still, with thousands of regional and local variations, the last 20 years of the century have seen not only a rebirth of the former Christian churches (as also of Buddhist, Taoist and Muslim communities, the other 'recognized religions' – if not without their full share too of tricky moments and awkward pressures) but also an astonishing flowering of Christian commitment and evangelism such as the churches of the early part of the century could never have dreamed of.

As already noted, there has to be caution about quoting numbers. Yet where in 1949 it was generally considered that the Catholics were about 1,500,000 and the Protestants 800,000, by the year 2000 figures of the order of 10 million for the Catholics and 18 million for the Protestants are widely accepted as a minimum. These are still small proportions of the total population of 1.3 billion, a little over 2 per cent in all. But, as has been the case in Korea, even a small proportion who are convinced and committed to their beliefs can work unexpected wonders.

In 1980 the Protestants established a new China Christian Council (CCC) to oversee the life, teaching and development of the total church, responsible for 'church affairs', alongside the Three-Self Patriotic Movement, still responsible for relations between church and government. In fact these two bodies quickly agreed to do most of what they do in close harness, with at first the officers of the one serving also as officers of the other, at national and often also at provincial level. Numerous seminaries and Bible schools have been set up, all under the guidance of a commission of the CCC, and in relation to the Nanjing Union Theological Seminary, created in the 1950s from several earlier colleges, as the one university-related institution, training not least the future staff for them all. Still more, in the mid–1980s, Christian leaders established the Amity Foundation, not as a body in any way limited to Christians but which carries through distinctively Christian commitments within society, and which looks to the churches in other countries for significant financial and personnel support. Its overall task is to serve and help to develop truly human lives and hopes in the poorer and neglected areas of Chinese society.

Similarly the Roman Catholic Church established in the early 1980s a Catholic Bishops' Conference alongside the Patriotic Association, several seminaries in different parts of the country, and a great network of convents for the large number of new sisters becoming professed. From the city of Shijiazhuang (capital of Hebei Province in the north) a series of initiatives in Catholic Social Work arose in the 1990s which are serving as models for the wider Catholic community.

But of course these are no more than the outer contours of institutions. What matters so much more, and which again and again in many different settings thrills visitors to the Chinese churches, is the sense of eager excitement and expectation that can be felt in congregations from the grand 'Beitang' (Northern Cathedral, Catholic) in Beijing to humble village churches in distant and immeasurably poorer rural provinces. The worshippers, as always of course with infinite varieties among them, are aware – as comparatively few now seem to be in comfortable western Europe – that it is in Christ that the truest and most profound hope for the future of humanity is to be discovered and celebrated. See *SCM Core Reader*, 9.13, 'Good News for the Poor', for Raymond Fung's profoundly important call, from his experience among workers in Hong Kong, for a very different form of 'missionary movement' in the new century.

A wholly new chapter of this summary of the current 'presence' of the Christian faith in China has to be reserved for the intellectual communities. Where in the seventeenth century with Matteo Ricci, and then again in the nineteenth or early twentieth, it has been only with great insight and energy that foreign Christians have been able to have converse with Chinese scholars, in the 1990s there started a remarkable upsurge of interest in Christian faith among university teachers and students. Wholly unexpected, this almost certainly finds its roots in the otherwise total lack of concern for any overarching sense of meaning or purpose in Chinese life today – 'there must be more to life than simply making money' – and in the evident need, now that China is so open to foreign exchanges, in culture as much as in trade or sports, for ways of discerning truth and commitment that can be shared across the barriers of language, culture and politics. One amazing illustration of this interest comes from Professor He Guang-hu, the scholar who translated into Chinese the solid, 500-page, digest of European Christian wisdom *Principles of Christian Theology* by John Macquarrie of Oxford University. This was accepted for publication in China by a big general publisher, and printed in the mid-1990s in a first edition of 150,000 copies, which were sold out in 18 months! By the end of the century there were hundreds of university teachers in different faculties who were making time and space to teach religious studies, often with a particular concentration on Christian studies, even if this is not an 'official' part of the curriculum, and with hundreds of students attending these sessions.

And so, while John Mott's characteristically high hopes for China (*SCM Core Reader*, 9.7) may have seemed totally unrealistic a century ago, today his closing line, 'When China is moved it will change the face of the globe', is no longer so exaggerated. The gift of the Olympic Games in 2008 has been seen in the early years of the new century as the strongest possible affirmation that the new China has come of age. There will be more. One may even dare to believe that the mutually enriching dialogue between the great culture of China and Jesus of Nazareth, so long hoped for, is at last really getting under way.

Further reading

The Pacific

C. W. Forman (1982), *The Island Churches of the South Pacific: Emergence in the Twentieth Century*, New York: Orbis Books. An admirable survey of the first three-quarters of the century.

J. Garrett (1982), *To Live among the Stars: Christian Origins in Oceania*, Suva: Institute of Pacific Studies of the University of the South Pacific, and Geneva: WCC Publications.

J. Garrett (1992), *Footsteps in the Sea: Christianity in Oceania to World War II*, Suva: Institute of Pacific Studies of the University of the South Pacific, and Geneva: WCC Publications.

J. Garrett (1997), *Where Nets Were Cast: Christianity in Oceania since World War II*, Suva: Institute of Pacific Studies of the University of the South Pacific, and Geneva: WCC Publications.

Three large and highly detailed volumes cover the entire area with devoted thoroughness.

Japan

S. Endo (1978; originally published in Japanese, 1967), *Silence*, tr. William Johnston, London: Quartet Books. An unforgettable story based on the tragic events that dismissed the early Christian missionaries to Japan in the seventeenth century, by a well-known Japanese writer who is a Roman Catholic. His later *The Samurai* (1982), London: Peter Owen, also a novel, not direct history, brings the wider contexts of those events to life.

R. Lee (1967), *Stranger in the Land: A Study of the Church in Japan*, London: Lutterworth Press. A thorough empirical study made by a North American, one of the 15 referred to in Chapter 1 (p. 14) under the auspices of the World Council of Churches.

K. Koyama (1984), *Mount Fuji and Mount Sinai: A Pilgrimage in Theology*, New York: Orbis Books, and London: SCM Press. A profound, personal meditation about the deep differences between the history and culture of Japan and the biblical tradition, by a Japanese who has spent most of his adult life as a Christian missionary outside Japan.

Korea

J. Huntley Grayson (2002), *Korea: A Religious History*, rev. edn, London and New York: Routledge Curzon. This covers also the distant history of Korea and the various other 'religious traditions' to be found there down the centuries. The author is a Protestant academic whose account of the churches, though only one element in the book, is rounded and accurate.

Australia and New Zealand

R. C. Thompson (1994), *Religion in Australia: A History*, Melbourne: Oxford University Press. This is a relatively short book, chiefly interested in the way the Christian churches have related to society in Australia over the 200 years since the faith arrived there. It is a survey rather than a detailed history, but useful and readable.

A. K. Davidson (1991), *Christianity in Aotearoa: A History of Church and Society in New Zealand*, Wellington: Education for Ministry. This is very much more detailed, and thus longer, recalling the many names which have helped to shape developments in a number of fields over a slightly shorter time span.

China

B. Whyte (1988), *Unfinished Encounter: China and Christianity*, London: Collins Fount Paperbacks. This remains the best single account of the long history of Christian faith in China, with particularly full consideration of the 'new beginnings' since 1979.

A. S. K. Lam (1997; Chinese edn 1994), *The Catholic Church in Present-Day China: Through Darkness and Light*, Hong Kong: The Holy Spirit Study Centre and Leuven: Ferdinand Verbiest Foundation. Only a few pages on the history before 1949, but a very thorough study of what has followed, with many of the key documents in the appendices.

R. Fung (1983), *Households of God on China's Soil*, New York: Orbis Books. Fourteen Chinese Christians telling their own stories of the rebirth of church groups after the Cultural Revolution.

J. and P. Wickeri (eds) (2002), *A Chinese Contribution to Ecumenical Theology: Selected writings of Bishop K. H. Ting*, Geneva: WCC Publications. Eighteen articles and addresses by Bishop Ting, in English and spanning the years 1940–2000, which provide an indispensable Christian 'view from inside' of the tumultuous changes and challenges of this whole period.

Notes

1 C. W. Forman (1982), *The Island Churches of the South Pacific: Emergence in the Twentieth Century*, New York: Orbis Books, p. 227.

2 J. Garrett (1982), *To Live Among the Stars: Christian Origins in Oceania*, Suva:

Institute of Pacific Studies of the University of the South Pacific, and Geneva: WCC Publications, p. 2.

3 Garrett, *Among the Stars*, p. 3.

4 Garrett, *Among the Stars*, p. 33.

5 J. Garrett (1997), *Where Nets Were Cast: Christianity in Oceania since World War II*, Suva: Institute of Pacific Studies of the University of the South Pacific, and Geneva: WCC Publications p. 145.

6 Kozaki Hiromichi (1933), *Reminiscences of Seventy Years*, Tokyo: Kyo Bun Kwan, p. 20, quoted in R. Lee (1967), *Stranger in the Land: A Study of the Church in Japan*, London: Lutterworth Press, p. 32.

7 These and other figures from Lee, *Stranger in the Land*.

8 Usefully studied in M. Mullins (1998), *Christianity Made in Japan: A Study of Indigenous Movements*, Honolulu: University of Hawaii Press.

9 R. Drummond (1971), *A History of Christianity in Japan*, Grand Rapids MI: Wm B. Eerdmans, p. 241.

10 1,098,000 in a total population of 122 million, says the *Japan Christian Yearbook*, 1989.

11 Lee, *Stranger in the Land*, pp. 174–5.

12 Quoted by Mullins, *Christianity Made in Japan*, pp. 192–3.

13 See Allan K. Davidson (1991), *Christianity in Aotearoa: A History of Church and Society in New Zealand*, Wellington: Education for Ministry, pp. 20–7, for a careful account of this still much discussed and disputed Treaty, including the Maori text as well as two very different English versions, the one a more or less literal translation of the Maori, the other the one published at the time by the Governor's office. No shortage of room for major misunderstandings, then and ever since.

14 Quoted from the Epilogue of Davidson, *Christianity in Aotearoa*, pp. 183f.

15 R. C. Thompson (1994), *Religion in Australia: A History*, Melbourne: Oxford University Press, pp. 127ff.

16 As is recorded on the 'Nestorian Tablet' of 781, rediscovered in 1625 and now housed in the Provincial Museum in Xian.

17 B. Whyte (1988), *Unfinished Encounter: China and Christianity*, London: Collins Fount Paperbacks, p. 38.

18 The Mongol name for the later Beijing (literally: Northern Capital).

19 Quoted by Whyte, *Unfinished Encounter*, p. 59.

20 Whyte, *Unfinished Encounter*, p. 62.

21 Whyte, *Unfinished Encounter*, pp. 65–9.

22 Who, only a few years earlier, had written a moving poem about the crucifixion of Jesus, quoted by Bishop K. H. Ting in his lecture 'A Rationale for Three-Self', delivered in September 1984 at Doshisha University, Kyoto, Japan, and republished in J. and P. Wickeri (2002), *A Chinese Contribution to Ecumenical Theology: Selected Writings of Bishop K. H. Ting*, Geneva: WCC Publications, p. 115.

23 Used by Prof. Jonathan Spence as the title of a detailed retelling of this paradoxical episode (London: HarperCollins and New York: W. W. Norton, 1996).

24 Whyte, *Unfinished Encounter*, p. 147.

25 Whyte, *Unfinished Encounter*, p. 205.

26 Though Chen Kai-Ge's deeply moving film *Farewell, My Concubine* is widely recognized as an accurate reflection.

10

Latin America and the Caribbean

Torn between the cruelties of yesterday and a vivid hope for tomorrow

A name that reveals more than one expects

The very name of this continent points to some of the vital starting points for understanding its distinctive history, especially regarding its experience of Christian faith. In 1492 Christopher Columbus reached the islands that for many years were to be known, quite wrongly, as the 'West Indies'. His arrival, on a sea voyage undertaken in loyalty to King Ferdinand of Aragon and his Queen Isabella of Castile, who had recently become joint rulers of the whole of Spain, and were launching that country on 'the age of its greatest power and the decisive construction of its image as the standard-bearer of Catholicism',[1] set off a process of invasion and conquest that was to mark the entire continent for hundreds of years.

In fact the word 'America' was coined, we know not by whom, but clearly as part of the excitement arising from the wide publication and translation throughout Europe of some letters, from a voyage in 1501 across the Atlantic that reached Brazil on behalf of the ruler of Portugal. These letters were written by an Italian, Amerigo Vespucci, whose Christian name was twisted into a name for this huge new continent. Its 'discovery' gave a wholly new shape to the 'inhabited universe'. The adjective 'Latin' for the southern half of the continent will have been added some time later, in response to the need to distinguish between the northern part, under parallel occupation by British and French, and the southern, claimed by Spain and Portugal as their own. In respect of both halves, of course, the names showed – and still show – a total disregard for the indigenous inhabitants.

That very disregard was taken a great deal further, and from the earliest contacts, by what can only be called the gross cruelty and oppression with which the Europeans treated most of the indigenous peoples. By this – together with the unpredictable effects of infectious diseases brought from Europe – the majority of the indigenous peoples, starting with the Arawak and Caribs in the islands, were in fact killed off in a startlingly high proportion of their total numbers, and within a few generations of the European invasion in each area. Nowadays there are some attempts to recover a name for the continent based on an indigenous language (Abya-Yala in parts of Central America, for instance), but none has yet achieved any wide acceptance.

The division of the southern continent, into the Portuguese ownership of the 'bump' sticking out into the Atlantic, with the heart of the continent behind it, and the Spanish of all the territories 'round the other edges', arose from the Treaty of Tordesillas signed in June 1494 by both powers after negotiations with Pope Alexander VI ('a Spaniard and a rogue if ever there was one on the papal throne'[2]). None of them could have known much about these new lands at the time. The treaty simply offered a line drawn from north to south in the open Atlantic at a supposedly calculable distance from the Cape Verde islands. It was intended to safeguard both the existing Portuguese 'gains' from earlier explorations of the African coasts, and the recent Spanish landfall in the islands, clearly further over to the west. Already in 1493, barely a few months after the outcome of Columbus' voyage had become known, the same pope, no doubt responding to requests from the two powers, had granted to them both total control and ownership of whatever lands were yet to be discovered, with all their wealth and peoples, along with the patronato – the total responsibility, without further reference to Rome, for the evangelization and future Christian faithfulness of all the peoples there. It even included the choice of all bishops and – as later exercised – total responsibility for the activities of the Inquisition in all the realms claimed by either power.

As soon after the conquest as December 1511, Antonio de Montesinos, one of the first group of Dominican friars who had been sent to Hispaniola, had preached, after careful consideration by the whole group, a sermon fiercely denouncing the cruel ill-treatment of the indigenous people by the Spanish settlers. It was this sermon which 'converted' the 30-year-old Bartolomé de Las Casas, son of an adventurer who had taken part in Columbus' second voyage and had himself travelled across the ocean when just 18 to become one of the early settlers there. Under Dominican influence he gave up his allotted lands in the island, apologized for his cruelty to the natives who had been working for him, returned to Spain and became the outstanding and lifelong, eloquent and bitter critic to the Spanish throne of what the settlers were doing in the king's name (see *SCM Core Reader on World Christianity in the Twentieth Century*, 10. 1). His memory is treasured,[3] but it has to be acknowledged that even if on occasion he persuaded the Spanish rulers to think again and order their governors to ensure better treatment of los indios (= the Indians, as the Spaniards went on calling them, long after they knew better), it was so difficult to execute such orders, or to check that they were being obeyed, that Las Casas largely failed to achieve the goal of his campaigning.

In 1513 Balboa, another Spanish captain, crossed the Isthmus of Panama to 'discover' the Pacific Ocean, and in 1519 Hernán Cortés invaded and conquered the empire of the Aztecs, centred on Tenochtitlán, now Mexico City, although the whole empire was renamed at the time by Cortés as 'New Spain'. In 1532 Pizarro invaded the Inca Empire on the West Coast, locally known as Tawantinsuyu, now Peru, with its capital high in the Andes mountains at Cuzco. In both cases, Catholic priests were key players in the invading forces, using their religious 'powers' to admonish the demons at work in the regimes being overthrown, and trying to 'persuade' the defeated rulers and their subjects of the truths of the new, Christian religion. This apparent full identity, indeed the all-in-one totality of Christian religion with the power and greed of the invading armies, was to mark – one may well say 'deform' – the coming of Christian faith to the entire continent, even if of course there was endless diversity in exactly what happened in different areas at different times among different peoples. For the best part of 500 years the resulting Catholic 'supremacy', as *the* religion of Latin America, remained as good as unchallenged, alike by the rest of the world and – if with very different degrees of understanding and acceptance – by the peoples of Latin America. The Portuguese think of themselves as sometimes a little less harsh in the way they treated the indigenous peoples in their 'empire' of Brazil, but these differences were actually very minor in regard to the total result.

Church life rooted in an autocratic, discriminatory pattern of society

It will be obvious from this brief summary that the resulting pattern of church life, as of politics throughout the continent, was predominantly autocratic, top-down, centralized on the cities of power and economic domination (Mexico and Lima to begin with, later Asuncion in Paraguay, Santiago in Chile, Havana in Cuba, Buenos Aires in Argentina, and Rio de Janeiro and Sao Paulo in Brazil), and almost always exercised through networks of 'favourites' and 'clients' from which virtually all native persons and others of 'lower' standing were strictly excluded. The dominance of this unilateral 'Latin' culture and power cannot be overstated. It was for hundreds of years the characteristic 'style' of Latin America, and still today is to be sensed in the frequency with which the economic and class barriers it relied on continue to play a part in 'normal' life.

On the other hand there is evidence that the indigenous peoples, again with wide diversities in detail, were by no means totally hostile to the religion of the invaders. For one thing, it had abundantly displayed its power by the obvious 'success' of the conquest. At the risk of making a huge generalization, which historians and anthropologists would doubtless take apart in each specific situation, the indigenous peoples let themselves be impressed, and indeed for the most part integrated into the patterns and expectations of this new religion, not least as it allowed for some harmony, if not exactly acquiescence, in the comparable patterns and expectations of their own earlier religious beliefs and practices. For instance in the veneration of saints, most obviously that of the Virgin of Guadalupe whom a poor indigenous man called Juan Diego was reported to have seen in a vision in December 1531, in effect replacing the earlier existing temple for the veneration of Tonantzin, 'mother of the Gods' in Tepeyac, where the new vision was seen – though it took over 200 years for this story to be fulfilled by the building of a large new basilica, with the backing of all the Mexican dioceses, in 1746.

Rushing ahead in time, it was the Napoleonic Wars, when the rulers of both Spain and Portugal were overthrown in battle and were seen to lose their effective power, that set off the complex process(es) of 'independence', always linked with such names as Simon Bolivar and José de San Martin, which by 1824 ensured that the entire continent from Mexico to Chile and Argentina (but not including more than a few of the Caribbean islands), now in some 20 separate units (including small British territories in Belize and British Guiana, along with small French and Dutch colonies in Guyane and Surinam), was being ruled by 'local' people – if in Brazil's case still as 'the empire' by the son of the earlier Portuguese king. The details of these many struggles and their aftermaths are indeed very different, so that in practice generalizations about 'Latin America' as a whole are often quite as dangerous as in any other part of the world. In particular, the social and religious situations in Brazil, which had imported very many more African slaves than had been taken to any other part of the continent except the Caribbean islands, must never be assumed to be similar to those in the formerly Spanish colonies, different as these are among themselves too.

'Independence' under the rule of the descendants of the Spanish settlers, some, though not many, now with *mestizo* (that is, mixed) blood in their veins, did not in itself change the religious situation. In Brazil the public expression of lasting African religious sensitivities and practices gradually became more possible and more public. Especially as the Vatican in Rome, at the heart of a growingly worldwide Catholic Church, was able to exercise more influence and control over local bishops from the First Vatican Council of 1870 onwards, so the identity of Latin American Catholicism was loosened from the current influence of Spain and/or Portugal. Yet for many years – in effect until the Second Vatican Council of 1962–65 – the overall 'feel' of the Catholic Church remained much the same as it had been since the conquest.

In regard to general social change, not even the two World Wars in the first half of the twentieth century affected the continent much – although Paraguay became in the later 1940s a frequent refuge for former Nazis escaping from Europe. The huge changes that have strongly affected Latin America in the second half of the century can be seen as stemming above all from a change of heart and purpose in the USA. Itself the decisive victor in the Second World War, yet in 1949 banished from China, it was looking for new ways of growing its wealth from influence in other areas, especially from the southern parts of 'its own' continent of America which it had already in the Monroe Doctrine of the 1820s claimed as 'its' due area of influence. So it was the arrival of the big North American multinational firms that more than any single other influence 'assisted' Latin America to 'enter the modern world'. With no shortage of money to invest, yet also with high expectations of the profits to be made from such areas as mining, agricultural products if farmed by industrial methods on huge land-holdings, mass media of communication and many other novelties, they soon found allies and partners in the upper-class elites of the cities. Add to that the intensity of the USA's concern, in the age of the 'Cold War' between the West and the Soviet Union, for 'security' against anything stemming from 'Communism', incarnated for nearby example in Castro's Cuba, and Latin America became in the 1950s and 60s an open field for the US-dominated 'globalization' which has come to be a key feature of the total world scene at the outset of the twenty-first century.

Developments in the wider Church

In this same period there were at least four initiatives in the worldwide Church that have had significant influence on Christians in Latin America, hardly in these cases forcing novelty on them, but helping to open up paths of exploration which by now – and with many quite specific Latin American forms of their own (see below) – have led to very considerable and important, if very much unfinished, changes – advances or losses, according to your particular point of view.

First, within the Roman Catholic Church, after the developments arising from the conservative emphases of the early twentieth century, the *aggiornamento* (renewal) sought by the Second Vatican Council of 1962–65 came as a welcome throwing open of many doors. These included that of relationships with the Jewish people and with other faith communities by the Council's document *Nostra Aetate,* that of openness to a more liberal and democratic type of society by *Gaudium et Spes,* and that of the contemporary ecumenical movement gathering the different Christian churches together by the *De Oecumenismo* (on all of which and more, see Chapter 3 above). This came as a great breath of new hope, faith and life to many, not least to many Catholic bishops, in Latin America. Perhaps the most outstanding single figure in this was Dom Helder Camara, Bishop of Recife, a particularly poor and deprived area in north-east Brazil, who was not afraid to say crucial truths during the time of military rule in Brazil from 1964 to 1985. He refused to live in his official episcopal palace, but instead occupied three rooms in the outbuildings of a convenient nearby church. His words were greatly respected, not only in the church but also by many people in political circles, despite the banning order on his books, and other signs of official disapproval. In particular, it was he who took the lead to call together leaders of the different churches in Brazil with a view to forming a national Council of Churches, one of the first such national bodies in which the Roman Catholic Church was a full member from the outset. It is thus above all from within Brazil that many Protestants and Orthodox have felt, since the Vatican Council, that the Roman Catholic Church has become at last essentially an ally in their hopes and strivings, not the big, dominant enemy of all Christians other than themselves that it has seemed for so long, especially in Latin America.

Second, the international ecumenical movement began to make an impact within Latin America in the second half of the century. The World Missionary Conference in Edinburgh in 1910 had quite deliberately left Latin America out of its agenda, on the widely held view (that is, in Europe!) that it was 'an already evangelized Roman Catholic territory'. Nonetheless John Mott met informally at Edinburgh with several of the delegates who were concerned with Latin America, in a conversation that led to a conference in 1913 on missions in the continent, and in 1916 to a first Congress on Christian Work in Latin America, held in Panama.[4] This gathered representatives from both the relatively small 'immigrant' Protestant churches and the missionaries from the same areas reaching out to evangelize those who had not heard the gospel before. Decades later, much helped by ecumenical youth movements and an influential body on church and society (ISAL) in the 1960s, the present

Consejo Latinoamericano de Iglesias (CLAI) was formed as a regional body associated with the World Council of Churches. Especially in the last 30 years, since the International Congress on World Evangelization, held in Lausanne, Switzerland, in July 1974, there has also been a parallel movement of gatherings among Evangelicals in Latin America who prefer to stay apart from the CLAI and the bodies associated with it. As this is being written, there is a Confraternidad Evangelica Latinoamericana (CONELA) which gathers not so much separate churches as groups from within many churches, even from local congregations who are unhappy with their own leadership.[5] One group which over a good many years has played an influential role in pursuing the appropriate debates between people in these separate movements is the Fraternidad Theologica Latinoamericana (FTL), with leading members including Samuel Escobar and Rene Padilla who have striven to keep alive some appropriate debates and attitudes between these non-communicating constituencies as a sign of a potentially healing process.

Third, since the 1950s, there has then been a very considerable body of North American Protestant, mostly rather conservative evangelical, mission agencies who, unable to work any longer in China, and unwelcome in various other parts of the world (for instance the Muslim-majority countries), came newly into Latin America to see if they could be of service there. The majority of these are 'faith missions', that is, relying on God to provide them with the contacts and finances they will need, and/or televangelists who look to opportunities of broadcasting, mostly by television, to discover new and willing audiences and eventual followers. Some of these will have strengthened the bodies mentioned in the last paragraph, yet some keep right away from even that kind of association with others, preferring to stick to what they already know. These have considerably added to the multiplicity, even the confusion, of Protestant witness in the continent, just when the Roman Catholic Church is at last open to meet, share, pray together with and indeed welcome friendly Protestants as partners in caring for the continent in which it has been so long the only Christian institution.

Fourth, there has also been a considerable entry into the continent of Pentecostal witness. Hundreds, possibly even thousands, of Pentecostal churches had, by the end of the twentieth century, found themselves responsible for a tumultuous movement into Christian faith of many people hardly touched by any of the foregoing. This strand in the total Christian presence goes back surprisingly far, to several small beginnings in the early years of the century, almost all of which had some relatively direct contact with the 'happening' in an old Methodist church on Azusa Street, Los Angeles, in April 1906 when 'the fire came down' on a congregation being led in prayer by William J. Seymour. That is frequently counted as the origin of the modern Pentecostal movement. (See Chapter 5 for a much fuller exposition.)

In 1910 two 'simple Swedish workers',[6] Daniel Berg and Gunnar Vingren, arrived as missionaries in the northern Brazilian town of Belem, by their own initiative, having learned to preach and received the vision that called them to go to Brazil while in Chicago. There they had attended the church of W. H. Durham, one of the participants in the Azusa Street revival a few years earlier. Out of the witness of those two Swedes grew what is often seen as the largest Protestant church in Latin America, the Assemblies of God. Also in 1910, there arrived in Sao Paulo, the capital of Brazil, an Italian American, who had similarly learned his particular form of witness in Durham's church in Chicago. At first he was able to gather some former Italian Waldensian Protestants into one congregation, and into another in a different area some former Roman Catholics, but soon his 'Congregação Cristã' had started to spread, purely by word of mouth, into other towns and areas in and beyond the city.

A year earlier, a missionary from the USA, Willis C. Hoover, had caused 'a certain scandal'[7] in Valparaiso, Chile, where he had for some years been leading that city's Methodist Episcopal church. His wife had been sent from India, in 1907, by an American friend who had also been in Los Angeles and had taken some part in the revival there, a leaflet outlining 'a clear and distinct baptism of the Spirit, as a complement to justification and sanctification which we had hitherto believed to comprise the whole of Christian experience'.[8] As this congregation found itself in turn caught up into a quite new range of emotional and religious expressions, it met with strong dismay, criticism, even condemnation, from the rest of the Chilean Methodist Church. The local paper, *El Mercurio*, thundered against 'dangerous fanaticism' among a group who have been condemned by their own Methodist Church yet who pursue their 'strange rites, with the blood of sheep, trances, the expulsion of demons, apparitions and other hysterical accidents as shared between the people who fall into this type of exaltation'.[9] This is the church, one of whose members almost 50 years later met Braulio Mamani, from the highlands of North Chile, invited him home for the night and introduced him to Christian faith and worship in a way that led to Mamani's remarkable ministry of evangelization in his home province over the following 30 years. In 1992 a census could discover that in his county 60 per cent of the people considered themselves *Evangelicos*, while only 34 per cent considered themselves Catholics (see *SCM Core Reader*, 10.5).[10] This is also one of the two first Pentecostal churches, both from Chile, which sought and gained membership in the World Council of Churches in 1961.[11]

Two major Latin American 'renewal' movements

With all this in the background, Latin American Christians had themselves over the last 40 years of the twentieth century initiated and carried forward two widespread and significant movements of renewal in the Christian Church. These are in many ways wholly different, even quite directly antagonistic, each in no important way dependent on the other, still less intentionally related to the other. Yet both are of the highest significance, even if exactly what this will mean in the long run is still at the time of writing relatively unclear. Either could be of high significance for the future of Christian faith in the continent as a whole, quite possibly affecting significantly the future of Christian faith in the wider world.

The first is in the Roman Catholic Church in the twin phenomena of the grass-roots Christian communities (*communidades cristianas de base*) and of liberation theology. Second, in the Protestant sphere of influence, though reaching far beyond what that has meant in earlier periods in Latin America, there has recently been a huge expansion of Pentecostal witness, in literally thousands of 'churches' and organizations with different types of names, to the point where an enthusiastic observer can risk the overall statistic of 141 million Pentecostals/Charismatics/Neo-Pentecostals in the continent in the year 2000, half of them in Brazil.[12] As mentioned above, in Chapter 1,[13] any such figure is dangerous, and will be seriously out of date by the time this is read.

What matters in both in the long run is the *quality* of the faith and of the witness, not the *quantity*, however that be calculated. Both movements have been and still are strong in some countries and contexts, weaker in others, and will change with the passing years. Yet both have already been remarkably influential in their different ways, inspiring and revealing different facets of the deepest beliefs and hopes of people in many different parts of the continent. Meanwhile *SCM Core Reader*, 10.8, from an essay by the outstanding Argentinian Methodist theologian José Míguez Bonino, will provide what many consider a 'central' theology of mission.

The preferential option for the poor

The 'local' trigger for setting off the twin movements in the Roman Catholic Church throughout the continent was the Second General Conference of Latin American Bishops (CELAM), held at Medellín, Colombia in 1968, relatively soon after the end of the Second Vatican Council. This conference, probably to its own surprise, produced two short but ringingly clear texts, one on Peace (for which see *SCM Core Reader*, 10. 3), the other on Church and Society, which brought forward the distinctive slogan 'God's preferential option for the poor'. In its Message to the Peoples of Latin America, the conference voiced the Church's commitment to the entire population of the continent, pointing to the intolerable state of underdevelopment which prevents any possibility of human flourishing for the large majority of the people, and calling this directly 'a situation of sin'.

The conference thus gave encouragement, without actually mentioning them, to what would come to be known as the 'grass-roots' Christian communities, to which Archbishop Camara gave the fullest possible support in his own diocese, and of which the group on the island of Solentiname, in Nicaragua, eagerly discussing the stories of the Bible with their pastor Ernesto Cardenal sj, (see *SCM Core Reader*, 10. 2) have become, thanks to the book he made from their recorded conversations, the best known example and forebear.

This initiative responded to several acute needs in the Catholic Church. At one level it was a creative response to the acute lack of priests. The requirement of celibacy was no doubt largely responsible for this situation, which had been partially covered by the importing of hundreds of Catholic priests from Europe and North America in the 1960s, but which was becoming very severe. So, many bishops actively encouraged their parishes to set up groups of lay Christians in the different areas of the parish who would meet regularly for prayer and Bible study. Leaders were offered some elementary training. At another level this policy met the urgent need for such Christians to feel that the church was theirs, not just the property of the priest or the bishop to lay down from on high what shall happen. Now there was a real chance for ordinary local people to run their own meetings, to voice their own prayers and feelings in worship, and to propose their own priorities and actions. In practice, naturally enough, these met better than the formal parish structures some of the urgent social and community needs of the total population of the area. At yet another level, these groups were naturally more open to other persons, not necessarily of any official standing in the Catholic Church, possibly of other Christian churches, or simply of general good will without any definite faith, to join in at least the actions of the group, and often also in the meetings for prayer and Bible study. So that these grass-roots communities also became natural evangelizers among their own neighbours, to the lasting good of the Church.

Some areas, especially in Brazil and Guatemala, saw large numbers of such communities spring up remarkably quickly, especially where there was warm encouragement from respected and well-loved bishops such as Helder Camara and Paulo Arns in São Paulo. Others were more hesitant, with a consequently slower rate of take-up, if any, for this sort of idea, as in Argentina and Colombia.

At much the same time, the 'theology of liberation' burst upon the scene at the level of intelligent believers, with the book by Gustavo Gutiérrez, chaplain at a Catholic university in Peru, *Teología de la liberación: Perspectivas* coming out in 1971 (in English, *A Theology of Liberation: History, Politics and Salvation*, New York: Orbis Books, 1973) and being read widely throughout the continent – and soon the world – within a few months. Other authors joined in, perhaps most notably the Brazilian Leonardo Boff, whose book *Church: Charism and Power – Liberation Theology and the Institutional Church* (1981; in English, from New York: Crossroads and London: SCM Press, 1985), very much reflecting the experiences of the grass-roots communities, was to lead to a four-hour conversation between the author and the then Cardinal Ratzinger[14] in 1984, which in turn led to Fr Boff being silenced and forbidden to teach for a year.

This 'wing' of theological exploration was widely held, in the circles anxious about or hostile to it, to be drawing on Marxism for too much of its social critique, and thus dangerously sympathetic to Fidel Castro's Cuba, itself dangerously close to the Soviet 'empire'. Yet at the same time it struck the great majority of its readers, especially those in the poorer areas and active in the grass-roots communities, as a fountain of encouragement for breaking out of the limited expectations that had dominated their lives for centuries. (See the martyr witness of Fr Ellacuria (*SCM Core Reader*, 10. 4), identifying the central purpose of his Jesuit University in San Salvador as to serve the needs of the poor.) Yet this was all happening at a time when right-wing, often military governments were dominating most of the continent – Brazil after the military coup of mid-1964, Argentina under those who invaded the Falkland/Malvinas islands in 1982, Chile under General Pinochet, Nicaragua under the Somozas until 1979 and Guatemala from 1954 under a 50-year succession of military rulers, including briefly (1982–83) even a staunch Pentecostal General Rios Montt, probably the most brutal of them all in its cruelty to the indigenous rural population. So there was a considerable degree of tension in the air. The more cautious bishops were by no means easily won over.

These tensions came to a head, within the Roman Catholic Church, in the preparations for the Third General Conference of the Bishops, planned to take place in Puebla, Mexico, in early 1979. In the years since the Medellín Conference the CELAM had elected new officers, including the later Cardinal Lopez Trujillo as its Executive Secretary. Under his leadership, draft papers were prepared for the Puebla conference to work on, yet which aroused such a wave of indignant opposition from those sympathetic to liberation theology that they were withdrawn. The conference was left to write its own reports and Message. The newly elected Polish Pope, John Paul II, was to visit Latin America for the first time for that conference and was known to have a strongly anti-Communist attitude, though what he saw in the poorer areas he visited clearly led him at the time to express himself more openly in favour of social change than many had expected. Nonetheless, and although there was much in the Puebla texts to encourage the grass-roots communities, in 1984 the Vatican published an Instruction from the Congregation for the Doctrine of the Faith (Cardinal Ratzinger's office) which was sharply hostile to liberation theology. A subsequent Instruction from that office on 'some aspects' of that same theology a few months later seemed a little more understanding and friendly. There is little doubt that these internal debates and hostilities did great harm to the Catholic Church's reputation in the continent, and greatly lessened its 'official' commitment to the grass-roots communities and to liberation theology, even if those active in these movements took some heart from the number and wisdom of those supporting them, clearly at some points if not others including Pope John Paul II. It must also be said that while liberation theology in the strict sense of the term was intended to be a 'theology for Latin America', it was also widely welcomed in educated circles in many other parts of the world as a movement from which many other Christians could learn much.

Confidence in the power of the Holy Spirit

During the same years the many Pentecostal communities and their leaders were beginning to have a massive effect in a population whose numbers were now soaring, thanks to more modern medicine and care. The numbers of 'new' Christians could be counted by those following it all in millions rather than thousands. Again, there could be no denying that this whole movement was literally a God-send to huge numbers of people who had moved into the poorer shanty-town areas of the major cities in hope of the kind of 'modern' jobs and lives the US-dominated TV companies were exhibiting every night in their programmes. As David Martin shows (*SCM Core Reader*, 10. 6) it was overwhelmingly the lower-class communities in the slums who were thrilled by the invitation to follow the Pentecostal path to a salvation that quite directly involved taking hold of one's life and determinedly ensuring that one's money was carefully husbanded, one's emotional and sexual desires were held within the family, one's social and political yearnings were expressed and worked on within the new fellowship of believers, in a way that no other movement, let alone Christian Church, had effectively offered to these sorts of people.

To understand exactly how the Pentecostals managed this sort of 'uprising' from below requires at one level an extraordinary degree of care over the hugely diverse details of each individual process. There is obviously a huge difference between the story of Braulio Mamani (*SCM Core Reader*, 10. 5) in his Chilean rural highland area, and that of a former Brazilian state lottery official, Edir Macedo, and his 'Universal Church of the Kingdom of God' setting up thousands of new meeting points in the huge and ever-growing cities of Brazil, then in other countries of Latin America, and by the early twenty-first century also around the world.[15] By the 1990s, Anderson reports, this was 'the fastest growing church in Brazil' with 'well over a million members, a television station costing 45 million US dollars ... a political party participating in national politics and a "Cathedral of Faith" seating 10,000 worshippers in Rio de Janeiro'. Note also that 'members, who are mostly poor people, are encouraged to bring cash to church in order to receive the blessings of God'.

But such differences – and there are hundreds of other examples of 'Pentecostal churches' – go much deeper than the outer forms and practices. Among the considerable number of foreign academic 'experts' who have written about Latin American Pentecostals there is still debate about the extent to which their leaders are driven by a genuine Christian faith and inspiration, how much by a hard-headed awareness of how one can best lead congregations of people in these difficult contexts into paths of hope and obedience, even if the preaching visionaries may have rather different personal goals and expectations. There are those who see this huge and totally unforeseen Pentecostal 'advance' as a twenty-first-century equivalent to the European Reformation, leading to wholly new forms of religious, social and economic independence for ordinary people, as of political leadership for the nations of Latin America. But also those who see it as a breakthrough by leaders of the lower classes in an autocratic and 'top-down' style not so very different in fact from what Latin America has known for so long, if earlier exclusively from the 'Latin' Spanish and Portuguese Catholic cultural traditions. Others again take it to represent the triumph of a US-style personalized evangelical leadership likely in the long run to foster a North American colonialization of the entire southern half of the continent. *SCM Core Reader*, 10. 7, provides a particularly interesting comparison of these two movements by a British academic, himself with Jewish forebears, who has for many years been a specialist in Latin American social and political affairs and has only more recently studied what has been going on in the churches.

Only time will tell which of these analyses, if any, are more or less true to the admittedly vastly diverse and puzzling evidences available to outsiders. Meanwhile an unforgettably outstanding invitation was offered at the Ninth Assembly of the World Council of Churches, held in 2006 in the Brazilian city of Porto Alegre, by an Argentinian Pentecostal preacher, Norberto Saracco (see *SCM Core Reader*, 5.7), pleading in his sermon to the representatives and leaders of other churches to accept Pentecostals simply and directly as fellow Christians and friends, without rushing to vast generalizations about precisely what might have got them started on the path they so clearly see as their simple obedience to Jesus, Son of God and Christ, crucified and risen.

History, as always, moves on. By the time this is being read, it could well be that some 'new thing' has appeared on the scene in parts of this great continent. It would be particularly interesting, and by no means impossible, if some integration of these two movements were to take place, say if Pentecostals discovering their own forms of obedience as Latin American citizens for the first time were to adopt liberation theology as their slogan and pathfinder – no doubt from their fellow Christians in the grass-roots communities rather than from the academics. The only generalization in which one can indulge in the early twenty-first century is that Latin America will continue to deserve attention as at least as active and inventive a context for Christian obedience as any other part of the world.

The Caribbean – same 'beginning', very different story

Christian faith first 'arrived' in the Caribbean with Christopher Columbus, as mentioned above (p. 167). While 'officially' (as far as royal proclamations went) the sharing of Christian faith was among the objects of the Spanish adventurers, it was in practice left entirely to those few Catholic religious, mainly Dominicans and later Jesuits, who took this seriously, while being invariably cruelly disregarded by the other Spaniards, however 'Christian' they may have claimed to be. The first concern of the latter was to make the indigenous Arawak and Caribs, followed all too soon by African slaves, perform the services the 'masters' required, however much these affected their health, indeed their very life. Within a generation, in all the islands the Spaniards had occupied, the indigenous peoples had died out, and the productivity of the land was depending entirely on the new workforce brought over in appalling conditions from Africa.

It was not long before British and Dutch ships also started arriving in the Caribbean area – John Hawkins in 1562 and Francis Drake in the 1570s. In 1625 the British took possession of Barbados, while the Dutch took Curaçao and Aruba. Before long both the Danes and the French had joined in, so that for a couple of hundred years there were innumerable 'conquests' and exchanges between these European powers, especially during the Napoleonic Wars, indeed with the USA joining in in the late nineteenth century to take Puerto Rico and Cuba. Between the landowners and rulers being invariably of European descent and the workers of African, until a large number of East Indian workers were shipped in to some of the British-held islands after the practice of slavery was eventually and all-too-slowly banned in the course of the nineteenth century, the entire prospect of any shared and lasting Caribbean identity only really arrived in the later twentieth century and is still a matter of profound uncertainty, as of glaring differences between the different classes in the many island societies.

Moreover, while the monks had achieved a measure of evangelistic 'success' among some of the slaves, the Protestant clergy who in small numbers accompanied some of the incoming British, Dutch and Danes saw themselves purely as 'chaplains' to their fellow countrymen. Quakers, of whom a small party were banished from England to the Caribbean in 1665, stood out for non-conforming behaviour, though it was not until 1755 that they decided no Quaker could be allowed to own a slave. The first Christians who came to live among the slaves were the two Moravians, Leonard Dober and David Nitschmann who arrived in 1732, as mentioned in Chapter 1 (p. 9). But it was only in 1782, in a party of Baptists under George Liele who had fought with the British against the American revolutionaries in the War of Independence up north, that a 'Black-led' church appeared on the Caribbean scene and started to win adherents. And only in 1823, for the first time, that an Anglican bishop was solemnly charged, by the colonial Governor of Jamaica, to care for and report on how the slave population was flourishing under current conditions.

So it is no surprise to learn:

> Up to quite recently, religious affiliation on the part of the Caribbean people was linked to their places on the social scale. Those places were not unrelated to the distribution of power in the society, or at any rate to the perception as to how power was distributed. Thus, in a British colony, Anglicans would be high in the social gradation, with Methodists and 'Scots' Presbyterians sharing a middling position, and Congregationalists and Baptists being fairly low. The most deprived classes would hold to some form of cultic beliefs which represented ... some form of syncretism. Because the social consensus recognizes only membership in the Christian Church as one of the symbols of social worth, where there were Hindus and Muslims these were relegated to the fringes of society. So, also, were those practitioners of 'African' rites who did not belong to Christian congregations.[16]

That same historian offers in his *History of Religions in the Caribbean*[17] an overview of various ways in which many among the black population of the Caribbean have been able to blend African and European religious practices. The Rastafarian movement, originally indigenous to Jamaica, is probably the one best known in the twentieth century. It took off from Marcus Garvey's saying that when a king was crowned in Africa, the time of Africa's resurgence was near. So 'when Ras Tafari was crowned in November 1930 as Emperor Haile Selassie of Ethiopia, King of Kings, Lord of Lords, Conquering Lion of the Tribe of Judah, many blacks saw in the coronation the fulfilment of Garvey's prophecy' and built their movement on that Messianic and millenarian promise.[18]

In areas with considerable numbers of people of East Indian descent, there are Hindu temples and Muslim mosques in plenty, though very little as yet by way of careful, let alone socially fruitful interfaith dialogue.

Meanwhile, in the second half of the twentieth century, the ecumenical movement had taken form in many places, not least at the regional level in the Caribbean Conference of Churches (CCC), whose first Assembly was held in November 1973 in Kingston, Jamaica. Its preamble is distinctive:

> We, as Christian people of the Caribbean, separated from each other by barriers of history, language, culture, class and distance, desire because of

our common calling in Christ to join together in a regional fellowship of churches for inspiration, consultation and cooperative action. We are deeply concerned to promote the human liberation of our people, and are committed to the achievement of social justice and the dignity of man in our society. We desire to build up together our life in Christ, and to share our experience for the mutual strengthening of the kingdom of God in the world.

It had grown out of the slightly earlier inauguration of a far-reaching programme of 'Christian Action for Development in the Caribbean' (originally 'Eastern Caribbean' because of a US-financed survey of the needs in the Windward and Leeward Islands) in which the social and economic needs of the population had been identified as among the first priorities for attention from the Christian churches. The CCC has ever since been active in promoting human and social development in various fields, as is witnessed in the Verdun Proclamation it drew up for the five-hundredth anniversary of the arrival of Columbus, in partnership with the Caribbean/African American Dialogue (CAAD), the final part of which, headed 'Towards a Caribbean Theology', is to be found in *SCM Core Reader*, 10.9.

The CCC identified, in the run-up to the twenty-first century, four large social phenomena as needing to be grappled with: endemic poverty, including food security; the second highest incidence in the world of HIV/AIDS infection, with some 400,000 adults and children living with the disease in 2000, already then the leading cause of death among 15–45-year-olds; drug trafficking and addiction; and the phenomenon of uprootedness as people are, for various reasons, internally displaced. 'By their very nature, the churches, as civil society actors, are well-poised to have a real, sustainable and positive impact on some of these seemingly intractable social problems.'[19]

In order to face up to such a programme, the churches will, however, also need to take account of four other, yet all contributing, challenges:

- The economic problem that 'dependency continues to perpetuate the colonial heritage both of the Caribbean and of those who offer paternalistic support. The economic system that provides the funding for a significant number of projects is the same system that exploits the people.'
- 'National Councils of churches, individual denominations and local churches need to commit themselves to grassroots ecumenical projects, integrating development and liberation projects with the religious needs and aspirations of the people in the pews.'
- Interfaith issues must be given due place. 'In the past the emphasis on issues of development and justice have marginalized the spiritual life and fervour of the region. Can the CCC and other ecumenical bodies articulate the theological relationship between material and spiritual need? How will a Caribbean theology of religions respond to the voices of those lacking the basic necessities of life? How will a Caribbean theology of decolonization include a theology of religions perspective?'
- 'Will the CCC and its member churches be able to establish relationships with the many Pentecostal and neo-Pentecostal movements in the region? These churches represent an increasing majority among Christians and the poor.'[20]

In conclusion, Caribbean Christianity now has a worldwide arena. For it is not only in Britain that the churches have been enriched by the arrival of considerable numbers of Christians from the Caribbean over at least two generations. This is not the place for any careful report on what has happened as a result, which has had its disappointing moments as well as much that is positive. But the sheer fact of this migration points strongly to the recognition that while the Caribbean experience of Christian faith may be relatively small in regard to numbers, as compared to other regions of the world, it has now a worldwide impact which matters very considerably to many other areas. The ways in which responses are found for the challenges laid out above will have an impact well beyond the islands from which they take their origin.

Further reading

The books from which the documents in the corresponding chapter in the *SCM Core Reader* have been taken are all worth looking into further, as well as the list below. Those who read Spanish and/or Portuguese should consult the nearest university library to see if they have a representative collection which you could borrow from.

A. Hastings (1999), 'Latin America', in his *A World History of Christianity*, London: Cassell, is an excellent 40-page presentation of the more than 500 years that Christian faith has been present in the continent.

From inside, there are two valuable essays by writers who have themselves been actors in much that they write about:
E. Dussell, 'The Catholic Church in Latin America since 1930', and
José Míguez Bonino, 'The Protestant Churches in Latin America since 1930', both in L. Bethell (ed.) (1995), *The Cambridge History of Latin America*, vol. VI /2, Cambridge: Cambridge University Press.

For a close but discerning story of several of the crucial episodes of the material in this chapter, two books by Philip Berryman provide good reading and reliable evidence:
P. Berryman (1984), *The Religious Roots of Rebellion: Christians in the Central American Revolutions*, New York: Orbis Books and London: SCM Press.
P. Berryman (1994), *Stubborn Hope: Religion, Politics and Revolution in Central America*, New York: Orbis Books and the New Press.

Quite different but also attractive, the novel written by R. Bolt (1986), *The Mission*, London: Penguin Books, and the film subsequently made out of it with the same title, both tell in a way that is essentially accurate, even if many of the details are of course invented, the important, if finally tragic, story of the Jesuit *reducciones* (settlements) in Paraguay in the seventeenth and eighteenth centuries – rich alike in what Christian mission in Latin America at its best could, and there did, look like, and in how the 'Latin' appetite for power so disastrously ruined it.

Two key Roman Catholic texts, mentioned above, each author and each book in their own ways an important actor in the key developments within that church of the last 25 years of the century:

G. Gutiérrez, (1973), *A Theology of Liberation: History, Politics and Salvation*, New York: Orbis Books and London: SCM Press.

L. Boff (1985), *Church: Charism and Power: Liberation Theology and the Institutional Church*, London: SCM Press.

And for a full, detailed, critical study of Protestantism in Latin America in its various forms, very much including the recent surge of Pentecostal churches, those who read French cannot do better than search out the long book by J.-P. Bastian:

J.-P. Bastian (1994), *Le Protestantisme en Amérique Latine: une approche sociohistorique*, Geneva: Labor et Fides. It is also available in Spanish and German, but not yet in English.

The Caribbean is known to enjoy a primarily oral culture. Books giving an overall picture are few and far between. One source readily available in other parts of the world:

G. Mulrain (2004), 'The Caribbean', in J. Parratt (ed.), *An Introduction to Third World Theologies*, Cambridge: Cambridge University Press, pp. 163–81.

Notes

1 A. Hastings (ed.) (1999), *A World History of Christianity*, London: Cassell, p. 328.

2 Hastings, *World History*, p. 329.

3 For example, in the 680 pages of Gustavo Gutiérrez (1992), *Las Casas: In Search of the Poor of Jesus Christ*, New York: Orbis Books.

4 See R. Rouse and S. Neill (eds) (1954), *A History of the Ecumenical Movement 1517–1948*, London: SPCK, p. 396.

5 A feature stressed in José Míguez Bonino (1995), *Faces of Latin American Protestantism*, Grand Rapids MI and Cambridge UK: Wm B. Eerdmans, p. 45.

6 As described in W. Hollenweger (1972), *The Pentecostals*, London: SCM Press, p. 75.

7 As quoted by Jean-Pierre Bastian from a local paper, *El Mercurio* of 3 November 1909, in his (1994), *Le Protestantisme en Amérique Latine: une approche sociohistorique*, Geneva: Labor et Fides, p. 135.

8 As quoted in C. L. d'Epinay (1969), *Haven of the Masses: A Study of the Pentecostal Movement in Chile*, London: Lutterworth Press, p. 7, from W. C. Hoover's (1931) own account of it all, *Historia del Avivamiento pentecostal en Chile*.

9 See note 7 above.

10 Figures quoted by J. Sepúlveda (1997), *The Andean Highlands: An Encounter with Two Forms of Christianity*, Geneva: WCC Publications, no. 17 in the Gospel and Cultures Series, p. 27.

11 Along with a sister church, the Mision Iglesia Pentecostal, both reacting to diatribes by the 'extreme American fundamentalist, C. McIntire', on which see Hollenweger, *The Pentecostals*, pp. 438ff. For their acceptance into WCC mem-

bership, see (1962), *The New Delhi Report: The Third Assembly of the World Council of Churches*, London: SCM Press, pp. 9–10 and 69–70.

12 Quoted in A. Anderson (2004), *An Introduction to Pentecostalism*, Cambridge: Cambridge University Press, p. 63, referring to D. B. Barrett and T. M. Jonson, 'Global Statistics', in S. M Burgess and E. M. van der Maas (eds) (2002), *New International Dictionary of Pentecostal and Charismatic Movements*, Grand Rapids MI: Zondervan.

13 See pp. 12–14 in Chapter 1 above.

14 At the time of writing, Pope Benedict XVI.

15 See Anderson, *Introduction*, pp. 73–4.

16 D. Bisnauth (1982), 'Religious Pluralism and Development in the Caribbean: Questions', *Caribbean Journal of Religious Studies* 4, September, p. 22.

17 D. Bisnauth (1996), *History of Religions in the Caribbean*, Trenton NJ: First Africa World Press.

18 Bisnauth, *History*, pp. 185–93.

19 *Caribbean Regional Development Programme*, Caribbean Conference of Churches, Port of Spain, 2000, quoted in J. Briggs, M. Oduyoye and G. Tsetsis (eds) (2004), *A History of the Ecumenical Movement: Volume 3, 1968–2000*, Geneva: WCC Publications, p. 530.

20 From the chapter by C. F. Cardoza-Orlandi (2004), 'Caribbean', in Briggs et al. (eds), *A History*, pp. 531f.

11

North America

It is difficult to review the story of Christianity in the USA and Canada during the twentieth century without taking into consideration, consciously or unconsciously, the developing role of the USA in the international arena during the century, as one of the major world powers during the Cold War period and as the major power by the end of the century. Most especially, it is difficult to assess this story without recalling the horrific tragedy of 11 September 2001, when three passenger planes were deliberately flown into the twin towers in New York and the Pentagon in Washington. Over 3,000 people were tragically killed on that day. The nation that had become a major, indeed *the* major, power had become vulnerable, a target of international terrorism.

This interweaving of power and vulnerability will inevitably shape any perspective on the story of Christianity during the century. Moreover, some of the most important developments within twentieth-century Christianity, such as Pentecostalism and feminist theology, had their origins within the USA, although their subsequent development meant their being reshaped and transformed by particular local and national contexts in countries around the world. How did the churches find ways of empowering and liberating the vulnerable and marginalized in US society during the century? How did the churches enable wider society in the USA to celebrate diversity rather than seek uniformity? How did an increasingly conservative understanding of Christianity find ways of recognizing and relating to more liberal and inclusivist perspectives of the Church and society at large? These are questions to which we shall have to return. But this chapter will also need to be aware that although Christianity in Canada, during the century, has inevitably been in some ways overshadowed by its larger neighbour, and trends within the USA have influenced church life in Canada too, as our study will show, Canada has its own distinct history of Christianity, with its own approach and identity.

The United States of America

In many ways, the history of the USA has been shaped by immigration, transmigration and internal conflict, not least with the American Indians. The vast majority of the present population trace their origins back to immigrant communities. American society is, therefore, inevitably very diverse in terms of ethnicity, identity, language, culture and religion. This diversity has had a fundamental effect on Christianity. Similarly, the Evangelical Awakening of the end of the eighteenth century, the continuation of European immigration (among whom was a growing number of Catholic Christians), the American Civil War and the anti-slave movement, all contributed to shaping early twentieth-century America.

The early twentieth century

A number of trends that were influencing Christian thought in other regions of the world, not least in Europe where many of them had their origins, were challenging perceptions and convictions in America. The Darwinian 'revolution', the related disputes about biblical authority, the growth of the social gospel and liberal theology were formative during the early years of the century. Walter Rauschenbusch (1861–1918), one of the foremost theologians within this latter tradition, claimed that 'the fruits of the Kingdom would be a social redemption that would complement spiritual redemption ... [The] triumph of co-operation over competition, fraternity over coercion and public good over private gain.'[1]

This was also the period of the origin and development of Pentecostalism (see Chapter 5). The Azusa Street revival meeting in 1906 had inaugurated a movement which would have transforming effects not just in North America but worldwide during the subsequent century. Its powerful consequences, displaying the charismatic gifts of the power of the Holy Spirit, had a profound effect not least among the African-American community.

Alongside these largely Protestant debates and developments, there were debates also about the place of the Roman Catholic Church. As we have seen, the church was a very large and significant Christian family within North American society. Some of its leaders – such as Archbishop Ireland (1838–1918) and Archbishop Corrigan (1839–1902) – tried to work towards social integration (though not, of course, doctrinal or ecclesial convergence) in a predominantly Protestant society. However, in 1899, Pope Leo XIII promulgated an encyclical to Cardinal Gibbons, Archbishop of Baltimore, 'Concerning new opinions, virtue, nature and grace, with regard to Americanism' (*Testem Benevolientiae Nostrae*).[2] In this encyclical, Leo XIII expressed deep anxiety about and opposition to trends to 'novelty' (or 'new opinions') within what he described as 'Americanism', and to which he believed the Roman Catholic Church in America was in danger of succumbing, in order to attract people into (or back into) the church.

However, as the century progressed, the Roman Catholic Church did grow in prominence within the USA. One of the great achievements of the church was to maintain the integrity of a church community which was largely made up of immigrants from Europe and elsewhere. Latourette describes this as 'one of the most striking achievements in the history of Christianity ... From being an alien intrusion into a land predominantly Protestant in background, the Roman Catholic Church became more and more an integral element of the country's life.'[3] And yet, Mullin claims that 'until the 1960s, American Catholics and Protestants would inhabit quite different intellectual worlds'.[4]

The Eastern Orthodox community within the USA at the beginning of the century was largely an immigrant community. Over the years, a number of independent Orthodox churches were set up reflecting the ethnic and religious origins of these diverse communities, including Albanian, Bulgarian, Greek, Romanian, Russian, Serbian, and Ukrainian Orthodox churches. It was not until 1945 that a federation of Orthodox churches was set up to enable mutual understanding and collaboration among these churches.

Ethnic identity and integration of Native Americans was also a key issue during the early years of the century, although not as significant in the minds of the white population as it had been in the previous two centuries. By 1914 it was estimated that between one-third and a half of the Native American population was Christian or closely influenced by Christianity, more or less equally divided between Catholicism and Protestantism.

There were more African Americans (at that time referred to as 'Negroes') than Native Americans. Latourette[5] quotes a figure of 9.2 million by 1910. It was a moving population, with families moving from rural to urban settings and also from southern to northern states, mainly because of economic inequality and discrimination. The great majority of African Americans were Protestant (mainly within 'Black-majority' churches rather than in mainstream Protestant churches), with only 52,000 being Roman Catholic in 1916, increasing to 138,000 by 1936.[6]

The inter-war years

Inevitably, the First World War (1914–18) was a key turning point for Christianity in the USA. This is not the place to examine the issues of war and peace as such (see Chapter 13). Mullin claims that America entered the First World War 'an inward looking, idealistic nation, confident in its values ... [with the] pre-eminence of the Protestant heritage largely unchallenged'.[7] He believes that, after the war, America 'was shown to be far more pluralistic than previously supposed' and the conservative–liberal divide, briefly described above, had become 'acrid controversy'. Mullin claims that the conservative–liberal or fundamentalist–social gospel divide within Protestant Christianity ultimately led, during the post-war years, to the domination of a fundamentalist understanding of Christianity with its 'combative vision reflecting a strict doctrinal orthodoxy' having no compromise with liberalism.[8]

One factor in this critique of liberalism and the social gospel was the Great Depression of 1929. Stock prices fell by 40 per cent, 9,000 banks went out of business and 9 million savings accounts were wiped out. Wages fell by an average of 40 per cent and 15 million people became jobless, an increase in the unemployment rate from 9 to 25 per cent. An economic crisis of this magnitude raised fundamental questions for Christians about the validity of the theology of human progress in building the Kingdom on earth.

One of the more important contributions to the theological response to this crisis was that of Reinhold Niebuhr (1892–1971) and his brother Richard Niebuhr (1894–1962), the former teaching Christian ethics at Union Theological Seminary, New York, and the latter teaching theology at Yale Divinity School. Reinhold Niebuhr, probably the more influential of the brothers, rejected the social progress paradigm and instead introduced a theological analysis of social and political life based on the doctrine of sin. In his renowned book, *Moral Man and Immoral Society*,[9] he argued that the triumph of love in the world 'would have to come through the intervention of God'.[10] This call to abandon the progress paradigm and to adopt what came to be regarded as a Barthian neo-orthodoxy became, during subsequent decades, a prophetic clarion call not just to Christians in the USA but in Europe too, as they struggled with the moral implications of the Depression and the disillusion with the social gospel theology.

Emerging themes post-1945

The decades following the Second World War (which Latourette believes did not affect the USA as profoundly as Europe[11]) were transformative for American Christianity. This chapter cannot examine the dominant themes of the second half of the century thoroughly but the 'Further reading' suggestions at the end of the chapter will direct readers to sources for more detailed study.

The transformation of American Christianity

Paul A. Crow Jnr quotes Ahlstrom who argues that the 1960s (which he characterized as 'the end of "a Great Puritan Epoch" in Anglo-American culture') was a time 'when the old foundations of national confidence, patriotic idealism, moral traditionalism, and even Judeo-Christian theism, were awash ... The nation was confronting revolutionary circumstances whose effects were irreversible.'[12]

This period was also characterized by political realities that shaped American (and global) society for the remainder of the century. Not least among these was the power struggle of the Cold War, in which the USA and the USSR represented the dominant powers in a world divided between the 'Communist' Eastern bloc and the 'Democratic' Western states. The political and military tensions and conflicts that arose from these competing political hegemonies shaped the world's history during the middle decades of the century. Towards the end of the period under consideration, the collapse of the USSR and the consequent democratization of the former Eastern bloc states transformed the world political scene, giving the USA political, cultural and economic domination in a world increasingly influenced by rapidly emerging economic powers such as China and India.

The years immediately after the Second World War saw a growth in church membership, so that by 1960, 69 per cent of Americans were associated with a religious community.[13] Mullin questions, however, whether this was necessarily the result of growth in faith, and argues that it was more likely to have been caused by a rise in anti-communism and demographic changes in society. Crow argues that, later during this period, the churches no longer enjoyed 'the privileges of an unofficial establishment'. In Crow's words, 'A common civil faith that once united Americans around the same national values and identity lost its power to hold people together.'[14]

During this period also the traditional Protestant hegemony within American society was lost with the gradual increase in the membership and public influence of the Roman Catholic Church (especially after the Second Vatican Council, 1962–65) and the election of John F. Kennedy as the first Catholic President (in 1961) and the dramatic growth in Evangelicalism (see below) and Pentecostalism (see Chapter 5). This meant a move towards the centre-right in political terms. During the final decades of the century, this centre-right perspective on political and moral issues (which occasionally brought together fundamentalist and Catholic Christians) became increasingly influential in the political life of the USA. However, there were also radical and prophetic voices, not least from within the Catholic Church, on socio-economic as well as other issues (see *SCM Core Reader on World Christianity in the Twentieth Century*, 11.1, for the 1986 Pastoral Letter on Economic Issues from the US Catholic Bishops).

It should be noted that, by the end of the century, 85 per cent of the population of the USA was Christian, representing 66 million Catholics, 63.5 million in traditional Protestant churches (including the Episcopal Church (Anglican), almost 6 million Orthodox and over 80 million Independent (the majority of which were Evangelical or Pentecostal).[15] The Protestant family of churches includes denominations and churches with very significant membership numbers, such as the two major African American Baptist Conventions with total membership of approximately 12.5 million, the American Baptist Churches, with 1.4 million members, the Evangelical Lutheran Church (see below) with 5 million members, the Episcopal Church in the USA, with 2.5 million members, three African American Methodist churches with a total of just under 5 million members, the United Church of Christ with 1.4 million members, the Christian Church (Disciples of Christ) with 830,000 members and the largest Protestant church, the United Methodist Church with over 10 million members.[16]

The call to co-operation and unity

The story of the development of the ecumenical movement within the USA is a long and complex one. The National Council of Churches of Christ in the United States of America (NCCC USA) was founded in 1950 as a successor to the Federal Council of Churches USA, established in 1908. There were 29 founding churches and denominations, 25 Protestant and 4 Orthodox. The Roman Catholic Church was not a member of the NCCC. It is, however, a participating church in Christian Churches Together in the USA (CCTUSA), which has been in formation since 2001 and is due to be formally organized in 2008.[17]

Among the notable early achievements of the NCCC were the publication of the Revised Standard Version of the Bible (1952) and its successor, the New Revised Standard Version (1989). International aid and development was a major element of the NCCC's programme and, at one point, accounted for between 70 per cent and 80 per cent of the budget. During the Cold War years, it played a key role in peace-making and reconciliation, holding a series of seminars for church leaders in the USA and the USSR with a view to fostering dialogue between them. In social and public affairs, a radical agenda – in areas such as human rights, peace and racial integration – characterized its activities, and, in Crow's view, represented 'a minority liberal conscience'.[18]

At the end of the century, there was a significant challenge to councils of churches as expressions of ecumenical partnership (which was not, of course, confined to the USA) that sprang from changes in church leadership, a distrust of institutions, a postmodern critique of consensus, the challenge of pluralism and a sharp decline in contributions and resources.[19] It may be significant that the basis for the newly established CCTUSA omits a key phrase, which was included in the basis of the NCCC USA, namely, 'These communions covenant with one another to manifest ever more fully the unity of the church.' This marks a move away from a commitment to visible unity, which had been such a key driving force during previous decades.

This is not to say, however, that the search for visible church unity has been entirely devoid of positive results. For example, there were a number of acts of union between churches that belonged to the same denominational family. Thus, in 1968 the United Methodist Church was formed from the Methodist Church (itself the product of unity between the Methodist Episcopal Church [South], the Methodist Protestant Church and the Methodist Episcopal Church in 1939) and the Evangelical United Brethren Church (formed in 1946 when the Church of the United Brethren in Christ and the Evangelical Church united), a church which, according to its own self-description, 'reflects the diversified society of the nation'.[20] Similarly, in 1983, the Presbyterian Church in the USA (predominantly a southern denomination, which came into a divided existence following the Civil War), was reunited with the United Presbyterian Church in the USA to form the Presbyterian Church (USA). There was a similar merger among Lutheran churches in 1988 when the Lutheran Church of America, the American Lutheran Church and the Association of Evangelical Lutheran Churches joined to form the Evangelical Lutheran Church in America. This united Lutheran Church describes itself as representing 'historical continuity for Lutherans from colonial days as well as the weaving together into one body of all the threads of Lutheran history in North America'.[21]

Another impetus towards visible unity was represented in the Consultation on Church Union (COCU) formed in 1960. It involved the United Presbyterian Church, the Episcopal Church, the Methodist Church, the United Church of Christ, the African Methodist Episcopal Church, the African Methodist Episcopal Zion Church, the Christian Methodist Episcopal Church, the Christian Church (Disciples of Christ) and the International Council of Community Churches. It developed a model of covenant communion as a basis for the commitment to unity between these churches, which was formalized in 1988 in a document entitled, 'Churches in Covenant Communion: The Church of Christ Uniting'. Crow describes the goal of this covenant as 'becoming one in faith, sacraments, ministry and mission ... a unity [that] was visible and organic, whether or not organizational structures were to be consolidated'.[22]

When these proposals had been before the churches for a decade, it was decided that a new impetus was needed. Consequently, in 1999 a proposal for a new covenant relationship to be known as Churches Uniting in Christ

(CUIC) was agreed, that included nine 'visible marks' (see *SCM Core Reader*, 11.2).[23] Crow comments:

> [T]he potential of Churches Uniting in Christ represents a new depth and vitality in American churches' search for faithfulness, reconciliation and renewal ... The presence of the three African American churches requires the other communions to address the question of racism – the most divisive reality in America – and to search for visible unity with justice and inclusiveness.

Bilateral dialogues were also a significant aspect of the response to the call to unity in the USA. The Second Vatican Council provided the impetus for bilateral dialogues worldwide (see Chapter 2) such as the Anglican–Roman Catholic International Commission (ARCIC). These encouraged growth towards theological consensus on a number of key church-dividing issues, both ecclesial and social. Similar dialogues were begun in the USA, immediately following the Second Vatican Council. The Lutherans held bilateral dialogues with the Reformed, Episcopal, Baptist, Orthodox and United Methodist Churches and the Roman Catholic Church held dialogues with the Christian Church (Disciples of Christ), the Southern Baptist Convention, the Lutherans and the Oriental Orthodox.

Segregation, civil rights and black theology

From its modern origins in the seventeenth century, the USA has been a multiracial society. Relations between the indigenous Native Americans and the early settlers, relationships between settlers from different national and ethnic backgrounds, the coming of slaves from Africa and the Caribbean and the subsequent abolition of slavery and the growing presence of former slaves and their descendants within American society, and more recently the arrival of migrants from Central and Latin America as well as the Middle East and the Far East, have all shaped contemporary America. This brief review of Christianity in the USA, in all its social and cultural complexity, cannot possibly cover all these aspects. We will have to focus on some (only) of the issues that revolve around the African American communities that trace their origins to Africa and the Caribbean.

Even within this community, the ecclesial identities are complex. Some African Americans were drawn into the traditional, largely Protestant, churches, and have maintained that relationship. Others founded their own churches and developed a pattern of worship and Christian life and witness that reflected their own culture and tradition. Others have forged partnerships and union with other 'white' churches that reflect an inclusive and multiracial Christian identity.

During the early years of the twentieth century the African American population saw considerable growth (an increase of around 3 million in the 30 years between 1910 and 1940). There was also a trend towards urbanization as well as a movement from south to north as the community sought improved economic and social conditions. Racial segregation was the norm throughout the USA during the early decades of the century. It affected schools and colleges, hospitals and medical facilities, employment and welfare benefits, transport and social provision. It was in the mid-1950s that the American Civil Rights Movement began to challenge this situation.

There were challenges to legalized school segregation and trials of 'whites' who were accused of murdering 'black' citizens. Desegregation required the intervention of President Eisenhower. There were similar struggles in relation to segregated transport (leading to the famous Montgomery bus boycott, in which Rosa Parks, a black citizen who refused to give up her seat to a white person, was a key figure), and campaigns for the right to be served at lunch counters alongside other citizens.

At the formation of the NCCC USA, in 1950, a Department of Racial and Cultural Relations was set up within the council from the beginning. In the early period its work focused on congregational life and education, but as the struggle against segregation gained momentum, the NCCC USA became active in the Civil Rights Movement, helping to organize the march for jobs in Washington in 1963, for instance. Its newly formed Commission on Religion and Race provided a focus for this work.

One leader within the African American Christian community stood out at this time. From the 1950s onwards Martin Luther King, who had been minister of Dexter Avenue Baptist Church, Montgomery, Alabama, from October 1954, became increasingly involved in the Civil Rights Movement.[24] Inspired by the pacifist ideal (see Chapter 13, and *SCM Core Reader*, 1.6) and by Mahatma Gandhi's powerful non-violent advocacy on behalf of the Indian untouchables during the 1940s, he sought to focus the Civil Rights Movement on the ideals of non-violent protest and struggle. He was a leading figure in many of the key events in the struggle, such as the protest march in Birmingham, Alabama, in March 1963, for which he and others were imprisoned (see an extract from *A Letter from Birmingham Jail*, *SCM Core Reader*, 11.3), the march on Washington, in August 1963, where he delivered his powerful 'I have a dream ...' speech, the planned Montgomery march to appeal to Governor Wallace (a march that the Governor refused to allow) and the Montgomery march on 25 March 1965.

In November 1963, President John F. Kennedy was assassinated. Kennedy had been a powerful advocate for civil rights. His assassination was a severe blow to the Civil Rights Movement. But his successor, Lyndon Baines Johnson, not only continued Kennedy's advocacy but also translated the rhetoric into powerful federal legislation. On 2 July 1964, President Johnson signed the Civil Rights Act. In King's words:

It was a great moment. The legislature had joined the judiciary's long line of decisions invalidating state-compelled segregation [as well as] the office of President with its great tradition of executive actions, including Lincoln's Emancipation Proclamation, Roosevelt's war decree banning employment discrimination, Truman's mandate ending segregated Armed Forces units, and Kennedy's order banning discrimination in federally aided housing ... [The Act] is historic because its enhancement was generated by a massive coalition of white and Negro forces. Congress was aroused from a century of slumber to a legislative achievement of rare quality.[25]

This was not the end of King's leadership in the struggle for equality and civil rights, however. The Montgomery March (March 1965), the Chicago Campaign (1965–66), his response to the rise of Black Power, King's call for a halt to the Vietnam War and his involvement in the Poor People Campaign (focusing, among others, on sanitation workers), were all major contributions to the Christian advocacy of freedom, rights and justice within American society.

Martin Luther King was assassinated in Memphis on 4 April 1968, a week or so after leading a protest march on behalf of sanitation workers there.

During the subsequent 40 years, significant strides have been made. There have been African Americans among presidential candidates, state governors, US senators, mayors and congress members, as well as holders of senior offices of state, such as Colin Powell and Condoleezza Rice. However, despite the progress made, the socio-economic position of many African Americans remained a matter of grave concern at the end of the century.

The engagement of African American Christians with the Civil Rights Movement and the struggle for desegregation provided an impetus towards the development of black ecumenism[26] and black theology. According to Crow, black ecumenism's 'agenda is empowerment and liberation. Their goal is participation as equals among equals in an ethnically pluralistic American society and in a universal Christian church, comprised of culturally defined particularities. Their strategy is co-operative ...'[27] Two factors became significant in pursuing this goal. One was the full participation of African American churches in the ecumenical movement, both within the USA and globally. The second was the development of organizations such as the Congress of National Black Churches (founded in 1978) and the National Black Evangelical Association, committed to the unity and collaboration of the African American churches. Such bodies had a different set of agenda goals from many other churches. Crow argues that economic and racial empowerment (through 'identification with poor and marginalized people' and 'through the struggle for justice') had a higher priority than 'theological consensus'. 'Christian unity is possible only when justice has been achieved.'[28] But also there was, and continues to be, a considerable commitment within the larger ecumenical movement in the USA both to an inclusive Christianity and an engagement in the continuing struggle for liberation and justice, for example, through the Partners in Ecumenism project within the NCCC USA from 1978 to 1988. For other testimony to this commitment, see the marks of union of the Churches Uniting in Christ in *SCM Core Reader*, 11.2, and the resolution on the Threat to Civil and Religious Liberties in Post-9/11 America, in *SCM Core Reader*, 11.5.

Black theology emerged as a theological engagement with the African American context. As a theology, it is rooted in black, largely Protestant, communities in the USA but, in due course, it also reflected and incorporated the Catholic perspectives on the analysis and biblical interpretation developed particularly by Gustavo Guttiérez in Latin America (see Chapter 11).[29] The extract from the article by James H. Cone, described by Alister McGrath as 'the most significant writer within the movement'[30] (*SCM Core Reader*, 11.4). provides a brief outline of the key insights, perspectives and affirmations of black theology. Two key aspects may be highlighted here. First, it began with a recognition that African American theology and its understanding of the gospel needed to be set free from the dominant 'white' framework. Second, the distinctiveness of the black experience became a dominant theological premise. A statement by the National Committee of Black Churchmen in 1969 emphasized these themes:

> Black theology is a theology of black liberation. It seeks to plumb the black condition in the light of God's revelation in Jesus Christ, so that the black community can see the gospel is commensurate with the achievement of black humanity. Black theology is a theology of 'blackness'. It is the affirmation of black humanity that emancipates black people from white racism, thus providing authentic freedom for both white and black people.

It was this interweaving of contextuality, experience and engagement that not only gave black theology a key role in articulating the gospel's promises and claims for African American Christians but also enabled this theology to become a key paradigm for similar theological articulations in contexts such as South Africa and the Caribbean.[31]

The growth of evangelicalism

From its earliest beginnings, an 'evangelical' understanding of Christianity has been prominent within Protestantism in the USA. But during the second half of the twentieth century, it grew to much greater prominence. Wolffe[32] quotes surveys by a number of scholars who estimate that there was a growth in the number of Evangelicals from around 12 per cent in 1990 to 33 per cent in 1998, the greatest proportion of these being within southern states and smallest proportion within north-eastern states. He believes that this resurgence may be traced back to the 1940s and 1950s, and particularly the formation of the National Association for Evangelicals in 1942, under the leadership of Harold Ockenda and J. Elwin Wright. He quotes a recent analysis by Christian Smith:

> The vision and program these young, restless reformers began to develop ... can best be described as 'engaged orthodoxy' ... [They] were fully committed to maintaining and promoting confidently traditional, orthodox Protestant theology and belief, *while at the same time* becoming confidently and proactively engaged in the intellectual, social and political life of the nation.[33]

Evangelical Christianity is characterized by a number of key beliefs and approaches, including the ultimate authority (and for many the inerrancy) of the Bible in matters of belief and moral behaviour, the uniqueness of Christ and his cross as a satisfaction and atonement for sin, and the imperative of evangelism with its goal of personal conversion. (See *SCM Core Reader*, 11.6, for an example of a typically evangelical Statement of Faith and Belief from the Southern Baptist Convention.)

Another feature of much of American evangelicalism was the development of what came to be known as 'the new right'. This powerfully influential movement began in the late 1970s and early 1980s, and was exemplified, for example, by Jerry Falwell's Moral Majority and Pat Robinson's Coalition for America. These became powerful moral and political forces that generally supported the political right (that is, Republicanism), focusing most particularly on moral issues such as abortion and homosexuality. At the time of writing, it is generally agreed that this movement no longer has the same political influence in post-9/11 and post-Iraq-war USA. But in the early years of the Bush administration, they wielded considerable influence.

In order to illustrate key aspects of American evangelicalism during the century, we offer below three cameos, one of an Evangelical church and two of key Evangelical leaders, which may help readers to understand some of the current trends within evangelicalism.

The Southern Baptist Convention

This was established in 1845 in Augusta, Georgia. Currently, it has over 16 million members who worship in more than 42,000 churches throughout the United States. Southern Baptists sponsor about 5,000 home missionaries as well as 5,000 foreign missionaries in 153 nations of the world. Working through 1,200 local associations and 41 state conventions and fellowships, Southern Baptists share 'a common bond of basic Biblical beliefs and a commitment to proclaim the Gospel of Jesus Christ to the entire world'. A statement on 'The Baptist Faith and Message' (*SCM Core Reader*, 11.6), highlights their position on many key issues. One example of its generally conservative approach was a resolution agreed at its 2002 Convention meeting to advise its members and organizations not to use the most recent version of the New International Version of the Bible because it had altered the originally gender-specific terminology to be more inclusive.

The Convention is not a member of the NCCC USA or the World Council of Churches. But, significantly, towards the end of the century, the Southern Baptist Convention engaged in conversations with the National Conference of Bishops of the Roman Catholic Church, with a view to deepening mutual understanding, particularly in relation to the nature and authority of the Bible and approaches to biblical interpretation. For some within the Convention, this was a very controversial decision, but clarifications of the meanings of key terms, such as revelation, infallibility and inerrancy which emerged from these discussions may well be important foundations for further mutual understanding and closer relationships in the future.

Billy Graham

Billy Graham has been one of the key figures in twentieth-century evangelicalism, globally as well as in the USA. Born in 1918 and brought up within the Southern Baptist Convention he felt called to ministry and to evangelism. He conducted his first evangelistic crusade in 1947 and continued to conduct missions and campaigns, around the world – including Eastern Europe and the Soviet Union – for almost 60 years, the last being in New Orleans, following the floods there, in 2006. In the 41 crusades Graham conducted during this period, it is estimated that he addressed more than 200 million people in more than 185 countries and brought many thousands to evangelical Christian conviction. He became a major Christian figure in the USA, has served as minister and adviser to US Presidents (and participated in presidential funerals), has been received by the pope, and honoured in the USA and elsewhere for his notable contribution to religion.

One of his major contributions to global evangelicalism was to convene the Lausanne Congress for World Evangelization in 1974,[34] which has been described as the largest and broadest gathering of Protestant Christians. The Lausanne Covenant (see *SCM Core Reader*, 5.2), whose chief architect was John Stott (an English Anglican who was another major influence on worldwide evangelicalism) and which was agreed at the Congress, was a foundational statement of globally accepted evangelical and evangelistic principles and beliefs. Its emphasis on holistic ministry and mission and its re-emphasis on the urgency of reaching the unreached peoples of the world with the gospel have been formative among evangelical Christians in subsequent years.

Alongside his deep concern to proclaim the gospel of Jesus Christ, Graham was also committed to social engagement. He opposed segregation in the USA (and was responsible for bailing Martin Luther King from jail on more than one occasion). He also denounced apartheid in South Africa and refused to conduct a crusade there unless black, coloured and white citizens were allowed to sit together at his meetings.

Jim Wallis

Jim Wallis is also a leading evangelical voice, but offers a radical evangelical perspective, especially on issues of justice and peace both with America and globally. As a young theological student, he participated in the civil rights campaign and in protests against the Vietnam War. He founded the Sojourners community in 1971. His most recent book, *God's Politics*, with its subtitle *Why the right get it wrong and why the left don't get it*, claims:

> *God's Politics* offers a clarion call to make both our religious communities and our government more accountable to key values of the prophetic religious tradition – that is, make them pro-justice, pro-peace, pro-environment, pro-equality, pro-consistent ethic of life (beyond single issue voting), and pro-family (without making scapegoats of single mothers or gays and lesbians). These are the values of love and justice, reconciliation, and community that Jesus taught and that are at the core of what many of us believe, Christian or not. His driving concern is to be a radical evangelical voice within contemporary America.

These very brief portrayals of two key figures in American (and global) evangelicalism, remind us that this is not one uniform movement. Although they both define themselves as Evangelicals, Billy Graham and Jim Wallis stand in sharp contrast to one another and both are far removed in theology, and in moral and social perspectives, from tele-evangelists such as Jerry Falwell and Pat Robinson. Within American evangelicalism there is considerable diversity.

Wolffe concludes:

> it may well be ... that the multifarious nature of American Evangelicalism is actually its greatest strength. It offers under the capacious umbrella of belief in the need for conversion and the authoritative status of the Bible, such numerous forms of religious and cultural expression that it has proved to be adaptable to any context.[35]

The USA: final reflections

We may now return to the questions we posed in our introduction to this chapter. How has Christianity in the USA responded to the challenges of diversity and unity, vulnerability and power, inclusiveness and segregation during the century?

First, while it is true that the Christian right became a particularly powerful social and political as well as religious force during the last half of the century, galvanizing its members in support of a generally conservative moral and political agenda, there is recent evidence of the decline in their influence. Moreover, during the same period, other Christian groups have become more radical and liberal. For example, the Episcopal Church in the USA (a member of the worldwide Anglican Communion) had, among its diocesan bishops, Bishop John Shelby Spong, a very radical voice in theological and moral matters during recent decades. It was the first Anglican province to elect a woman (Barbara Harris) as a bishop, the first to elect a female bishop (Katharine Jefferts Schori) as the Presiding Bishop of the church and, amidst considerable controversy, elected Gene Robinson, an openly gay priest, as Bishop of North Carolina, thus threatening a serious split in the worldwide Anglican Communion. But alongside this radical, inclusivist approach there were others in other traditions who argued strongly against this 'modernizing' approach on the grounds, for some, that it compromised traditional catholic principles and threatened the larger unity of the Church and, for others, undermined biblically authorized Christian morality. The principle of inclusivity in terms of race, gender, sexual orientation, differently abled etc. has become fundamental for some, but is seen by others (within Catholic, Orthodox and Protestant communities) as a threat to the inherited understanding of the Church. And as we have seen, this diversity is found not only between what might be described as evangelical and ecumenical Christianity but also within each of the families of Christianity.

Second, while many of the traditional churches and denominations have been committed members of the Federal Council of Churches of Christ in the USA and its successor body, the National Council of Churches of Christ, and have found their membership to be a source of enrichment for the life and witness of their churches, others have eschewed any involvement with such ecumenical bodies because they believed that such partnerships would compromise the fundamental principle of biblical inspiration and inerrancy which was at the heart of their Christian identity. Indeed, it may be said that while the latter decades of the century saw – in the USA as well as in Western Christianity generally – what many described as 'an ecumenical winter', it is also true that, both in the formation of Christian Churches Together in the USA in 2001 and in the agreement of the COCU churches to move to the deeper commitments of Churches United in Christ, with its nine marks of Christian unity, there may be discerned signs, not of 'winter', but of a renewal of ecumenical commitment, partnership and unity. Particularly significantly, Churches Together also includes the US Conference of Catholic Bishops – which has been playing an increasingly significant role in providing a Christian critique upon US society during recent decades – as full ecumenical partners for the first time.

Finally, during this period, there was also a trend towards radicalization in some of the churches' witness and engagement in social and political affairs, nationally and internationally. The protests against the Vietnam War, the churches' involvement in the Civil Rights Movement that sought to end segregation of and discrimination against African Americans, and the attempts, towards the end of the century and into the twenty-first century, to provide what the Sojourners community has described as 'the values of love and justice, reconciliation, and community that Jesus taught', were radical challenges to the status quo. It is important to recognize this political radicalization within the Christian community in the USA, not as a 'merely' political response but as a witness to the Kingdom values of the Christian gospel.

At a time when the dominant public perception – certainly among Christians outside the USA – has been of a growing conservatism (but also of a recent decline in the influence of the 'right') this witness to an inclusive community, to a vision of unity and to a just society, has continued to be a central thrust of the Christian presence and a powerful prophetic critique of the more reactionary forces at work in the USA. This witness has not only been a key influence within the USA itself, but in a world increasingly influenced by it, politically, culturally and religiously, it has contributed in formative ways to the shaping of global Christianity into the new century.

Canada

The first settlers in what is now known as Canada were the French, who settled predominantly in the St Lawrence Valley. The British conquest of Canada occurred in 1760. Following the American Revolution, in the latter decades of the eighteenth century, the 13 American colonies that rebelled against rule from London tried to persuade Canada to join them. But this failed. The northern colonies became a haven for refugees from the south and attracted emigrants from Britain. So by the late eighteenth century, Canada consisted of the original inhabitants (now known as First Nations), the first French colonizers (focused in Quebec province) and the British settlers in the other provinces. The mid-nineteenth century saw efforts towards confederation, that is, a unity between the provinces. The Law of Confederation was passed in 1867 and this was the beginning of modern Canada, a confederation of eight provinces. Canada achieved independence from Britain in 1931 (retaining its place within the British Commonwealth) but in subsequent years, and especially during the 1970s, French Quebec has felt deeply uneasy, to say the least, about its own identity and recognition as French Canadian in a country dominated by English-speaking Canadians. As a consequence to this history, Canada has been and remains a diverse country, with First Nations inhabitants, French-speaking and English-speaking Canadians and immigrants from many parts of the world. Canada has, therefore, seen itself as a multicultural society and seeks to develop social, cultural and political frameworks that will give to this multiculturalism a sense of integrity. Christianity in Canada during the twentieth century, inevitably, reflected these diversities and occasional tensions and conflicts.

The churches and ecumenical relationships

In a population of around 32 million, it is estimated[36] that 80 per cent are Christian, 1.3 per cent, Jewish, 1.7 per cent Muslim, 1.3 per cent Buddhist and 1 per cent Hindu. The Christian population includes 14 million Catholics, 5.5 million Protestants (including Anglicans), 600,000 Orthodox and 1.7 million Independent.

Catholicism came to Canada with the French settlers, and, at a much later date, Anglicanism took root here with the arrival of settlers from Britain. As European immigration increased, so did other denominations and traditions find their place within Canadian society. As a result, a range of Protestant and Orthodox communities have developed during recent centuries.

The Anglican Church of Canada is a member of the worldwide Anglican Communion, in full communion with the Evangelical Lutheran Church in Canada, and became an independent Anglican province (independent from the Church of England) in 1964 when the Church of England in Canada became the Anglican Church in Canada. The Roman Catholic Church is the largest and oldest Christian community in Canada. Its earliest beginnings are in the coming of the first Europeans to this land in the sixteenth century. The Evangelical Lutheran Church in Canada is the result of a merger, in 1986, of the Evangelical Lutheran Church of Canada and the Lutheran Church in America – Canada Section, and currently has just under 200,000 members. Although it has a number of members of German and Scandinavian origin, its main language is English. In the first half of the century, especially, it played a key role in enabling immigrants from Europe to integrate into Canadian society.

The Orthodox community includes Eastern Orthodox dioceses (Orthodox Church in America, Greek Orthodox and Ukrainian Orthodox) as well as Oriental Orthodox communities (Armenian, Coptic, and Ethiopian). A number of smaller Christian communities, such as the Baptists, the Religious Society of Friends, the Christian Church (Disciples of Christ) and the Mennonites, are also significant in the Christian life of Canada.

Particularly noteworthy within the Canadian (and worldwide) scene, however, is the United Church of Canada (UCC). Although it claims a total membership of 608,000 members, it ministers to close to 3 million people and is therefore the second largest non-Catholic church. It was formed in 1925 (and was, therefore, the first united church in the world during the modern period to bring about unity across historical denominational lines) when Congregational, Methodist and Presbyterian churches united. This act of union brought together the formative traditions of these churches, as the Basis of Union affirmed:

> We affirm our belief in the Scriptures of the Old and New Testaments as the primary source and ultimate standard of Christian life and faith. We acknowledge the teaching of the great creeds of the ancient Church. We further maintain our allegiance to the evangelical doctrines of the Reformation, as set forth in common in the doctrinal standards adopted by the Presbyterian Church in Canada, by the Congregational Union of Ontario and Quebec, and by the Methodist Church.[37]

In 1968, the Canada Conference of the Evangelical United Brethren Church also joined the United Church of Canada. Recently, discussions with the Anglican Church of Canada have resumed. Lois Wilson, a former Moderator of the United Church and one of the Presidents of the World Council of Churches between 1983 and 1991, writing in 1982[38] almost 50 years after the formation of the United Church, and in anticipation of the welcoming of the Sixth Assembly of the World Council of Churches to Vancouver in 1983, refers to the parochial tendencies of the Church and the marginalization of Christianity. In the same issue of IRM, James Taylor could write about 'Mission and Justice: The Dual Mandate of the UCC'.[39]

Twenty years later, the United Church's self-description in the WCC *Handbook*[40] could recognize:

> Canadian society is multicultural and multifaith. It is a culture in which the pervasive economic worldview impacts relationships, values, identities, and understanding of the church ... Through advocacy and outreach, the church ministers to those marginalized in this economy of exploitation, in addition to providing the traditional ministries and pastoral care. A growing area of work is with ethnic ministries and integration of churches brought to Canada by new immigrants ... Working in a framework of 'whole world ecumenism' focused on the mending of the world, the church has also supported processes of interchurch and interfaith dialogue.

The Canadian Council of Churches (CCC), founded in 1944, has been the main forum for ecumenical partnership and collaboration between the diverse traditions and Christian families in Canada. The Anglican, Catholic, Lutheran, Orthodox churches as well as the United Church of Canada and a number of other smaller Christian churches (a total of 20 in all) are member bodies of the Council. It collaborates well with the Evangelical Fellowship of Canada, which provides a forum for Evangelical churches ('gathering Evangelicals together for impact, influence and identity in ministry and public witness').

Since 1995, the CCC has reconstituted itself as a Forum. Within the Forum

> all participants in any ecumenical action speak and make commitments only with the authentic voice of their own church. Explicitly or implicitly,

action-decisions of the CCC carry the full approval of the magisterial authoritative office within each member church ... All ... recognize this definition
of ecumenism to be honest, true to present historic circumstances, faithful
for every member church, and yet still workable and effective. The result is a
major contribution to the history of Christianity in the twentieth century.[41]

Whereas this assessment may well be overconfident and overoptimistic, nevertheless this development does represent a significant move towards deeper
unity and closer partnership between the member churches of this Forum.

Seeking right relationships with First Nations

During recent decades, First Nations has been adopted as the preferred term
for the original inhabitants of Canada, the Yukon and Northwest territories,
and the northern parts of British Columbia, Quebec and the Labrador Peninsula, which have been homelands for Indian and Inuit peoples for thousands
of years. For many decades, they have struggled and campaigned for self-government and aboriginal rights, especially land rights. Lands have been used,
without any agreements, for mineral exploration and exploitation, and to develop transport and other public amenity infrastructures. The churches' role
in this field has been crucial. Since they contributed in the past to the marginalization and subjugation of the Indian and Inuit peoples, they now recognize
fully that they have a clear role in the struggle for justice and rights.

Project North was developed in 1975 by the Anglican, Catholic and United
churches, together with the Lutheran, Mennonite and Presbyterian churches,
as well as the Quakers, to support the struggles of the Indian and Inuit peoples
for justice and self-determination (including in areas such as industrial development and education).

Coalitions in response to social and humanitarian issues

One of the innovative developments within Christianity in Canada during
the 1980s was the setting up of 'coalitions' to enable co-operative social action
by churches and other groups in response to specific social and public issues.
Their beginnings may be traced to the period following the Second Vatican Council, when there was growing co-operation between Protestant and
Catholic Churches in the field of social justice. An attempt at establishing a
Coalition for Development did not survive as a national organization, but the
model would become a key mechanism for future collaboration.[42] The coalitions focused on issues such as peace (Project Ploughshares), self-determination
for First Nation peoples (Project North, see above) and the death penalty (Task
Force on Responsible Alternatives to the Death Penalty).

Hutchinson describes coalitions as 'experiments in Canadian pluralism',
and sees them as strategic groups aimed at seeking changes in the socio-
economic system. They were crucially influenced by the Roman Catholic concept of subsidiarity (which insists that 'what *can* be accomplished by small

groups *ought* to be"[43]) and the principle of socialization (which 'acknowledges the need for greater public intervention in relation to the provision of basic economic needs').

This ecumenical engagement in social action for justice was set, at least to some degree, within the theological and missiological framework of the justice, peace and integrity of creation process that emerged from the Vancouver Assembly of the World Council of Churches (1983). By the end of the twentieth century, KAIROS: Canadian Ecumenical Justice Initiatives was established, 'dedicated to promoting human rights, justice and peace, viable human development, and solidarity'.[44] It brings together the ten coalitions that had been set up in the previous decades to respond to particular issues and focuses on issues within Canada as well as internationally.

Responses to socio-political diversity

Relationships between French-speaking Canada and English-speaking Canada have been a matter of considerable dispute and conflict within Canadian society over very many years, and continued into the later decades of the twentieth century. The growing engagement of the Roman Catholic Church in ecumenical relationships gave this issue a greater priority within the ecumenical family. One example of the churches' attempt to set out the basis for dialogue in relation to this divisive issue was 'A Montreal Declaration'[45] (see *SCM Core Reader*, 11.7). It arose (in the late 1970s) within the United Church of Canada, had wide repercussions within Canadian churches as well as within society generally and was well received within the French-speaking community. Its structure of Affirmation and Lament in relation to a number of key aspects of this relationship offers a framework of vision and faith, repentance and action for future action and dialogue. One paragraph of this declaration gives an indication of the church's approach:

> We affirm that we are prepared to live in Quebec as part of a minority; we intend to be a creative element within that minority, to support the vision of a better society as it inspires many of our leaders, and to be vigilant for human dignity according to our Christian understanding of the nature of humanity.
> We lament for this reason any remnant of false pride which may still keep us and our English-speaking compatriots from accepting the posture of such a minority, wishing instead to play a dominating role.[46]

This brief review of some of the key developments in Canadian ecumenical relationships and the churches' ecumenical engagement in public and international affairs indicates that Christianity in Canada, despite declining membership and support in many churches and denominations, shows a deep commitment to unity and partnership, within Canada itself as well as in the global Christian community. It also testifies to the ways in which the churches have engaged in social critique, witness and action that could offer a vision and model for other churches in other contexts.

Final reflection on North American Christianity

At the end of a chapter on 'North America', we must now ask what this term means in socio-political as well as religious (and specifically, Christian) terms. Is it merely a convenient geographical designation or does it have a deeper meaning, especially in terms of the Christian presence? There is no simple answer to this question. There are clearly common characteristics that mark both societies, which, to a greater or lesser extent, have shaped Christianity in the continent. There have been ongoing attempts to recognize the particular identity of the indigenous peoples of the USA and Canada and of forging just societies (and churches) in which their culture and rights (not least the right to land) are more fully recognized.

Another key feature that marks both nations is the struggle to recognize social and religious diversity, both in terms of those, mainly from Europe, who were the original settlers, and the immigrant communities having their roots in other regions of the world, that have become an increasingly significant element of North American society. This cultural diversity has been a key factor in the story of Christianity during the twentieth century.

In church terms, although most of the major traditions are present alike in both nations, all the churches have 'separate' identities and structures within the USA and Canada, and have formed separate ecumenical and collaborative structures. There has been a commitment in both countries to the search for Christian unity, although they have developed along separate paths. The churches in both the USA and Canada have had strong relationships with global ecumenical organizations such as the World Council of Churches, in which many church leaders from both countries have played prominent roles (with Eugene Carson Blake, a US Presbyterian, for example, serving as the second General Secretary of the WCC and the Most Revd Ted Scott, Archbishop of the Anglican Church of Canada, serving as Moderator of its Central Committee). And although North America has been a 'region' of the WCC from the beginning, unlike other world 'regions' there has never been a North American regional body. Rather the NCCC USA and the Canadian Council of Churches have worked in partnership when regional issues have needed to be tackled.

So what does the term 'North America' mean in this context? It certainly designates a geographical area and points to a range of common challenges that have been highlighted above. Yet, despite some military and economic collaboration, the two nations function as entirely separate political entities and bring different insights and priorities to bear within the international community. Similarly, despite the common features alluded to above, Christianity in Canada is very different from Christianity in the USA, and it can hardly be claimed that there is a North American Christianity as such, any more than there is an African or an Asian Christianity other than an interweaving of the rich diversity of contextual perspectives and responses that characterize Christianity in the various nations that constitute these continents. At the end of the twentieth century, global Christianity is marked more by diversity than by uniformity and the goal of the ecumenical movement has been to forge a true unity that will hold these diversities together in mutually enriching ways. Christianity in North America has contributed in crucial ways to this global commitment.

Further reading:

For an excellent review of the history of Christianity in the USA over the centuries:

R. B. Mullin (1999), 'North America', in A. Hastings (ed.), *A World History of Christianity*, London: Cassell.

Reinhold Niebuhr (1963), *Moral Man and Immoral Society*, London: SCM Press (first published in the USA by Charles Scribner's and Sons, 1932). One of the classics of the century, it provides an invaluable insight into one theological response to the liberal theology of the early decades of the twentieth century.

For an authoritative account of ecumenical developments in the USA during the century:

P. A. Crow Jnr (2004), 'North America', in J. Briggs, M. Oduyoye and G. Tstetsis (eds), *A History of the Ecumenical Movement: Volume Three 1968–2000*, Geneva: WCC Publications. The author has been at the heart of the ecumenical movement not only in the USA but worldwide over many decades.

James Cone (1984), *For My People: Black Theology and the Black Church*, Maryknoll: Orbis Books, provides an overview of this distinctive theological development by the most influential theologian of black theology in the USA.

C. Carson (ed.) (1998), *The Autobiography of Martin Luther King Jnr*, London: Little, Brown and Co., the official autobiography of the best known and one of the most influential leaders of the American Civil Rights Movement.

C. Smith (1998), *American Evangelicalism Embattled and Thriving*, Chicago: University of Chicago Press, is a useful resource for anyone wishing to study this topic more thoroughly.

For a comprehensive review of issues of Christian witness, mission and unity in Canada in the years up to 1982, see a wide-ranging series of articles in:

International Review of Mission, vol. LXXI, no. 283, July 1982, Geneva: WCC Publications.

Notes

1 W. Rauschenbusch (1945), *A Theology for the Social Gospel*, New York: Abingdon Press, p. 226 (for further information see http://www.rauschenbusch.org/rauschenbusch.php)

2 For the full text of the Encyclical see http://www.papalencyclicals.net/Leo13/113teste.htm

3 K. S. Latourette (1958–62), *Christianity in a Revolutionary Age: A History of*

Christianity in the Nineteenth and Twentieth Centuries, New York: Harper & Brothers, vol. III, p. 126.

4 R. B. Mullin (1999), 'North America', in A. Hastings (ed.), *A World History of Christianity*, London: Cassell, p. 442.

5 Latourette, *Christianity*, p. 134.

6 Latourette, *Christianity*, p. 136.

7 Mullin, 'North America', p. 446.

8 Mullin, 'North America', p. 448.

9 R. Niebuhr (1963), *Moral Man and Immoral Society*, London: SCM Press (first published in the USA by Charles Scribner's and Sons, 1932).

10 Niebuhr, *Moral Man*, p. 82.

11 Latourette, *Christianity*, p. 155.

12 P. A. Crow Jnr (2004), 'North America', in J. Briggs, M. Oduyoye and G. Tsetsis (eds), *A History of the Ecumenical Movement Vol. 3 1968-2000*, Geneva: WCC Publications, p. 609.

13 Mullin, 'North America', p. 451.

14 Crow, 'North America', p. 609.

15 H. van Beek (ed.) (2006), *A Handbook of Churches and Councils*, Geneva: WCC Publications, p. 353 (which gives a detailed account of the NCCC member churches).

16 van Beek, *Handbook*, pp. 555ff.

17 For further information on the Roman Catholic Church, see Chapter 3 and the section on the USA Catholic Bishops' *Pastoral Letter on Just War and Nuclear Warfare*, in Chapter 13 (see *SCM Core Reader*, 13.6).

18 Crow, 'North America', p. 614.

19 Crow, 'North America', p. 615.

20 van Beek, *Handbook*, p. 579.

21 van Beek, *Handbook*, p. 563.

22 Crow, 'North America', p. 622.

23 For more information, see Crow, 'North America', pp. 623f.

24 See C. Carson (ed.) (1998), *The Autobiography of Martin Luther King Jnr*, London: Little, Brown and Co.

25 Carson, *Autobiography*, pp. 243-4.

26 See M. R. Sawyer (1994), *Black Ecumenism: Implementing the Demands of Justice*, Philadelphia: Trinity Press.

27 Crow, 'North America', p. 628.

28 Crow, 'North America', p. 629.

29 For an account of the history and development of black theology, see J. H. Cone (1984), *For My People: Black Theology and the Black Church*, Maryknoll: Orbis Books, and G. S. Wilmore and J. H. Cone (eds) (1979), *Black Theology: A Documentary History, 1966–1979*, Maryknoll: Orbis Books.

30 A. McGrath (1993), 'Black Theology', in *The Blackwell Encyclopedia of Modern Christian Thought*, Oxford: Blackwell, pp. 56f.

31 For an evaluation of the significance of black theology as a liberation theology, see E. Antonio (1999), 'Black Theology', in *The Cambridge Companion to Liberation Theology*, Cambridge: Cambridge University Press, pp. 63–99.

32 J. Wolffe (2002), *Global Religious Movements in Context*, Milton Keynes: Open University Press and Aldershot: Ashgate, pp. 49ff.

33 C. Smith (1998), *American Evangelicalism Embattled and Thriving*, Chicago: University of Chicago Press, pp. 10f.

34 See http://www.lausanne.org/home.html
35 Wolffe, *Religious Movements*, p. 63.
36 van Beek, *Handbook*, p. 547.
37 United Church of Canada, Basis of Union, para. 2.0, from http://www.united-church.ca./history/overview/basisofunion
38 L. Wilson (1982), 'How I See My Country, My Church', *International Review of Mission*, vol. LXXI, no. 283, July, Geneva: WCC Publications, pp. 320ff.
39 *International Review of Mission*, July 1982, p. 275.
40 van Beek, *Handbook*, p. 552.
41 Taken from the website of the Canadian Council of Churches at http://www.ccc-cce.ca/english/home/history.htm
42 For an account of the origins and development of coalitions, see R. Hutchinson (1982), 'Ecumenical Social Witness in Canada: Social Action Coalitions', *International Review of Mission*, July, pp. 344ff.
43 *International Review of Mission*, July 1982, p. 351.
44 See http://www.kairoscanada.org
45 *International Review of Mission*, July 1982, p. 295.
46 *International Review of Mission*, July 1982, p. 296.

12

Europe

The odd one out?

Hardly a success story

The twentieth century is unlikely to be one on which the Christians of Europe will look back with pride. The European Union (EU) is presiding at the turn of the century over a much expanded group of nations, which has had remarkable success, at first in overcoming the damage and tensions left by the Second World War, and then by economic growth in a free-trade area that has often been referred to as the envy of many other parts of the world. Still more, when Communist rule over central and eastern Europe collapsed in 1989/90, it was the possibility of joining the EU that nerved most of the new leaders in the former Soviet-controlled nations and which has become true for most of them, if not all, by the early years of the twenty-first century. But this type of 'success' hardly affects the outward appearance of Christian practice in the continent, where the rates of regular churchgoing have shown a sharp and continuing decline in almost all areas since the early 1900s – Romania and Albania perhaps the main significant exceptions as the twenty-first century begins. The degree of public interest in, or of the popularity of, Christian ideas and conviction for most of the century has been far from what Christian leaders have hoped for. And this despite – indeed to a significant extent probably because of – the enormous growth in both printed and electronic media of mass communication in this as in other continents.

So this chapter, written unlike the others by an author who cannot but be very much 'inside' the continent to which these pages are devoted, will largely concentrate on a consideration of the factors underlying this long 'decline' and then of how today's and tomorrow's Christians can hope to stand firm despite its apparently unstoppable force. The basic situation of the Christian churches across the continent remains as briefly indicated in Chapter 4, p. 61, with the qualifications to which the following paragraphs are devoted. The major events and factors that have affected them in the twentieth century are then indicated in the next section.

Europe has in fact considered itself a – for many Europeans *the* – Christian continent since the later part of the first millennium, when the Nordic and Baltic peoples were the last to be evangelized. Over the centuries since, European Christians have known only two significant minorities of people of another faith. First, and with the deepest roots in European history, the Jews. After particularly difficult times in the Middle Ages, when many were killed or expelled, especially at the western end of the continent, they have been relatively numerous in Poland and Russia, if for much of the time isolated in their own villages (and at times horribly persecuted), until in the later part of the twentieth century many chose to emigrate to Israel. In both France and Germany, despite being relatively few, Jews have been strongly represented in the economic and cultural life of both nations, as also in the Netherlands and other areas. Unfortunately they have been more than visible enough to attract several outbreaks of antisemitism, culminating in the appalling Holocaust under the Nazis of Germany, with the long-term result that educated European Christians cannot but have a guilty conscience about their treatment for generations yet to come. The other community, chiefly in the south-east of the continent, consists of the long-standing minorities of Muslims in the European areas of the Ottoman Empire, especially in Albania, Bosnia and Bulgaria. These also have never, since the repulse of the Turkish invasions in the seventeenth century, expected to play a major role in the continent as a whole. Yet they have long served as a crucial indicator of the worldwide importance of Islam. Both groups have long since accepted that Europe was and is a Christian-majority area.

So Europe is readily still today identified with Christian faith. Yet the inward health of that faith was at best shaky by the beginning of the twentieth century. Names such as those of Marx, Darwin, Nietzsche and Freud were then gathering storms of critique and unbelief around them. Mary Heimann's diagnosis for western Europe (*SCM Core Reader on World Christianity in the Twentieth Century*, 12.1), that 'late seventeenth century Christianity was generally presumed to be true unless there seemed good reasons to doubt, whereas by the 1990s Christianity was usually presumed to be untrue unless good reason could be given to believe', will be agreed by many to be a fair summary – even if she goes on in her chapter to show how misleading in detail it is.[1]

That immediately raises the huge problem of how best to summarize the experience of a whole continent. Europe is by no means alone in being a continent about which people in other regions speak as if it is a single whole, while its own peoples invariably think of it as a tangle of very different, even contradictory and highly singular, largely national realities! Not least when trying to analyse its religious realities, a careful study of particular places and peoples will throw up a wide span of differing results, almost always refusing the over-easy generalities that make the headlines. Robin Gill's masterly study of churchgoing in various parts of England, in his *The Empty Church Revisited*,[2] shows how important it is to be able to examine the range of factors involved, some available to sight and measurement, many others not so readily. But there are also indeed the large and general factors which have their effect too, even if it is extraordinarily difficult to trace the exact relationship between the two 'levels'.

Major events and developments

A quick run through some of the major events and developments during the twentieth century may summarize some main features of what has been happening to Christian faith and practice:

- The First World War brought about the dissolution of four major empires, three of which had been strongly identified with a specific form of Christianity, the fourth with Islam – the Austro-Hungarian (Roman Catholic), the Russian (Orthodox), the Prussian (Protestant) and the Ottoman (Muslim). It also caused much critique, even cynicism, among those fighting on all sides, let alone in the elites, about the role of the churches and of Christian faith (see *SCM Core Reader*, 12.3).
- The 1920s saw the rise of atheist Communism in Russia, developing into the huge Union of Soviet Socialist Republics, and then of Fascism in Mussolini's Italy and Hitler's Germany. All three of these totalitarian powers in one way or another ensnared and disabled most Christian contributions to their national life other than abject obedience. *SCM Core Reader*, 2.5, gives a vivid illustration.
- The economic disaster of the 1929 Wall Street slump, when the New York stock exchange lost much of its value and gravely disturbed almost all international trade and thousands of jobs also across Europe. Its huge effects brought extremities of poverty and unemployment to the often newly industrialized and urban communities that had thought they were escaping the penury known for so long by their rural ancestors.
- In 1936 Spain was torn apart in the Civil War between republicans and Generalissimo Franco's nationalist, traditionalist Catholic-supporting forces, which achieved victory in 1939.
- The Second World War then brought the horrors of the Holocaust for Jews and Gypsies, huge loss of life, especially in the USSR, the ruin by aerial bombardment of countless cities and industries, the sinking of many ships and threats to others – and much else. It ended with the monstrous sign of atomic weaponry – not directly used in Europe, but produced by the leading academics and deployed by the leading politicians of the 'Christian West'.

The second half of the century brought, thank God, on the whole considerably more happy and encouraging developments, but not without continuing sores and threats. For example:

- The disbanding of the British and French colonial empires, mostly by relatively peaceful processes, though not without full-scale wars in Ireland (already in the 1920s), Israel/Palestine and Algeria, each with consequences still unreconciled at the end of the century, and each in its own way reflecting serious religious enmities.
- The long, often relentless struggles between state and church in the Communist countries. The worst single episodes of persecution of Christians

were those in the USSR under Stalin in the 1930s and under Krushchev in the 1960s. But almost all of the Communist nations experienced disgraceful pressures and imprisonments, let alone deaths, in their often very different contexts, as well as many individual stories of Christian faithfulness and resistance, including those among Orthodox grandmothers in the USSR, of the more intellectual Protestants carrying further in the German Democratic Republic the heritage of the Confessing Church under Hitler, or those of the more populist Catholic patterns of protest and subversion that blossomed in Poland in the Solidarity movement of the early 1980s.

- The former Yugoslavia, which had seemed so comparatively peaceful under Marshal Tito, fell apart after his death into its earlier constituent 'nations', with increasingly violent wars involving Serbia and its increasingly hostile former partners, again with the factor of contrasting religious allegiances playing a major role.
- The rise of the global economic empire of the multinational business corporations of the USA, in close cultural harmony with its parallel powers of mass communication, pillaging the natural resources, especially mineral, of the 'underdeveloped' nations. This was the largest factor which in effect divided the world into an ever-widening gulf between the richer, persons and nations (many of them in Europe), and the many poorer.

To set against these, what can 'Christian' Europe claim that will continue to have health-giving effects in the twenty-first century and beyond? Perhaps at least a major share in two lasting areas of concern:

- The League of Nations in the aftermath of the First World War, and then the United Nations Organization (UNO) after the Second. Both of these have proved far from adequate to the tasks of building and preserving world peace, although of the two the UNO has been able to outlast its less effective moments. It may yet be reformed into an appropriate anticipation of the international decision-making forum and agency that our single world community undoubtedly and badly needs. Europe cannot boast any specific contribution, apart perhaps from those of the first two General Secretaries of the UNO, Trygve Lie from Norway, and Dag Hammarskjöld from Sweden. But it has provided much lasting public support for the efforts of both bodies.
- Since the end of the Second World War, several European countries and, then the European Union as a whole, have been in the forefront of developing patterns of 'welfare state' or 'social market economies'. These, in their variety and with many weaknesses, are committed to reducing the gaps between richer and poorer in a way that can promise a reasonable degree of mutual respect and empowerment between the two ends of the social pyramid. Their early stages were made to suffer not a little from the 'Washington Consensus' of the Reagan/Thatcher alliance in the 1980s, dedicated primarily to increasing the wealth of the already richer. But they remain in the minds and hearts of many Europeans a most important encouragement in the long struggle for justice and peace within each nation.

Turning then more specifically to what Christians may have been able to contribute positively within this large picture, there are at least four areas that deserve to be remembered and carried through into the new century:

- On the worldwide scene, the growth and flourishing of the ecumenical movement, with its figurehead in the World Council of Churches, based in the Swiss city of Geneva alongside the League of Nations and the International Red Cross, has been a notable contributor to a better future. For Europe, a parallel Conference of European Churches was founded in 1959, consisting not only of the churches that were already members of the WCC, but also of a number of smaller churches that needed the support of an all-European body. In later years it has arranged, in partnership with the Conference of European Catholic Bishops' Conferences, three large European Ecumenical Assemblies (Basel, 1989; Graz, 1997; and Sibiu, Romania, 2007), which have succeeded in providing a strong sense of a pan-European identity and commitment to churches often earlier rather isolated.
- In the Roman Catholic Church, the Second Vatican Council and its far-reaching outworkings around the world have in many ways mirrored a parallel development to the ecumenical movement, including of course the Catholic Church's own newly rediscovered and profound commitment to that same unity, mission and renewal of the total Church of Christ.
- Through leading figures such as Archbishop Nathan Söderblom, Professor Karl Barth, Archbishop William Temple, Pastor Dr Willem Visser 't Hooft, Père Yves Congar OP, Pope John XXIII, Archbishop Anastasios of Tirana – and many others, Europe has provided inspiration and leadership to a host of theological and faith-related movements that have contributed more than any of us can adequately map to both the new strength of the civilized patterns of life in today's Europe and to the best thinking and liturgical creativity of today's churches in and for Europe.
- Let the names of Dietrich Bonhoeffer, Franz Jägerstätter and Petru Dumitriu stand for the thousands of martyrs, during the World Wars and under Communist regimes, who have accepted a cruel death as the price of their faith in Christ, and whose witness is still inspiring and strengthening many others for the tasks that face us today and tomorrow.

The constant and dismaying question of church decline

This has become in recent decades, though the awareness of it is by no means new, the peculiar burden of Europe's Christians, a never-yet-ending topic for further research, and a major cry for help in a time of profound perplexity.

Grace Davie sets out in her admirable study *Religion in Modern Europe: A Memory Mutates* a characteristic set of figures.[3] Church attendance figures for western Europe were found in 1990 by the European Values Systems Study Group, a highly reputable trans-national academic project, to be as follows (in percentages of the total populations):

Countries	At least once a week	On special occasions	Never
Belgium	23	13	52
France	10	17	59
Ireland	81	6	5
Italy	40	23	19
Portugal	33	8	47
Spain	33	15	38
Great Britain	13	12	56
Netherlands	21	16	47
West Germany	19	16	41
Northern Ireland	49	6	18

Church attendance (in percentages of total populations)

Once a month or more (these come from another survey by the same group):

Denmark	11
Sweden	10
Norway	10

As has been suggested above, any such figures deserve the most careful testing, and will always be found to need complementing by a wide range of specific factors, let alone causes. In Ireland, in 1990, the possible resolution of the conflict between Unionists (strongly identified with Protestantism) and Republicans (likewise with Catholicism) was still very tentative. By 2003 the picture was shifting rather closer to the European 'norms'. But the overall picture is clear, namely that regular church attendance in all these countries is now relatively slight – the 'average' for the countries surveyed came to 29 per cent weekly attenders – and has fallen off by high proportions since the beginning of the twentieth century. Gill[4] reckons that for England the census of 1851 is the point of the highest recorded regular attendance, and that the decline set in at about the turn of the century.

The causes of this steep decline are many and various, but some major generalizations may be risked:

- The first, surprisingly ancient, is that almost from its beginnings, Christian faith in Europe has been a top-down affair. Most people became Christians, centuries ago, because their king, their landlord, their admired leader, said they should. The event is long forgotten, but until and unless people have received fresh cause to lay hold on their faith anew – as in, say, the rise of Methodism in England in the mid-eighteenth century – they will one day lose their hold on it. The conditions of modernity and post-modernity strongly encourage such a loss.

- Slightly more recent, traceable at least to the Reformation, is the long-term effect of the divisions within Christianity. All too many wars in Europe have been fought between different sorts of Christians. Still today people all too easily expect Christianity to be a divisive force. Notice how the public media, the press, films, etc. almost only give 'religion' a serious amount of space when there is some quarrel, some split, some unhappiness to report and discuss. It is rare to find an item simply giving a straight report on some discussion or project which a church or group of Christians has been pursuing that has been going well. See David Martin's summaries (*SCM Core Reader*, 12.5) of ways in which three major Catholic-majority nations in Europe have been reacting in recent generations to changes within and around them.
- This affects not least church–state relationships. Again and again in European history, there has been some set pattern of this relationship to try and cope with the divisions – such as, the *cuius regio, eius religio* of the Peace of Westphalia that ended the Thirty Years War in the 1640s, by which all the citizens of each 'nation' were required to follow the faith of its ruler. The *laïcité* of France, imposed by an Act of 1903 which rigidly excludes anything religious from the concerns of the state, was a later attempt at a similar overall pattern that has proved no less questionable. Sooner or later any such arrangement proves inadequate in one way or another. The search for even more appropriate ones will continue for generations yet.
- Coming then to the intellectual factors to which Mary Heimann is pointing,[5] it is undeniable that all the arguments unleashed by the Enlightenment of the eighteenth century, backed up by much in what the world thinks of as 'modern science', have spread the sense that Christianity not only cannot be proved but has been positively proved not to be true. Look up her chapter for some of the arguments that deserve to follow on that sweeping statement, but it is sure that all too many 'ordinary' Europeans will say something of the sort to those who ask them about their faith, or the lack of it.
- A parallel social reason is that since the settled rural people of Europe started to flock into the towns and cities for urban forms of work – in Britain in the late eighteenth and early nineteenth centuries, in other countries later – and in some, Poland for instance, still today – there has been a sharp break with the patterns and culture of their rural life. Many families and communities for whom in their rural lives churchgoing had been a normal part of their week have found that they no longer need or want to bother with it in the city. Cox's study of what happened in Lambeth, a part of London just south of the Thames (*SCM Core Reader*, 12.2), is illustrative of just how this sort of factor affected one specific urban area at the turn of the twentieth century.
- The mobility that is characteristic of 'modern' life is now affecting ever-higher proportions of the population. It goes hand in hand with the individualism by which in today's Europe no child expects her or his parents to take any decision for her or him after the teenage years – which Peter Berger in the 1970s saw as a profound 'homelessness' affecting people badly (*SCM Core Reader*, 12.4). Both these are influential in more or less unconsciously pushing younger people away from any regular church attendance.

- Another important, if also largely unconscious, factor is that of modern technology. Thanks to so many recent inventions, most Europeans can take it for granted that if they want something to change they can find the right machine to make it do so. If the right machine is not yet to hand, we imagine we have only to sit down and invent it ourselves. In fact, of course, not so many of us are born inventors. But Europeans are all very accustomed to thinking that they and their fellow human beings are totally 'in charge' of their own lives. They have no need of an 'outside' deity to help them make the most of life.

- Finally in this all too sketchy list of major, general factors, is the affluence so many people in today's Europe enjoy. Yes, many people are still relatively poor. But even they expect one day to be much better off, and then to have at their disposal at any time, as the majority already do, whatever they want by way of entertainment, pastime or pleasure. Any of these distractions can readily push church on Sunday morning out of sight as an appropriately desirable – or even understandable – part of life.

These are the more 'outward' factors that affect almost all people in Europe today. But there is also no shortage of more inward factors, which it is impossible to generalize about. One frequently mentioned is the degree of hurt caused when a Christian says or does something that rejects the other party in a conversation. For some deep reason in the psyche, this seems often to hurt far more deeply than it deserves to, let alone is meant to. When some minister, for instance, has been slow to agree to baptize a new baby, and has suggested that the parents should come and share in some sessions of a baptismal preparation group or class before a decision is taken, those parents may hold it so bitterly in mind that they never go near a church again!

One particularly striking finding of many surveys is that, positively, the degree of continuing belief in the main teachings of Christianity – about God, Jesus of Nazareth, sin and salvation – is much higher than the regularity of churchgoing. On the other hand, those rarer surveys that directly ask people why they do *not* go to church any more (as over against the habits of their parents or grandparents) are almost always told: 'There was no particular reason, I can't really remember when we first stopped ...' Few people have decided to follow any particular alternative system of belief, let alone been 'converted' by modern science or any other general theory. It has more usually been a matter of growing indifference, of unthinkingly slipping away from something that one's forebears may have seen differently but of which today's people have not had occasion to discover the value for themselves. Life is already too busy with other things people want to do, with having a working and playing life so full and rewarding, that any spare time, on Sunday or whenever else, is best spent at home.

Towards appropriate responses

It often seems as if European Christians are so spellbound by the inevitability of decline that they overlook how impressed they would be if, say, the number of Christians in China (as it soon well may) were to grow so far as to show the rate of regular churchgoing that Europe can still rely on. So why not accept that a certain era of top-down Christianity has now passed away and face the actual future with the strengths presently available? There is no need for, nor any conceivable advantage in, defeatism. Grace Davie's closing chapter (extracts in *SCM Core Reader*, 12.8) points to several ways in which it remains desirable and appropriate for Christians to make the most of what they and their faith still stand for.

One hopeful sign from several surveys is that a majority of those who are still actively engaged in their churches have taken a deliberate, personal and in its own way costly decision that they believe in Jesus Christ as Son of God and Saviour, and will make the time to put that into what they see as coherent and meaningful practice. If this is true – as it must be, more or less – then it means that the general quality of Christian discipleship and commitment must be higher than our churches have perhaps ever known before. There is of course no straightforward correlation between quality and quantity, but of the two there can be no doubt that it is quality that counts in the long run, let alone in the sight of God.

A second such sign has to do with the higher rates of 'belief' than of 'belonging' uncovered by most surveys. No fewer than 72 per cent of the total UK population declared themselves to be 'Christian' in the national census of 2001. How can their churchgoing fellow Christians best help such people explore more deeply into the joys and potential of that than most of the 72 per cent so far seem to be doing? The great central questions about the meaning and purpose of life are of course all the more difficult to handle when lives are so dominated by the everyday matters of work, money, social relationships, etc. that it is easy to understand how many people never really, personally, make the time to 'come apart and ponder' them. But they are still inevitably there, under the surface, and from time to time showing themselves as necessary or urgent questions. Few people can wholly escape having to face up to times of major decision or of disturbing failure. The European churches clearly need to find new ways of opening up these questions for the widest possible exploration and follow-through, for which events like the German Kirchentag or the British Greenbelt, or the many courses like those called Alpha, have begun to model appropriate processes. If people can feel they are finding their own ways of exploring these central questions, and of coming to their own conclusions and decisions – rather than simply accepting those that somebody else is putting to them – then a good many will positively want the sense of community in obedience that the churches are there to embody.

A third, perhaps surprising, conclusion to which these surveys point is that it is potentially helpful that in European cities there are present nowadays people and communities of virtually every major faith from around the world. For the last 50 years, school children have been learning that there is Christianity, there is Hinduism, there is Islam, along with Buddhism, Judaism and a few more. In the abstract, that piece of knowledge has probably often served to encourage the teenager to think, and sometimes say, 'I'd rather like to explore one of the others more than Christianity.' Today that can often be positively pursued, not merely thought. Yet a common experience in meeting someone of a different faith to one's own is in fact to find oneself strengthened in one's own, not least by realizing how inadequately one has explored it. Europe's newly multicultural societies, with several major faith traditions represented articulately within them, will surely in the long run throw up many new possibilities which will be a challenge for each and all of those faiths. But already the chance of making one's own explorations, and thus of coming to more lastingly meaningful conclusions for oneself within some degree of interfaith contact or dialogue, can only be healthy alike for the individuals involved and for society as a whole.

Added to that can be the undoubtedly positive effects that the various diasporas that Europe has been able to welcome over the last century are having on their former home traditions, as well as on those Europeans who learn so much from them. The Russian Orthodox diaspora, for example, that arrived in Paris in the early 1920s and spread out from there has long made a great contribution to the enrichment of the faith and worship of many different Christian communities throughout Europe. Those same Orthodox have also learnt from their interaction with people of other backgrounds how their own tradition can be refreshed and renewed to face up to the challenges and demands of a very different world than that of the Russian emperors. On a very different front, the arrival at Tilbury, near London, in June 1948 of the *Empire Windrush*, carrying 492 Jamaicans, was the beginning of an Afro-Caribbean diaspora that has brought large numbers of Afro-Caribbeans seeking work and a prosperity most often earlier denied to them. They have brought to Europe also a whole family of sizeable 'new churches', with their own sorts of leadership and patterns of worship and obedience. The 'historic' European churches have not a little to learn from these too. One hopes that the Afro-Caribbean fellow Christians are in turn encountering in Europe significant new patterns of faith and obedience which can in the long run refresh the experience and expectations of the peoples they came from.

Another whole range of positive effects has been opened up, though too often hemmed in by the prevailing social conditions, by the arrival of large populations of North African Muslims into France, Turkish Muslims into Germany and Pakistani and Bangladeshi Muslims into the UK. These, together with people of the other world faiths, have also brought a wake-up call to European Christians. They are living symbols that all faiths now need, each and all in their own ways, to grow into the role of enabling their members to live in the one world we all share, with all the wider and deeper challenges that brings. None of our faiths can any more be satisfied with one small part of the world to relate to. They each need to grow into their potential calling as faiths for the one world, the entire human community, in ways that will surely prove of high significance in the century ahead.

Finally, today's new situation, as Davie points out so well in her analysis of the 'vicariousness' of Christian faith (*SCM Core Reader*, 12.8), calls European Christians – and their fellow citizens of other major faiths – to learn in a quite new way to explore and make meaningful to others the 'public' purpose, meaning and service of the faith one holds to. It is not just for one's personal, family or local life, but has been from the beginning – why else those three kings from afar visiting Jesus in the manger? – a faith for all humankind, and thus also for the great affairs of state and the universal human family.

Large areas of as yet unexplored interfaith listening and discerning are here opened up for which much time and patience will be required. Both Archbishop John Habgood's essay on the values at the root of concern for human rights (*SCM Core Reader*, 12.6) and Prime Minister Garret Fitzgerald's list of 'revolutions in our political thought' in recent years (*SCM Core Reader*, 12.7) point in precisely this direction, uncovering the deep and often hidden service which the Christian tradition, if interpreted appropriately, can render to our public life and planning. In regard to the huge threats we clearly have to face in the twenty-first century, whether that from climate change or those of the 'conflicts of civilization' that some prophets are warning about, any real degree of mutual understanding and mutual trust that can be found in the sharing of fellow citizenship in Europe between Christians and neighbours of other convictions, not least Jews, Muslims, Hindus, Sikhs and Buddhists, will be hugely important for the common future.

Further reading

G. Davie (1994), *Religion in Britain since 1945: Believing without Belonging*, Oxford: Blackwell.
G. Davie (2000), *Religion in Modern Europe: A Memory Mutates*, London and New York: Oxford University Press.
R. Gill (2003), *The Empty Church Revisited*, London: Ashgate.
D. Martin (2005), *On Secularization : Towards a Revised General Theory*, London and Burlington VT: Ashgate.

For the period of Communist rule in East and Central Europe:
T. Beeson (1982), *Discretion and Valour: Religious Conditions in Russia and Eastern Europe*, rev. edn, London: Collins, Fount Paperbacks.

For a more general survey of the European churches at the end of the twentieth century:
K. Clements and T. Sabev (2004), 'Europe', in J. Briggs, M. Oduyoye and G. Tstetsis (eds), *A History of the Ecumenical Movement: Volume 3 1968–2000*, Geneva: WCC Publications, pp. 533–64.

Notes

1 M. Heimann, 'Christianity in Western Europe from the Enlightenment', in A. Hastings (ed.) (1999), *A World History of Christianity*, London: Cassell, pp. 458ff.
2 R. Gill (2003), *The Empty Church Revisited*, London: Ashgate, pp. 256, taking further the exploration begun in his book (1993), *The Myth of the Empty Church*, London: SPCK.
3 G. Davie (2000), *Religion in Modern Europe: A Memory Mutates*, Oxford and New York: Oxford University Press, pp. 218ff.
4 Gill, *Empty Church Revisited*, p. 8.
5 Hastings, *World History*, pp. 458ff.

13

War and Peace

The twentieth century was marked by tragic wars and conflicts. Two World Wars (1914–18 and 1939–45) left many millions of combatants and civilians dead and caused economic and social devastation in countries around the globe. There were more 'local' wars in which some of the major powers were engaged, such as Korea (1950–53), Vietnam (1959–75), Afghanistan (1979–88), the Falklands/Malvinas War (1982) and the first Gulf War (1991). There were wars of independence in many African countries and border disputes that have led to conflicts and wars in Africa, Asia and elsewhere. There were internal guerrilla conflicts in Central and Latin America, Asia and Africa. There were devastating conflicts and wars between various nations in the Middle East during much of the second half of the century (see Chapter 6).

Some of the chapters on Christianity in various regions have touched on some of these events. This chapter cannot possibly examine, in any comprehensive way, the Christian responses to all these military disputes. Our intention, therefore, is to explore some of the principles on the basis of which Christians have made judgements on the moral issues of war and peace, to examine the responses of the churches and ecumenical agencies to the two World Wars, and to outline Christian ethical perspectives on nuclear weapons. The chapter will end by examining some of the causes and consequences of the many wars that have marked the latter decades of the twentieth century, and by exploring aspects of the Christian responses to these conflicts.

The morality of war

Traditionally, Christians have adopted two contrasting sets of principles in reaching judgements about the ethics of war. Pacifism goes back to the earliest days of Christendom and is likely to have been the foundation of Christian attitudes to war in the first three centuries. Based predominantly on the teaching of Jesus, as represented, for example, in 'the Sermon on the Mount' (Matthew 5—7), pacifism rejects all use of violence both in personal relationships and in relationships between peoples and states. It claims that the only genuinely Christian attitude is that of non-violence. Thus it rejects all war as being in conflict with the teaching of Jesus. A number of peace churches have adopted this approach to war during recent centuries. Notable among these has been the Religious Society of Friends (Quakers). A statement of their position issued in 1915 (that is, in the very early months of the Great War) by the London Yearly Meeting, set out this position clearly:

> Meeting at a time when the nations of Europe are engaged in a war of unparalleled magnitude, we have been led to recall the basis of the peace testimony of our religious Society. It is not enough to be satisfied with a barren negative witness, a mere proclamation of non-resistance ... We must search for a positive, vital, constructive message. Such a message, a message of supreme love, we find in the life and death of our Lord Jesus Christ. We find it in the doctrine of the indwelling Christ ... leading as it does to the recognition of the brotherhood of all men. Of this doctrine our testimony as to war and peace is a necessary outcome ... [calling us] to the peaceable spirit and the rule of love in all the broad and manifold relations of life.[1]

Throughout the twentieth century, a large number of Christians and many churches and denominations, have maintained this, at times costly, pacifist witness. (See, for example, *SCM Core Reader on World Christianity in the Twentieth Century*, 1.6, for Gandhi's influence on Martin Luther King, and for a more recent evaluation of this pacifist tradition, see the address by John Habgood, then Archbishop of York, to the Anglican Pacifist Fellowship in 1987, in *SCM Core Reader*, 13.2.)

However, it is probably true to say that another approach has had greater prominence within most of the churches. This is the 'just-war' tradition. This dates back to the fourth century, when the conversion to Christianity of the Emperor Constantine meant that Christians – having in general held a pacifist position – had to struggle for the first time with the question of whether it was morally acceptable for Christians to engage in war in the name of an empire that was now ruled by a Christian emperor and had at least accepted Christianity as a recognized and legitimate religion. It was St Augustine of Hippo (334–430) who proposed the principles of a just war. He proposed two key principles, namely, that the war had to be authorized by a legitimate authority and that the war was being fought with the right intention. In the thirteenth century, St Thomas Aquinas (1224–74) expanded on these principles (*SCM Core Reader*, 13.1). His version of the just-war theory has been deployed by Christian churches throughout the subsequent centuries.

In a Pastoral Letter on war and peace (issued in May 1983, focusing particularly on the question of nuclear weapons, which we shall examine later) the Catholic bishops of the USA confirmed and developed the just-war principles, dividing them between *jus ad bellum* (justice in approaching war) and *jus in bello* (justice within warfare) (*SCM Core Reader*, 13.6). In the preamble, the bishops state:

> just-war teaching has evolved as an effort to prevent war. Only if war cannot be rationally avoided does the teaching then seek to restrict and reduce its horrors. It does this by establishing a set of rigorous conditions which must be met if the decision to go to war is to be morally permissible. Such a decision, especially today, requires extraordinarily strong reasons for overriding the presumption *in favor of peace* and *against* war.[2]

This crucial emphasis on the need to avoid war and to see just-war principles as a set of 'rigorous' principles to be applied only if recourse to war is the only option available, needs to be emphasized, lest these principles are seen as an easy justification for a state's engagement in war. Indeed, the US bishops and other Christian leaders and organizations, as we shall see, have been very articulate and firm in their opposition to twentieth century wars in which the USA and other nations and states have been engaged.

As we review some examples of ways in which Christians and Christian churches have responded to wars and conflicts during the century, these principles will be seen to be fundamental.

The Great War

In many ways, the Great War (1914–18) was a European war, although other nations and states became involved. Direct military action left at least 10 million people dead; many more died of disease and starvation during and after the war and it had devastating economic consequences. Commenting on this war and the Second World War (1939–45), J. M. Roberts writes:that 'though [the Great War] sucked into itself other conflicts and jumbled together many issues, Europe was at the heart of it. In the end, self-inflicted damage would deprive [Europe] of her world hegemony ... [that] would become undeniable only in 1945.'[3] The early years of the twentieth century saw transformational changes 'in politics and society' as well as 'upheavals in ideas and even personal behaviour' and Roberts comments:

[In] these huge transformations, some of whose origins lie very deep indeed, what came to be called the 'Great War' was a major catalyst. It was the bloodiest, most intensely fought, and most costly struggle that had ever taken place. These uniquenesses explain its other striking features, its unprecedented psychological and cultural effects.[4]

In its aftermath, new republics were created: Latvia, Lithuania and Estonia in the Baltics, a revitalized Poland, a new republic of Czechoslovakia, an Austrian republic, a reduced Hungary and a new South Slav kingdom.

Naturally, the Great War had an enormous impact on Christians, on Christian churches and on Christianity as a whole. Two such consequences may be mentioned here. The first is the impact of the Great War on theology. It led to a transformation, a sea-change, in Christian theology which had a lasting influence on the twentieth century. At the heart of this theological revolution was Karl Barth (1886–1968), a Swiss theologian regarded by many as the greatest Reformed theologian of the twentieth century. He was trained and taught within the liberal tradition of Reformed theology with its emphasis on 'the social gospel' and its belief and confidence in human progress and social evolution, rooted in, shaped by and in fulfilment of the Kingdom of God on earth. The Great War destroyed Barth's confidence in this theological paradigm. How can Christians believe in God-given human progress and the establishment of God's Kingdom on earth, through human agencies, when those very human agencies were prepared to engage in and uncritically support a war that had such devastating human consequences? As a result of this self-questioning, the second edition of his commentary on the Epistle to the Romans (1922) marked a turning point in twentieth-century Protestant theology. His theology has been described as a theology of crisis, emphasizing both the crisis of God's judgement and the cultural crisis created by the Great War. This crisis of confidence in the possibility of human progress led Barth to articulate a theology in which all the initiative was God's, in which God proclaims a 'no' to any human achievement and God's 'yes' through the raising of Christ from the dead. In David Ford's words: 'With explosive vehemence and vivid rhetoric'[5] Barth proclaims the Jesus Christ that he discovers through the Epistle to the Romans: 'We stumble when we suppose that we can treat of Him, speak and hear of Him – *without being scandalized.*'[6] Ford comments that 'each moment of time confronts the judgement of God and only because of the "impossible possibility" of faith in the gospel is there a way through'.[7] In a sense, all theology after Barth's commentary on Romans was shaped in one way or another, either as a development of or a reaction against, by his dialectic understanding. To a large extent, it signalled the end of a liberal theology with its confidence in the possibility of human progress.

The second consequence of the Great War may be seen in an ecumenical response to the devastation, enmity and division it brought, especially within Europe. The first universal conference on life and work, created and convened largely at the initiative of Archbishop Nathan Söderblom of Sweden in 1925, was motivated, among other things, by the sense of war-torn humanity left by the war. It analysed the nature of the crisis of post-war Europe and emphasized, in response to what the Message from Stockholm called 'the sins and sorrows, the struggles and losses of the Great War and since' the vision of a 'Christian fellowship that transcends denominational oppositions and national antagonisms'.[8] The conference offered

> principles of a Christian internationalism, equally opposed to a national bigotry and a weak cosmopolitanism. We have affirmed the universal character of the Church ... We summon the Churches to share with us our sense of the horror of war, and of its futility as a means of settling international disputes, and to pray and to work for the fulfilment of the promise that under the sceptre of the Prince of Peace, 'mercy and truth shall meet together, righteousness and peace shall kiss each other'.[9]

The crucial significance of this event was not so much what it said about war but that, through this Life and Work Universal Conference (perhaps an overambitious description of the event), those Protestant and Orthodox (but not Catholic) leaders from a broad family of churches worldwide were able to speak together about an event that so transformed considerable areas of the world. (For further reflection on the First World War, see *SCM Core Reader*, 16.3.)

The Second World War

The war that was to continue until 1945 began on 1 September 1939 with the German bombing of Polish cities. Two days later Britain and France went to war against Germany in defence of Poland and to seek to prevent German domination of Europe. In Roberts' view, although it was not obvious at the time, these early years of the war 'marked a break in European and world history like no other one. Those years register the final, no longer deniable fact that the history of Europe had come to an end as a self-contained, coherent, self-explanatory entity.'[10] Many European countries were occupied by Germany (which had been joined by Italy). German attempts to attack the USSR were not successful and led to the USSR joining the struggle against German forces. By 1941, the United States of America was also offering support to those opposing the German advance, and in December of that year, Hitler, the German Chancellor, declared war on the United States. Japan had already attacked British, Dutch and American territories in the Pacific. So, in Roberts' words, 'Europe's future was now to be settled not by her own efforts but by the two great powers on her flanks, the United States and Soviet Russia.'[11]

In December 1942, Japan executed an air attack on the American fleet in Pearl Harbor, all but wiping out American air units, though it did not destroy the US navy. This transformed the war into a 'World War' in a much more real sense than the Great War had been. North Africa, the Atlantic, Arctic, Pacific and Indian oceans as well as the Mediterranean, were part of the vast conflagration. In due course, the nations allied against Germany and Italy won costly victories in these theatres of war. Europe was gradually regained, again at great cost. Germany capitulated on 7 May 1945, following Hitler's suicide five days earlier. The war in the Far East still continued. On 6 August 1945 the USA dropped atomic bombs on Hiroshima and Nagasaki with horrific consequences. On 2 September Japan surrendered and the war was over.

The brutality of this war and its cost in human lives was at an unprecedented scale. Five to six million Jews were killed in the Holocaust, more than fifty million people were killed as a result of military operations, including possibly twenty million people lost in Russia alone, and around half that number in China. Famine caused the death of millions more and the bombing of Nagasaki and Hiroshima had devastating effects not only in their immediate aftermath but also over succeeding generations. 'It was probably true that no one before 1939, however fearful of war, would have guessed that human society could endure such bloodshed and survive.'[12]

In evaluating Christian responses to the horror of this war, we can only highlight a few examples. The first highlights the struggle between the principles of pacifism and the moral requirement of resisting one of the most cruel and inhuman acts of what can only be described as genocide in recent history. In struggling with this question, Bonhoeffer the pacifist became Bonhoeffer the conspirator.[13] Clements distinguishes between a pacifism which rejects violence 'in an aggressive national cause' and a pacifism which leads to 'complicity in the greater guilt of allowing ... genocide to continue'. He quotes Bonhoeffer's last known words, in a message to George Bell, Bishop of Chichester, shortly before his final court martial: 'Tell him, that with him, I believe in the principle of our universal Christian brotherhood which rises above all national interests and conflicts, and that our victory is certain.'

Within Germany, one of the key responses to the Second World War was the Stuttgart Declaration submitted by leaders of the German Confessing Church to ecumenical representatives in a meeting in Stuttgart in October 1945 (*SCM Core Reader*, 13.4). It makes a declaration of guilt and a commitment to a new beginning:

> With great pain we say: By us infinite wrong was brought over many peoples and countries. That which we often testified to in our communities, we express now in the name of the whole church: We did fight for long years in the name of Jesus Christ against the mentality that found its awful expression in the National Socialist regime of violence; but we accuse ourselves for not standing to our beliefs more courageously, for not praying more faithfully, for not believing more joyously, and for not loving more ardently.
>
> Now a new beginning is to be made by our churches. Based on the Holy Scripture ... they start to cleanse themselves of the influences of beliefs foreign to the faith and to reorganise themselves.
>
> ... We hope to God that by the common service of the churches the spirit of violence and revenge, which today again wants to become powerful, will be directed to the whole world, and that the spirit of peace and love comes to predominate, in which alone tortured humanity can find healing.[14]

This declaration became an important step in recognizing the failure of the churches in the cause of justice and peace, and contributed to creating a new union of churches in the Protestant Church in Germany and to opening the door to the German churches to play their part fully in the ecumenical movement which was in process of formation and in the search for peace. For another key statement 'The Barmen Declaration of the Confessing Church in Germany', which predated the war, see *SCM Core Reader*, 1.3.

At the first Assembly of the World Council of Churches, three years after the end of the war, George Bell contributed to the debate on Section IV of the Assembly Report, 'The Church and International Disorder'. The report presents his comment as follows:

> The Bishop of Chichester said that ... [m]odern war was a violation of order and justice in a supreme degree ... One of the great tasks of the Christian Church was to mitigate ... barbarism and to distinguish between just and unjust wars. A just war was fought for just causes with just means, and terminated with a just peace. But a great change occurred in the twentieth century ... In the second World War, total war became unrestricted war and means were employed that no one could call human – obliteration bombing and the indiscriminate use of atomic force. The distinction between just and unjust war had disappeared. We had returned to barbarism. Even if we had a just cause, the means by which we defended it were not just. It was time for the Christian Church to urge the world to recognize the harsh fact: that modern war brings barbarism and cannot be an act of justice.[15]

The significant point in this intervention is that George Bell does not argue from a pacifist perspective but from a just-war perspective and claims that the very nature and methodologies of modern warfare, even during the years of the Second World War, undermined the moral authority of the just-war principles. During subsequent decades, as we shall see below, these same principles would be questioned even more comprehensively with the development in nuclear armaments by the dominant world powers. But it is noteworthy that Bell was questioning their validity, even at this relatively early stage in the development of atomic weapons, as they were then called. The Section Report upon which Bell was commenting was approved unanimously by the Assembly, stating that 'War as a method of settling disputes is incompatible with the teaching and example of our Lord Jesus Christ ... In [the circumstances of modern warfare] the tradition of a just war, requiring a just cause and the use of just means, is now challenged' (see *SCM Core Reader*, 13.5, for the full text of the relevant portion of the report).

On the twenty-fifth anniversary of the formation of the United Church of Christ in Japan (Kyodan) a similar statement was issued repenting of the atrocities committed by Japan during the Second World War. The final paragraph read:

> ... in the name of the Kyodan, we issued a statement [*in 1941*] at home and abroad in which we approved of and supported that war, and encouraged prayers for victory.
>
> Indeed, even as our country committed sin, so we too, as a church, fell into the same sin. We neglected to perform our mission as a 'watchman.' Now, with deep pain in our hearts, we confess our sin and ask the Lord for forgiveness. We also seek the forgiveness of the peoples of all nations, particularly in Asia, and of the churches therein and of our brothers and sisters in Christ throughout the world; as well as the forgiveness of the people in our own country.[16]

There is a moral quandary for Christians as they hear church leaders in Germany and Japan asking for forgiveness, while realizing also how much their people suffered at the hands of the Allies. Christianity should always guard against making over-easy judgements about the allocation of blame and moral responsibility in complex situations such as the Second World War.

There has been considerable debate about the role of the Roman Catholic Church in relation to the war. In his encyclical of 1937, Pope Pius XI makes his resolute opposition to the rise of National Socialism in Germany very clear:

> Whoever exalts race, or the people, or the State, or a particular form of State, or the depositories of power, or any other fundamental value of the human community – however necessary and honorable be their function in worldly things – whoever raises these notions above their standard value and divinizes them to an idolatrous level, distorts and perverts an order of the world planned and created by God; he is far from the true faith in God and from the concept of life which that faith upholds.[17]

Pope Pius XI died before the outbreak of the war, to be succeeded by Pope Pius XII who, as Secretary of State, had made a concordat with Hitler, set aside an encyclical against racism and antisemitism and resisted a public condemnation of National Socialism. Küng comments that 'he was almost predisposed (as a professional diplomat) to a pragmatic anti-Communist alliance with totalitarian Nazism (but also with Fascist regimes in Italy, Spain and Portugal)'.[18] There was no protest about the bombing of Poland in 1939. There was no excommunication 'for the "Catholics" Hitler, Himmler, Goebbels and Bormann ... he was silent about the Holocaust, the greatest mass murder of all times.'[19] This Küng regards as a 'moral failure'. It was left to his successor, Pope John XXIII (elected in 1959), to represent a changed attitude to the Jews (greeting them on one occasion outside a Berlin synagogue with the words from Genesis, 'I am Joseph, your brother').

Reflections on responses to two World Wars

A number of lessons may be learned from these illustrations of Christian responses to the two World Wars. First, it soon became clear that the traditional ethical principles by which moral judgements have been made on issues of war and peace were increasingly questioned during both wars. Both the absoluteness of traditional pacifism and the moral principles set out by the just-war tradition were thought by many to be inadequate to tackle the developing realities of modern warfare. This process of moral re-evaluation would continue throughout the century.

Second, the role of the churches came increasingly under the microscope. Offering Christian support for the moral and political aims of a regime or government always carried with it the danger of becoming uncritically complicit in their actions during conflict and war, and the voices of those who spoke a prophetic word of protest and challenge was often unheard or, if heard, ignored or silenced. The ending of war often gave new perspectives and frequently led to confession and repentance and a shared search for the possibilities of renewal and transformation.

Third, in the case of both World Wars, enmities and conflicts between peoples and nations, and the cruelties inflicted on fellow human beings, stimulated new commitments to developing closer fellowship between Christian communities and churches, across national as well as denominational boundaries. Modern warfare proved to be too powerful and too cruel for a divided Church. The formation of the World Council of Churches was, at least in part, a consequence of the forces of destruction and the longing for healing and reconciliation that were unleashed by both wars.

Finally, the ending of the second World War did not in any way reduce the commitment of the churches to the search for peace and the ending of war. One crucial example may be found in *Gaudiem et Spes: The Constitution on the Church in the Modern World* issued by the Second Vatican Council in 1965, 20 years after the ending of the war (*SCM Core Reader*, 13.6). While refusing to deny to nations and states the right to go to war to defend fundamental rights and principles, the statement also calls for a deeper commitment to bring all war to an end and, in particular, to end the arms race, by multilateral rather than unilateral means:

> [T]he arms race is an utterly treacherous trap for humanity, and one which ensnares the poor to an intolerable degree. It is much to be feared that if this race persists, it will eventually spawn all the lethal ruin whose path it is now making ready ... If we refuse to make this effort, we do not know where we will be led by the evil road we have set upon.
>
> It is our clear duty, therefore, to strain every muscle in working for the time when all war can be completely outlawed by international consent ... Since peace must be born of mutual trust between nations and not be imposed on them through a fear of the available weapons, everyone must labor to put an end at last to the arms race, and to make a true beginning of disarmament, not unilaterally indeed, but proceeding at an equal pace according to agreement, and backed up by true and workable safeguards.[20]

The morality of nuclear weapons

Hiroshima and Nagasaki were the first (and, thankfully, still the only) cities to have suffered the horrific consequences of atomic bombs. But humanity has failed to learn the lessons of those devastating attacks. The powerful nations have committed (and still commit) vast sums of money to developing nuclear arsenals. At the end of the Second World War, only the USA possessed an atomic bomb. By the end of the twentieth century, there were nine nuclear powers, and others, despite international treaties and commitments, sought to develop and possess such weapons. Non-proliferation treaties have been agreed and some weapons have been destroyed. But the dangers persist.

So, during the decades after the war, the churches gave particular attention to this question of the possession and use of nuclear weapons. One of the most important statements was issued in 1983 by the US Conference of Catholic Bishops, *The Challenge of Peace* (*SCM Core Reader*, 13.7). Recalling *Gaudiem et Spes* (see above), the Pontifical Academy of Science's *Statement on the Consequences of Nuclear War* (1981) and Pope John Paul II's World Day of Peace Message (1982), the bishops questioned whether the just-war criteria of proportionality (namely, that retaliation must be proportionate to the threat) and discrimination (that is, that the weapons of attack must be capable of distinguishing between military and civilian targets) can ever be satisfied given the indiscriminate and destructive power of these weapons. They conclude their comprehensive statement by affirming that 'decisions about nuclear weapons ... involve fundamental moral choices' and

> The whole world must summon up the moral courage and technical means to say 'no' to weapons of mass destruction; 'no' to an arms race which robs the poor and the vulnerable; and 'no' to the moral danger of a nuclear age which places before humankind indefensible choices of constant terror or surrender.[21]

In July and August of the same year (1983), the Sixth Assembly of the World Council of Churches was held in Vancouver. A Public Issues Committee minute on the elimination of nuclear arms stated:

> Churches must prevail upon governments until they recognize the incontrovertible immorality of nuclear weapons. From its birth as a fellowship of Christian churches the WCC has condemned nuclear weapons for their 'widespread and indiscriminate destruction' and as 'sin against God' in modern war (First WCC Assembly, 1948), recognized early that the only sure defence against nuclear weapons is prohibition, elimination and verification (Second Assembly, 1954) and called on citizens 'to press their governments to ensure national security without resorting to the use of weapons of mass destruction' (Fifth Assembly, 1975).[22]

In view of this sustained opposition to nuclear weapons, the Assembly affirmed a challenge to the churches: 'We believe that the time has come when the churches must unequivocally declare that the production and deployment as well as the use of nuclear weapons are a crime against humanity and that such activities must be condemned on ethical and theological grounds.'

In these two statements by the US Bishops (which became foundational in subsequent ethical discussions about these issues) and the WCC Assembly we have an important Christian consensus that condemns the production, deployment and use of nuclear weapons as contrary to Christian morality. Although it could be argued that the ecumenical consensus may well still accept the principles of just war as relevant and valid for conventional warfare – although a very significant number of Christian traditions and churches would condemn all warfare and adhere to a pacifist stance as a confessional position – during the last decades of the twentieth century there was general agreement that these principles could not be applied to nuclear weapons, and that the possession and use of such weapons are absolutely immoral.

Interestingly, in exploring the moral demands of *Creating a Just Future* (1989), Jürgen Moltmann proposes that what is in fact a deliberately secular ethical theory, namely, Kant's Categorical Imperative, should be used as a basis for humankind's rejection of the nuclear option, so as to ensure the survival of humankind. Kant's maxim of universal law, as set out by Moltmann, is as follows: 'So act that the maxim of your action through your will becomes a universal law for all men and women and the universal law for all men and women becomes the maxim of your actions.'[23] Unless the possession and use of nuclear weapons can be available to all peoples and nations, they cannot be available to any. They cannot be available for universal use, therefore, they cannot be available for use by any nation. Moltmann describes this as 'the categorical imperative for the survival of humankind'.

The last decades of the twentieth century saw the end of the Cold War. The early years of the twenty-first century brought changes to the international military threat, not least because of the commitment to 'the War on Terror' following the attacks of 11 September 2001. While the major powers have been, rightly, vociferous and determined in seeking to prevent new states from developing and possessing nuclear weapons, they have been less committed than could have been wished in honouring proliferation treaties and in reducing their own stocks of nuclear weapons. There has been a danger that the churches, and the international community generally, may have been less vociferous in their witness against nuclear weapons during this recent period than in the past.

Local and regional conflicts: causes, consequences and Christian responses

The years since the end of the Second World War have seen innumerable wars and conflicts within and between nations and states in most regions of the world. We cannot examine these in any detail in this chapter. The focus in this section will be on some of the underlying causes and consequences of these conflicts and the responses to these events by individual Christian leaders, as well as by churches and ecumenical agencies, with a view to discovering whether there has been an emerging consensus within Christianity on issues of war, conflict and peace during this period.

Some of the most devastating conflicts of the latter half of the twentieth century were around land and territory. As we have already seen, some of the wars in which Israel was involved in the Middle East were initiated in order to gain or regain land and territory which they regarded as theirs. The Falklands/Malvinas War was focused on the historical rights to the islands, which had been the subject of dispute and diplomacy between Britain and Argentina ever since Britain took possession of the islands from Argentina following the conflict of 1833. In this and similar situations the question of the legitimacy of territorial claims, either on the basis of, for example, ancient historical or religious tradition or the 'spoil' of wars, is always morally debatable. Some Christian leaders, such as Cardinal Basil Hume, the Presiding Archbishop of the Bishops' Conference of the Roman Catholic Church in England and Wales at the time, argued that the British defence of the Falkland Islands (Islas Malvinas) could be regarded as a 'just cause' as defined by just-war principles (though others voiced strong opposition to this view). Argentinian leaders as well as CLAI (the Latin American churches' regional ecumenical organization) argued that, for historical, geographical and cultural reasons, the Islands were legitimately Argentinian territory and that, in this sense, at least, their invasion of the Islands was also a 'just cause'. The difficult moral question in this and similar situations is: how do Christians (and others) resolve such a moral dilemma when both parties in a conflict can claim that justice is 'on their side'?

Another major cause of conflict during this period was the struggle for independence from colonial rule and the felt – and legitimate – need to establish national sovereignty. The years before the partition of India (as well as the years immediately following independence) saw costly and bloody conflict. Some of the internal wars in Africa were of this kind. Southern Rhodesia (later to become Zimbabwe) and Kenya (both of which had been under British colonial rule), and Angola and Mozambique (which were under Portuguese rule) are examples (from among many) of costly conflicts in which many lives were lost both from among colonial military personnel and from among liberation armies and innocent civilians in many situations around the world. Whereas some former colonies achieved independence without such conflict, many emerging independent states faced guerrilla rebellions. In many ways, Christian voices in response to such conflicts were often ambiguous. Generally, the majority of churches, both denominationally and ecumenically, within such countries as well as within the international Christian community, were clearly in favour of independence for former colonies. They understood and defended the longing of the people of Africa, Asia and Latin America, for example, for liberation, freedom and sovereignty, but found the guerrilla methods of the liberation armies in Africa, for instance, unacceptable. While being sympathetic to the goals of liberation they condemned some of the methods employed for achieving these goals. One example of the Christian response to these costly conflicts – costly not only financially but more significantly in the loss of human life and devastating suffering – was the Programme to Combat Racism, inaugurated by the World Council of Churches following the Uppsala Assembly of 1968. Whereas this programme was not primarily a direct response to wars and conflicts of liberation from colonial rule, it did seek to respond to the racial and racist consequences of many such conflicts and used what were described as the humanitarian agencies within the liberation movements to channel aid and assistance to those who suffered the worst consequences of these conflicts. The enormous controversy (as well as the significant support) generated by this programme – and the perception that through this aspect of the WCC's work, the churches were siding with the liberation movements – was symptomatic of the considerable and deepseated disagreement and conflict within the Christian community, not least in the North and West, over actions that generally were welcomed by Christians and churches in the directly affected countries of the South.

Religion itself, of course, has been an underlying factor in many of the conflicts that have marked the latter decades of the century. Conflicts such as those in the Balkan states, in the Middle East, in Northern Ireland and in regions within Asia had clear religious dimensions. But it would be misleading to attribute the conflicts directly and solely to religious causes. In most such situations, religion had been a powerful influence in shaping the social, cultural, ethnic and political life and realities of these communities. The divisions that led to internal conflict were often rooted in religious divides. But the historical consequences of these divisions, as expressed in socio-economic injustice or political disenfranchisement, were usually more significant factors than the religions themselves. In our own context, we are aware that the 'troubles' in Northern Ireland, as they came to be known, might have appeared to be religious in origin since the conflict seemed to be between Catholic and Protestant communities, the former having nationalist goals while the latter were committed to retaining loyalty to the British monarchy. But the situation was much more complex than such a simplistic analysis suggests. Religion clearly was a factor, but far more significant was the reality of social, economic and political inequality, and the communal divisions and suspicions that were the consequences of these realities. One of the most impressive aspects of the situation in Ireland (the whole of Ireland, Northern Ireland as well as the Republic of Ireland) has been the ability of the churches, all of which have a presence in the whole of the island, to bear witness to and work towards reconciliation among the nationalist and loyalist communities specifically because they were able to recognize a degree of unity, reconciliation and healing among themselves which became symbolic of the possibility of social, economic and political reconciliation and healing within the community as a whole.

Ethnicity has been a another major cause of conflict during recent decades. The cruelties of the Balkan conflicts and the genocide in Rwanda, for example, were largely ethnic in their origins. Following the disintegration of the Yugoslav Federation, the 1990s saw war in Croatia and conflict in Serbia and Bosnia where there was 'ethnic cleansing' of Muslims on a horrific scale. Roberts notes how paradoxical it seems that Europeans who appear, in so many ways, not to be, generally, very different from their fellow Europeans in other nations and states, could commit such 'barbarities' for what are basically ethnic motivations: 'In the Balkans in recent years the full repertoire of the barbarities of the Middle Ages has erupted anew; yet those who launch pogroms, murder, mass rape and intimidation against their ethnically different neighbours also wear clothes like those of other Europeans.'[24]

A message from the Central Committee of the World Council of Churches, issued in January 1994, expressed ecumenical solidarity with those involved. The message recognized that religious symbols and language were being manipulated, and called 'on our member churches ... especially to resist every attempt to use religious sentiment and loyalty in the service of aggressive nationalism'. McCullum comments that this message restated 'the first principle, the over-riding need to remain faithful to the call of Christ to be peacemakers, while pointing to the dangers of ethnic cleansing and unbridled nationalism'.[25]

Four years later, a WCC message to a conference on peace and tolerance in Kosovo, following the conflict there between Serbian forces and ethnic Albanians, called for a negotiated settlement 'based on the establishment of full democracy and respect for the human rights of all communities, majority and minority'.[26]

Similarly, the genocide in Rwanda in 1994 was largely the result of ethnic conflict. Hundreds of thousands of ethnic Tutsis and moderate Hutu sympathizers were brutally murdered, largely at the hands of extremist Hutu militia groups. At least 500,000 Tutsis and thousands of moderate Hutus died in the genocide. Some estimates put the death toll between 800,000 and 1 million. In this conflict, Christians were killing Christians, and there has been long debate about the complicity of Christians and the Christian churches in the genocide. When Archbishop Desmond Tutu visited Rwanda in 1995, as President of the All-Africa Conference of Churches, he counselled Rwandans against pressing for 'total justice' in response to the genocide, since 'justice had to be tempered with mercy'. The greatest need was to stop the cycle of reprisal and counter-reprisal. 'The only way to do that was to move beyond retributive justice to restorative justice and forgiveness'[27] – a path that he was to follow later in South Africa as Chairman of the Truth and Reconciliation Commission.

Among the most difficult regional wars and conflicts to evaluate effectively are those that have involved major world powers. At first sight, they appear to be regional in their focus. But it soon emerges that there are other factors at work. More often than not, the political, economic or commercial interests of the major powers involved play a much more pivotal role than any local or regional factors. Three examples serve to illustrate this.

The Korean War, during the 1950s, was rooted in the division of Korea into North and South along the thirty-eighth parallel, following Korean liberation from the Japanese in 1945, at the end of the Second World War. The north, which was a mainly industrial area, was soon occupied by Soviet Union forces and the south, which was mainly agricultural, was occupied by the Americans. However, after the withdrawal of these forces in 1950, North Korean forces invaded southern Korea. This act was seen as a key moment in the Cold War and the USA believed that it had to take decisive action. The conflict within Korea soon became drawn into the Cold War between what were perceived as western democratic powers and Soviet supported communist interests. The conflict ended with an armistice in July 1953 with many millions of lives lost and an estimated 10 million families divided from one another. More than 50 years later, North and South Korea are still divided, with a largely closed North and a commercially vigorous and internationally open South Korea. There is a longing among many Koreans for reconciliation and a restoration of unity between North and South, including among Christian churches and ecumenical and other organizations in South Korea. But despite many attempts at healing and re-unification, they have not as yet borne fruit.

A statement issued in 2003 (*SCM Core Reader*, 13.8), on the fiftieth anniversary of the ending of the war, called on North Korea to abandon its nuclear ambitions because they believed that 'Any attempt to possess nuclear weapons [would] endanger security and [could] result in enormous tragedy and destruction. North Korea must clearly declare its willingness to give up its nuclear weapons development program for the sake of the life and very existence of its people.' Similarly the statement calls on South Korea

> to make every effort to eliminate the threat of war and pave the way for a peace settlement by combining our commitment to solidarity between North and South and our commitment to the US–South Korea alliance. We denounce war under any circumstances in Korea. We do not want to repeat the agony and suffering of the Korean War. We call on the South Korean government to do its best to dismantle the Cold War structures by extensively enhancing the ongoing South–North peaceful coexistence.[28]

There are lessons here that need to be learned at the beginning of the twenty-first century not just in Korea but throughout the international community.

Similar processes were at work in the Vietnam War in the 1960s and early 1970s. America's support of non-Communist South Vietnam as 'essential for (US) national security'[29] and Chinese and Soviet support for the North and for Viet Cong guerrilla movements into the South, led to Kennedy's sending 23,000 military advisers into South Vietnam in 1962, early in his presidency. By 1968, the year when troop withdrawal began, there were 500,000 US military personnel in Vietnam. A ceasefire was signed in 1973. Some 57,000 American soldiers had died. More than 3 million Vietnamese had been killed and countless other innocent civilians have had to live with enormous suffering.

At the height of the war, Martin Luther King expressed the mind of many, not just in America but around the world. In an address given at Riverside Church in New York on 4 April 1967 (*SCM Core Reader*, 13.9), he called for a revolution of values:

> [A] positive revolution of values is our best defense against communism. War is not the answer. Communism will never be defeated by the use of atomic bombs or nuclear weapons. Let us not join those who shout war and, through their misguided passions, urge the United States to relinquish its participation in the United Nations. These are days which demand wise restraint and calm reasonableness. We must not engage in a negative anti-communism, but rather in a positive thrust for democracy, realizing that our greatest defense against communism is to take offensive action in behalf of justice. We must with positive action seek to remove those conditions of poverty, insecurity, and injustice, which are the fertile soil in which the seed of communism grows and develops.
>
> These are revolutionary times. All over the globe men are revolting against old systems of exploitation and oppression, and out of the wounds of a frail world, new systems of justice and equality are being born. The shirtless and barefoot people of the land are rising up as never before. The people who sat in darkness have seen a great light. We in the West must support these revolutions.[30]

Our final example is the first Gulf War in 1990 following Saddam Hussein's invasion of Kuwait for a mixture of historical (an old border dispute) and commercial (Kuwait was an oil rich state) reasons. Very soon after the invasion, the USA had sent troops to the Gulf, managing to build up a consensus of world opinion against Iraq, including some key Middle Eastern states. The allies struck in January 1991. Within one month, Iraq yielded to their supreme military might. Roberts argues:

> Hussein's attempt to inspire an anti-Israel Islamic crusade had found no takers ... The main losers were the Palestinians. Israel had gained most ... [Yet] he did not seem to have lost his grip on Iraq ... The United States was frustratingly unable to assure itself that the threat posed by 'weapons of mass destruction' ... had gone away ... [The] crisis in the Gulf appeared to have revealed that the oil weapon had lost much of its power.[31]

As the war intensified, the Seventh WCC Assembly was being held in Canberra, Australia. During an intense debate, a statement was issued (*SCM Core Reader*, 13.10) which noted that 'a war of terrible proportions is being waged in the Gulf ... Kuwait and Iraq are being destroyed by bombardment of unprecedented intensity ... [claiming] a mounting toll of victims.'[32] This Assembly had a deep concern for the global impact of the war, and noted, for example, that 'the oil spillage which has already occurred in the Gulf, and the estimated consequences for the global warming of the earth's atmosphere should the oil wells of Kuwait, Iraq and Saudi Arabia be set ablaze, show that the potential of this war for widespread, even global ecological destruction is exceptional.[33] Furthermore, it recognized the devastating consequences for the poorest people in the developing world:

> eliminating major markets for primary exports, causing prices for fuels and petroleum products and for basic foodstuffs like rice and grain to skyrocket ... The war has led to new acts and threats of terrorism in several parts of the world ... [and] has fanned the flames of religious, ethnic and regional conflicts in many countries, especially in Asia.

The tragedy of 11 September 2001, the subsequent second war in Iraq in 2003, the overthrow, ensuing trial and execution of Saddam Hussein, the continuing crisis in the Middle East and the costly struggle of the USA and its allies to support the establishment of their version of democracy in Iraq and to defend themselves against the nations that have been identified as 'the axis of evil', continue to hold the world in a state of fear and terror at the beginning of a new century. The predictions of the Canberra statement are becoming increasingly realized in a global community under threat from so many directions.

Final reflections

At the end of our review of a century which experienced war and its devastating loss of human life on an unprecedented scale, what conclusions can be drawn with regard to Christian responses to war and conflict?

The first, and fairly obvious, conclusion is that the complexities and destructiveness of the global consequences of contemporary wars and of the powerful weapons at our disposal point to the inappropriateness of the old categories and the need to develop new moral foundations for tackling war and conflict in the future. Increasingly, faced with contemporary conflict and warfare, Christians have questioned the validity of just-war principles. Most particularly, the impossibility of targeting the effects of nuclear weapons on military as opposed to civilian targets and of using such weapons for anything that could be described as a proportionate response, invalidates the just-war principles. In this context, Moltmann's proposal that there should be adopted as a fundamental ethical principle, faced with such destruction, 'the categorical imperative for the survival of humankind' seems to offer a pointer to a new ethical framework. In some ways, of course, given the powerful weapons at humankind's disposal, a strong argument could be made – on biblical and theological grounds – for a complete rejection of war under any and all circumstances, a newly formulated global pacifism which enshrines within it Moltmann's principle of 'the survival of humankind'. The difficulty with such an attractive moral principle for many Christians is that such a position fails to provide appropriate means to counteract the inhuman cruelty of oppressive and powerful regimes, not least towards the poor and vulnerable.

How can there be developed a pacifist realism, rooted in the rich traditions of the world's major religions, which can both oppose oppression and cruelty and offer a just and peaceful hope to humankind?

Second, the growing availability of nuclear weaponry and the growing ambitions of those who wish to possess them have raised new moral and political questions. Nuclear proliferation treaties have been warmly welcomed by Christian churches and organizations as well as by the international community generally. However, the effectiveness of these treaties is, to say the least, questionable. In fact, if anything, the growing threat to humankind from terrorism and other subversive activities has made the proliferation of nuclear weapons more rather than less likely. In addition, as we have observed earlier, there is a moral ambiguity at the heart of this debate, since it is those globally powerful states that already possess nuclear weapons and are reluctant to lose their defensive (and perhaps offensive) potential that are also the states that oppose any desire by 'new' nation-states to acquire such weapons. From a Christian – and indeed a humanitarian – perspective, no state can justifiably call for non-proliferation unless it is prepared to forgo such weapons itself. A new understanding of a fair and equal global community where the rights of all have equal significance in political decision-making needs to be developed by the international community before nuclear proliferation treaties are likely to become redundant and ineffective. But we have to ask whether such an ambitious and idealistic goal is likely to be achieved, given the current international situation.

Third, the end of the Cold War has not meant the reduction of the threats to humankind. Indeed, the global threat is as great at the beginning of the twenty-first century as it was at the height of the Cold War. It is only the nature of the threat that has changed. There remains the continuing danger of the ambitions of global political, economic and military powers such as the USA and, increasingly, China. This is likely to mean that there will need to be very urgent international efforts to increase the powers and effectiveness of the UN as a global organization for peace, justice and ecological sustainability that is not constantly subject to the control of the interests of the major powers. Christians, in partnership with the other major world religions, have a moral responsibility to strengthen the capability of the UN organization, but to do so in a way that makes it a credible instrument for peace and justice, not just from the perspective of western 'democratic' states but of all the nations of the South and North, developing and developed. Such strengthening of the UN will need to be an urgent priority if the world is to have a possibility of avoiding global catastrophe through war and conflict in the future.

Fourth, the commitment of the World Council of Churches to convene a Global Christian Forum will be a crucial means for developing, maintaining and strengthening a strong global Christian voice for peace and justice. The wide range of churches and Christian organizations that will participate in the Forum will provide a key gathering place for the broadest range of views and perspectives. Küng's proposal for a global *ecumene* of religions which embraces all religions could provide a key forum and instrument not only for fostering mutual understanding between religions but also to engage in common action towards peace with justice at global, regional and national levels.

These initiatives could contribute in vital ways towards making the voice of religions heard within a revitalized United Nations organization.

Finally, there is an urgent need to address the devastating effects of war on the global environment and on the poor of the earth, and to develop more effective global institutions and binding agreements to prevent, or at least reduce, such possible horrific consequences. However, more fundamentally, there will be the need in the next period to address questions of poverty, injustice and oppression, which continue to be at the root of many conflicts and wars. The UN Millennium Goals (including the target of halving the number of people in poverty in the world by 2015) will be an important contribution to this. To be effective, however, the written agreements and commitments will have to be translated into targeted and monitored actions by governments around the world, most particularly those in the economically developed world.

Further reading

Most textbooks on ethics will include chapters on issues of war and peace. Two may be noted here:

R. Gill (ed.) (2001), *The Cambridge Companion to Christian Ethics*, Cambridge: Cambridge University Press.

R. Gill (2006), *A Textbook of Christian Ethics*, new edn, Edinburgh: T and T Clark.

Two books very helpfully focus specifically on issues of war and peace in the current context:

D. Francis (2004), *Rethinking War and Peace*, London: Pluto Press.

C. Reed (2004), *Just War? Changing Society and the Churches*, London: SPCK.

Notes

1 'Quakers against World War', a statement issued by the Quaker London Yearly Meeting 1915, in *Quaker Faith and Practice*, para. 24.08, quoted in H. Bettenson and C. Maunder (eds) (1999), *Documents of the Christian Church*, Oxford: Oxford University Press, p. 369.

2 http://www.americancatholic.org/Newsletters/CU/ac0883.asp See R. Gill (1995), *A Textbook of Christian Ethics*, second edn, Edinburgh: T & T Clark, pp. 328ff.

3 J. M. Roberts (1999), *Twentieth Century: A History of the World, 1901 to the Present*, London: Penguin Books, p. 243.

4 Roberts, *Twentieth Century*, p. 244.

5 D. Ford (1995), 'Karl Barth', in A. E. McGrath (ed.), *An Encyclopedia of Modern Christian Thought*, Oxford: Blackwell, p. 30.

6 K. Barth (1968), *The Epistle to the Romans*, trans. E. C. Hoskyns, Oxford: Oxford University Press, p. 280.

7 Ford, 'Karl Barth', p. 31.

8 A. J. van der Bent (1992), 'Ecumenical Conferences', in N. Lossky et al. (eds), *Dictionary of the Ecumenical Movement*, Geneva: WCC Publications, pp. 325f.

9 'Message from the Universal Christian Conference on Life and Work, Stockholm, 1925', para. 8, in M. Kinnamon.and B. E. Cope (eds.) (1997), *The Ecumenical Movement: An Anthology of Key Texts and Voices*, Grand Rapids MI: Wm B. Eerdmans, and Geneva: WCC Publications, p. 266.

10 Roberts, *Twentieth Century*, p. 411.

11 Roberts, *Twentieth Century*, p. 422.

12 Roberts, *Twentieth Century*, p. 432.

13 K. Clements, 'Ecumenical Witness for Peace', in J. de Gruchy (ed.) (1999), *The Cambridge Companion to Dietrich Bonhoeffer*, Cambridge: Cambridge University Press, p. 158.

14 Taken from http://www.history.ucsb.edu/faculty/marcuse/projects/niem/StuttgartDeclaration.htm and translated by Harold Marcuse.

15 W. A. Visser 't Hooft (ed.) (1949), *The First Assembly of the World Council of Churches*, London: SCM Press, p. 102.

16 Confession on the responsibility during World War II, issued by the Moderator of the Kyodan, Easter Sunday 1967, taken from http://www.d2.dion.ne.jp/~m_osamu/edoc/UCCJresponsibilityWWII.htm

17 *Mit Brennender Sorge*, Encyclical of Pope Pius XI on the Church and the German Reich, March 1937, para. 8, taken from http://www.vatican.va/holy_father/pius_xi/encyclicals/documents/hf_p-xi_enc_14031937_mit-brennender-sorge_en.html

18 H. Küng (2002), *The Catholic Church*, London: Phoenix Press, p. 186.

19 Küng, *Catholic Church*, p. 189.

20 *Gaudiem et Spes* (1965), para. 81, taken from http://www.vatican.va/archive/hist_councils/ii_vatican_council/documents/vat-ii_cons_19651207_gaudium-et-spes_en.html

21 Gill, *Christian Ethics*, p. 338.

22 Statement on the Elimination of Nuclear Arms (1983), in Minutes of the Public Issues Committee, Sixth Assembly of the World Council of Churches, Vancouver 1983, taken from http://www.oikoumene.org/en/resources/documents/assembly/porto-alegre-2006/1-statements-documents-adopted/international-affairs/first-report-draft-for-action.html

23 J. Moltmann (1989), *Creating a Just Future*, London: SCM Press and Philadelphia: Trinity Press, p. 47.

24 Roberts, *Twentieth Century*, p. 846.

25 Hugh McCullum (2004), 'Racism and Ethnicity', in J. Briggs, M. Oduyoye and G. Tsetsis (eds) (2004), *A History of the Ecumenical Movement: Volume 3, 1968–2000*, Geneva: WCC Publications, pp. 368–9.

26 McCullum, 'Racism and Ethnicity', p. 369.

27 John Allen (2006), *Rabble-rouser for Peace*, London: Rider, p. 378.

28 From http://www.cca.org.hk/ccanews/local/kr/30401peace.htm (accessed 17 Oct. 07).

29 Roberts, *Twentieth Century*, p. 672.

30 Martin Luther King, *A Time to Break Silence*, downloaded from http://www.americanrhetoric.com/speeches/mlkatimetobreaksilence.htm

31 Roberts, *Twentieth Century*, pp. 768–9.

32 Michael Kinnamon (ed.) (1991), *Signs of the Spirit: Official Report of the Seventh Assembly of the WCC*, Geneva: WCC Publications and Grand Rapids MI: Wm B. Eerdmans, pp. 205ff.

33 Kinnamon (ed.), *Signs of the Spirit*, pp. 209–10.

14

The Response of Faith to Contemporary Science

Introduction

Twentieth-century Christianity inherited the responses of Christian faith to revolutionary developments in scientific understanding in previous centuries. Three such developments set the historical context for this chapter. In the sixteenth century, Galileo Galilei (1564–1642) argued for the Copernican understanding of planetary motion as against the Ptolemaic position. This led to a heliocentric (sun-centred) view of our universe rather than the geocentric (earth-centred) view that had held sway throughout previous centuries. The theological implications of this revolution were dramatic. The earth, the home of human beings and the arena of the biblical story of redemption, was no longer at the centre of the universe. At the time, while many theologians and Christian leaders, including John Calvin (1509–64), one of the chief authors of the Protestant Reformation, could accept scientific discoveries and their theological consequences, many did not. Galileo was condemned as a heretic by the Roman Catholic Church for theological novelty and for rejecting an understanding and interpretation of Scripture rooted in the early Fathers and the tradition of the Church.

The second revolutionary development was the result of the work of Isaac Newton (1642–1727). His mathematical laws of motion became accepted as not only describing motion on the earth's surface but were regarded as being valid for planetary motion also. The implication of Newton's laws was that the universe could be understood mechanically. It was seen as a machine the movements and actions of which were governed by immutable laws. The challenge for Christian theology focused around two implications of Newton's laws. First, if the universe could be seen as a 'machine' the intricate motion of which obeyed these laws, did this not strengthen the cosmological argument for the existence of God? Surely, the existence of a mechanical universe obeying stated laws implied the existence of an intelligent being who brought this universe and its governing laws into being. Second, however, Newton's universal laws challenged faith. Eighteenth-century Christians asked themselves questions such as the following: If this universe is a machine that obeys a set of immutable laws, even if such a universe was created by God, what place is there in such a universe for a God who sustains the world? God may be Creator, but is that God also Sustainer? If God is not Sustainer, then is faith not reduced to a deistic understanding of God rather than a theistic understanding of God as a divine being who both created and sustains the universe in its course and purpose?

The third revolutionary development during the mid-nineteenth century not only led to considerable controversy at the time but continues to be the cause of conflict and debate among Christians (and non-Christians) worldwide. It was, of course, the theory of evolution most famously propounded by Charles Darwin (1809–82) in two key books, *On the Origin of Species* (1859) and *The Descent of Man* (1871) but also proposed by Alfred Russell Wallace (1823–1913). This is not the place to expound this theory in any detail. It is adequate here to be reminded that Darwin's claim was that there was an evolutionary continuity between species throughout the plant and animal kingdom and that the development of species was the result not of a unique and specific act of divine creation, but of small but significant evolutionary changes in response to environmental and other factors. At the heart of this theory was the principle of the survival of the fittest: those changes that produced biological adaptations that offered a greater possibility of survival in a particular environment had led to the development by evolution of new species. All species, including human beings, were regarded as having been subject to this evolutionary process. The implications for Christian faith are well known. If Darwin's theory is accepted, it challenges a literalist understanding of the accounts of creation in the first chapters of the book of Genesis. These accounts were generally understood as envisaging that the creator God created each species by a special and individual act of creation and that human beings were the climax of these creative acts of God and had been formed 'in God's image' (Genesis 1.26ff.).

The conflict around these three revolutionary developments continued into the twentieth century and is as divisive today, at the beginning of the twenty-first century, as it was one and a half centuries ago. The focus of the conflict is the nature and interpretation of the Genesis accounts of creation, the compatibility of the Darwinian account of human origins with the Christian understanding of human nature and the divine–human relationship and the necessity (or indeed the possibility) of a role for a divine creative agent within the evolutionary process. We will return to this continuing conflict later in this chapter.

The remainder of this chapter will explore the Christian responses to key scientific developments during the twentieth century, focusing particularly on theological and ethical questions. As with the other thematic chapters in this volume, it will not engage in a historical survey (although it will include some historical material) so much as explore key theological and philosophical issues raised for Christians by these developments. Readers are directed to the 'Further reading' at the end of the chapter for fuller treatments of key issues. Generally speaking, more has been written in this field by Christian theologians in the North. Their perspectives may, therefore, be seen as over-dominant, although we will explore other viewpoints both here and in the accompanying *SCM Core Reader on World Christianity in the Twentieth Century*.

Some key twentieth-century developments

This section will focus on four areas: quantum theory and relativity, cosmology, DNA, and advances in medical treatment. It will give a brief outline of the key aspects of these developments and offer a preliminary exploration of the challenges they have posed for Christians. The next section of the chapter will provide a brief outline of ways in which different traditions have responded to some of these issues.

Quantum theory and relativity

Classical theories about the structure of matter (based, to a large extent, on a Newtonian world-view) maintained that it was possible to understand and describe the atomic structures that were the building blocks of matter in terms of mass, velocity, momentum, acceleration, etc. at the subatomic level. These explanations were not regarded as models but descriptions of physical reality. Quantum theory challenged this understanding and maintained that it is impossible to give a fully detailed and accurate description of the structure of matter. Two aspects of the theory illustrate this challenge.

First, our understanding of the behaviour of subatomic structures is dependent on how particular phenomena are observed and how they are measured. Subatomic structures sometimes seem to behave as particles and at other times seem to behave as waves. Quantum theory, therefore, approached matter not in terms of realism (as did classical Newtonian physics) but in terms of complementarity, that is, the holding together of two models that seem to be mutually contradictory.

The challenges to the traditional view of the world were clear. Was this complementary understanding the result of the lack of scientific knowledge (and therefore a step on the way to a full understanding) or was it the consequence of the fact that this is essentially how things are? For Christian faith, this raised the question of our theological understanding of the fabric of the universe and of the nature of the God who created and sustains the universe. Is this complementarity (or dual-nature) a fundamental characteristic of the world which God created? The old certainties were being challenged and replaced by possible ambiguities.

Second, quantum theory raised the issue of certainty in another way. The Heisenberg Uncertainty Theory claimed that it is impossible to know both the position and the momentum of any particular particle. Put over-simply, if its position is known we cannot know how fast it is moving. If we know how fast it is moving, we cannot know its position with certainty. This fundamental uncertainty clearly challenged classical determinism that believed the universe to be governed by immutable laws.

Again, there were implications for Christian faith. If the behaviour of the fabric of the universe is uncertain (to use the terminology of Heisenberg), does that also mean that it is unpredictable? Barbour answers that the future is unpredictable *because it is undecided*: 'the future is not simply unknown. It is "not decided". More than one alternative is open and there is some opportunity for unpredictable novelty.'[1] Does this mean that we have to abandon the belief that the future is in the hands of God? If we do have to abandon such a belief, what kind of God are Christians left with? Can we still claim that the future is in the hands of God, even when it is full of novelty that is, by definition, unpredictable – even to God? Perhaps we are being pointed to faith in a God who will hold and guide the cosmos and all life upon it, even in all its uncertainty and unpredictability. Perhaps we are invited to believe in a God who does not and cannot know what the future holds, but yet is Lord of whatever that future may offer and bring.

Einstein's theories of relativity have contributed to this fear of uncertainty. In classical physics, time and space were understood as separable and absolute; that is, they were not mutually dependent. Every object has a definable position within space and all time moves in definable ways for all objects and beings. Relativity challenges this fundamental certainty. Two events that can be coterminous in one time frame can be non-coterminous in another time frame. Such a universe is dynamic and interconnected, and the events of the universe are unified and interactive. Such an understanding challenged some traditional concepts of the immutability of God and the permanence and un-changability of the universe.

Cosmology

Twentieth-century cosmology proposed, largely on the basis of its calculated rate of expansion, that the universe began around 15 billion years ago. It had its origins, according to this theory, at a point of singularity, popularly described as the Big Bang, which set gravitational and nuclear forces into being which made possible the being of the universe and its constituent particles. Over subsequent billennia, subatomic particles and atomic nuclei, atoms and molecules, galaxies and planets, microscopic and more complex life forms came into being. If this explanation and time frame for the origins of the universe were to be accepted (as they have been by the vast majority of scientists), Christians had to ask: are these claims about the origins of the universe compatible with the traditional belief in God as Creator?

There have been two contrasting responses to this challenge. Some fundamentalist Christians, especially those that hold a literalist view of the Bible, have questioned the validity of the theory. For them, the biblical account of creation had to be taken as authoritative, and modern understandings of the universe and its origins had to be judged in the light of biblical truth. The nature of the Big Bang and its aftermath, and the timescale involved, was seen to be inconsistent with biblical truth as expounded in Genesis 1 and 2. Therefore, it had to be rejected. Those who held this position were (and are) normally opposed also to the Darwinian explanation of origins.

Other Christians rejected this negative response to recent cosmological theories and proposed a mythological approach to the Genesis accounts. This approach understood 'myth' not as a false or unreliable account but as an attempt to express in literary form a theological understanding of the true relationships between God and the universe. In mythological narratives that may have been influenced by surrounding cultures, such as the Babylonion creation myths, the traditions behind the Genesis accounts sought to express through myth their understanding not so much of the way in which the universe came into being but of the authors' fundamental faith that its existence owes its origins and purposes to God. On this basis, while denying that the Genesis accounts were in any way a scientifically accurate account of origins (and, therefore, should not be taken literally), they could nevertheless be seen as valid theological accounts of the origin of the universe and of the nature and purpose of human beings.

One of the most significant Roman Catholic responses to twentieth-century scientific developments was Pope Pius XII's enthusiastic endorsement of the Big Bang theory of the origins of the universe. In an address to the Pontifical Academy of Science in 1951 he said:

> [I]t would seem that present-day science, with one sweep back across the centuries, has succeeded in bearing witness to the august instant of the primordial *Fiat Lux* [Let there be Light], when along with matter, there burst forth from nothing a sea of light and radiation, and the elements split and churned and formed into millions of galaxies.[2]

The discovery of DNA

The conflict that the Darwinian theory of natural selection caused at the time of its publication in the mid-nineteenth century continued throughout the twentieth century. In the latter half of the twentieth century, the discovery of the structure and role of DNA (deoxyribonucleic acid), and the explanation of its role in genetics, in many ways exacerbated the conflict. At the heart of this explanation was that the DNA molecule incorporates the genetic code which determines the genetic characteristics of living forms. Specific characteristics were thought to be handed on from generation to generation as the genetic material from the parent generation combined in various ways to form the next generation. Biological evolution was further explained in terms of mutations of these genetic codes, over a number of generations, in response to environmental and other factors. The story goes that, when the discovery of the structure of DNA by James Watson and Francis Crick was announced in 1953, Watson is said to have exclaimed that they had discovered the secret of life! The potential for theological conflict is obvious. When Darwin's work on origins, subsequent work by Gregor Mendel and others on the processes of genetic inheritance, and the role of DNA, were put together, they were seen to offer a scientific explanation of the origins and development of the complexity and diversity of known life forms that was comprehensive and valid.

Watson himself believed that the discovery was a challenge to religion and showed that there was an entirely material basis for life. Neo-Darwinians such as Richard Dawkins share this view and regard these genetic explanations as rendering belief in God unnecessary (a significant word: unnecessary rather than, for example, impossible). He claims that the purpose of all life is the continuation of DNA. On this basis, he and others have claimed that adhering to a religious explanation and understanding was to deny proven scientific facts and to live on the basis of falsehood.

A number of fundamental theological questions have been raised by these debates. If the genetic explanation were to be accepted, is there a place for a purposeful universe? Dawkins has argued that DNA is fundamentally purposeless and indifferent. It exists merely to replicate itself, and all life forms, including human beings, are subject to its otherwise purposeless action. Keith Ward, on the other hand, during a debate with Dawkins, denied this conclusion and argued that evolution displays characteristics that are perfectly consistent with belief in a God of wisdom and purpose, and that religious belief and scientific explanation may enrich and inform each other.

Another key question was whether everything could be reduced to genes (and, therefore, ultimately, to chemistry), that is, whether the principle of reductionism was acceptable. Crick has been quoted as saying that 'it will be possible to explain everything in biology in terms of the level below it, and so down to the atomic level ... The knowledge we already have makes it very unlikely that there is anything that cannot be explained in terms of physics and chemistry.'[3] But the question for Christians was (and, of course, remains): can there be meaning beyond the physical and chemical explanations?

Genetic manipulation

The technology that has been developed from the biochemical understanding of genetic processes raises equally important moral questions. Genetic engineering enables the manipulation of genetic material and its transference between biologically different organisms in ways that would be impossible by natural means. This technology can be used for medical, agricultural and, of course, commercial purposes. Moralists generally and Christian moral theologians in particular need to grapple with the ethics of such procedures. If they are beneficial (in developing a cure for cystic fibrosis, for example) are they ethically acceptable? If they are commercially advantageous but pose a developmental threat (for example, producing a variety of rice that can be grown in adverse weather conditions, but which increases the cost of production for poor farmers in the South) are they still ethically acceptable? If such techniques produce more acceptable produce – such as tomatoes that have a more consistent appearance and a longer shelf-life – can these be approved morally?

Most problematic of all in this field has been the issue of genetic cloning, manipulating the reproductive process in order either to eliminate undesirable mental or physical abnormalities, or to produce a replica of the parent organism. The question of whether such techniques are acceptable in general for Christian faith has been an issue of considerable debate, and has become even more controversial in relation to the possibility of extending the presently available techniques into the field of human cloning.

Advances in medical treatment

The twentieth century saw vast progress in the development of medical treatments. Some diseases, such as smallpox, were all but eliminated by the end of the century. Treatment for other diseases, such as tuberculosis, was greatly advanced. But new diseases, such as HIV/AIDS, reached epidemic proportions in many areas of the world. In general, these advances and areas of research did not raise fundamental questions for faith – although they continue to raise questions about the key relationship between epidemiological patterns (the patterns of the spread of diseases) and poverty that should constantly challenge Christians. However, other areas of medical advance, for example, in relation to the beginning and end of life, have raised crucial theological and moral issues.

These questions may be illustrated by briefly examining questions around abortion and euthanasia. By the end of the twentieth century, enormous advances had been made in relation to the viability of very premature babies. There were cases of babies of 22 weeks gestation surviving outside the womb with very advanced specialized medical support, and developing into normal childhood and adulthood. These developments raised ethical questions about permitting abortion at 24 weeks (the statutory maximum period for an abortion in the UK in 2007). In view of medical advances, should the threshold be reduced to 22 weeks, thus making abortion less easily available? It continues to be the case, however, that the majority of Christians – notwithstanding these advances and the possible changes to the threshold – would still be opposed to abortion at any stage in pregnancy unless the life of the mother was in danger.

Similar questions were being raised in relation to the end of life. There has been considerable pressure in the UK, for example, for the legalization of euthanasia. Such legislation was already in place (under carefully controlled medical and ethical conditions), in the Netherlands, for instance. Christian responses to these questions have focused on the belief that human beings are created 'in the image of God' and are, therefore, worthy at all times of being treated with dignity. (It should be noted, incidentally, that this argument could be deployed both in favour and against euthanasia.) Another matter of concern for Christians (and others) has been the fact that there have been cases where patients have recovered from what had appeared to be an irreversible terminal illness. The vulnerability of patients facing death to the consequences of criminal acts by those in whose care they have been placed has also been a cause of considerable concern to those who have opposed legalizing euthanasia. Many Christians have shared the conviction that the taking of human life – either that of others or one's own – is always contrary to the will of God.

Christian responses to scientific advances

This section will focus on three sources as illustrative of responses within world Christianity during the century: first, responses from the Roman Catholic Church; second, responses from evangelical and fundamentalist Christians; and, third, ecumenical responses as represented by reports and statements, predominantly from the World Council of Churches.

Before we explore these responses, it will be helpful to outline Barbour's paradigm for the complex inter-relationship between religion and science. His scheme has become a classic model. He proposed a fourfold typology.[4]

He described the first category as *conflict*, in which religion was understood as being in conflict with the principles and methodology of science. The second he described as *independence*. Science and religion could coexist provided they were recognized as referring to different aspects of life and as employing different kinds of language to answer different questions. He described the third category as *dialogue*. Barbour's understanding of dialogue recognized that, although science and religion each had their own integrity and generally answered different kinds of questions, fruitful connections and interactions could be possible which were mutually enriching. Science could lead to questions that religion could contribute to answering and may contribute to a greater understanding of religious affirmations and beliefs. Finally, Barbour proposed *integration* as a description of a closer partnership between the two disciplines that can enable theology to be reinterpreted in the light of new scientific understanding and scientific understanding to be integrated more fully with a theological and philosophical system. The following explorations of the responses of various Christian traditions to contemporary science will illustrate these four models as well as occasionally indicating ways in which Christians and Christian traditions have made a shift from one category to another. (For Barbour's full description of this typology see *SCM Core Reader*, 14.1.)

The Roman Catholic Church

Two episodes illustrate how the church responded to the way in which science challenges faith. The first is the case of Galileo. The Pontifical Academy of Science was founded in 1936 by Pope Pius XI, who gathered a group of scientists to keep the Holy See informed about scientific developments and thus aid the church's theological and moral reflection on the issues raised. More than 40 years later, in 1979, Pope John Paul II, addressing the Pontifical Academy at the beginning of his pontificate, called for an investigation into the case of Galileo so that any errors committed by anyone could be recognized. His motivation for this initiative was revealing. It was 'to remove the distrust that this case still generates, in the minds of many people, placing obstacles thereby in the way of fruitful concord between science and faith'.

The Pope established a study commission in 1981 to study the Galileo case and to help to clarify the appropriate relationship between faith and science. The commission concluded, first, that 'no one at the time understood adequately the relationship between data and theory and between data and theory and their philosophical and theological frameworks'.[5] Second, it concluded that 'the theologians in the Galileo case, failed to grasp the profound, non-literal meaning of the Scriptures when they describe the physical features of the created universe. This led them unduly to transpose a question of factual observation into the realm of faith.' Sherwen comments that 'John Paul exhibits in his writings a real affection for Galileo', not least because of 'the insight Galileo exhibits concerning biblical interpretation'.

The second example illustrates the way in which the church developed its response to modern scientific theories and developments. In August 1950, Pope Pius XII issued his encyclical, *Humani Generis* (*SCM Core Reader*, 14.2).[6]

He was a deeply conservative pope, yet this encyclical contained some revealing statements about the church's attitude towards scientific developments. First, he generally encouraged taking science seriously:

> [T]aking these sciences into account as much as possible ... would be praiseworthy in the case of clearly proved facts; but caution must be used when there is rather [a] question of hypotheses, having some sort of scientific foundation, in which the doctrine contained in Sacred Scripture or in Tradition is involved.[7]

The key here is the relationship between scientific understanding and biblical and doctrinal truth as understood by the church. Where there is no relevance with respect to doctrine, scientific research and the exploration of what the Pope describes as 'proven facts' is to be encouraged as 'praiseworthy'. But where there is a conflict between scientific 'hypotheses' and the teaching of the church 'the demand that they be recognized can in no way be admitted'. That is, generally speaking, the church's approach to scientific hypotheses was to be determined not on the basis of the science itself but from the authoritative perspective of 'the doctrine revealed by God'.

Pius XII goes on to examine the church's approach to evolution. He states that 'the Teaching Authority of the Church does not forbid that, in conformity with the present state of human sciences and sacred theology, research and discussions, on the part of men experienced in both fields, [should] take place with regard to the doctrine of evolution'.[8] His encouragement of 'research and discussion ... with regard to the doctrine of evolution' was particularly significant given the hitherto cautious and conservative attitude of the church to scientific developments and expressed support for the process of scientific research, exploration and debate, provided the doctrinal authority of the church was not thereby undermined.

In an address to the Pontifical Academy of Sciences in 1996, Pope John Paul II, commenting on some of the principles enunciated in *Humani Generis*, stated that 'new knowledge leads the theory of evolution to be no longer considered as a mere hypothesis'. He thereby recognized that 'this theory has progressively imposed itself on the attention of researchers following a series of discoveries made in the various disciplines of knowledge'.[9] However, this address not only built on the previous Catholic understanding of the theory of evolution, but explored in very perceptive ways the Catholic understanding of science and in particular its role in relation to the nature and origins of human beings.

This examination of Roman Catholic responses to scientific developments during the century has shown a readiness on the part of the Church hierarchy to take seriously the scientific challenges that confronted Christian faith and to respond creatively. The generally traditional conservatism of Catholic theology meant that such a creative response often involved a slow process that called for considerable theological and philosophical struggle. Nevertheless, in many ways the church made significant and often courageous strides in moving from its response to Galileo in the sixteenth century to a position of considerably greater openness to the insights and theories of contemporary science in the last decades of the twentieth century.

Evangelical and fundamentalist approaches

Space does not allow a thorough examination of ways in which evangelical and fundamentalist theology responded to twentieth-century scientific developments. We shall focus in the following section on questions raised by theories of cosmic and human origins.[10]

As we have seen, as soon as Darwin's theory of evolution was made public, evangelical Christians saw it as undermining the Genesis account of God's work of creation. It was understood as a threat to biblical authority and to the truth of Scripture. 'Special creation' had already been proposed as one explanation for natural and human origins. According to this theory, species were created 'individually' through an act of 'special creation'. Darwin rejected this theory in favour of an evolutionary approach. But 'special creation' was clearly more in accord with the general Christian understanding of creation in the mid-nineteenth century. In due course, the term 'creationism' came to be accepted as an expression that sought to encompass this traditional Christian view. Its key principle was to assert that God's act of creation as set out in the Genesis account should be taken as authoritative, that the scientific evidence adduced in support of evolution was inconclusive and that the scientific 'facts' could as easily and more correctly be adduced in support of an explanation of origins that was consistent with the Genesis accounts.

As the support for evolutionary theories strengthened within the scientific community, creationism gradually became the overall framework for those who opposed these theories. It came to incorporate a number of theories that sought to express the compatibility between the emerging evidence and the biblical accounts. One of the key issues at stake here was the age of the universe. As we have seen, the emerging scientific consensus was that the universe had its origins 15 billion years ago in what has been described as a Big Bang. Whereas Pope Pius XII declared that the church saw no inconsistency between the Big Bang theories of cosmic origins and biblical belief in God as the Creator of all things, others have seen this timescale as inconsistent with the biblical account. Consequently, Young Earth Creationism emerged, rooted in an uncompromising biblical literalism. Its key claim, in opposition to the scientific consensus, was that the earth is 'young', having come into existence no more than 6,000 to 10,000 years ago. Young Earth Creationists further claimed that all life forms were created by God 'each after their kind' (Genesis 1.24). Any theory that undermined the belief that God was directly responsible for the creation of each and every species was rejected.

Closely related to Young Earth Creationism is Creation Science, which seeks to employ scientific and empirical methods to support the biblical accounts of creation. The theological beliefs of the proponents of Creation Science were similar to those of Young Earth Creationists. Current models of evolution and geological origins were rejected, as were the theories that emerged from the mainstream scientific community on the age of the universe and the common descent of all life forms. Creation Science offered a number of theories which claimed to be 'scientific' but which the scientific community regarded as 'pseudoscience'. These included creation biology and flood geology. Creation biology asserted that biological evolution was false, since there was, in their view, no evidence of the interim forms of life that should have existed if natural selection was true (the 'missing links argument'). Another key theory was 'flood geology'. The heart of this theory was that much of the earth's geology, as well as fossils and fossil fuels, was formed as a result of a global flood described in Genesis 8 and 9. It also rejected radiometric dating (that is, dating rock formations etc. on the basis of isotopic half-life measurements), which was one of the fundamental tools of mainstream geology, as inaccurate and unreliable.

Similar support gathered around the theory of Intelligent Design. Whereas evolutionary theory was premised on a random process of natural selection, which had no purpose or design, Intelligent Design theory was premised on there being an Intelligent Designer and design behind the universe. It was claimed that this was an alternative scientific explanation for the origins of the natural world, that could be set alongside of or seen as superior to, other scientific theories preferred by mainstream scientists.

However, many Christians found all of these theories unacceptable on the basis both of their understanding of the biblical texts and their support for the general thrust of evolutionary theory. So a final example of attempts to develop explanations of origins which were consistent with the Christian understanding of God as Creator was Theistic Evolution. The heart of this approach was to accept micro-evolution (the detailed mutatory processes of natural selection) and macro-evolution (the large-scale developments leading to the creation of new species in response to genetic mutations, environmental conditions, etc.), but to claim also that this was not a random, purposeless process but the consequence of the work of a Creator God. Evolution was seen as the mechanism by which God brought the earth, and the life upon it, into being. It was argued that this approach was consistent with both a deist and theist understanding of God (see above) and faithful to the scientific data. Supporters of theistic evolution claimed that scientific theory and the Genesis accounts served essentially different functions. The former answered the 'How?' question; the latter answered the 'Why?' question (for examples of these views see *SCM Core Reader*, 14.3 and 14.4).

Ecumenical responses through the World Council of Churches

In general, discussions within the World Council of Churches (WCC) of the impact of contemporary science on Christian faith focused primarily (though not exclusively) on the ethical issues that were raised by scientific developments rather than the theological questions. In the inaugural Assembly of the WCC (Amsterdam 1948), this concern expressed itself in terms of the way in which technology was applying scientific discoveries. Technical developments within industry, for example, were seen as having 'relieved men and women from much drudgery and poverty, and are still capable of doing more'.[11] However, there was a concern that such developments were not more equitably shared: 'Justice demands that the inhabitants of Asia and Africa, for instance, should have benefits of machine production.' But there was also a cautionary note: 'They may learn to avoid the mechanisation of life and the other dangers of an unbalanced economy which impair the social health of older industrial peoples.' The key question seems to have been whether technological society contributed to fullness of life: 'There is no inescapable necessity for society to succumb to undirected developments of technology, and the Christian Church has an urgent responsibility today to help men [*sic*] to achieve fuller personal life within the technical society.' Alongside this concern about full personal lives was the concern for the relevance of their faith to the problems of the technological society: '[Our churches] have often failed to understand the forces which have shaped societies around them, and so they have been unprepared to deal creatively with new problems as they have arisen in technical civilization.' These quotations indicate that the Assembly was less concerned about the theoretical questions raised by science and more concerned with the way in which technology harnessed these developments for the benefit as well as the disadvantage of individuals and communities.

This concern for technological change hints at concerns that would become more significant half a century later. Ruth Conway comments:

> Within a few short centuries we human beings have transformed the face of the earth, laying hold of the resources of the planet and constructing environments matched to the perceived needs and aspirations of human communities ... But there is another side to the experience from which no one can be completely isolated. To a greater or lesser degree, people are aware of clouds of smog blanketing the cities; of rising sea levels threatening island and coastal dwellers; of land degraded, deforestation, reduced biodiversity, and small-scale farmers forced into poverty by the methods employed by multinational agribusinesses ... of the unresolved (and unresolvable?) problems of nuclear waste.[12]

One way or another, these positive and negative consequences of technology have been an outworking of scientific developments and focus very clearly the moral challenges for people of faith.

The World Conference on Church and Society held in Geneva in 1966 took as its theme 'Christians in the Technical and Social Revolutions of our Time'. One commentator expressed the view that the conference was 'more adept at talking about social than technological revolutions'.[13] However, it did encourage churches to welcome these developments as an expression of the work of the Creator God as well as the economic progress that they enabled. Such sentiments gave encouragement to the WCC to pursue these questions, especially through dialogues between scientists, technologists and theologians.

In 1967, and largely independently of the Geneva Conference, a report was presented to the Faith and Order Commission in Bristol on 'God in Nature and History' (see *SCM Core Reader*, 14.5).[14] In the introduction, the report recognizes that scientific developments over the previous century had changed the Christian world-view and that this raises important theological challenges. However, it sets itself a limited task of discovering 'the relations between the biblical message and the modern world-view ... [in] the hope that it will help many to overcome in their hearts and minds the gap between their Christian faith and their expectations and embarrassments as modern men'.

Given the significant controversies about the relationship between science and Christian faith over the centuries, the concluding paragraph of the chapter on 'The Biblical and the Modern World-View' was significant as an ecumenical approach to a controversial topic:

> Christian faith is not identical with modern science or any world-view claiming to depend upon it. But it is deeply indebted to modern science, because the scientific approach and its results have compelled Christians to re-examine their convictions and to free their faith from elements which, though long thought to be integral to the Christian message, are now seen not to be so. Christians should therefore be grateful for the way in which God has used science to clarify and deepen the insights of faith.[15]

Subsequent chapters consider themes such as the following: Nature and Man; Nature, Man, Sin and Tragedy; Nature in God's History with Man; Christian Faith and Technology; God in Universal History; and History and Nature in Consummation. The Section Report on 'Christian Faith and Technology' (frequently referred to in the text as 'technics') is illuminating:

> [We] do not advocate a stop to technical development. Man has to do not less, but more. He has to subjugate his technical possibilities to the other relations of his life, instead of allowing technics to supersede these other relations ... Everywhere, however, man has to be reminded of the fact that what seem to be ambiguities of technics are in reality the ambiguities of man himself, and that in view of the immense power which he now possesses, it is high time for him to seek a fresh understanding of his nature and destiny.[16]

During the subsequent decade, faith, science and technology became a major theme of the WCC Sub-unit of Church and Society.[17] The work culminated in the World Conference on 'Faith, Science and the Future' which was held at the Massachusetts Institute of Technology in July 1979 (see *SCM Core Reader*, 14.6).[18] The reports of this conference are crucial resources for any study of the ecumenical engagement with the issues of science, technology and faith during the twentieth century and represent one of the fullest accounts of the churches' response to the key issues raised in this chapter. In his introduction to volume 2 of the Report, Paul Abrecht, the Director of the Sub-unit, notes that there were three imperatives behind the conference, namely, to set the science, faith and society discussion within a world perspective, to relate ecological and technological sustainability to the concern for justice and participation, and to develop a critique of science and technology in terms of faith.[19] These themes were explored in a series of wide-ranging section reports from the conference on topics such as The Nature of Science and the Nature of Faith; Humanity, Nature and God; Ethical Issues in the Biological Manipulation of Life; Technology, Resources, Environment and Population and Science/Technology, Political Power and a More Just World Order. One of the most significant sections, which drew on the expertise of all the other sections, studied the ethical implications of developments in science and technology under the topic of 'Towards a New Christian Ethic and New Social Policies for the Churches'.

It is impossible here to give a detailed account of these substantial reports, but a few reflections may provide a fuller understanding of the response of world Christianity – as represented in this conference – to these issues during the second half of the century. First, it is noteworthy that the section on 'The Nature of Science and the Nature of Faith', set out possible ways of inter-relating faith and science which closely reflected the paradigm suggested by Barbour (who was present at the conference).[20] A critique of the various positions was offered but none was commended by the Section as its preferred approach. Rather, each was passed on for further study by the churches etc. This suggests that the representatives of the world of science and technology as well as the world of theology were divided – as the churches were and are – on this question. It did recognize, however, that there was an important theological task of formulating 'a strong theology of nature and a reassessment of the doctrine of creation ... in terms of a new ecological sensibility ... [and] our responsibility for nature as God's creation'.[21] It was clear from the report, that delegates believed that science and theology needed each other if humankind was to face the future in hope.

Important as these theological reflections were (and are), it is clear that ethical issues dominated the thinking of the conference, with seven of the ten conference sections discussing aspects of the ethical challenge of developments in science. The report highlights a number of interrelated roles and responsibilities in the task of developing this ethical approach, including those of scientists, citizens, governments, international organizations and non-governmental institutions (including the churches). Some key ethical issues also emerged, including biological manipulation, the role of technology, the environmental crisis, secure energy, the economics of a just, sustainable and participatory society, and political power, military technology and peace. It was awareness of the centrality of these issues that led to the insights of this conference being one of the key contributory elements in developing what came to be one of the dominating ecumenical themes of the 1980s, 'Justice, Peace and the Integrity of Creation'.

One of the controversial aspects of the conference focused on these ethical issues. A number of participants from Africa, Asia, Latin America, the Middle East and the Pacific expressed considerable dissatisfaction with the 'historical and current use of science and technology by industrially and technically advanced societies to serve military and economic interests which brought about great suffering to the peoples of the third world' (SCM Core Reader, 14.7).[22] This was a stark reminder that science cannot be an isolated academic study but needs to be seen both as being shaped by and shaping the local as well as the global context. It is the context that should, and frequently does, determine issues of research funding, technological development and ethical response.

Stanley Harakas, in an essay that offers a comprehensive account of ecumenical developments in this field, assesses the significance and impact of the conference as follows: 'Arguably ... [it] was one of the most sustained, inclusive, reflective and honest ecumenical efforts in the twentieth century regarding faith, science and technology ... [It] became a springboard for continuing ecumenical concern.'[23] Many of the issues that were highlighted in the conference did indeed become urgent issues in subsequent decades. Among them were ecological questions (focused around the Earth Summit in Rio de Janeiro in 1992), issues around genetic manipulation (as explored, for example, by the Science, Religion and Technology Project of the Church of Scotland) and climate change (which became one of the most urgent issues for the global community towards the end of the decade and in which the WCC was actively involved through the early years of the twenty-first century).

Final reflections

In summing up a century of exploration of the relationship between science and Christian faith, a number of insights may be offered. First, although many were critical of science as offering explanations of the natural world that they judged to be contrary to their understanding of Christian truth, the majority of theologians in the West and the North who reflected on these issues understood theology and science as being complementary rather than in conflict. Theology asks 'Why?' or meaning questions, science asks 'How?' or process questions. This understanding of the functions of the two disciplines helps to clarify issues and questions that have been the cause of deep and wounding divisions in previous centuries, and to the forging of new insights and perspectives on some of the fundamentals of faith. However, as we have seen, the tension still remains and it is true to say that many Christians in the rapidly growing churches and traditions around the world still view any theological position that in any way undermines the literal truth of the accounts of creation in Genesis as a fundamental threat to the authority and claim of God's revelation in the Bible. Whatever the other challenges of the twenty-first century may be in this field, it will be centrally important, both for the worldwide Church and for the scientific community, that the dialogue between faith and science continues in as open and constructive a context as possible. Neither Christians (nor scientists) can occupy closed worlds.

Second, Barbour's typology for the interrelationship between religion and science – conflict, complementarity, dialogue and integration – was reflected in exploration of the responses of various traditions. Indeed, there were instances, within the Roman Catholic Church for example, where a tradition moved from one category of response to another, as new insights became available to the Church. At their best, theology and science have been perceived as mutually enriching. A theological perception of the world as 'created' has enabled scientists – even those who have been extremely sceptical about the claims of Christianity – further to explore questions of meaning and purpose as they have developed their understanding of the cosmos. The frequent claim that there is more to be said than is offered by scientific theory alone is, to a degree at least, a perception gained, directly or indirectly, from Christian philosophical and theological reflection.

Third, the nature of scientific exploration and explanation threw new light on the nature of theology. There is always the danger of seeing theology as a body of immutable or unchanging truth about God, the universe and humanity which needs only to be interpreted and explained. Twentieth-century scientific advances (as those of previous centuries) have contributed to challenging this view. Theology must be shaped as much by the changing understanding of the world in which is acted out the story of God's engagement with the universe and with human destiny, as it must be by the understanding of God handed on from generation to generation. Maintaining the tradition and enabling theological renewal have to be held together in creative tension in theology as much as in any other discipline. Twentieth-century science helped to foster this more open and exploratory approach to the theological task, an approach that was warmly welcomed by some and severely criticized by others.

Fourth, however, it was mainly Christians in the North that were concerned for the theological and philosophical issues raised by science. They were the questions that arose, on the whole, in scientifically and technologically advanced societies. The examination of the ecumenical responses, in particular, indicated that, from the perspective of global Christianity, some of the philosophical and theological questions explored by theologians were viewed with less urgency. In many parts of the world, such as the poorer nations of Africa, the fundamental questions have been those of economic survival, unjust deployment of scientific domination and power and the need to give priority to potentially fatal infectious diseases such as malaria and HIV/AIDS. The key moral question remains: is a disproportionate amount of scientific funding and expertise being devoted to research and development projects which do not touch the poor and which divert resources away from research that could and should be targeted at their economic and medical needs? The theological challenge is to discover whether or not the Creator God is most clearly discerned in the scientific advances per se or whether this God is challenging the scientific community to harness scientific understanding in areas such as gene therapy, genetic engineering, cloning, etc. to meet the urgent demands of the poor of the earth. Unless this shift in perspective occurs, Christian theology in the North could be accused of an unjust approach to theology by focusing on the philosophical challenges posed by science rather than questions of applying scientific advances more directly to create a more just and moral world.

Finally, Harakas' Afterword to his essay on the ecumenical response helpfully points to the challenge of contemporary science for faith at the end of the twentieth century and sets a direction for this continuing reflection into the twenty-first century:

Any science-based technology is capable of helping to improve life. However, often unintended negative consequences can arise for some or all, especially for those on the periphery. Christians concerned for the well-being of others must speak and act on behalf of those who cannot speak and act in the halls of power and authority ... Concern for issues of faith, science and technology has moved in the final half decade of the twentieth century to practical questions, and it is clear that there will be continued ecumenical involvement with these issues as a consequence of the churches' commitment to Christian ethics and action in obedience to the triune God of all creation.[24]

The engagement of Christians of every culture and background with these issues must continue to be central if Christian witness is to be faithful to the theological articulation of the faith, to the proclamation of the gospel and to its commitment to the search for justice, peace and the wholeness of creation into the twenty-first century.

Further reading:

I. G. Barbour (1998), *Religion and Science: Historical and Contemporary Issues*, London: SCM Press, gives the most comprehensive examination of the philosophical and theological issues across the range of this extensive subject.

R. Conway (1999), *Choices at the Heart of Technology: A Christian Perspective*, Pennsylvania: Trinity Press International, clearly and succinctly explores the issues around technology that became increasingly important during the century.

P. Davies (1993), *Science and the Mind of God: Science and the Search for Ultimate Meaning*, London: Penguin, provides a scientifically authoritative and theologically sympathetic exploration of the themes from a scientist who does not, in his own words, 'subscribe to a conventional religion'.

S. S. Harakas (2004), 'Science, Technology and Ecology', in J. Briggs, M. Oduyoye and G. Tstetsis (eds), *A History of the Ecumenical Movement: Volume 3 1968–2000*, Geneva: WCC Publications, pp. 373–402, provides a comprehensive and rich account of the ecumenical and confessional engagement with these issues during the century.

H. M. Morris and J. C. Whitcomb (1989), *Genesis Flood*, Philadelphia: Presbyterian and Reformed Publishing, proposes a way of unifying and correlating scientific data on the earth's early history and a biblically based system of creationism and catastrophism.

J. Polkinghorne (1998), *Science and Theology: An Introduction*, London: SPCK and Minneapolis: Fortress Press (as well as his many other books), provides a sound exploration of both the science and theology of these issues.

E. C. Scott (2004), *Evolution vs Creationism: An Introduction*, Berkeley: University of California Press, provides an excellent study by a scientist of the science behind evolution and creationism.

J. C. Whitcomb (1994), *The Early Earth: Introduction to Biblical Creationism*, rev. edn, Grand Rapids MI: Baker Book House, provides a brief introduction to creationism.

Notes

1 I. G. Barbour (1998), *Religion and Science: Historical and Contemporary Issues*, London: SCM Press, p. 173.

2 Pope Pius xii, 'The Proofs of the Existence of God in the Light of Modern Natural Sciences', an address to the Pontifical Academy of Sciences, 22 November 1951, para. 44, taken from http://www.papalencyclicals.net/Pius12EXIST.HTM

3 Barbour, *Religion and Science*, p. 230.

4 I. G. Barbour (2000), *When Science Meets Religion*, San Francisco: Harper-SanFrancisco, pp. 1–4.

5 M. Sherwen OP, 'Reconciling Old Lovers: John Paul on Science and Faith' at http://www.catholic.net/RCC/Periodicals/Dossier/0708-96/article4.html (accessed 4 Dec. 06).

6 *Humani Generis* at http://www.vatican.va/holy_father/pius_xii/encyclicals/documents (accessed 4 Dec. 06).

7 *Humani Generis*, para. 35.

8 *Humani Generis*, para. 36.

9 M. S. Sorondo (2003), *The Pontifical Academy of Sciences: A Historical Profile*, Vatican City, p. 2.

10 For a scientifically informed study of the debate, see E. C. Scott (2004), *Evolution vs. Creationism: An Introduction*, Berkeley CA: University of California Press, which includes a detailed examination of the issues as well as extracts from key publications.

11 W. A. Visser 't Hooft (ed.) (1948), *The First Assembly of the World Council of Churches: The Official Report*, London: SCM Press, p. 75.

12 R. Conway (1999), *Choices at the Heart of Technology: A Christian Perspective*, Pennsylvania: Trinity Press, p. 2.

13 R. Shinn (1991), 'Science and Technology', in N. Lossky et al. (eds), *Dictionary of the Ecumenical Movement*, Geneva: WCC Publications, p. 904.

14 See 'God in Nature and History', in G. Gassmann (ed.) (1993), *Documentary History of Faith and Order, 1963–1993*, Geneva: WCC Publications, pp. 289ff.

15 Gassmann, *Documentary History*, p. 298.

16 Gassmann, *Documentary History*, p. 305.

17 For a brief summary of the sub-unit's work on this topic during this period see (1983), *Nairobi to Vancouver, 1975-1983: Report of the Central Committee to the Sixth Assembly of the WCC*, Geneva: WCC Publications, pp. 99ff.

18 R. Shinn (ed.) (1980), *Faith and Science in an Unjust World, Vol. I*, Geneva: WCC Publications, and P. Abrecht (ed.) (1980), *Faith and Science in an Unjust World, Vol. II*, Geneva: WCC Publications.

19 Abrecht, *Faith and Science*, pp. 2–3.

20 Abrecht, *Faith and Science*, pp. 14f.

21 Abrecht, *Faith and Science*, p. 22.

22 Abrecht, *Faith and Science*, p. 171.

23 S. A. Harakas (2004), 'Science, Technology and Ecology', in J. Briggs, M. Oduyoye and G. Tsetsis (eds) (2004), *A History of the Ecumenical Movement: Volume 3, 1968–2000*, p. 385.

24 Harakas, 'Science, Technology and Ecology', p. 400.

15

From the Perspectives of Women

At the beginning of the twentieth century, women were largely disenfranchised and disadvantaged compared to men. Although the issue of the status and rights of women had been raised, certainly in Europe and North America, during the nineteenth century, with words and phrases such as 'feminism' and 'the women's movement' being introduced into the vocabulary, the majority of women were unaffected by these issues, even in Europe and America, and even less so within the other regions of the world. By the beginning of the First World War, women had been granted the vote in a handful of countries, and the struggle for greater rights for women was gaining strength. As the century progressed, there were a few examples of women being elected to high political office, in countries such as Sri Lanka, India, Pakistan and the United Kingdom. But even at the end of the century, such countries remain small in number. Notwithstanding their role in the highest offices of state, however, the role and status of women progressed enormously in many regions of the globe during the last century in a wide range of fields such as medicine, law, education, politics, commerce and business. In very many countries, they have the same status, rights and opportunities as men, although there are still areas of discrimination and inequality even in countries where there appears, officially, to be legal and economic equality. This is not equally true around the world, however, and in many countries, for a range of cultural and religious reasons, women continue to suffer discrimination and inequality in strongly patriarchal societies ruled by men, in which women have lower status, freedom and opportunities as compared to men.

This global pattern has been reflected to a large extent within Christianity during the century. At the beginning of the century, the Church was largely dominated by male leadership, although a large percentage (often the majority), of church members were women. Ordained ministry was almost universally confined to men. There were very few female academic theologians teaching in the universities. The vast majority of representatives in major church conferences were nearly always male. By the end of the century, many churches had welcomed women into ministry, including, in some cases, episcopal ministry. Women have been prominent in theology, both in writing and teaching, and have offered perspectives and approaches that have been unique to women. Denominational and ecumenical organizations have been increasingly conscious of the need to ensure equal participation of women and men in the life, worship and mission of the churches, as well as in their decision-making bodies. In many contexts, theological and liturgical language has been adapted and changed in order to be more inclusive.

However, we cannot sound too triumphalistic in these matters. In many churches, traditions and contexts, many problems remain and women are still deprived – for theological as well as cultural reasons – from playing their full part in church life. For very many women around the world, there is still a long way to go.

Inclusive community

Over recent decades, many churches have sought to address the challenges of inclusive relationships for Christian koinonia (communion or fellowship), and have given especial attention to the relationships between women and men within the Church. Those who have encouraged Christians to reflect within the life of the churches the greater equality between women and men that has developed over recent decades within society, in many though not all nations and regions, have often found it difficult. There clearly have been cultural factors. Churches, as well as individual Christians, inevitably reflect, in their attitudes and relationships with one another and with those around them, the cultural norms of their own society, often shaped by many centuries of tradition and history. But in many areas of the world, not least with the encouragement of the developed vision and priorities of ecumenical organizations such as the regional ecumenical councils and the World Council of Churches, establishing the community of women and men in the churches has been a priority.

Indeed, the WCC played a decisive role in this field not least through pioneers such as Madelaine Barot and Brigilia Bam.[1] Pauline Webb, a Methodist laywoman from the UK, was appointed the first female Vice-Moderator of the WCC Central Committee. In recognition of her pioneering role, she was invited to preach at the opening worship service of the Sixth Assembly of the WCC, Vancouver, 1983 (see *SCM Core Reader on World Christianity in the Twentieth Century*, 15.1). Thankfully, many women have followed her in leadership positions within the WCC.

One of the realities of this period (and, of course, of subsequent decades) was that there was a diversity of approaches to these issues among women themselves, set as they were in such a variety of cultures and traditions. For women in the North, the women's 'movement' and the socio-political drive for legal, economic and social equality and freedom became increasingly important within society as a whole, as well as, more gradually, within the churches. But for women in the South, questions of economic survival, health, education and cultural, racial and social freedom, were often more pressing. For them developing partnerships for liberation from oppression, injustice and poverty for everyone was seen as demanding a higher priority.

Gradually, these two priorities began to be integrated. 'Sexism', incorporating every aspect of injustice and oppression against women, became one of the overarching paradigms for this aspect of the ecumenical agenda. Rooted in the social analysis and theological framework of Latin American liberation theology, an analysis of sexism within Church and society in different contexts around the world opened the door to a deeper understanding of the issues and a greater collaborative engagement, not only by women but also by many men, in seeking to address the relational and theological issues that were at its heart.

During this time, the WCC Faith and Order Commission adopted the vision of 'The Community of Women and Men in the Church' and established a study process which captured the imagination of many churches around the world. The idea of this study process was accepted by the WCC Assembly in Nairobi in 1975. Its adoption as a Faith and Order study meant that there was a recognition that inclusive community raised questions and concerns about the fundamental nature of the Church and the search for Christian unity. The study, launched in 1978, would encourage participation by local churches and women's organizations. Regional meetings were called, and an international conference was held in Sheffield, England, as the culmination of the study process. One sign of the success of this process was that 65,000 copies of a study booklet, in 13 different languages, were produced. Constance Parvey, the director of the study, quotes Philip Potter, the then General Secretary of the WCC, as seeing in the responses from this worldwide study 'the incredible pain and agony of it all – and with it the extraordinary love and patient endurance and perseverance which lie behind it'.[2] The report of the study to the 1981 meeting of the WCC Central Committee noted that 'its framework has not been illness, but health and healing, not brokenness but new community'.[3]

Inclusive language

During the first half of the twentieth century, there was very little discussion of inclusive language within the churches. In theology, liturgy and church relationships and structures, language was almost exclusively masculine. However, as with inclusive community, the growing women's movement, feminist concerns and the struggle for equality for women within male-dominated societies challenged linguistic usage also. Gradually, during the second half of the century and especially from the 1960s onwards, it became increasingly unacceptable to use phrases such as 'God created man in his own image' or 'We pray for all men according to their need' or the first line of the well-loved hymn, 'Stand up, ye men of God'. For some these issues cause irritation, but for others they are priority concerns for the Church, since, in Elisabeth Raiser's words, 'language is the most effective mirror of cultural reality. It creates as well as interprets relations between human beings in a particular cultural context; every current language expresses superiority and subordination, reveals or keeps quiet about particular realities of life.'[4]

Recent decades have seen progress. There have been excellent examples of prayers and collects for the Christian Year being written using inclusive language.[5] There have been attempts, too, to offer inclusive translations of the Bible. For example, the note 'To the Reader' in the New Revised Standard Version of the Bible (1989) notes that the mandate given to the translators was that 'in references to men and women, masculine-orientated language should be eliminated as far as this can be done without altering passages that reflect the historical situation of ancient patriarchal culture'.[6]

It is fair to note, of course, that such attempts at inclusive language have not been without their critics. Elisabeth Raiser notes, for example, that for many within the Orthodox tradition, inclusive language is seen as 'damaging the holy Tradition brought down to them'.[7] Similarly, the Roman Catholic Church found it impossible to employ inclusive language in its English language version of *The Catechism* which was issued with the full authority of Pope John Paul II in October 1992. The first paragraph of the text reads:

> God, infinitely perfect and blessed in himself, in a plan of sheer goodness freely created man to make him share in his own blessed life. For this reason … God draws close to man. He calls man to seek him, to love him with all his strength. He calls together all men, scattered and divided by sin, into the unity of his family, the Church … In his Son and through him, he invites men to become … his adopted children.[8]

For many, such language now sounds at best strange, and at worst unacceptable. But it is fair to say that the greatest controversy has focused on the search for an inclusive language for the Triune God. While there has been wide agreement that there is no gender in God and that God is neither male nor female, the inevitability of having to use gender-specific vocabulary in most languages has challenged those who have been seeking to develop renewed liturgical texts. While many welcome such changes as genuine attempts to express, at the heart of their faith, something of the felt reality of God in their lives, others find them unacceptable because they seem to reject the inherited language of liturgy and faith in favour of what is seen as the product of a 'cultural trend' that has developed in certain contexts.

The role of women in ministry

There is a vast diversity within worldwide Christianity – both in terms of the response of particular ecclesial traditions and in terms of different regional cultural and historical contexts – in relation to the leadership and ministry of women. Many churches and denominations within the Protestant and Reformed families, though not all, enthusiastically welcome women's leadership and ministry and so have, in Elisabeth Raiser's words, 'put the issue of women's ordination on the ecumenical agenda'.[9] There is no doubt that the full partnership of women in ordained ministry has greatly enriched these churches, bringing unique pastoral, theological, liturgical, spiritual and personal gifts into the life, leadership and ministry of the churches. A series of 'propositions' (in fact, they were stated in the form of questions) issued by the WCC Faith and Order Commission in 1979 highlights the importance of these gifts but also notes that there are differences of view among the churches:

> Many say that the Church especially needs the caring, nourishing and nurturing that women have traditionally provided. Some emphasize that

these qualities in women will bring a style of leadership to the Church that encourages partnership rather than domination/submission. Others believe that emphasizing these qualities in women leads to assigning them to specialized and/or secondary roles. Another way of addressing this problem may be: Can there be wholeness in the life of the Church and its ministry before both men and women fully contribute and participate in it?[10]

Many churches have, of course, recognized the importance of these gifts by electing women to ministries of oversight and leadership within the church. For example, some Reformed and Lutheran churches have appointed female bishops or moderators during recent years as have some provinces of the Anglican Communion. Women are full partners in all aspects of ministry in other Protestant traditions also, such as Baptist, Congregational, Methodist and Presbyterian churches, as well as in the Salvation Army.

The Provinces of the Anglican Communion (each province having independence of jurisdiction but within a partnership of all the provinces through the worldwide Anglican Consultative Council), on the other hand, rooted as they are within both the Catholic and Protestant traditions, struggled for considerable time with this question. Florence Li Tim-Oi was ordained priest in the Diocese of Hong Kong and Macao in 1944. When the diocese brought the issue of women's ordination to the Lambeth Conference of all Anglican bishops in 1968, it was resolved that the theological arguments for and against women's ordination were inconclusive and that no province should ordain women to the priesthood without giving serious consideration to the view expressed through the Council. However, the first meeting of the Council itself, two years later in 1970, advised the Bishop of Hong Kong and Macao that 'if he were to proceed to the ordination of a woman his action would be acceptable to the Council, and that the Council would ... encourage all provinces of the Communion to continue in communion with that Diocese'.[11] At the next Lambeth Conference, in 1978, when four provinces had ordained women to priesthood and another eight had accepted the principle, the Lambeth Conference recognized the legal right of each province 'to make its own decision about the appropriateness of admitting women to Holy Orders'.

A few years later, but before women were ordained within the Church of England, Mary Tanner, later to be moderator of the WCC's Faith and Order Commission, writing in *Feminine in the Church*,[12] quotes one woman's experience:

I sincerely believe that women should be ordained, but I cannot believe that I would feel any different or more open as a channel for the Holy Spirit if I could say certain prayers and perform certain actions. I feel ordained now – as one of the parishioners wrote to me last Christmas: 'While the Church argues whether women should or should not be ordained, it has already happened in this parish.' It is felt by others, I feel it too. The ordination of women has much opposition which hides a lot of anger and aggression, I believe, having its roots deep in our experience of sexuality, and our belief in God. We must not fight with anger or prejudice other people's deep feelings. We take the hurt that comes through the denial of our recognition by the Church of England and go on ministering in love, speaking and working for the truth as we see it, in love. In these ways we may be instruments in bringing new life into our Church and in our Christian communities.

Mary Tanner comments:

> These stories contain their own power. They are not about militant, strident women claiming their rights, equal rights with men in the public institution of the Church. They are stories of women who, against all the odds, have experienced slowly, and often painfully and fearfully, a growing sense that God is calling them to ministry ... [The story] is told with amazement that God should, through others, be asking of them a priestly ministry.[13]

Another ten years later, in 1988, the Lambeth Conference had to face the question of the ordination of women to the episcopate (that is, to serve as bishops), after the US Episcopal church had agreed 'not to withhold consent' for such ordination. The Conference resolved that each province should 'respect the decision and attitudes of other provinces ... without such respect necessarily indicating acceptance of the principles involved'.[14]

At the time of writing, the position of the Roman Catholic Church is very different. In his Apostolic Letter *Ordinatio Sacerdotalis*, on Reserving Priestly Ordination to Men Alone, issued on 22 May 1994 (see *SCM Core Reader*, 15.2), Pope John Paul II made two particularly important points. First, the Letter seeks to underscore the importance of the presence and role of women in the life and mission of the church and quotes a previous Apostolic Letter, *Mulieris Dignitatem* (issued in 1988), which affirms that 'By defending the dignity of women and their vocation, the church has shown honour and gratitude for those women who – faithful to the Gospel – have shared in every age in the apostolic mission of the whole people of God', not least by passing on the Church's faith and tradition 'by bringing up their children in the Spirit of the Gospel'.[15] Second, in seeking to make it clear that the church's unequivocal position is that ordination is reserved to men alone, Pope John Paul II reminds Catholics of what he wrote when the issue of ordination to the priesthood was raised within the Anglican Communion. He writes:

> [The Church] holds that it is not admissible to ordain women to the priesthood, for very fundamental reasons. These reasons include: the example recorded in the Sacred Scriptures of Christ choosing his Apostles only from among men; and her living teaching authority which has consistently held that the exclusion of women from the priesthood is in accordance with God's plan for the Church.

In the light of this, and other arguments, he declares that 'the Church has no authority whatsoever to confer priestly ordination on women and that this judgement is to be definitively held by all the Church's faithful'.

This is the authoritative teaching of the Roman Catholic Church. But there are other voices. For example, <www.womenpriests.org> is one of the largest international websites on women and ministry. It focuses on the Roman

Catholic Church but draws on theological insights from other Christian traditions. While fully accepting the authority of the pope, they believe that 'the Pope and his advisors in Rome are making a serious mistake by dismissing women as priests ... Our aim is to enable the Church to reform its way of thinking and its practice so that women, as much as men, will be admitted to all the ordained ministries.'[16]

In a theological article included on the website, Reimund Bieringer, a Dutch Catholic theologian, argues that the scriptural grounds upon which *Ordinatio Sacerdotalis* bases its argument for reserving priesthood to men, are unsustainable (see *SCM Core Reader*, 15.3). He argues: 'According to our exegetical analysis it is impossible at the hands of the New Testament to prove that it is historically certain that Jesus chose his apostles only from among men ... [or that] the male sex of those chosen was essential for their mission.' He concludes that 'the apostolic letter reconstructs facts, which cannot be substantiated with historico-critical proof'.[17]

Eastern Orthodox theology, faith and order are based on the teaching of the early Fathers of the Church and on the seven Ecumenical Councils (see Chapter 2). The Orthodox churches' understanding of ministry is, therefore, rooted in the ancient tradition. So priesthood is strictly limited to men. The Orthodox position is based on many of the arguments referred to above in relation to the Roman Catholic Church. First, God became human, in a gender-specific way, in Jesus Christ. Since the priest is an ikon of Christ, then only men can be priests. During his earthly ministry Jesus deliberately chose 12 men to be his apostles, and they were the forerunners of a male priesthood. Any suggestion that the Church has misunderstood the mind of Christ is, therefore, rejected as misplaced. It is also argued that there is no evidence in the Bible that women were engaged in ordained ministry in the early Church.

Women have, of course, always played a central role in the life and witness of Orthodox churches. They play key roles in the transmission of the faith within the family and through education, as catechists and liturgical musicians, and in some churches as members of parish and diocesan councils. Orthodox women theologians have been playing an increasingly significant role both within the Orthodox family and ecumenically.

A consultation in Agapia, Romania, in 1976 focused on 'Orthodox Women, Their Role and Participation in the Orthodox Church'.[18] The consultation recommended opening up theological education, diaconal ministry and service on decision-making bodies to women. But it was ten years later that it was unanimously agreed to restore the diaconal ministry for women. While it is the case that, generally, Orthodox women have not been vociferous about ordination to the priesthood, there have been significant voices that have sought to encourage the Orthodox churches to give more sympathetic consideration to the ministry of women. Given the growing presence of Orthodox communities in contexts where there is not an established Orthodox tradition there is always the possibility that what Behr-Sigel (see below) has called 'a marriage of different cultures' may have an impact on Orthodox life and theological perspectives.

In an article written in 1998, Elisabeth Behr-Sigel concludes:

[I]t is the supreme will of God that the Church becomes that which she is: a community in faith, hope and love, of men and women, of the mystery of individuals, ineffably equal yet different, in the image and radiance of the divine Trinity. Such is the grand ecclesiological vision of the Orthodox Church. What remains is to translate it into our historical, empirical existence.[19]

(For another perspective on the same topic see *SCM Core Reader*, 15.4.)

Given this diversity of understandings of the role of women within the ministry of the Church, it may be helpful to recall the affirmations made within the WCC's report, *Baptism, Eucharist and Ministry*.[20] Although this document was published in 1982, it still represents in a helpful way the areas of agreement and debate within the ecumenical community 25 years later:

Both women and men must discover together their contributions to the service of Christ in the Church. The Church must discover the ministry which can be provided by women as well as that which can be provided by men. A deeper understanding of the comprehensiveness of ministry which reflects the interdependence of men and women needs to be more widely manifested in the life of the Church.

Though they agree on this need, the churches draw different conclusions as to the admission of women to the ordained ministry. An increasing number of churches have decided that there is no biblical or theological reason against ordaining women, and many of them have subsequently proceeded to do so. Yet many churches hold that the tradition of the Church in this regard must not be changed.

The commentary on this section of the text draws particular attention to the deeply held convictions that inform these different positions:

Those churches which practise the ordination of women do so because of their understanding of the Gospel and of the ministry. It rests for them on the deeply held theological conviction that the ordained ministry of the Church lacks fullness when it is limited to one sex ... Those churches which do not practise the ordination of women consider that the force of nineteen centuries of tradition against the ordination of women must not be set aside. They believe that such a tradition cannot be dismissed as a lack of respect for the participation of women in the Church. They believe that there are theological issues concerning the nature of humanity and concerning Christology which lie at the heart of their convictions and understanding of the role of women in the Church.

In view of these convictions, dialogue within and between the churches will need to continue in order to bring the churches to a deeper understanding of one another and of the gospel's vocation to ministry for all God's people.

Feminist perspectives on theology

Daphne Hampson begins the Introduction to her book *Theology and Feminism* with these words:

> Feminism represents a revolution. It is not in essence a demand that women should be allowed to join the male world on equal terms. It is a different view of the world. This must be of fundamental import for theology. For theology, as we have known it, has been the creation of men; indeed, of men living within a patriarchal society. As women come into their own, theology will take a different shape.[21]

It must be recognized, first of all, that there has been some discussion about the most acceptable term for what is being described here. Not all female theologians feel comfortable with the term 'feminist theology'. Some women theologians in the South see it as a western phenomenon that reflects a more strident and militant attitude towards the relationship between women and men than they would wish to espouse, and would feel more at home with a phrase such as Asian/African/Pacific women theologians. In what follows, we will use the terms that seem to be most appropriate to what is being described.

In the early decades of the twentieth century, Karl Barth saw God as 'wholly Other', a transcendent being, above and beyond the created world and human existence, but reaching out to human beings only in and through the incarnation, life, death and resurrection of Jesus Christ, in whom, therefore, the transcendent God becomes immanent. Many female and feminist theologians (as well as many male theologians) reject this concept of God as a denial of a truly incarnate understanding of God. Feminist theology (which is not a homogenous discipline but a complex of approaches to theology from the perspective of women in diverse contexts around the world) is more than a matter of exploring the potential for developing new language about God, language that is inclusive and not patriarchal. It is rather about seeking to articulate, using different metaphors and models, a transformed concept of God.

Carter Heyward writes, for example, of Dorothee Soelle's attempt to understand God 'in the "crossing over" – or "transcendence" – that occurs between and among us … God is the living, active, breathing dynamic of love that we experience in relation to one another … or God is not at all'.[22] So God is not so much almighty as all-loving; God is not so much with us in our suffering as suffering alongside us. This is the crossing-over of the transcendent God. Sallie McFague[23] suggests the metaphor of God as 'friend' and this reflects something of the understanding of God offered by Soelle. Friendship suggests mutual relationship and partnership rather than hierarchy and dominance, interdependence rather than submission.

Theologians have always argued that the doctrine of the Trinity is essentially relational. Its heart is the relationships within the being of God, between Father, Son and Spirit or Creator, Redeemer and Sanctifier. Traditionally, these realities of God, or perhaps better, this reality of God, has been understood in terms of co-equality, co-eternity, being undifferentiated in nature and substance. However, Daphne Hampson[24] comments that 'when all is said and done it is unclear to me whether [McFague] is in fact speaking of God, or rather of an attitude to life. In all this, what I miss is "theology": talk of God.' She concludes her book by suggesting that

> [the] interest which feminists have shown in the relationship of the self to its world may enable us to think in subtle and complex ways about the relationship between what we mean by self and what we mean by God ... [so as to] allow us to think about receptivity to the presence of God in our world [and] find new ways to conceive the presence of God in our world.[25]

Clearly there is more at stake here than appropriate use of inclusive language. These reflections point us towards a renewed approach to the concept of God in terms of vulnerable love rather than all-powerful coercion, in terms of relationship and partnership rather than hierarchical domination. It remains to be seen, however, whether this aspect of feminist theology can effectively transform not only the approach of academic theology to the concept of God but the contours of the faith of Christians in diverse contexts around the world.

Creative and potentially renewing as these theological struggles are, however, it has to be recognized that whereas for some Christians they are refreshing and encouraging, for others they challenge inherited theological metaphors and language and, as such, are in danger of undermining the inherited Christian tradition of the centuries. This fundamental tension within world Christianity over recent decades is not likely to be easily and swiftly resolved. It is also true to say that this debate about theological language and concepts is dominated by feminist theologians in the North. As we shall see, for women in the South, issues of justice, liberation and reconciliation take on much greater significance and a more urgent priority. But there is no doubt that feminist perspectives on theology do offer the potential, in Daphne Hampson's words,[26] for a 'revolution', for 'a different view of the world' and for a process of exploration that could give theology 'a different shape'.

Women doing theology in context

Theology does not happen in a vacuum. Theology is shaped by particular religious, cultural and socio-economic contexts. A few examples will have to suffice to illustrate this reality in relation to women's theology. But we should first pause to note the use of the phrase 'doing theology'. The term points to the need for theology to be rooted in a particular context, taking the experiences and realities of the lives of women (in the present case) as an essential resource in the theological task. It also recognizes that theology is not a static body of knowledge and understanding of God that 'merely' requires interpretation in diverse periods and contexts, but that it is rather a dynamic process which requires theologians (in partnership with all the people of God in a particular place) to be engaged in a process of creative reflection arising from a dialogue between the theological perspectives of the tradition and contemporary contexts. 'Doing theology' therefore offers the possibilities for

264 WORLD CHRISTIANITY IN THE TWENTIETH CENTURY

transforming theology, so as to make it contemporary and relevant in the lives and experiences of persons in particular contexts. In this way, theology is grounded in day-to-day realities.

So, for example, Angela Wong Wai-ching affirms that 'the theological reflection of women in Asia must not be only a kind of speculative activity, but an active engagement in response to women's confessions in their daily living experience and a commitment to strive towards full humanity. It must liberate and empower women in their living contexts.'[27] Wong goes on to quote Kwok Pui-lan who argues that 'Asian feminist theologians cannot afford to engage in the academic exercise of mental gymnastics, when so many are daily dehumanized or die of malnutrition and unsafe drinking water.'

Asian women's theology, then, draws on a range of resources from Christian and other religious sources, in folk art and literature, and in ancient mythology, in order to explore images, metaphors and narratives that could bring new paradigms and perspectives into a contextual theology rooted in Asian women's lives. One of the most notable, and most controversial, women engaged in 'doing theology' in Asia by drawing on these sources during the latter years of the twentieth century has been Chung Hyun Kyung in Korea. Her keynote address to the Seventh Assembly of the World Council of Churches (1991) – an invitation encouraged mainly by women theologians in the USA, where she was teaching at the time, rather than by Korean Christians – caused excitement and consternation (see *SCM Core Reader*, 15.6). In exploring the Assembly theme, 'Come, Holy Spirit – Renew the Whole Creation', she drew on *Han*:

> *Han* is anger. *Han* is resentment. *Han* is bitterness. *Han* is grief. *Han* is broken-heartedness and the raw energy for struggle for liberation ... The *Han*-ridden spirits ... are all over the place seeking the chance to make the wrong right ... These *Han*-ridden spirits in our people's history have been agents through whom the Holy Spirit has spoken her compassion and wisdom for life. Without hearing the cries of these spirits we cannot hear the voice of the Holy Spirit ... For us they are icons of the Holy Spirit who became tangible and visible to us. Because of them we can feel, touch and taste the concrete bodily historical presence of the Holy Spirit in our midst.[28]

This address exposed some sharp and fundamental questions around 'doing theology' in this way. Some responded warmly and passionately to her insight and appeal. Others were equally passionately critical, claiming that her attempt at drawing on these mythical religious and cultural insights in service of Christian theology resulted in syncretism – a process that draws on a variety of religious sources to produce a theology in which the fundamental truth of Christianity is lost or marginalized. A statement from Orthodox representatives emphasized:

> [W]e must guard against a tendency to substitute a 'private' spirit, the spirit of the world, and other spirits for the Holy Spirit who proceeds from the Father and rests in the Son. Our tradition is rich in respect for local and national cultures, but we find it impossible to invoke the spirits of 'earth, air, water and sea creatures'.[29]

Another aspect of women's theology in Asia (although it is not in any way confined to women theologians) is its attempt to grapple with the pain of the poor. Kwok Pui-lan, for example, sees Asian feminist theology as 'a story of suffering' that has been sometimes caused and often deepened by the western colonial presence:it will be 'a cry, a plea and invocation. It emerges from the wounds that hurt, the scars that hardly disappear, the stories that have no ending. Feminist theology in Asia is ... scribed on the hearts of many that feel the pain, and yet dare to hope.'[30]

There has been a similar emphasis among women engaged in theology in Africa. One of their key concerns is the relationship between theology and culture. Elizabeth Amoah writes:

> While [African women] accept African culture as a basis for theology, they go on to demand a critique of African culture. This critical stance is extended to the unquestioning use of the bible as the source of theology. [Many women] recognize the dehumanizing effects, especially on women, of certain aspects of African beliefs and practices. Such persistent customs as widowhood rituals, food taboos, traditional laws on inheritance and female circumcision impinge on the health and rights of women ... African women experience the effects of racism, poverty, social, economic and political problems ... even more than their male counterparts. Such pressing issues also form the content of African women's theology.[31]

One example of cultural impact is the issue of polygamy within African society. SCM Core Reader, 15.7, gives one example of a theological response. Musimbi Kanyoro suggests that until recently polygamy has been seen as a moral question: is polygamy acceptable within a Christian morality of marriage? African women, however, have called for a different perspective, so that polygamy is seen not as a moral issue but as an issue of equality, 'an institution that is oppressive to women',[32] and concludes that '[failure] to teach true equality between the two sexes is failure to instil into society that the superiority of man over woman is contrary to God's intention for human beings'.

Amoah also calls for African women in theology to have high on their agenda international policies that have an effect on the lives of women, such as structural adjustment programmes and international trade systems (which include the questions of 'third world debt').

Similarly, the pain and suffering of women have been formative influences on the theology of women in Latin America. Ana Maria Sales Placidino describes the spiritual experience of women encountering the black, feminine face of God:

> God is like the woman who braids hair, who, as she braids the hair of the little girls, is keeping black culture alive ... God is a hungry, abused, enslaved little girl. God is a young black woman, militant and sensitive to the pain of the age in which she is living ... This vision of the God of life was a silent thread running through the long years of suffering ... But the moment has arrived: what was conceived in the silence of the night is being born in the hubbub of the day![33]

These three examples from Asia, Africa and Brazil, remind us that the concerns of women doing theology in these contexts are often very different from those of women in the North and West. Exploring inclusive language and developing new philosophical categories become less important than the more urgent task of enabling women to grapple with the challenge to theology of the pain and suffering inflicted on women (and, of course, on others) by oppressive cultural traditions and unjust international systems.

The Ecumenical Decade of Churches in Solidarity with Women

The Ecumenical Decade was launched by the WCC at Easter 1988. Among its objectives were the following:

- empowering women to challenge oppressive structures in the global community, their churches and communities;
- affirming ... the decisive contributions of women in churches and communities;
- giving visibility to women's perspectives and actions in the work and struggle for justice, peace and the integrity of creation;
- encouraging the churches to take actions in solidarity with women.[34]

The title should be noted – it was the Decade of the *Churches* ... – and this became one of its main difficulties: enabling the churches to recognize the Decade as theirs and to place its concerns at the centre of their agenda rather than within the remit of their women's organizations. From 1993 onwards a series of team visits was organized as 'living letters' to churches and national councils of churches to discuss the concerns of the Decade and to learn about the ways these concerns impacted on various situations around the world. Some 330 churches, 68 national councils of churches and 650 women's groups were visited![35] At the halfway point of the Decade[36] a number of key issues were identified, as a result of visits and consultations, that would be the focus for the remaining years. These included the participation of women in the life and ministry of the Church, the effect of the international economic crisis on women, the increasing violence against women in every region of the world both within and outside the Church, and the effect of rising racism and xenophobia on women. The striking feature of this assessment is that the concerns of women doing theology in regions within the South that we identified in the previous section came to dominate the agenda, though not, of course, to the exclusion of the issues that have continued to be fundamental in other regions of the world.

Immediately before the Eighth Assembly of the WCC in Harare, Zimbabwe, in November 1998, a Decade Festival was held to mark the end of the Decade. The letter issued by this Festival[37] (see *SCM Core Reader*, 15.8) made a number of key affirmations which were presented to the WCC Assembly and its member churches. These included, first, the importance of encouraging participation of each and every one in the life of the churches. Second, it called for the elimination of all violence in various forms and of the culture of violence (declaring that violence against women within the Church was, in particular, 'an offence against God, humanity and the earth'). Finally, it affirmed the 'vision of a world of economic justice, where poverty is neither tolerated nor justified'.

The debate about these issues in the Assembly itself inevitably heard voices of solidarity and deep criticism but at the end of the debate a series of recommendations was adopted that included calls for the churches 'to provide opportunities for women to speak out about violence and abuse'; 'the use of languages and policies' that support inclusion 'in all aspects of the life of the churches, where this is in harmony with the churches' self-understanding'; the denunciation of 'commercial sexual exploitation'; support for 'the development of just economic systems and structures in church and society' and to 'keep the goals of the Decade before them'.[38]

Ten years after the end of the Decade, there is still deep division among the churches on questions such as inclusive community and inclusive language, some of the traditional doctrines of faith and the place of women in the ministry of the churches at all levels. And although dialogue continues between the Christian communions about these issues, there are no signs that the areas of deep disagreement are likely to be resolved in the immediate future. Already, however, the growing voice of women in the churches has been theologically creative. New metaphors, models and paradigms, as well as renewed theological language and hermeneutics, have resulted from the explorations in which women (and occasionally male) theologians have been engaged. At a world level, there is a clear tension between those who seek to highlight issues of language, theology and partnership within the Church and those for whom the pain, suffering and oppression of women must take on a deeper and more pressing priority. So one of the key tasks that will need to exercise the churches during the early decades of the twenty-first century will be to develop new ways of being in solidarity with women (and with all marginalized persons) in societies where injustice, oppression and inequality are causing profound suffering and pain, while also continuing the theological dialogue that will enable women to be full partners within the life and mission of the churches.

Further reading

A number of articles and chapters in key textbooks and encyclopedia give a balanced account of the story told in this chapter. Among these are the following:

A. Carr (1993), 'Feminist Theology', in A. E. McGrath, *The Blackwell Encyclopedia of Modern Christian Thought*, Oxford: Blackwell, pp. 220–28, which also includes an excellent bibliography, provides a good résumé of the key issues, both theological and practical, around this topic.

R. Muers (2005), 'Feminism, Gender and Theology', in D. Ford and R. Muers (eds), *The Modern Theologians*, Oxford: Blackwell, pp. 431ff., offers insightful summaries and reflections on key issues and personalities.

E. Raiser (2004), 'Inclusive Community', in J. Briggs, M. Oduyoye and G. Tstetsis (eds) (2004), *A History of the Ecumenical Movement: Volume 3 1968–2000*, Geneva: WCC Publications, pp. 243ff., provides a very helpful summary of the ecumenical aspects of the issue during the latter decades of the century.

Books on this topic include:

M. Furlong (ed.) (1984), *Feminine in the Church*, London: SPCK, which includes an excellent range of essays by leaders and theologians.

M. R. A. Kanyoro (2002), *Introducing Feminist Cultural Hermeneutics: An African Perspective*, Sheffield: Sheffield University Press, explores, from an African perspective, one of the key theological issues within the debate about theology and culture.

Kwok Pui-lan (2000), *Introducing Asian Feminist Theology*, Sheffield: Sheffield Academic Press, which is widely regarded as the best introduction, at the time of writing, to the topic, from an Asian perspective.

O. Ortega (ed.) (1995), *Women's Voices: Theological Reflection, Celebration, Action*, Geneva: WCC Publications, offers a wide range of articles by women from many backgrounds and cultures around the world.

N. Slee (2003), *Faith and Feminism: An Introduction to Christian Feminist Theology*, London: Darton, Longman & Todd.

N. Watson (2004), *Feminist Theology*, Guides to Theology series, Grand Rapids MI: Wm B. Eerdmans.

Notes

1 E. Raiser (2004), 'Inclusive Community', in J. Briggs, M. Oduyoye and G. Tsetsis (eds) (2004), *A History of the Ecumenical Movement: Volume 3, 1968–2000*, Geneva: WCC Publications, pp. 243ff.

2 C. F. Parvey (ed.) (1983), *The Community of Women and Men in the Church: The Sheffield Report*, Geneva: WCC Publications, p. 25.

3 C. F. Parvey, in an unpublished paper, quoted in M. May (1986), *Bonds of Unity: Women, Theology and the Worldwide Church*, UMI Dissertation Information Service, p. 56, and quoted in Briggs et al., *A History*, p. 250.

4 Raiser, 'Inclusive Community', p. 255.

5 See, for example, J. Morley (1992), *All Desires Known*, London: SPCK.

6 NRSV, Nashville TN: NCCCUSA, 1989.

7 Raiser, 'Inclusive Community', p. 256.

8 *Catechism of the Catholic Church*, London: Geoffrey Chapman, 1992, p. 7.

9 Raiser, 'Inclusive Community', p. 251.

10 C. F. Parvey (1979), *Ordination of Women in Ecumenical Perspective: Workbook for the Church's Future*, Geneva: WCC, ch. VI, quoted in G. Gassmann (ed.) (1993), *Documentary History of Faith and Order: 1963–1993*, Faith and Order Paper no. 159, Geneva: WCC Publications, p. 156.

11 See *The Windsor Report* (2004), London: Anglican Consultative Council, p. 14.

12 M. Tanner (1984), 'Called to Priesthood: Interpreting Women's Experience', in M. Furlong (ed.), *Feminine in the Church*, London: SPCK, p. 161.

13 *Windsor Report*, p. 14.

14 *Windsor Report*, p. 15.

15 *Ordinatio Sacerdotalis*, para. 3, from http://www.vatican.va/holy_father/john_paul_ii/apost_letters/documents/hf_jp-ii_apl_22051994_ordinatio-sacerdotalis_en.html (accessed 8 Oct. 07).

16 www.womenpriests.org (opening page).

17 R. Bieringer (2001), 'The Scriptural Argument in *Ordinatio Sacerdotalis*', trans. J. Wijngaards, *Bijdragen* 62, p. 142, from www.womenpriests.org/scriptur/biering.asp (accessed 15 Nov. 07).

18 See the report of the same title, Geneva: WCC Publications, 1977.

19 E. Behr-Sigel (1998), 'Women in the Orthodox Church', trans. D. Takles, *St Nina Quarterly*, vol. 2, no. 2, Spring, final paragraph, downloaded from the online version of the journal at http://www.stnina.org// (accessed 15 Nov. 07).

20 *Baptism, Eucharist and Ministry*, Faith and Order Paper no. 111, Geneva: WCC Publications, 1982, Ministry para. 18.

21 D. Hampson (1990), *Theology and Feminism*, Oxford: Blackwell, p. 1.

22 C. Heyward (2003), 'Crossing Over: Dorothee Soelle and the Transcendence of God', in S. K. Pinnock, *The Theology of Dorothee Soelle*, Harrisburg/London/New York: Trinity Press International, pp. 221ff.

23 S. McFague (1987), *Models of God*, Philadephia: Fortress Press.

24 Hampson, *Theology and Feminism*, p. 154.

25 Hampson, *Theology and Feminism*, p. 170.

26 Hampson, *Theology and Feminism*, p. 173.

27 Hampson, *Theology and Feminism*, p. 1 (see the quotation at the beginning of this section).

28 Angela Wong Wai-ching (2004), 'Women Doing Theology within the Asian Ecumenical Movement', in N. Koshy (ed), *A History of the Ecumenical Movement in Asia, Volume II*, HongKong: WSCF/YMCA/CCA, pp. 100–1.

29 Chung Hyun Kyung (1991), 'Come, Holy Spirit – Renew the Whole Creation', in M. Kinnamon (ed.), *Signs of the Spirit: Official Report of the Seventh Assembly*, Geneva: WCC Publications, p. 39.

30 Chung, 'Come, Holy Spirit', pp. 15f.

31 Kwok Pui-lan (2000), *Introducing Asian Feminist Theology*, Sheffield: Sheffield Academic Press, p. 32.

32 E. Amoah (1995), 'Theology from the Perspective of African Women', in O. Ortega (ed.), *Women's Voices: Theological Reflection, Celebration, Action*, Geneva: WCC Publications, pp. 1f.

33 M. R. A. Kanyoro (2002), *Introducing Feminist Cultural Hermeneutics: An African Perspective*, Sheffield: Sheffield University Press, p. 87.

34 Quoted by R. S. de Oliviera, 'Feminist Theology in Brazil', in Ortega, *Women's Voices*, p. 68.

35 Raiser, 'Inclusive Community', p. 260; see also M. Oduyoye (1990), *Who Will Roll the Stone Away?*, Geneva: WCC Publications.

36 Raiser, 'Inclusive Community', p. 261.

37 For a mid-decade assessment of the Decade, see A. Gnanadason (ed.) *The Ecumenical Review*, vol 46, no 2, April 1994, Geneva: WCC Publications.

38 See D. Kessler (ed.) (1999), *Together on the Way: Official Report of the Eighth Assembly of the World Council of Churches*, Geneva: WCC Publications, pp. 243ff.

39 Kessler, *Together on the Way*, p. 251.

16

Christians and Our Neighbours of Other World Faiths

One of the great challenges facing Christians in the twenty-first century is that of facing up to the fact that we share this planet with several other major world faith traditions. These are usually listed as those of the Hindus, Jews, Buddhists, Sikhs and Muslims. They will accompany us, in some senses rival us, perhaps in some ways outdo us, and in any case remain unmistakably present in the same world as us, whether we like it or not. Their sheer presence will constantly call in question the claims we may make about the truth and value of our own faith. People accustomed to looking out over the planet as a whole will know that this has long been so – only Islam and the Sikh teachings have come onto the world scene since Christianity. But those accustomed rather to living in religiously more enclosed societies, whether Christians or of another faith, still find it challenging to learn to deal with believers in another tradition as near neighbours.

The history is long and complex. The ancient Hindu Vedic teachings, like those of Lao-tzu known through the Chinese Taoist tradition, took shape many hundreds of years before Jesus of Nazareth (from whose supposed birth-date Europe has dated history for most of the last 2,000 years). At around the same time, Abraham was called by God to leave his home in the land of the Chaldees with the promise 'I will bless you, and make your name great ... and in you all the families of the earth shall be blessed' (Genesis 12.2–3). Both Confucius in China and Gautama the Buddha in Northern India lived in the sixth century before Christ, while the Prophet Muhammad began to receive the teachings gathered in the Qur'an in the year 610 after Christ, and the Sikh Guru Nanak and his nine successor Gurus were active between 1500 and 1708. Both the teachings of the Buddha and those of Jesus of Nazareth were responsible for what one might call a 'reform movement' in their native Hindu and Jewish traditions, neither welcome to the then leaders of the 'parent' community. Yet both have spread and grown more widely than the older tradition.

Often involved in conflict

So there is nothing new about the fact of different faith traditions living and growing alongside one another, even within the territory and society claimed by one of the others as distinctively theirs. Still less is it new to find 'religions' taking up aggressive stances towards one or more others, whether internally, as Christians have long experienced throughout Europe, not least between Catholics and Protestants in Northern Ireland throughout the twentieth century, or externally, as at the turn of the twenty-first century in certain Islamic movements calling for *jihad* (= struggle) against 'unbelievers' such as that headed by Osama Bin Laden in Afghanistan. In every part of the world, relations between the faith traditions today are profoundly determined by their local history and its heritage in community outlooks.

Relations between Buddhists and Hindus in Sri Lanka, for instance, reflect the pride of the Sinhala people who accepted for their own, many centuries ago, the teachings of the Buddha which the Hindus of his own homeland in north-east India had refused to honour. The more recently arrived Tamils of the island's northern and eastern coastal areas have long been looked down on as some sort of advance party for a wholly unwanted domination from the vast and overcrowded neighbour to the north. Relations between Christians and Muslims in Nigeria, a very different situation, still bear the stamp of hostilities between the incoming British invaders, accompanied by new Christians from the tribes of the south, and the pride and valour of the northern Muslim horse-riding tribes ruling over their huge, semi-desert domains. Every local situation will have some sort of comparable heritage behind what one can see in action today. It is important always to learn as much about such factors in the context as one possibly can before coming to any judgement about the best way ahead.

In particular, wherever there has been a 'religious' conflict of some sort, there will always have been a complex of social, economic and power factors involved. These will often have been at the root of the conflict more strongly than the religious factor. At the same time, the involvement of a religious factor often makes the task of peaceseeking and peacemaking even more difficult because there is no clear model or agreement available by which the religious dimension of the conflict can be resolved. Even if the hostile parties each insist that God wills peace, the fact that they reflect an age-old and unbridgeable religious divide means that there seems no hope by which God's will for peace and harmony can be expected to resolve whatever are the specific political, social or other reasons for the conflict.

In many of the major traditions there have been examples of devoted believers risking much to try and bring peace to situations of bloodshed and hatred. Christians look back to St Francis of Assisi. He visited the Muslim ruler Saladin, who had reconquered Jerusalem from the Crusaders towards the end of the twelfth century, and found him to be a model of chivalry, sensitivity and openness to debate. There have undoubtedly been many other examples of peacemakers, for instance in both the Buddhist and Sikh traditions, even if often alongside dauntingly powerful and cruel fellow believers known for their military prowess even in those peaceseeking traditions!

The part of the world that has experienced, perhaps more than any other, the heights and the depths of relationships between different faiths over the centuries is the Indian subcontinent. This is the area which gave birth to the Vedas and the entire range of Hindu traditions, while also providing humanity with the person of the Buddha, with the tradition of the Sikh Gurus, with the distinctive teaching and practice of the Jains – and much else. Yet it has also known grievous conflicts between religious groups, even the splitting of the nation of India into two (later three) because of the enmity between Hindus and Muslims. It has nonetheless enriched humanity with many teachers and leaders in the exploration of interfaith understanding and respect – think of the Bengali poet Rabindranath Tagore or the activist pacifist Mahatma Gandhi in the earlier part of the twentieth century, of the Dalai Lama and of Mother Teresa of Calcutta later in the century. Each has stood in their own tradition yet widened the awareness of many people beyond that.

There are few easy answers in this long problematic field. Yet for well over 100 years now there has been a growing sense that humanity need not be locked into the apparently inevitable conflicts between the great faiths. If only humanity could learn to obey the deepest and truest teachings in all the traditions we would discover there a power for peace and mutual understanding rather than the cause of hatred and cruelty that has so often disfigured human behaviour.

How do Christians understand God's intentions for different faiths?

In 1846 F. D. Maurice of King's College, London, published *The Religions of the World and their Relations to Christianity*, a set of lectures which was to serve as a leading light for all subsequent teaching and exploration in the West towards a more friendly and open-minded approach to 'other' religions than had been followed earlier. Indeed, the rubric which governed the annual 'Boyle' lectureship that Maurice was fulfilling that year had specified in 1691 that 'Eight Sermons should be preached each year in London for proving the Christian religion against notorious Infidels, to wit, Atheists, Theists, Pagans, Jews and Mahometans; not descending any lower to any controversies that are among Christians themselves'![1]

Kenneth Cracknell draws out of these lectures ten leading 'principles'.[2] These may serve as a starting point for the exploration of 'relations with other faiths' in which so many Christians, and their colleagues in the other faith traditions, are now engaged.

1 The phenomenon of religion is always to be understood theologically.
2 Christianity is the key to the reconciliation of religions.
3 Creation in the image of God is the basis for evaluating all other religious traditions.
4 All religions are part of human history which itself points to a completion.
5 The insights and testimonies of the religions of the world find responses within the Christian revelation.
6 Christians must never cease to look for all that is good in the world's religious traditions.
7 The encounter with other religious systems will help to detect the errors into which 'Christianity as a System' is also prone to fall.
8 The encounter with other religious traditions may offer correctives to Christian theological formulation.

9 All Christians are to proceed in their relations with followers of other paths by dialogue and not by polemic.

10 All Christian theology of religion flows from and feeds back into a theology of Christian mission.

Over the years since, Christian thinkers have striven long and hard for an appropriate understanding of how Christians should think of, approach and expect results from their contact with believers of the other faiths. These debates have gone through many stages, which we cannot nor need not set out here at length. Yet there have been remarkable, and at the time largely unexpected, results from this search, which deserve to be chronicled – if only to help avoid any repetition of what have proved to be inadequate positions.

At the extraordinarily important World Missionary Conference at Edinburgh in 1910 (on which see Chapter 1, p. 18) its Commission IV brought forward a report which both affirmed and demonstrated the overwhelmingly clear conviction, in virtually all the material from serving missionaries that had contributed to it, that 'the true attitude of the Christian missionary to the non-Christian religions should be one of true understanding and, as far as possible, of sympathy' and that 'the true method is that of knowledge and charity' (*SCM Core Reader on World Christianity in the Twentieth Century*, 16.1). That has admittedly not been universally followed since, but should still be regarded as a basic starting point.

Within the circles that were to become, from 1948 onwards, the World Council of Churches, the debate following up on that Edinburgh conference has been long, at times tortuous, and still at the time of writing by no means ended. The next world conference called by the committee established at Edinburgh, by then entitled the International Missionary Council, took place at Jerusalem in 1928. This was dominated by an awareness of the growing 'secularism' in Europe rather than by any question about 'other faiths'. Not so its successor in 1938, which took place in India, at Tambaram, near Madras, now Chennai. For this, the Dutch theologian Hendrik Kraemer, who had spent nearly 20 years living among university-trained Muslim leaders and thinkers in Indonesia, wrote *The Christian Message in a Non-Christian World*. This book offered a distinctive theological starting point in the 'radical' Christocentrism of Karl Barth, which many from outside the circles where Barth was admired and followed found distasteful, even unacceptable. See, for instance, the passage where Kraemer uses for his purposes Barth's famously massive dictum that between God and humankind 'there is no point of contact' (*SCM Core Reader*, 16.2).

This same area of question played an important part in the Second Vatican Council of the Roman Catholic Church in the 1960s. There, what was at first planned as a text on Christian relations with the Jews, became a short but extraordinarily influential text (*SCM Core Reader*, 16.3, reprints the greater part of it), opening up a new sense of neighbourhood, respect and friendship with people of all the other faiths.

Soon after, the debate was strongly taken up again from 1968 onwards in the WCC. Stanley Samartha, an Indian theologian, was appointed to serve a working group on 'Dialogue with People of Living Faiths'. This held an impressive series of meetings in the 1970s, both for Christians to debate among themselves (in increasingly effective teamwork with the parallel Vatican Secretariat) and bringing together members of the several major traditions. The clearest theological results from that group are to be found in the book, *Faith in the Midst of Faiths: Reflections on Dialogue in Community*,[3] resulting from a conference in Chiang Mai, Thailand in April 1977.

In the 1970s and 80s the parallel debates in western church circles – and often in other areas too – concentrated on three possible approaches to the other religions. The first was labelled the *'exclusive'* approach. This affirms God's revelation in Jesus Christ to be unique and final. Whatever truth and goodness there may be in other faith traditions, salvation can only come in and through Jesus Christ. This is not to say that God's love and mercy are for Christians alone, let alone that God is dismissive of the other faiths. But it does emphasize the belief that it is in Jesus that human beings of any and every background and culture can see and meet God in the life, death and rising of the man from Nazareth in a way that no other faith can offer. The second was the *'inclusive'* approach. This claims that any grace and any understanding of the truth and salvation available to humanity comes ultimately from the God whom Jesus knew as 'Father', however much the realities and value of it may have been learned in or from a community of another faith. The Austrian Jesuit Karl Rahner referred to some people as 'anonymous Christians', that is, persons who may be regarded as Christians even if they are not themselves conscious of the origins in Christ of the faith and obedience they practise. The third was then the *'pluralist'* approach, which suggests that all religions have a common heart or essence, so that all religious traditions and communities may be seen as offering some genuine possibilities of a spiritual path towards God. This approach was widely seen as that of Christians willing to accept the other traditions as comparable religious realities to their own, and so offering equally valid and mutually enriching teachings. These three approaches were argued over for several years, and still are in some circles.

Yet at the international level many who have worked with these categories have reached at least two interim conclusions. First, that any strict or total 'exclusiveness' cannot be seen as compatible with the attitudes Jesus showed to people he met, however much Christians may feel it right to doubt or disagree with any specific assertion(s) of another faith. Second, that to settle for a 'pluralism' which simply allows us all to live alongside one another, without trying to resolve our evident disagreements, is in fact seriously to undervalue the profound convictions related to the central and distinctive features of each faith. These must be respected, even if they point to definite disagreements between the faiths, and must be allowed to be honoured and practised in mutually accepted tolerance.

In the earlier stages of these debates, evangelical Christians were often found in sharp disagreement with what was being said in ecumenical gatherings. But this antagonism has also considerably softened over the years. *SCM Core Reader*, 16.7, for instance, is from a book written at the end of the century by Vinoth Ramachandra, an Indian Evangelical, whose arguments will be widely respected and agreed with by many fellow Christians who by no means identify themselves as evangelical.

Perhaps the single most valuable outcome of this whole period of debate is to be found in the report of a section of the 1989 WCC World Mission and Evangelism Conference in San Antonio, Texas. This (see *SCM Core Reader*, 16.6) stresses that 'We cannot point to any other way of salvation than Jesus Christ', but goes straight on to affirm that 'we cannot set limits to the saving power of God'. There is necessarily a 'tension', which is to be 'appreciated' even if the writers decide not to 'attempt to resolve it', between what God has so clearly made known and available in Christ, and what God can do in and through people of other faith traditions, not least for Christians in mutually supportive dialogue with them.

Complementarity rather than competition

Meanwhile thinkers such as S. Mark Heim (see *SCM Core Reader*, 16.8) have begun to explore ways in which the major faiths may be seen not as directly in contradiction with one another, so much as addressing themselves variously to somewhat different 'ends'. They thus bring to bear their distinctive convictions and obedience in ways that are not essentially contrasted with, let alone directed against, those of others. Careful, mutual listening and understanding can instead open up greater appreciation of a certain complementarity in belief, as of potential areas of alliance in practice.

As Archbishop Rowan Williams, speaking as a Christian among Christians, said to the World Council of Churches' Assembly in Porto Alegre in 2006 (see *SCM Core Reader*, 16.9): 'We are not called to win competitions or arguments in favour of our "product" in some religious market place', but simply to accept the place that Jesus gives us to occupy and there behave and react as nearly as we can in the ways he did in his own time. It is not our job as Christians to judge what others confess and insist on – that is for God, not us. But it is our job to react in friendship and sympathy, and then see what next steps we are both and all being led into by the Holy Spirit.

Priority to practice

Already in 1981, under the leadership of Kenneth Cracknell, its first ever Secretary for Inter-Faith Relationships, the British Council of Churches produced a set of four surprisingly short but endlessly true, rich and encouraging 'Principles':

1 Dialogue begins when people meet each other.
2 Dialogue depends on mutual understanding and mutual trust.
3 Dialogue makes it possible to share in service to the community.
4 Dialogue becomes the medium of authentic witness.

See *SCM Core Reader*, 16.4, for the original, brief expositions which accompanied these. They show not least that it is in how we actually behave in regard to one another, across the lines of faith, culture and tradition, that we can best discover the mutual respect and trust that is the base line for all further exploration. In particular, many have discovered that the Holy Spirit can guide and lead us more genuinely by the movements of our hearts and wills (stimulated *in and through our practice of dialogue*) than by our supposing that we do best *to think out first our theological presuppositions* in detail. The surprises and demands of practice have again and again proved more creative and positive than any prior theological statement of what God intends by and for the others, especially when this is seen in contrast to what God intends by and for Christians.

In particular, these four Principles have frequently proved helpful also for what they point away from. For instance, the first, by stressing that it is always *persons* that meet one another shows that it is never 'religions' that meet or need to relate, only always particular persons or groups of actual people. The second, stressing *mutual respect and trust*, shows that we will only get anywhere in such relationships if we can discover how to grow to respect and trust the other person and her or his companions. So also the third, by insisting that the point of any dialogue is not in our own good fortune or enjoyment, emphasizes that the service we can now give together to *the wider community* is a more worthwhile purpose than anything directed only at our own fellow believers. Most important of all is the fourth, in its surprising juxtaposition of *dialogue* and *mutual witness*. This shows that the possibility of one day sharing one's deepest convictions about the truth of one's own specific faith, and in such a way that these can be understood and welcomed by our friends of another tradition, is much more likely to arise in a situation of mutual trust, caring and appreciation than when there is any remaining hint of rivalry or self-assertion.

Difficulties ahead

Looking around the world, the experience of interfaith practice that the twentieth century has left for its successors is by no means all creative and positive. If anything, in the aftermath of western colonialism, which often – consciously or unconsciously – gave the impression that the Christian way was bound to be the best, the 'other' traditions have bounced back and strongly reclaimed both their members and their cultural and political traditions. This has in turn often given rise to an expectation of conflicts, both internal (for example, as between different Muslim traditions in Iraq) and between the religious communities (such as, Buddhist Singalese confronting largely Hindu Tamils in Sri Lanka). Indeed the early years of the new century have been dominated in many quarters by the threat and dismaying experience of all-out conflict between the inheritors of 'western Christian civilization' and those who inherit rather the ambitions of political Islam as the 'final' prophecy for all humankind. Experience in regard to Afghanistan, to the destruction of the Twin Towers in New York in September 2001, to the war on Iraq and its aftermath, and to the continuing threats of major attacks by al-Qaida, all share in that particular context. So there can be little doubt but that a very high priority remains appropriate for any and every attempt to work through in active practice the best possible approaches, in all possible local, national and international settings, to interfaith dialogue and intercultural collaboration.

One early initiative to encourage the practice of interfaith relationships at the international level was the first 'World's Parliament of Religions', held in Chicago in 1893. This was long remembered for the contributions of the Hindu teacher and evangelist Swami Vivekananda. Each religious tradition and community was enabled to present its own faith and hope in its own way, yet in a common and shared setting. Its tradition was renewed in 1993, with a meeting in Cape Town under the same title and in the same style. But by then, while the provision of space and time for each faith to present itself in its own way was still appropriate, many who attended felt a yawning emptiness in its disregard of actual dialogue or collaboration. Fortunately, these can now be found at the international level in several active voluntary organizations, including the International Association for Religious Freedom (from 1900), the World Congress of Faiths (from 1936) and the World Conference on Religion and Peace, more recently known as Religions for Peace (from 1965). All of these have depended considerably so far on North American money, though with the Japanese *Rissho Kosei-Kai* (a Buddhist movement established in Japan in 1938) also contributing a great deal, as an initiative and 'impulse' which 'still comes overwhelmingly from the Christian side'.[4]

Ninian Smart has put one conclusion from this long striving rather neatly in his dictum: 'From a Christian perspective we can say that God put other faiths there to keep us honest'![5]

At the national level, we remember with some astonishment how Stanley Samartha's successor in the WCC, the Sri Lankan Wesley Ariarajah, remarked to us in 1982 that 'you British are probably the most favoured nation in the world in regard to the possibilities of inter-faith dialogue'. One particularly impressive exploration has seen the creation and development of the Inter-Faith Network. This consists of leaders of the various faith traditions, each and all carefully chosen and commissioned by their own constituencies, working together at national level for the sake of the nation as a whole. Over twenty and more years, this Network has grown into a dependable and creative partner to government, and was able to hold a particularly noteworthy public celebration of the new century in January 2000 in the British House of Lords. Through this Network, the faith communities offer, and can be seen to carry through, their best services in every part of the United Kingdom. And this not in competition or rivalry, but by encouraging one another and discovering patterns by which people of very different backgrounds can nevertheless bring out the best in each other and make that available to the wider population.

Learning to speak clearly and truly about each other

Another vital strand in the continuing search has come from the Canadian Islamic scholar and Harvard Professor Wilfred Cantwell Smith in his outstanding book *The Meaning and End of Religion*. He is here writing out of an awareness that

> Unless a Christian can contrive intelligently and spiritually to be a Christ-
> ian not merely in a Christian society or a secular society but in the world;
> unless a Muslim [or] a Buddhist can carve a satisfactory place for himself as
> a Buddhist in the world in which other intelligent, sensitive, educated men
> are Christians and Muslims – unless, I say, we can together solve the intel-
> lectual and spiritual questions posed by comparative religion, then I do not
> see how a man is to be a Christian or a Muslim or a Buddhist at all.[6]

So he proposes that we abandon the word 'religion' as a noun, especially in
the plural, since this cannot but be seriously misleading in any attempt to
seize hold of the wholeness of the relationships that all faiths, in their very
different ways, are concerned with. Rather he bids us speak, when handling
those things that can be seen and measured in each community, of 'cumu-
lative tradition(s)', and when touching on those aspects that are essentially
unseen, unprovable and unfathomable, of 'faith'. That care to use a vocabulary that allows for both likeness and deep difference between the faiths is
exemplary.

Where are we going?

A question frequently raised in regard to the diversity of world faiths is: precisely what are we aiming at? What do we see as the appropriate goal for all
the dialogues and strivings? In a particularly brash discussion of this among
friends, Kenneth Cracknell once formulated four possible 'answers':

1 The ultimate triumph of one religious tradition over all others.
2 The deliberate creation of a new, deliberately syncretistic religion, in which
  all people are enabled to find fulfilment.
3 The conscious decision by religious communities to live and let live, within
  various forms of splendid isolation, and
4 Something as yet to be guessed at, a wholly new action of God, to which I
  give the wholly ungrammatical code name 'You ain't seen nothing yet'.[7]

It was then, and still is now, hardly surprising to realize that of these four
'answers' only the last can possibly be believed and followed through in practice. To decide finally and only for any of the other three, however tempting it
may seem at the time, could only lead to quite impossible situations. It is precisely a matter of peculiarly 'religious' obedience to believe and trust that no
one but God alone, whom no human has ever seen, can, in God's good time,
produce the 'solution' to this major puzzle.

What human beings can do meanwhile, each of us in our own setting and
in accordance with our own specific belief, is to obey the guidance we believe we have received from God. Christians will follow as best they can the
example of Jesus, while others will comparably follow their best teacher(s).
We shall then all be able to respond with sensitivity, generosity and imagination to what happens when and as we take actual next steps in mutual understanding and collaboration. In and from such *practice* of active and loving

relationships with our neighbours of the other faiths – as with any and every other sort of neighbour – God the Holy Spirit can allow, indeed enable us to serve the coming of his Kingdom. In his good time he may even perhaps let us begin to sense for ourselves that it is now coming!

Further reading

There is of course a vast number of relevant books and articles on the theme of this chapter. Each country involved, each language area and indeed each faith community will have a significant quantity from which useful reading can be selected. So here, for English-speaking readers in Europe, are a few titles to start with. Many of these will in turn provide further suggestions.

N. Smart (1989), *The World's Religions: Old Traditions and Modern Transformations*, Cambridge: Cambridge University Press (also in later paperback). Well illustrated and covering the history, both ancient and modern, and the contemporary developments in the faith and practice of all major traditions and cultures.

J. Sacks (1995), *Faith in the Future*, London: Darton, Longman & Todd. Short chapters by the UK Chief Rabbi setting out a way of understanding what modernity is doing to us all and how a Jew makes sense of his own tradition within that.

C. Lamb (1985), *Belief in a Mixed Society*, Tring: Lion Publishing. Both an empirical study of how different faith communities experience different aspects of living in the UK today and of how Christians can behave and witness in full friendship and respect of their neighbours. A foretaste of what the twenty-first century is bringing us all.

W. Cantwell Smith (1962), *The Meaning and End of Religion: A New Approach to the Religious Traditions of Mankind*, New York: Macmillan and London: SPCK, 1978. A fascinating, scholarly exposition of the terms best used in discussing humanity's various 'religious' traditions, which is enlightening in many different and profound ways.

K. Cragg (1956), *The Call of the Minaret*, New York: Oxford University Press. The first major book by the outstanding interpreter of Islam to Christians in our time. Deeply researched and experienced, it is not difficult but not to be read quickly. Among his many later books, *Sandals at the Mosque* (1959), London: SCM Press, and *Muhammad and the Christian: A Question of Response* (1984), London: Darton Longman & Todd and New York: Orbis Books, would for beginners be worth trying first.

H. Kraemer (1960), *World Cultures and World Religions: The Coming Dialogue*, London: Lutterworth Press. No longer exactly the latest, but still a most useful and penetrating survey by a master of this field in his generation. Based on lectures given at Princeton University.

S. M. Heim (1995), *Salvations: Truth and Difference in Religion*, New York: Orbis Books. Deeply interesting study of the different 'ends' of traditional religious seeking in the different world faiths, and thus of how they can all be seen as complementing rather than competing with each other.

Notes

1 K. Cracknell (1995), *Justice, Courtesy and Love: Theologians and Missionaries Encountering World Religions, 1846–1914*, London: Epworth Press, p. 39.

2 Cracknell, *Justice*, pp. 44–59, with full expositions of each of these principles.

3 S. J. Samartha (ed.) (1977), Geneva: WCC Publications.

4 I. Selvanayagam (2004), 'Interfaith Dialogue', in J. Briggs, M. Oduyoye and G, Tsetsis (eds), *A History of the Ecumenical Movement, Volume 3, 1968–2000*, Geneva: WCC Publications, pp. 149–73.

5 N. Smart and S. Konstantine (1991), *Christian Systematic Theology in a World Context*, London: Marshall Pickering, quoted in Christopher Lamb's 1997 lecture, 'Yours Interfaithfully: An English Christian Tries to Stay Honest', Birmingham: Selly Oak Colleges, p. 7.

6 W. Cantwell Smith (1962), *The Meaning and End of Religion: A New Approach to the Religious Traditions of Mankind*, New York: Macmillan, and (1978), London: SPCK. The quotation here is from the Introduction, p. 15, in the 1962 edition.

7 Published in the World Council of Churches' journal, *Current Dialogue* 26, June 1994, pp. 10–22. The list of four 'shapes for the religious future' and the discussion of these is on pp. 16–18.

17

Final Reflections

'Looking back; looking forward'

As we come to the end of our review of world Christianity in the twentieth century, we must take time to reflect on the story we have told, asking two crucial questions. What has happened to Christianity during the twentieth century? What pointers have we found to the future of Christianity in the twenty-first century? Neither of these questions is capable of being answered comprehensively and objectively. We can only hope to share our own personal perspectives on the story we have been telling, to draw on the insights of others who have ventured their own reflections and to take a hesitant view towards the distant horizon. Readers who have shared this journey with us may well see the past differently and have different perspectives on the future. We can only hope that these final reflections will stimulate and encourage others to find their own path through this meandering history. It has been a basic premise of our journey that Christianity in any one place and among a particular people cannot be separated from the culture, history and identity of those places and peoples. The story of world Christianity as a whole, similarly, cannot be separated from the story of global human community among whom Christians live out their faith. So we begin our reflection with a brief reminder of our changing world.

A changing world

In the Retrospect to his magisterial book, *Twentieth Century*, J. M. Roberts recognizes that the twentieth century saw change on a scale hitherto unknown in any previous century, 'unprecedently radical, intense and compound in effect'.[1] As evidence for this claim, he cites, among other factors, the great upheavals of the century such as up to 100 million lives lost in war and conflict and the birth and demise and human cost of international communism, both signalling 'a more damaging release of evil impulse than ever before'. The world population more than trebled during the century, from some 2 billion to well over 6 billion, and the majority of these have been and still are living in poverty in an increasingly wealthy world. Alongside this unprecedented population growth and its undeniable problems of equality and shared opportunity, we have also seen at least the beginnings of an international struggle to set out a legal framework and a structure, albeit fragile and by no means universally accepted, for implementing basic human rights and justice.

The century has also seen revolutionary changes in humanity's scientific understanding, technological power and what Roberts calls 'mastery of the material world',[2] but these too have affected human beings in diverse and often unequal ways. The benefits have often had greater advantageous effects on those in wealthier nations. Technological breakthroughs have been directed, often deliberately, more to the advantage of the already developed nations than towards a more just sharing of resources and opportunities. Particularly significant has been the transformation of communications technology. More information is available than ever before, it is more easily available and it is available to a greater proportion of the world's population. But here too, despite the ease of electronic communication technology, its dependence on access to the basic technological hardware often means that the poorest in the community do not reap its benefits (though we have to recognize that it is not all benefit) as fully and as advantageously as they should in a more equal world.

At the political level, the century saw the demise of empires (most of them European) and the growth of independent sovereign states, with their very diverse range of consequences for their populations. Alongside this seismic change, there has developed also, again for good and ill, a globalized international community, not least because of the revolutionary changes in communication already noted. But financial institutions (such as the World Bank), commercial links and global business interests (such as transnational companies, some of which are many times wealthier than the total gross national product of a number of the poorer states added together), as well as the political machinery of bodies such as the United Nations have also contributed to shaping this global community. This has meant that, in Roberts words, 'human destinies are now linked round the world'.[3] Increasingly during the century, human beings in vastly different cultural, economic and political contexts have come to share in a global community and culture of which Coca Cola may be a trivial symbol.

From the perspective of religion, too, there have been dramatic changes. Roberts observes that in the Middle Ages there was a general belief in a transcendent God and 'religious belief was at the very root of most [people's] lives'.[4] By the end of the twentieth century, however,

> At least in Europe, we confront ... populations for the most part taking in their daily lives no account at all of whether there is a God or not ... Religion – across all creeds and systems – seems to have lost much of the enormous advantage it once possessed as virtually the universal source of consolation, explanation and hope to men and women trapped in an unchanging order.

This is, as we shall see, a questionable conclusion, but for the moment we recognize that it does represent at least one aspect of the changes in religious belief and practice that has occurred in one section of the global family during the last hundred years.

In an article entitled, 'Beware Apocalypse', published in January 2000 (*SCM Core Reader on World Christianity in the Twentieth Century*, 1.11), and already referred to in Chapter 1, the late Adrian Hastings predicts that 'by the middle of the twenty-first century ... almost everything that has mattered hitherto will get worse and worse'.[5] His main concern is global warming, which, he predicts, will change the whole ecological balance of the world, leading to coastal erosion, the disruption of food chains, and consequent mass migration. He believes that these global problems can only be solved by strong global government. But the international institutions will be incapable of taking the necessary steps unless there is fundamental change in their approaches and structures. Hastings calls for two kinds of responses:

> First, to do all in our power to bring the world's leadership to its senses while something can still be done to limit the scale of the disaster. Secondly, to recognize that global catastrophe is in the judgement of hard realism very likely to come upon us and, therefore, to prepare ourselves and small communities of sanity and faith to live undespairingly within it.

The year 2001 brought unprecedented acts of terror in Washington and New York (on 11 September) which had their origins in the growing extremism of the last decades of the twentieth century. If such extremism had its origins in religion, it was increasingly shaped by political and cultural critique and ambition. Modern radical Islam – which by no means represents anything like the majority of those who follow Islam as faithful and peaceful believers – has created among some of its followers such a powerful and fundamental critique of western-dominated civilization that it has led them to believe that the only possible response must be one of violence and terrorism. So, despite the horrors and tragedies that human beings experienced during the twentieth century, the new century too began with a sense of foreboding and fear about the terrors and threats that it might bring. The continued ambition of a number of states to own and be able to deploy, if necessary, nuclear weapons is only one of the continuing threats to exacerbate this sense of foreboding. There is a sense in which the story of human progress and development, and even hopefulness, in its apparently inevitably partial and unequal ways, has not penetrated nearly far enough among the poorer sections of the world's population to dispel this sense of gloom that is overshadowing us.

Christianity tranformed

This inevitably brief, personal and partial overview of the century sets out a context or, better perhaps, contexts, which have shaped, from a human perspective, the changes within Christianity during the twentieth century. Before we offer our own response to these changes, it will be stimulating to reflect briefly on ways in which others have viewed the past century and the present 'new' century. There is general agreement among many analysts that the most significant change in Christianity during the century was what has been described as the southward shift. The nations of the northern and western world are no longer the centre of the global Christian community. The focal point has moved to the South and the East. McGrath comments:

Christianity, while surviving the twenty-first century, will undergo major changes as a result of the continued expansion of Christianity in the non-western world and its likely diminishing role in the west ... [It] is essential not to judge the future of Christianity by its fate in the west. Its future lies in the largely unreported growth in Africa and Asia. In the west we may hear little more than the melancholy low roar of an ebbing tide. Yet elsewhere the tide is flowing and new possibilities are emerging.[6]

In his study of what he describes as *The New Christendom*, Philip Jenkins also recognizes this crucial shift in Christian demography.[7] He suggests that what he describes as southern Christianity, is

the Third Church, [which] is not just a transplanted version of the familiar religions of the older Christian states ... It is a truly new and developing entity ... In this encounter, we are forced to see the religion not just for what it is, but what it was in its origins and what it is going to be in the future.

He goes on to suggest that this southward shift will inevitably lead to a shift in perspective since the majority of Christians will be living in economic poverty and their gospel perspectives, increasingly focused on the Beatitudes of Jesus (Matthew 5.1–12), will be very different from those of Christians in the North and West. 'Christianity', he claims, 'is flourishing wonderfully among the poor and persecuted, while it atrophies among the rich and secure.'[8]

We will come later to offer our own perspectives on some of these observations but, for the moment, it is worth noting Jenkins' recognition that the demographic changes that he (and McGrath, above) observes are not merely statistical shifts but have been leading to transformations in Christian experience, perceptions and, indeed, articulations of the faith. These will have inevitable consequences for Christian worship, discipleship and theology in the coming century.

Hans Küng's erudite and perceptive book, *Christianity: The Religious Situation of Our Time*, was written because of a deep concern about Christianity into the third millennium, 'how and why Christianity became what it is today – with a view to how it could be'.[9] In what he calls, 'Not an epilogue', he notes (in 1994) that Christianity has to face a number of challenges.[10] These include:

• recognizing the polycentric nature of Christianity in a polycentric world;
• taking up the opportunities for a more Christian Christianity;
• pursuing the possibilities for a more peaceful world *ecumene*, founded on renewed relationships with the other world faiths;
• forging a new synthesis in which theology embraces the insights of natural sciences, psychotherapy, politics and aesthetics; and
• forging a Christianity for humankind that is cosmic, holistic, liberating and ecumenical.

These are surely visionary insights as we seek to travel the road before us.

In these three contributions from McGrath, Jenkins and Küng, we have three significant pointers to the nature of the changing Christianity whose story we have attempted to tell. They draw into our horizon three interrelated realities. First, there is no doubt that the demographic shift from North and West to South and East is highly significant. It recognizes changes in patterns of belief in both areas of the world. A faith that seems to have become estranged from the majority of the population in those countries where Christianity has been the dominant religion in the past has become, partly as a result of worldwide mission and, most importantly, as a result of local, indigenous, contextual Christian witness, a believable faith lived out by rapidly growing Christian communities in vibrant worship and committed discipleship.

But, as we have seen, there is more than statistics at work here. The south-ward shift has meant a transformation in what we might call theological perception, which has only gradually been articulated in structured and systematic ways during the last decades of the century. It is the result of a change of context from relative wealth in the North and West to relative (and, sometimes, abject) poverty in areas of the South and East. It has often been most clearly articulated (or, perhaps better, experienced) as a theology from within poverty and oppression. Latin American theology of liberation and the Korean *minjung* theology are notable examples of this theological shift shaped by a context of poverty and oppression. The coming period is likely to offer further examples of transforming theological insight and articulation.

Küng's comment, however, takes us one step further. Not only does he rec-ognize that these shifts have happened, and that they have created their own theological responses among particular peoples and contexts, he also believes that world Christianity itself, in the North and West as well as in the South and East, needs to be transformed by these challenging changes if it is to 'survive' through the third millennium. His vision of polycentrism, his call for rebirth, renewal and reformation, his commitment to a new vision of a peaceful *ecumene* (or *oikoumene*, God's house for the whole of humankind) and his desire that there should be forged a global Christianity that is cosmic, holistic, liberating and ecumenical, are all fundamentally dependent on *the whole global Christian community* taking seriously into their own thinking and believing the diverse articulations of Christian faith and discipleship which have been emerging among those communities and peoples where Christian-ity has been growing. It is not just a matter of accepting that a demographic shift has occurred. It is, more importantly, a matter of allowing that shift to shape the future of Christianity as a whole.

The ecumenical movement

Since the two of us who have written this volume have spent much of our Christian life within the fellowship and service of the worldwide ecumenical movement, there is, for us, an obvious preliminary question. It is this: to what extent has the ecumenical movement succeeded in enabling different sorts of Christians in very diverse contexts to collaborate more effectively in Christ-ian witness and service, to understand each other more deeply, and to reach agreement on fundamental dividing issues? It is impossible to give a simple and brief answer to such a question, but some insights might be helpful.

There is no doubt that the ecumenical pilgrimage that began in Edinburgh 1910 (which was itself shaped by previous ecumenical efforts) has transformed church relationships around the world. In many, probably most, situations – locally, nationally and regionally – there has been collaboration in development projects, in serving local communities, in being witnesses for, and agents of, peace, liberty and justice, in challenging and working in partnership with governments, in witness and evangelism, in forging relationships and engaging in dialogue with other faith communities.

Stimulated by Edinburgh 1910 and its recognition that worldwide Christian mission required greater mutual understanding and, indeed, fuller unity, the search for agreement and understanding in relation to some of the fundamental questions of faith and the related issues around the nature of the Church, the calling to mission and ministry, and the essence of Christian sacraments and worship, have occupied an enormous amount of time and energy. One important result of this was the WCC's 1982 report, *Baptism, Eucharist and Ministry*.[11] The subsequent worldwide debates on the issues raised have enabled churches of different traditions to grow towards greater understanding and consensus in some of these crucial areas of church life. Similarly, bilateral dialogues, at a global level, between different world communions and, more locally, between different churches and denominations, have led, at the very least, to growing mutual understanding, and at their best to significant agreements. Most significantly of all, a number of united and uniting churches have been formed, beginning in Canada, moving through the Indian subcontinent, the Caribbean, Africa, Australia and Europe.

The World Council of Churches, the regional ecumenical bodies in Africa, Asia, the Caribbean, Europe, Latin America, and the Pacific, as well as the ecumenical partnerships in North America, and a large number of national and local councils of churches, are all – notwithstanding frequent questions about their goals and their failures in effectiveness – important witnesses still to the ecumenical vocation.

It is also true to say that many churches and Christian communities are not members of the various organizations of the ecumenical movement. Despite its deep commitment to the search for unity, the Roman Catholic Church is not a member of the WCC, although it is deeply involved in much of its work and is either a member or a partner in most of the regional and national ecumenical bodies. Similarly, while many Pentecostal and Evangelical churches are committed participants in the ecumenical movement, many others prefer to remain outside its fellowship and still others are opposed to its work and influence.

One key question in all of this is the nature of the relationships between Christianity and the other world faith communities. The last chapter has explored this question carefully, and we do not need to repeat any of that discussion here, but it is clear that the future of Christianity into the twenty-first century will depend crucially on the relationships being developed and forged between it and people of other faiths in seeking to shape what Küng has called 'a more peaceful world *ecumene*'. The role the ecumenical movement will have in relation to this particular vision will be especially challenging in the future.

The end of the twentieth century and the beginning of the twenty-first has, in fact, seen a re-visioning of the ecumenical movement, not least through the WCC. In part, this was in response to declining resources being made available from churches upon which bodies such as the WCC had been heavily dependent. It was, however, predominantly driven by a need to articulate the ecumenical vision in a new way for a new century. Chapter 1 has already drawn attention to the search for what the WCC Assembly at Harare in 1998 called 'a new ecumenical space' that would be more open and tentative and would allow a far broader range of relationships and commitments.

A statement 'Called to be the One Church',[12] approved by the Porto Alegre Assembly (2006), reaffirms the churches' commitment to full visible unity. It explores 'the conciliar relationship of churches in different places'. It also places an emphasis on catholicity, which

> expresses the fullness, integrity and totality of [the Church's] life in Christ through the Holy Spirit in all times and places ... Each church is the Church catholic and not simply part of it. Each church is the Church catholic, but not the whole of it. Each church fulfils its catholicity when it is in communion with other churches.[13]

These principles will contribute to shaping the search for unity in the new century.

In an address in New York in 2005, the General Secretary of the WCC, Dr Sam Kobia, explored 'The Challenges Facing the Ecumenical Movement in the 21st century'.[14] He notes, for example, that the shifting centre of Christian population will demand what he calls 'a re-conceptualization of relationships' and the creation of 'models of creative listening and clear communication' that will enable a new kind of listening between Christians in the North and West and those in the South and East, in terms of theological insights as well as Christian faith and witness. He also calls for 'a broader ecumenism' that enables Christians to inquire together 'as to God's purpose for us in a multicultural world characterized by a diversity of faiths'. Finally, he calls for 'a spirituality of engagement' that does not seek some kind of personal, psychological religious experience but 'takes hold of real-world as well as personal challenges, and will not let them go unresolved'. The parameters of the reconfiguring for which Kobia calls will inevitably lead to changes both in the ethos and the structures and patterns of the ecumenical movement during coming decades. They also reflect some of the perspectives that have emerged from our review in this book. We believe that they are clues to the future of Christianity in the twenty-first century.

Some personal perspectives

We offer, as pointers to the century that is past as well as to this new century, a series of tensions and contrasts which seem to us to characterize world Christianity at this time. These have to be set out here very briefly and in very general terms, but previous chapters should have enabled readers to gain a deeper understanding of some of the issues that are highlighted.

Quality of witness more crucial than quantity of growth

Chapter 1 indicated our reluctance to assess the health and growth of Christianity merely in terms of numbers and statistics. Admittedly, here and there in our review of the churches in the various regions, we have examined statistics. We see these, however, more as guides to the numerical strength of the churches in relation to each other and within the total context of their communities, rather than as an indicator of the quality and effectiveness of their Christian witness.

As we have seen in previous paragraphs, there is a danger of seeing the numerical decline of church membership in the North and West as signifying a decline also in the commitment, discernment and faith of believers. Similarly, some have equated numerical growth with a strengthened Christianity and a more effective Christian witness. While both of these analyses may be correct, we believe that a different perspective is necessary. We believe that we have discerned in the life of churches and Christians in the North and West a quality of Christian commitment and discipleship which bears powerful and effective witness to the Good News of the Kingdom, announced through, and embodied in, the ministry of Jesus of Nazareth. There may be found among them signs of the Spirit at work, in powerful ways, moulding and remoulding churches and communities to reflect Kingdom values and proclaim its judgement and hope. Small, fragile and, often, vulnerable communities can offer as powerful a witness as those that are numerically strong. Conversely, a church that is growing very strong numerically, and is characterized by prosperity, wealth and personal and communal influence and power, does not necessarily reflect and proclaim the justice and liberty and reconciliation being offered to the world in and through a crucified Lord.

From mission as sending to mission as mutuality

Many of the stories that have been told in this book have begun with accounts of the missionary enterprise that led to the establishment and growth of Christianity in the various regions of the world. This 'sending' approach to mission was still in place at the beginning of the twentieth century. It was largely a sending from the North and West to the South and East. The international missionary conference held in Edinburgh in 1910, which gave birth to so much of the ecumenical development of the century, was largely a conference for representatives of missionary societies and organizations. Its central concern was the challenge of the continuing missionary enterprise towards the proclamation of the gospel to the whole world 'in this generation', as the conference itself expressed it. But it was never narrowly about evangelism and conversion. The conference stimulated Christians worldwide to recognize that this missionary task could not be fulfilled without facing the challenges of Christian unity, engagement in social transformation (or life and work) and deeper partnerships in mission.

By the 1970s and 1980s, there were calls within international ecumenical conferences and gatherings for what came to be called a moratorium, a halt to the sending of missionaries from North and West to South and East. This was a hotly debated issue. A moratorium was never fully implemented, but the whole debate did lead to a refocusing of mission. Mission has come to be understood less in terms of sending and more in terms of mutuality, less in terms of conversion through evangelism and more in terms of the transformation of the whole person and the whole of society, less in terms of movement across cultural boundaries and more in terms of presence and witness in each place. The mission of each Christian community is now seen primarily in terms of its witness in and for the peoples and society in which it was placed rather than a constant calling to Christians to leave their own setting in order to witness to Christ in a 'foreign' land.

However, this changing paradigm and practice has not been followed universally. In very general terms, it may be said that those churches that have been closely involved with the ecumenical movement have acted according to this paradigm shift. Those churches that have been more closely aligned to the Lausanne Committee for World Evangelization (now better known as the Lausanne Movement) have generally had greater sympathy for the continuing need for cross-cultural mission that has evangelism and conversion as a fundamental goal. But these churches also recognize that Christian mission must offer and enable the transformation of persons and communities on the foundations of the Kingdom of God. We have seen how a sending missionary endeavour is still central to the life of many churches in, for example, South Korea, north-east India and the United States of America. Still more significantly, churches in the North and West are now increasingly encouraging fellow Christians from churches in the South and East to cross boundaries and come to share with them in enabling, re-visioning and resourcing their mission within their own difficult context.

Locally rooted and globally aware

We have discerned that, at their best, Christian churches and fellowships are both locally rooted and globally aware. The local or national context is clearly of utmost importance to Christian flourishing. No church or Christian community can claim to be fully Christian that does not take its own local community and environment in all its division and fragility into account. It has been frequently – and correctly – said that effective Christian witness is first and foremost local Christian witness. However, we also believe that, especially during the twentieth century, Christians have been enabled – not least through the worldwide ecumenical movement – to be catholic, in the original sense of that word, namely, worldwide in their sense of identity and belonging. Isolation within a local context, devoid of any awareness of dependence on or sense of responsibility for, the wider Christian community can rob churches and Christians of this truly multidimensional essence of being the people of God in each place *and* in all places.

The changes in communications, the growing global interdependence between peoples and the greater possibility of understanding something of the cultures and languages (in their broadest sense) of other peoples and communities have opened up for Christians exciting possibilities for truly catholic discipleship, spirituality and worship. We have discerned a danger in some churches and denominations – both in contexts of strength as well as in situations of decline – of withdrawal into themselves in order to conserve strength and resources or maintain identity or protect from external influences. We are fearful that such an inward-looking perspective blinds Christians to the exciting and risky things that God is doing within the whole inhabited earth.

Being pilgrims on the way while living in the tradition

Our review of world Christianity has revealed a myriad ways in which Christians have been open to the renewing powers of the Spirit. They have welcomed renewal in worship and spirituality, in evangelism and witness, in responding to human need and standing for social justice, in seeking news ways of being the Church and of reshaping Christian communities. The Christian pilgrimage in the twentieth century has been, in many different ways, a source of renewal and newness for all Christian traditions and families.

For example, the Second Vatican Council was specifically convened by Pope John XXIII to be a source and instrument of renewal within the Roman Catholic Church. There is no doubt that it achieved much towards this goal. In worship and spirituality, in opening up the possibilities and opportunities for new ecumenical relationships, in encouraging Catholics to challenge injustice and oppression in new ways and to enter into dialogue with other Christian traditions as well as other faith communities, as in many other ways, the Catholic Church was opened up to renewal. But this renewal occurred while the church was still firmly embedded in the tradition of the church, that is, in that understanding of the truth of the gospel and the doctrine of the church that has been handed down from generation to generation through popes and bishops. Such a process of renewal can also be traced in the life of many other churches and traditions during the twentieth century. At its best, such renewal has not meant an abandonment of the tradition of Scripture and doctrine upon which Christianity in all its diversity has been built. Being open to renewal and change while being creatively and dynamically rooted in the Christian tradition is an essential characteristic of the Church of God in all times and places.

Worship that is contextual and universal

Much of the growth and development of Christianity during the twentieth century can be attributed to the renewal of worship and spirituality. New people have been attracted into a particular church or fellowship because of the vibrancy of its worship and the power of its prayer. Truly vibrant worship, such as the worship of Pentecostal churches in Latin America or African Initiated Churches in Africa, has often drawn on local cultural expressions in music and dance, in movement and communication, in art and sculpture. This process of inculturalization of worship and spirituality, not least in churches that were, in previous periods, deeply influenced by the western missionary enterprise and inherited patterns of worship, has been freeing and liberating. But alongside this renewal of worship through drawing on local cultural traditions, there has developed, during the century, another equally creative wellspring of spiritual and liturgical renewal.

Both of us have shared in many international gatherings where a vast diversity of indigenous worship resources, in prayers, music, dance and other art forms, have been brought into liturgy, often intertwined with traditional words and patterns. This has enabled Christians gathered from around the world and from diverse traditions to praise God and celebrate their faith in ways which draw on the richness of the universal family of God's people. Some have accused such worship of being syncretistic, that is, of being so diverse in its 'ingredients' as to be no longer rooted in any particular Christian tradition. We believe this to be mistaken. Nor is it necessary for this drawing together of local cultural traditions for the enrichment of worship to be confined to international Christian gatherings. Worship, whether in local congregations or international gatherings, is always more enriching when it interweaves the local and the universal in the response of Christians to God.

Building up the church and acting for justice

At its best, Christianity in the twentieth century has recognized that the Christian community cannot live in isolation from those persons and forces that threaten local and national communities and humankind as a whole. There is nothing new in this. Christians and Christian leaders throughout the history of the Church have seen clearly that building up the Christian community and developing Christian discipleship must involve obedience to God's call to witness to peace and justice in a world of conflict and injustice as much as creating appropriate patterns for deepening and developing the internal life of congregations and fellowships. Christian discipleship at its best has always been seen as a holistic discipleship.

This demand for obedience and witness led Christians to challenge the growing power of National Socialism in 1930s Germany, to a courageous commitment to reconciliation between North and South Korea, to campaign against segregation in the USA, to engage in the anti-apartheid struggle in South Africa. In more recent years, it has involved engagement in costly witness for peace in places of conflict in Africa, the Middle East, Central America and elsewhere. It has meant martyrdom for some, imprisonment for others and torture for many. The costly witness continues for those who seek to act justly to strengthen the poor in an increasingly rich world, for those who seek dialogue with people of other living faiths in contexts of religious extremism and conflict, and for those who seek to explore an appropriate balance between economic progress and ecological responsibility.

Twentieth-century Christianity has recognized that these are not optional or additional aspects of the churches' witness but essential facets of how Christians need to live out the gospel, and key channels for sharing in the Spirit's renewal of the Church and of the human community. Like the Old Testament prophets, Christians have recognized that obedience to God must require God's people to act justly and not only to worship worthily. Indeed, it has been out of such contexts of costly struggle and witness that global Christian leadership has emerged, especially in the latter decades of the century.

This will increasingly be the case in the twenty-first century as the southward shift that we have noted continues. Christians in the North and West will need to be increasingly sensitive and alert to words of challenge and hope from the emerging leadership of the global Christian family. A global sensitivity, perspective and response in relation to the threats to the environment and to the future of the global human community will be essential, for the whole of humanity and not just for Christians, if we are, in Adrian Hastings' words, 'to live undespairingly' within a likely global disaster in the coming century.

It is as Christians increasingly recognize the crucial relevance of these tensions and contrasts to the realities of Christian obedience and witness in their own local, national, denominational and ecumenical contexts that they will learn to grow as Christians. This will not be because they will have all the answers to all the questions but rather because they will have risked fellowship with those with whom they may well disagree, but who they will also recognize as sisters and brothers. This will be an increasingly important lesson to be learned in the twenty-first century, not least at a time when so many churches and denominations seem to be withdrawing from their former commitment to the worldwide Church and the global Christian family, seeking to isolate themselves in their own safe and risk-free environment.

Ultimately, however, the future of Christianity is not in human hands – although human obedience is central to that future. At the end of his study of Christianity, Hans Küng asks:

> Why has this Christianity kept surviving ...? How is it that the essence of Christianity did not get lost as an orientation, criterion, model for the concrete life of the individual and the community of faith, for relations with fellow human beings, human society and finally with God?[15]

Here is part of his answer to his own question:

> It is remarkable that time and time again it was the spirit of the Nazarene which managed to establish itself even when persons, institutions and constitutions, failed, wherever there were not just words, but there was quite practical discipleship; for the truth of Christianity is not just knowledge of the truth but existential truth ... What is there about this spirit, that all down the centuries, in an unparalleled movement, it has continually motivated, indeed driven people to break down all the cultural, social, political ... fortifications, and take seriously the earliest Christian ideal of a love for neighbours and others more distant? Known names and countless unknowns ... have gone by the values of the man from Nazareth ... They show that where Christianity really goes by its Christ and allows him to give it strength, it can offer a spiritual home, a place of faith, hope and love ... This faith in Christ is no mere other-worldly consolation but a basis for protest and resistance against unjust situations here and now, supported and strengthened by a restless longing for the 'wholly Other'.

So Christians may be sure that Christianity has a future even in the third millennium after Christ, that this community of the spirit and faith has its own kind of 'infallibility'. However, this does not mean that some authorities in particular situations do not make mistakes or perpetuate errors, but rather, that despite all mistakes and errors, sins and vices, the community of believers will be maintained by the Spirit in the truth of Jesus Christ.

The story of world Christianity in the twentieth century, as told in these pages, has, we believe, borne witness to the truth of this remarkable claim and can equip human beings still 'to live undespairingly' through whatever the future holds.

Notes

1 J. M. Roberts (1999), *Twentieth Century: A History of the World, 1901 to the Present*, London: Penguin Books, p. 833.
2 Roberts, *Twentieth Century*, p. 840.
3 Roberts, *Twentieth Century*, p. 845.
4 Roberts, *Twentieth Century*, pp. 832–3.
5 A. Hastings (2007), 'Beware Apocalypse', *Tablet*, 8 January, pp. 8–9.
6 A. E. McGrath (2002), *The Future of Christianity*, Oxford: Blackwell, p. 118.
7 P. Jenkins (2002), *The Next Christendom: The Coming of Global Christianity*, Oxford: Oxford University Press, pp. 214–15.
8 Jenkins, *Next Christendom*, p. 220.
9 H. Küng (1995), *Christianity: The Religious Situation of Our Time*, trans. John Bowden, London: SCM Press, p. xxiv.
10 Kung, *Christianity*, p. 79.
11 *Baptism, Eucharist and Ministry*, Faith and Order Paper no. 111, Geneva: WCC Publications, 1981.
12 *Text on Ecclesiology: Called to Be the One Church* (2006), Document No. PRC 01.1 Rev., from http://www.oikoumene.org/en/resources/documents/assembly/porto-alegre-2006/1-statements-documents-adopted/christian-unity-and-message-to-the-churches/called-to-be-the-one-church-as-adopted.html
13 *Text on Ecclesiology* (2006), para. 6.
14 For the full text of the address, see: http://www.oikoumene.org/en/resources/documents/wcc-programmes/ecumenical-movement-in-the-21st-century/foundational-texts/22-10-05-challenges-facing-the-ecumenical-movement-in-the-21st-century.html
15 Küng, *Christianity*, pp. 795–7.

Index

CPSIA information can be obtained
at www.ICGtesting.com
Printed in the USA
LVOW04s2350220416
484938LV00008B/36/P